UNCHAINED MAN

MAN THE ARCTIC LIFE AND TIMES OF CAPTAIN ROBERT ABRAM BARTLETT

BOULDER PUBLICATIONS

MAURA HANRAHAN

Library and Archives Canada Cataloguing in Publication

Hanrahan, Maura, author
Unchained man : the Arctic life and times of Captain Robert
Abram Bartlett / Maura Hanrahan.

Includes bibliographical references and index.
ISBN 978-1-927099-94-0 (softcover)

1. Bartlett, Robert A. (Robert Abram), 1875-1946. 2. Explorers--
Canada--Biography. 3. Ship captains--Canada--Biography. 4. Arctic
regions--Discovery and exploration. I. Title.

G635.B3H36 2018   910.92   C2018-900154-2

© 2018 Maura Hanrahan

Published by Boulder Publications
Portugal Cove-St. Philip's, Newfoundland and Labrador
www.boulderpublications.ca

Editor: Stephanie Porter
Copy editor: Iona Bulgin
Designer: Tanya Montini
Printed in Canada

We acknowledge the financial support of the Government of Newfoundland
and Labrador through the Department of Tourism, Culture and Recreation.

Funded by the   Financé par le
Government   gouvernement   Canada
of Canada   du Canada

*This book is dedicated to Paul and Jemma
with love and gratitude*

TABLE OF CONTENTS

PROLOGUE

Explorers are not well-balanced ... Really competent
people would not undergo the trials of exploration.
You have to be a bit daffy to do that.

– Isaiah Bowman, president of the American Geographical Society roasting Bob Bartlett

I shall satiate my ardent curiosity with the sight of a part of the world
never before visited, and may tread a land never before
imprinted by the foot of man.

– Mary Shelley, *Frankenstein*

As a child in the 1970s, I spent a memorable two weeks in Brigus, mostly on one of the town's rocky beaches. Not far from where I stationed myself at the water's edge was a small grassy area with a weather-beaten schooner-shaped monument. The sculpture was a tribute to Captain Robert Abram "Bob" Bartlett, who was a hero to generations of Newfoundland children as well as their parents. Bartlett had been to the Arctic with Peary and had had all manner of icy adventures in places most of us would never see.

My father had a penchant for doggedly pursuing information, so he took us to visit Jim Hearn, then an old man, who had lived his whole life in Brigus. In Hearn's ancient house I heard firsthand tales of Captain Bob. These were made more real by the fact that Hawthorne Cottage, the explorer's childhood home, was just a stone's throw away.

In 2016, I stood on the Greenland shore, staring at the Baffin Bay water Bartlett loved so much. I'd written a draft of this book, after spending more than a decade delving into the life and times of a man who meant so much to Newfoundlanders and Arctic aficionados but who was known only superficially. Some might dismiss Bartlett as another of Newfoundland's old salty dog types, only more famous. But Bartlett made major contributions to science, expanding the collections of numerous museums and universities, advancing the understanding of the Arctic environment, and mentoring noted scientists like David Nutt, whose work is important in the history of climate change research. As an explorer, Bartlett had a central place on the world stage and hobnobbed with aristocrats and presidents. I understood this vaguely as a child.

Bartlett tried to play a role in "firsting," "discovering" places that are actually within the territory of others, as the Arctic was for the Inuit. But he did not reach the Pole. He played a larger role in "seconding," relegating Inuit to the background in exploration narratives. In some ways, this book is guilty of seconding, for its focus is Bartlett, not the Inuit. While I have tried to bring Inuit toward the foreground, my chief objective here is to understand, as much as possible, a single man who was driven by the urge to explore the north. In this, I respond to Laura Nader's call to study the colonizer.[1] Further, I hope that this focus on one person takes away from, rather than adds to, the "great man" theory of history.

Naturally elusive, achieving fame was just one of the ways Bartlett pushed himself. The internal and external constraints he faced throughout his life are evident, yet he remains, as he wanted to remain, mysterious. He had a rich inner life but was lonely, not as a result of circumstances but because that was his nature. He was smart, pragmatic, brave, and stoic. He was also insecure, isolated, given to petulance, and deeply spiritual. He was very human in all senses of the word and I have very much liked getting to know him.

Maura Hanrahan
Lethbridge, Alberta

ANCESTRY OF CAPTAIN
ROBERT ABRAM BARTLETT

BARTLETT FAMILY TREE

1   Captain <u>William</u> (Billy, Follow-On) BARTLETT (ca. 1749–1829) m. Ann?[*] (ca. 1758–1830)

2. Captain <u>Abraham</u> (Abram) BARTLETT Sr. (1788–1852) m. Ann RICHARDS (1799–1869)

3. Captain <u>Abraham</u> (Abram) BARTLETT Jr. (1819–89) m. Elizabeth Bellamy WILMOT (1821–1904)[†]

4. Captain <u>William</u> James BARTLETT Sr (1851–1931) m. Mary Jemima LEAMON (1852–1943)

5. **Captain <u>Robert</u> Abram BARTLETT (1875–1946)**

CAPTAIN WILLIAM JAMES BARTLETT SR. M. MARY JEMIMA LEAMON'S CHILDREN (BOB BARTLETT'S SIBLINGS)[‡]:

1. **Captain Robert (Bob) Abram BARTLETT (1875–1946)**

2. Beatrice (Triss) Stentaford BARTLETT DOVE (b. 1876) (mother of Hilda, Robert, and James DOVE)

3. Hilda Northway BARTLETT WILLS (1879–1905)

4. Emma Gertrude BARTLETT (1881–1959)

5. Mary Elizabeth (Betty) Wilmot BARTLETT ANGEL (father of Ruperta [Paddy] ANGEL MURPHY & Jack ANGEL) (b. 1881)

6. William Leamon Norman BARTLETT (1885–1885)

7. William James BARTLETT Jr. (1887–1957)

8. Lewis Goodison BARTLETT (1890–1966) (father of Supreme Court Justice Rupert BARTLETT)

9. Rupert Wilfred BARTLETT (1891–1917)

10. Winifred Grenfell BARTLETT (ca. 1892)

11. Blanche Eleanor BARTLETT (1894–1973)

---

[*]   Ann's surname is unknown.

[†]   Abram Jr. and Elizabeth were the parents of Captain John BARTLETT (ca. 1841-1925), Captain Sam BARTLETT (ca. 1848-1916), Captain Henry Bellamy BARTLETT (1863-94), and Captain William BARTLETT, father of Robert Abram BARTLETT.

[‡]   Although there were others, only the nieces and nephews mentioned in this book are included here.

SUSANNAH NORMAN'S FAMILY (SUSANNAH WAS THE GREAT-GRANDMOTHER OF BOB BARTLETT)

1. Mary MUNDEN's parents: Ann PERCEY m. Captain Azariah MUNDEN (1739–1825)
2. James NORMAN m. Mary MUNDEN
3. Susannah NORMAN (b. ca. 1805) (sister of Captain Nathan NORMAN, 1809–83) m. John LEAMON (Squire LEAMON) (1804–66)*

LEAMON FAMILY TREE

1. Robert LEAMON m. Mary COZENS
2. John LEAMON (Squire Leamon) (1804–66) m. Susannah NORMAN (b. ca. 1805)
3. Robert John Cozens LEAMON (1828–73) m. Mary NORMAN (1830–1909)
4. Mary Jemima LEAMON (1852–1943) m. Captain William James BARTLETT Sr. (1851–1931)
5. **Captain Robert (Bob) Abram BARTLETT (1875–1946)**

For a full list of individuals featured in this book, please see People starting on page 283.

---

* The succeeding generations of the family are as follows (and, as above): Robert John Cozens LEAMON (1828-73) m. Mary NORMAN (1830-1909); Mary Jemima LEAMON (1852-1943) m. Captain William James BARTLETT Sr. (1851-1931); and Captain Robert Abram BARTLETT (1875-1946).

CHAPTER ONE
THE LARGENESS OF LIFE: INSIDE THE QUEST FOR THE NORTH POLE

Bob Bartlett, pre-1910. *The Log of Bob Bartlett* (1928; St. John's: Flanker Press, 2006).

I think some mysteries are better off unsolved.

– Northern historian Kenn Harper talking to CBC, 2014

It was with no small sense of relief that the *Roosevelt* pulled away from Recreation Pier on the East River, New York, on 6 July 1908, with a crew of Newfoundlanders handpicked by Captain Robert Abram Bartlett, more often known as Bob.[2] The ship was on its way to the Arctic, and some of those on board wanted to be the first to stand on top of the world at the ice-covered North Pole, the northernmost point on earth. At least half a dozen expeditions had made the attempt; the expedition led by British naval officer William Parry in 1827[3] was one of the first. Others, in the name of Britain, the United States, Norway, Sweden, and Italy followed;[4] all were unsuccessful and the status and accolades of reaching the Pole remained unclaimed. As the *Roosevelt* left the pier, thousands cheered and whistled, which heartened Bartlett and Admiral Robert Peary after the financial struggles they had endured to mount the expedition.

A year before, crowds had similarly seen off Frederick A. Cook, the physician-explorer who had taken part in the Belgian Antarctic Expedition in 1887–89 and then in Peary's 1891–92 Arctic foray a few years later. Cook had headed for the Pole with the same goal as Bartlett and Peary. Cook's supporters had held a banner that read "We Believe in You!," a phrase that would seem ironic later.[5] By 1909, Cook would be Peary's archrival, with both asserting that their respective expeditions had reached the Pole and been the first to do so.

On their way to Greenland and, they hoped, the Pole, Bartlett, Peary, and the *Roosevelt* stopped at Oyster Bay, New York, to host Teddy Roosevelt, 26th president of the United States, and his son, 19-year-old Theodore III, whom the ever-observant Bartlett described as having "glistening teeth and squinting eyes."[6] The *Erik* met the *Roosevelt* at Sydney, Nova Scotia, providing 800 tons of coal and thus some relief from worry about fuel. At Cape Charles, Labrador, the *Roosevelt* took on 10 tons of whale meat, some of it already decaying and stinking, for dog food. They stopped at Turnavik in northern Labrador, where Bartlett's family long had a large and impressive fishing station; there, they met familiar faces and gratefully received 50 pairs of sealskin boots. At Etah, Greenland, the prey-obsessed millionaire Harry Whitney was dropped off for a spot of polar bear hunting; the *Roosevelt* then collected a further 500 tons of coal, another 70 tons of whale meat, and 246 dogs, "all fighting and screaming."[7] The going was rough from that point and the *Roosevelt*, a small ship for such a challenging voyage, "forg[ed] ahead by inches."[8] The crew reached their winter quarters near Cape Sheridan on 5 September and used sledges to carry their supplies 90 miles west to Cape Columbia, the "hop-off point to the Pole."[9] That expedition included seven white men, 19 "Eskimos," and 20 sledges, according to Bartlett.[10] On 22 February 1909 (George Washington's birthday, Bartlett noted), Peary left Cape Columbia for the Pole, supported by several "units," all headed by white expedition members and consisting of several Inuit who played supporting roles in the manner of Sherpas on modern-day Mount Everest climbs. It was a bracing -30°F and blowing a gale. Interestingly, Bartlett, who was not unencumbered by racism, included Matthew Henson, Peary's African-American assistant, in his list of white unit leaders; expedition rank superseded race in the odd caste system of Arctic exploration. Henson was officially listed as Peary's valet, generally the highest naval rank an African-American could attain at that time.[11]

Using a method carefully worked out by Peary over many years of northern experience, each unit had a sledge longer than Inuit sledges, devised by Peary to, Bartlett claimed, the delight of the Inuit. Each sledge carried 650 pounds, including 50 pounds of biscuits, 50 pounds of protein-rich "man pemmican"* for the driver, tea, clothing, and dog food.[12] The explorers eschewed sleeping bags, dozing, instead, on their snowshoes covered by a piece of animal skin. On snowshoes and using a lantern in the darkness, Bartlett led the pioneer party, which meant he had the daunting responsibilities of setting the course, determining distances, and breaking trail, the most difficult and demanding task. In Peary's words, "[Bartlett] was pioneering ahead of his own party, and that whole division was pioneering ahead of the main party."[13] On Peary's orders, Bartlett's unit did short marches of less than 10 miles at a time. It was fair going at first but the relatively easy early days were followed by "a month of terrible labour for all."[14] There was more open water than they expected, and the wind was relentless, almost mocking them. The temperature was consistently a brutal -50°F. Yet Bartlett shared Peary's determination to make it to the Pole. Of a meeting among unit leaders, he recalled, "We pledged each other we would fight to the bitter end and do all in our power to help Peary plant the Stars and Stripes at the Pole. I remember [chief scientist Ross] Marvin was especially moved ..."[15]

Two Inuit, Pooadloona and Panikpah, deserted near the top of the world. No one can be sure why; it may have been maltreatment at the hands of the unit leaders, conflict between the Inuit themselves, or the low pay offered by Peary. Scrimping was a habit for Peary; his 1898 expedition to northern Greenland had lacked sufficient crew members and those it did have were underpaid.[16] In the Arctic explorer tradition, the Inuit were certainly undervalued, and they knew it; as Peary wrote of them in 1910, "Their very limitations are their most valuable endowments for the purposes of Arctic work."[17] Most explorers looked down on the Inuit. Peary's view was typical. Vermont-born Arctic explorer Charles Francis Hall was an exception; he acknowledged Inuit women's skilful handiwork in producing the clothes that allowed the explorers to survive in the Arctic, and Inuit are otherwise central to his narrative, his reliance on them obvious.[18] This is not to say that Hall was liberal by today's standards; as historian Michael Robinson explains, "Hall's rebellion was a quiet one. He never abandoned the mantle of civilized character. Nor did his appreciation of Eskimo life

---

*   Pemmican is a paste made mainly of meat and fat. A North American Indigenous invention, it became associated with explorers and the Métis of Western Canada.

ever challenge the supremacy of American values." * [19] Frederick Cook, too, who claimed to have reached the North Pole a year before Peary did, clung to then-conventional wisdom about the Indigenous people of the Arctic, but he also made it a point to learn Inuit skills and even the language. [20] As to why the Inuit left Peary near the Pole, it is difficult to discern motives across cultures and time.

The Arctic as an idea has deep roots in western culture. The word *Arctic* comes from *Arktos*, the ancient Greek word for the Big Dipper in the northern sky. [21] A poem presumed to have been written by Homer alludes to the Arctic, which the Greeks then believed to be inhabited by the immortal Hyperboreans, for whom it was a paradise. [22] They would never know the Arctic as the land of the Inuit.

The first time the Inuit saw Englishmen was when they boarded Martin Frobisher's ship in the summer of 1576. Frobisher, a privateer, or licenced pirate, who would be knighted by Queen Elizabeth I, was in search of the Northwest Passage that would give England better access to Asia for trade. [23] His navigator Christopher Hall described the Inuit: "They bee like to Tartars, with long blacke haire, broad faces, and flatte noses, and tawnie in colour, wearing Seal skinnes, and so does the women, not differing in the fashion, but the women are marked in the face with bleue streekes downe the cheeks, and round the eyes."† [24] Relations deteriorated very quickly and the Inuit captured five of Frobisher's crew members; in return, Frobisher ordered his men to take their Inuit guide hostage. [25] Frobisher's kidnapped men were never seen again by Englishmen but Inuit oral history records them as having lived with the Inuit for several years. Ever since then, the history of western-Inuit relations is pockmarked with misunderstandings, often resulting in devastating consequences, especially for the Inuit. The attitudes of the explorers have long shaped ideas about Inuit. [26] As late as 1955, a reputable geographer and anthropologist would write of the Greenlandic Inuit, "Eskimos are notably incapable of dwelling

---

*   Hall died off Greenland in 1871, after suffering vomiting, paralysis, hallucinations, and seizures due to arsenic poisoning. Hall may have been ingesting arsenic for medicinal reasons, as was the practice at that time. As he neared death, however, he believed he had been poisoned.

†   These were facial tattoos, an Inuit women's tradition. These tattoos have various functions, one of which was to recognize the skills an individual woman acquired. The practice was stigmatized for a period following the arrival of Christian missionaries to Inuit lands but is now enjoying a revival in many Inuit communities in Canada. Jamie Jelinski, "Kakiniit and Other 'Strong Blue Speckes': Self-Representation and Qallunaat Images of Inuit Tattooing," (PhD diss., Concordia University, 2015).

for long on an idea that is unrelated to problems of hunting ..."[27] For most explorers, and certainly for Peary, Inuit were "cogs in the machine."[28] For some, such as those of the Oxford University Expedition of 1935–36, the Inuit were "more of a hindrance than an assistance."[29] After Pooadloona and Panikpah abandoned their units, Bartlett observed that the remaining Inuit were demoralized. Their bleak mood was ominous.

Personalities matter on an expedition like Peary's, where the line between life and death is so thin. Though he stopped short of criticizing Bartlett, Henson described him as occasionally excitable or nervous; Henson thought him young to be in charge of a vessel. Bartlett was 34, not a young skipper by Newfoundland standards and certainly not by those of the accomplished family from which he came. Henson noted Bartlett's rounded shoulders, made so, he thought, by rowing oars—although the captain's posture was more likely the result of being hunched over a book. Henson astutely wrote of Bartlett's eagle eye and concluded that "[h]is manners and conduct indicate that he has always been the leader of his crowd from boyhood up, and there is no man on this ship that he would be afraid to tackle."[30]

On 28 March on the way to the Pole, Henson found Bartlett's leading unit asleep in their igloo, completely exhausted; he made sure not to disturb them. Upon waking, Bartlett explained that that day's journey had taken 14 hours "under the most trying conditions."[31] It was much shorter for Henson's unit, since Bartlett's team had broken trail for them and the others. Yet Henson, too, was very fatigued, writing, "We staggered into camp like drunken men, and built our igloos by force of habit rather than with the intelligence of human beings."[32] When, later, a rapidly shifting ice floe nearly caused their deaths, both Peary and Bartlett were "too full of the realization of [their] escape to have much to say."[33] Despite their veteran status in the Arctic, neither Peary nor Bartlett had expected such formidable and unsettling travel; they were taken aback by the obstacles they encountered and feared that the Pole might prove elusive despite their herculean efforts.

Admiral Peary called Bartlett the "most valuable of all" his expedition members.[34] Yet Bob Bartlett of Brigus, Newfoundland, declared he had no ambition to become an explorer. Bartlett was an established and experienced northern mariner before he ventured into actual polar exploration with Peary. His uncles, Captains John and Samuel Bartlett, had sailed into Arctic waters long before him, John as early as 1848. Two decades later, John brought the Dr. Isaac Israel Hayes Expedition to Melville Bay in the Bartletts' vessel, the *Panther*.[35] Captain Sam Bartlett skippered the *Neptune* in 1903–4, a voyage that culminated in Ellesmere Island being claimed by King Edward VII and the establishment of Canadian law and customs in the Eastern Arctic with lasting consequences for the Inuit. A great-uncle, Captain Isaac Bartlett, rescued the Tyson Party in 1873, survivors of the *Polaris* Expedition who had been stranded so long on an ice floe they "were about to resort to cannibalism," as Bob Bartlett put it.[36] Isaac was given to garrulousness but, in the main, the Bartlett skippers were usually matter of fact about their skills and experience. When, in stormy seas, Captain Thomas Bartlett brought a ship alongside "as easy as a young mother would put her baby in a cot," he dismissed compliments, saying, "There's lots of men, sir, in [nearby] Harbour Grace wearing canvas jackets [who] can do the same."[37] In the Arctic, Bartlett's uncles and his father, Captain William Bartlett, restricted their activities to the traditional duties of ship's captain and, until 1909 with Peary, Bob followed their examples. During this phase of polar exploration, when the era was nearing its end, there was little crossover between the occupations of explorer and skipper, with the result that there were few captain-explorers. Despite their military origins, neither Sir Ernest Shackleton nor Sir Robert Falcon Scott, both of whom went to the Antarctic during what was called the Heroic Age of Antarctic Exploration,[38] were ship's captains; nor was Fridtjof Nansen, the Norwegian explorer, scientist, and, intriguingly, champion ice skater. Peary had graduated from Bowdoin College in leafy Brunswick, Maine, with a degree in civil engineering. Frederick Cook was a physician living in Brooklyn. Though the son of a captain, Donald Baxter MacMillan, in the *Roosevelt* with Peary and Bartlett, was a geologist and an accomplished speaker on the subject of the Arctic, as Bartlett would become.

In combining his duties and skills as a mariner with those of an explorer, Bartlett was both an innovator and a throwback to Captain James Cook, the 18th-century Briton who mapped Newfoundland, who became the first known European to reach Australia's east coast and Hawaii, and circumnavigated New Zealand, driving what has been called the invasion of the South Pacific.[39] Like Bartlett, Cook was a pragmatist and entirely devoted to advancing his seagoing career, whatever it took. Mistrusted by the Hawaiians,[40] Cook suffered an apparently* violent death on Valentine's Day, 1779, when one of their number stabbed him in the back and was joined by others who "shewed a savage eagerness to have a share in his destruction."[41] Cook, meanwhile, had made substantial contributions to ethnographic collections in the west, to western science, and to navigation, and, in this way, to the advance of empires.[42] Bartlett would do the same, annually collecting "veritable zoological treasure trove[s]"[43] for American museums.

Although spared a painful death far from home, Bartlett was, in many ways, Cook's heir. Cook sailed to the Pacific only three times, dying on his third voyage. Bartlett made numerous Arctic voyages, with Peary, on his own in his schooner, the *Effie Morrissey*, and with the controversial Icelandic-Canadian explorer Vilhjalmur Stefansson, whom he would come to despise. On these trips Bartlett collected specimens and information for at least 14 leading scientific institutions, including the American Museum of Natural History, the University of Michigan, the Museum of the American Indian, the Smithsonian Institution, the American Geographical Society, the Chicago Zoological Society, the Cleveland Museum of Natural History, and Vassar College. Collecting was a vital part of the colonial enterprise that would shape the map of the world,[44] and Bartlett's role in collecting, which is not well known, extended the reach of western empires. From another perspective, collecting might be interpreted as stealing; as a result, museum collections are frequently contested in the 21st century† and specimens, including Inuit corpses that were taken from graves, are sometimes returned to their original location.

Bartlett's work with Peary triggered his interest in exploration. From their first meeting, the seeds would be sown for Bartlett to add polar exploration to his resumé and to fashion a then-unique position as a navigator-explorer which would match his own inclinations and add to his public and personal appeal. Accident rather than design was at work, at

---

* The facts surrounding his death are disputed and Cook has been the subject of considerable lore and fantasy. Gananath Obeyesekere, *The Apotheosis of Captain Cook: European Mythmaking in the Pacific* (Princeton, NJ: University Press, 1997).

† The Greek or Elgin Marbles housed in the British Museum are, perhaps, the most famous of these contested treasures.

least in the beginning. Bartlett slowly fell into the role of explorer, emulating Peary, whom he put on a pedestal, as he had a tendency to do with "great men," and learning the necessary skills from the Inuit of Greenland. In Bartlett's ghost writer's words*—which would have been fashioned and approved by Bartlett—"I had no fancy dreams about exploration. I had no scientific education or training beyond the limited navigation and other nautical knowledge required by my mate's and master's papers. I didn't want to become a professional explorer. I had sense enough to realize my limitation in attempting any scientific work. But it was in my blood to keep to the sea and to push out into the wild spaces of the earth."[45]

The polar exploration tradition was entrenched by Bartlett's time, but, save for the odd foray north, it would enter its dying days during the Great Depression. Exploration for its own sake is an old tradition in the western world. Pytheas of Massalia, a Greek colony in Southern France, was the first Arctic explorer. Born about 350 BC, Pytheas travelled to Britain, then sailed for six days to a place he called Thule. This may have been Iceland, any of the Scottish Islands, Norway, or perhaps the Svalbard archipelago in the Arctic Ocean. Pytheas was halted by a "sea-lung," possibly an icefield but more likely a fog bank, which he conceptualized as "that mixture of earth, water, and mist which so terrified the Mediterranean people."[46] Other Europeans followed, including Norseman Leif Eriksson and possibly Ireland's St. Brendan, reaching North America hundreds of years before Sir Martin Frobisher. These ventures preceded those of Icelandic explorer Thorfinn Karlsefni Þórðarson, who, around 1010, landed on Baffin Island, Inuit land which he called Helluland.[47]

Captain Edward Fenton, Frobisher's second in command, called the Inuit "Country People" and was disappointed in his failure to speak with them: "Only having viewed as neare at hande they retired themselves without any staie of conference with us albeit we offered them trafique and show of all courtesie we could devise, which by no means could allure them to staie, but so rowed from us into a sounde a league of[f] …"[48] After Frobisher, John Davis was next to make his mark. In the summer of 1585 his 50-ton *Sunshine* was nearly shipwrecked in the northern reaches of

---

*   According to Harold Horwood, one of Bartlett's biographers, most of Bartlett's books were ghost written (*Bartlett: The Great Explorer* [1977; Toronto: Doubleday Canada, 1989]).

Greenland. Davis jumped in a small boat and thus discovered that his ship was "embayed in fields and hills of ice, the crashing together of which made the fearful sounds" that had beckoned him from the *Sunshine*.[49] As the ship drifted, the English crew were mesmerized by a jarring but startlingly beautiful vision; they "saw the tops of mountains white with snow, and a sugar-loaf shape, standing above the clouds; while at their base the land was deformed and rocky, and the shore was everywhere beset with ice, which made such irksome noise" that they could not help but christen this place "the Land of Desolation."[50] In 1869, Captain John Bartlett sailed to that same spot in the *Panther*, the beloved and storied family vessel. On board was American explorer Isaac Israel Hayes, who first went to the Arctic in 1853.[51] Hayes described John Bartlett as "a little rash and venturesome," although this did not affect the crew's high opinion of the skipper.[52] John Bartlett's nephew Bob would reach these shores long afterwards but, for Bob, this fierce, sublimely beautiful and threatening spot would never be Davis's Land of Desolation. Instead, the vast white Arctic was the only place that could liberate Bartlett from the feelings of desolation that dogged him.

Racism was at the foundation of all exploration activity, whether in the Arctic or in Africa, and exploration maintained and propelled racism. Exploration was carried out in the interests of empires and states in Europe and, later, North America. The extension of empire had at its foundation "a complex ideology," as historian John M. MacKenzie put it.[53] *Terra nullius* was the European legal doctrine that identified land not owned or used for agriculture as "empty" and, therefore, unowned.[*][54] The presumed emptiness of the Arctic led Europeans to see it as unoccupied land, claimed by no one. This meant that the land was "discoverable" and available for the taking. Europeans did not understand the unique geophysical environment of the Arctic and Indigenous land-use patterns, which involved seasonal land and sea use and the movement of dwellings, instead of permanent structures, year-round settlements, and fields developed for farming. Inuit land-use patterns were complex and reflected millennia of accumulated

---

[*]   *Terra nullius* shaped contemporary Australia and was the law in that country until 1992 (Stuart Banner, "Why *Terra Nullius?* Anthropology and Property Law in Early Australia," *Law and History Review* 23, no. 1 [2005]: 95–131), but it had a huge influence in other colonized lands, such as Canada (Boyce Richardson, *People of* Terra Nullius: *Betrayal and Rebirth in Aboriginal Canada* [Douglas & McIntyre, 1993]) and the Norwegian archipelago of Svalbard (Geir Ulfstein, *The Svalbard Treaty: From* Terra Nullius *to Norwegian Sovereignty* [Oslo: Scandinavian University Press, 1995].

Indigenous knowledge. Explorers saw Inuit as simple and inferior at worst and skilled in a narrow set of tasks at best. Thus, Inuit were sources of expedition support and the Arctic was, as it is today for the countries that claim it, an opportunity for natural resource exploitation.

In western ways of thinking, ownership requires presence; following Britain, Canada has tried to maintain a presence in the Arctic since the late 1800s. In Pierre Berton's words, "all this bumbling about in the ice streams seeking the lost Franklin party made it possible for Canada to claim the Arctic as its own."*[55] Writer Ariana Crachiun pointed out that the Franklin saga was a distraction and the Arctic was never British and therefore can never be Canadian: "The Arctic and its Northwest Passages are not transhistorical entities awaiting the inevitable arrival of explorers, authors, nations, and sovereignty exercises to give them meaning."[56] This is why the capital of Nunavut was renamed Iqaluit, the place of fish, from Frobisher in 1987 in an attempt to decolonize. Yet the Arctic was long perceived as silent, empty, passive yet savage, an object of discovery.

Part of the Arctic's appeal to countries with imperial ambitions was that it seemed to lack the labour-intensity and complications of other pushes. By the mid-19th century, Americans were worn out by the Mexican war and by the rapid expansion into the west, by slavery and by debates about what to do with the new western territories, acquired from the Native Americans.[57] In contrast, the alleged empty northern lands seemed simple; "Arctic exploration constituted a safer form of conquest, offering many of the advantages of war without the messy commitments of empire."[58]

These considerations were understood as an unquestioned part of political discourse. As archaeologist Robert McGhee put it, "North American governments did not stop to wonder whether they had the right to grant the resources of Arctic regions to those who wish to exploit them for industrial purposes."[59] Meanwhile, the Canadian government used Inuit like chess pieces to further stamp its sovereignty on the Arctic; in the 1950s, Ottawa moved small groups of Inuit to the High Arctic, far from their hunting grounds, to send a message to Cold War United States. The Soviets moved Indigenous people to Wrangel Island, a locale that

---

*   Sir John Franklin's ships, the HMS *Terror* and the HMS *Erebus*, were lost in the mid-19th century with 129 men. The ships were recently discovered in the Canadian Arctic, their resting place identified at least partly as a result of Inuit knowledge.

would loom large in Bartlett's life. These actions by the Canadians and the Russians had countless parallels in history. In fact, they mirrored those of Julius Caesar, whose military push conquered Britain and pushed the Celts to the west, and Alexander the Great, whose armies spread across the Persian Empire. It is hard not to conclude that there is something in human beings that, if unchecked, drives us to dominate others. For much of our history, we have built philosophical and ideological constructs that cater to a thirst for power. This has certainly been the case with the countries of Western Europe.

Terra nullius and related ideas rendered Indigenous people and communities invisible and, when visible, insignificant. As far as the Spanish, French, English, and Dutch were concerned, "discovery with symbolic taking of possession [was] an adequate basis for legal title ... in North America."[60] Thus, planting a flag on newly "discovered" land granted ownership. This was particularly true in the early days of exploration, but the logic of it was imbued in the actions of Peary, Scott, and all other flag-planters and monument builders in polar regions; Bartlett would join their ranks.

Against this backdrop, Bartlett the explorer was to become one of the most honoured and celebrated figures of the first half of the 20th century. Bartlett reflected the ideas, feelings, and goals of the era in which he lived and thus offers a portal into the "unspoken assumptions" of an age.[61] While these assumptions are challenged in some venues, such as Canada's Indigenous land claims process, they continue to influence the governments of Canada, Denmark, and other northern countries in the 21st century.[62] It is ironic that contemporary Inuit are still described as "nomads," denoting aimless and uncertain wandering, when it was actually the nomadism of the Europeans that facilitated encounter.

Inuit voices rarely appear in any of the many published and unpublished polar accounts and their actions, crucial though they were, are peripheral to narratives and celebrations of Arctic explorers. Thus, while Inuit shared stories with each other, these exploration stories are "silent accounts to the rest of the world."[63] This makes exploration narratives incomplete and even suspect.[64] Indigenous silence allowed explorers to criticize and blame Inuit. This happened, for instance, when Norwegian topographer Bjarne Mamen of the doomed *Karluk*, skippered by Bartlett, referred to Inuit as

"lazy swine" in his diary.[65] In common with mountaineering tales, such as *Into Thin Air*, Jon Krakaeur's narrative of the 1996 Everest disaster, dominant Arctic exploration accounts become myths and also spectacles, obscuring the interests of various parties, such as the British or Canadian governments.[66] Sherpas who support Everest climbs are usually portrayed as passive and mute, heard only through acts of "colonial ventriloquism."[67] There is a close parallel to depictions of Inuit in Arctic exploration accounts. When there is a plurality of voices, stories become more nuanced and complex, less sensational and less easily consumed, but this makes these stories less compelling.[68] Attention to Inuit voices would have solved many mysteries of Arctic exploration; they would have undermined, for instance, the rumours of missing men, suicides, murders, and cannibalism that swirled around the Franklin saga.

In common with other explorer accounts of the time, the texts attributed to and those written by Bartlett lack Inuit voices; thus, some events and issues, including tragic incidents, can never be resolved or fully understood. A simple example of this omission occurred in Greenland when Peary and Bartlett were both critical of the "spells" of Ahngoodloo, an Inuk, who was likely experiencing stress, perhaps in reaction to the inherent power relationships and power abuse in Arctic exploration.[69] After all, the Inuit gave Peary a name which meant "one who is feared."[70] The dearth of available Inuit analyses leaves this an open question.*

Bartlett first encountered Admiral Robert Peary at Turnavik, the Bartletts' fishing station in northern Labrador; Turnavik had become a favourite port of call for Peary on his trips to Greenland. In 1893, Peary went there in the *Falcon*, captained by Harry Bartlett. Peary was 42; Bartlett, still a teenager, was immediately struck by the admiral's tall, lean, rugged figure, recalling that Peary was garbed in a "black long-tailed coat, slouched hat and sealskin boots."[71] In the adoring tone he often used when speaking of Peary, he said, "there was a light in his grey eyes that I never forgot. It shone with the determination to win. Deep down inside me I thought at once, here is a man I'd like to follow."[72]

---

*   A notable but not especially well-known exception is Hans Hendrik, the Greenland native who wrote his memoirs (*Memoirs of Hans Hendrik, the Arctic Traveller, Serving under Kane, Hayes, Hall and Nares, 1853–1876*, ed. George Stephens [1878; Cambridge University Press, 2014]) and was honoured by the naming of Hans Island. Yet, for Anglophone readers, this is a translation.

Bartlett had a tendency toward hero worship, always directed at men, a trait not surprising in a young man who grew up in Brigus, populated by national heroes who had conquered the icefields. When not being instructed in the importance of classical music by his elegant and commanding grandmother Mary Norman Leamon, Bartlett spent his childhood absorbing tales of derring-do. His uncles were celebrities; his father was a household name in Newfoundland, with his remarkable success at the prestigious—and dangerous—seal hunt and following the *Panther*'s rescue of hundreds of the survivors of the 1885 Eskimo Coast disaster, the hurricane that led to the deaths of dozens of women and children who had been in the holds of fishing ships travelling home to Newfoundland from the Labrador summer fishery. What is interesting about Bartlett's assessment of Peary is his stated desire to attach himself to a leader. At that stage, Bartlett saw himself as a follower and he was searching for a man to look up to—but outside of his family, where there was no dearth of leaders.

Peary began his polar career after a holiday in Greenland.[73] Peary was admired by Bartlett's uncles and by his father, which predisposed Bartlett to respect the explorer. Before Bartlett first sailed with Peary in the late 1800s, his uncle Henry (Harry) Bartlett reported, in typical Bartlett speech, that Peary was "like a T-square ... he thinks in a straight line. And you can't bend him anymore than you can steel ... He's the kind that doesn't make it his business unless he knows it ... He doesn't ask a man to go where he wouldn't go himself."[74] Peary had an equally high opinion of himself and wrote to his mother in 1880, "I would like to acquire a name which would be an open sesame to circles of culture and refinement anywhere, a name which would make my mother proud, and which would make me feel that I was the peer of anyone I might meet."[75]

Uncle John Bartlett pointed out, rather bluntly and pragmatically, that Peary knew how to "use the Eskimos."[76] Bob Bartlett's father, William, said that an attachment to Peary and his expeditions was "a good way to get ahead," a route that would allow Bob to become master of his own ship, a typical family goal.[77] All of these judgments ring true; Peary was businesslike, calculating, and ambitious, and he was an expert in identifying, incorporating, and adapting all available resources, including

Inuit. More importantly, these qualities of Peary reflected values the Bartletts held dear: dedication, ambition, and the semi-aristocratic honour of deliberately but unselfconsciously mucking in with the lower ranks. As Harry Bartlett put it, Peary was not "a rough handler ... by our way of thinking."[78] This was high praise indeed.

What most attracted Bartlett to exploration was Peary's systematic and goal-oriented approach, and he became very familiar with this during four years with Peary at Ellesmere Island in the *Windward*. The ship had been a gift from Sir Alfred Harmsworth, who would become Lord Northcliffe, the hugely influential owner of the London *Times*, the *Daily Mail*, and the *Daily Mirror*. For many years, the boreal woods of central Newfoundland supplied much of the paper needed for production of these publications. The Dublin-born Northcliffe was educated in England, alongside H.G. Wells. Bartlett would later (ca. 1915) attend a dinner with Lord and Lady Northclifffe at the Plaza Hotel in New York. A Union club valet helped Bartlett dress; Bartlett also willingly submitted to a manicure in preparation for the occasion.

From the *Windward*, with Bob as first officer and the experienced Captain John Bartlett at the wheel, Peary and company mapped the northernmost islands of the Greenland archipelago and reached 83'50" North.[79] They managed this even though the ship was not as capable as they had hoped; she was slow and not especially fit for Arctic ice conditions. When the *Windward* could not get north of Cape D'orville in the Kane Basin, Peary sledged his supplies to where he wanted to go.[80] Although neither Peary nor the Inuit who guided him had been to that part of Greenland before, they travelled by night, the first time an Arctic explorer had journeyed by sledge in complete darkness. Bartlett was enamoured with anyone undaunted by the challenges posed by the natural world and, after this feat, Peary grew even higher in his estimation. Like Peary, Bartlett embraced a certain amount of risk-taking, understanding that risks are one path to innovation and advancement. Neither man was afraid of failing, at least in the small things, although the North Pole had to be attained no matter what. As Bartlett put it, "I always loved Peary for being a true sportsman and in taking chances where sometimes we won and sometimes we lost ..."[81]

It was on this *Windward* trip that Peary lost his toes. Two hundred miles from the ship, he was trekking alone and fell through the ice, knocking himself out. When he awoke, his legs and feet were frozen and most of his toes beyond repair. Yet he survived the two months it took him to return to the *Windward*, where he could have the surgery he so desperately needed. Peary had ridden on a sledge the entire time, bouncing helplessly as it went over rough ice.* On board ship, Bartlett held the can of ether as Peary's dead toes were chopped off. As a result of this mutilation, Peary could not walk properly until the middle of 1900. Although he could only hobble about, he told Bartlett, "One can get used to anything."[82] There would be times in Bartlett's life when he would recall this advice and try to derive inspiration from it. Meanwhile, the amputation permanently left Peary with "a peculiar slide-like stride."[83]

According to Bartlett, Peary never lost his good cheer through the ordeal and its aftermath, and the admiral's uncomplaining nature appealed to the Brigus Methodist in Bartlett. Recovering from surgery akin to butchery, Peary had to walk over rocky ground when the snow began to melt. "[It] was hell," Bartlett recalled. "Imagine—no, one cannot, how he walked over these stones through icy cold water, with the bones sticking out of the stumps of his feet and the flesh turned [black]. It is beyond me to just know how he did it, for the dogs had to be taken from the sledge and floated along in the streams and over the rocks; it was all the dogs could do to haul the empty sledge."[84] And then, using the dramatic language he reserved for those most dear to him, "No martyr in the old days of religious persecution suffered and endured as [Peary] did."[85] This comment shows that Bartlett was shaped by 19th-century Brigus and raised as the inheritor of the Bartlett family legacy, including that of his great-great-grandfather Captain William "Follow-On" Bartlett, who had a withered arm but was renowned for his seafaring prowess. It was not suffering Bartlett valued—he was no Roman Catholic and was annoyed by saints, piety, and elaborate ceremony—it was Peary's unfailing stoicism. Bartlett eulogized his mentor at the Explorers Club in 1920, "I knew no matter what happened that never a word of commiseration would come from him, hence my reason for always respecting and my willingness to serve him."[86]

---

* Anyone who has ridden in a wooden *komatik* or on a sledge knows how uncomfortable it is, even for a short time.

The Greenlandic Inuit were Peary's main tutors; wisely, he had embraced rather than ignored their knowledge and expertise. He made sure to establish his winter quarters near Inuit populations and he acknowledged Inuit travel techniques and the skill of Inuit women in producing the clothing so necessary for the explorers' survival.[87] Frederick Cook had the same approach, but it was Charles Francis Hall who had first turned to Inuit material culture in the 1850s, seeing it as vital to success. Stefansson expressed bafflement that Inuit technology had not been adopted earlier in the history of exploration.[88] It was the Greenland-born part-Inuit Danish explorer Knud Rasmussen who, in 1912, finally offered a comprehensive manual on Inuit material culture and methods of travel and survival in the Arctic.[89]

By 1898, according to Bartlett, "Peary was pretty much of an Eskimo," meaning that he wore Inuit clothing, ate Inuit food, and had acquired Inuit travel skills.[90] Bartlett did not include world view or cultural outlook in his concept of Inuitness. For Peary, the Inuit fit into a kind of 'primitive plus' category as "philosophic anarchists of the North." He wrote, "They are savages but they are not savages; they are without government but they are not lawless; they are utterly uneducated according to our standard, yet they exhibit a remarkable degree of intelligence."[91] He claimed that the Inuit felt gratitude toward him and compared his "gifts" of rifles and other items to "those of an imaginary philanthropic millionaire descending upon an American town and offering every man there a brownstone mansion and an unlimited bank account."[92] Peary rewarded Seegloo, Ooqueah, Ootah, and Egingwah, who were on the final trek to the Pole, with tents and whaleboats which, he said, they received like children with new toys.[93] Some 50 years earlier, Elisha Kent Kane, who had tried to find the lost Franklin expedition, asserted that the Inuit "mourned [his] departure [from the Arctic] bitterly."[94] Kane's and Peary's interest in the Inuit did not extend much beyond their own usefulness to them. In contrast to Cook, Peary did not bother to learn the Greenlandic language, relying instead on hand gestures and very basic jargon.

In most of this, Bartlett followed Peary. Bartlett absorbed Inuit expertise and learned to use grass to keep clothes dry, adjust skin clothing to enhance warmth, eat raw and decaying seal meat, include blubber in his diet to better his tolerance of cold weather, drive a dog team up to 60 miles at a stretch, travel over rocks, glaciers, hills and crevasses without injury, identify potential avalanche sites and iffy ice, deal with ever-present lice,* and protect his boot-clad feet from freezing.[95] He remembered his apprenticeship with Peary fondly: "It sounds like a rough life. But it wasn't ... When I got back home in 1902, I realized that I was committed to Arctic work ... I knew I would have to keep at it."[96] He was also committed to Peary. When his father told him he would have to get his own expedition to make money, Bartlett replied, "But I don't want my own expedition as long as I can go with Peary."[97]

If it was not for Captain John Bartlett, Bob might never have gone to the Arctic. John Bartlett got his masters certificate from Greenock, Scotland, in 1866, when he was 23.[98] Samuel Bartlett was awarded his masters certificate 12 years later.[99] The brothers were among the first Newfoundlanders to achieve these certificates, with John likely being the first. John Bartlett was the first Bartlett to venture north of the Arctic Circle, and his association with Peary dated to the 1890s when he commanded the *Diana*, followed by the *Windward*, the *Erik*, and the *Jeannie*.[100] Captain Harry Bartlett also sailed with Peary.[101] For the push to the Pole, Sam Bartlett was offered the captaincy of the *Roosevelt*, but he felt he was too old and recommended his nephew for the job.[102] Bob was delighted to receive an enthusiastic invitation from Peary to skipper the *Roosevelt* in 1905 and he accepted immediately: "[Peary's] pluck and energy just took hold of you, unless you were a dead one you couldn't help but feel the magnetic forces of the great man."[103] Bartlett compared his excitement to that of a child who receives a longed-for bicycle at Christmas.

The *Roosevelt*, the 181-foot luxurious steam-sailer built for Peary's next assault on the North Pole, was launched at Bucksport, Maine, on 23 May 1905.[104] Like Peary, Bartlett was sure they would have an easier time than they had had with the *Windward*, but they were in for more than a few surprises. The *Roosevelt* and her crew of 25 left New York City on 16 July 1905.[105] A few weeks later Bartlett wrote in the log: "touched

---

* Lice were a problem for the Inuit but it was widespread throughout the western world at this time. Bartlett said that Newfoundland fishermen believed that lice do not nest on unhealthy bodies; it was said that "lice always left a dead man as soon as he got cold" (John K. Crellin, *Home Medicine: The Newfoundland Experience* [Montreal and Kingston: McGill-Queen's University Press, 1994], 176). Bartlett also credited the Inuit with being extremely clean in defiance of persistent and wrong-headed ideas about Inuit hygiene and in spite of his own frequent lapses into the use of native stereotypes in his *Log* and elsewhere.

bottom no damage."[106] This near miss foreshadowed a great drama that started with a bang, literally, when two of the ship's three boilers blew up at Sydney, Nova Scotia; only luck prevented fatalities, but some crew members were scalded. They continued north without getting the boiler replaced, a process which would have taken several months and so had to be foregone. Although Peary's determination was the main motivating force for their haste, Bartlett was also exhibiting his tendency to take risks at sea. As biographer Harold Horwood said of Captain John Bartlett and his nephew Bob, "[John] seems to have been a foolhardy driver of a captain, even by Bob's standards, which weren't very exacting, for he himself was no paragon of caution when it came to handling a ship."[107] As Bartlett analyzed his uncle's methodology: "Uncle John ordered his crew not to shorten sail 'no matter how hard it blew, or how foggy it became ...' in my forty years at sea I've never seen a captain drive a ship the way he did ..."[108] Indeed, John was capable of getting a ship's speed up to an impressive 10 or 11 knots under sail alone. Bartlett would emulate his uncle many times as the *Roosevelt* went north in 1905; at times he would be forced to do so.

The rotting whale meat they had collected in Labrador for the dogs immediately began seeping into the wood of the ship's decks, creating an awful smell as well as a fire hazard, given that virtually everyone on board smoked. The inevitable happened near Etah, then a village of three igloos, after an Inuk dropped his pipe. Bartlett recalled, "It was bad enough to have [the ship] burning up but the smell of the smoldering whale blubber was enough to asphyxiate one. After a fight we got it out."[109] By June, the *Roosevelt* was jammed between ice and the land. Peary recalled this stressful time: "Clinging with Bartlett, high up in the vibrating rigging, peering far ahead for a streak of open water, studying the movement of the floes which pressed against us, I would hear him shouting to the ship below us as if coaxing her, encouraging her, commanding her to hammer a way for us through the adamantine floes."[110] Bartlett resorted to dynamite to destroy the ice, but he used too much and damaged the ship. Just a few days later, the ship was rammed by ice, with the impact driving her out of the water. Her propeller was wrecked and her rudder ripped apart.

To add to the misery and worry, Bartlett soon discovered a hole in the *Roosevelt*'s bottom big enough for a small boy to crawl through. For

Captain John Bartlett, Bob's uncle, who first went to the Arctic in the 1850s with American explorer Dr. Isaac Isreal Hayes, thus setting the stage for Bob. The photo was taken in the 1880s. *The Rooms Provincial Archives Division/S.H. Parsons.*

an excruciating 15 minutes, the ship was held by pressure, ice creaking all around her, her "groans" reminding Bartlett of a human being in pain. Expecting the *Roosevelt* to capsize completely, Bartlett ordered the crew to land provisions. But their incessant working of the pumps succeeded and the ship was saved. They blocked the hole with waste, oakum, and cement; such stopgap measures would become a trademark of Bartlett in a crisis. Repairs to the propeller took 48 hours, during which time a blizzard raged around the labouring men. Peary was inland at the time but nothing that had happened necessitated a report to him upon his return; as far as Bartlett was concerned, the explorer was too tired to be told of such nuisances.

Bartlett was inured to calamity by this stage in his career, having started marine life as a teenager, and he had a well-worn shipboard routine. His nephew Jack Angel, who sailed to the Arctic with him several times, said "the Skipper [as he called Bartlett] didn't change his clothes, you know, he never changed his clothes."[111] Bartlett slept with his oilskins on, his feet clad in sealskin boots, and was partial to catnaps. He was never more than an arm's length away from his chronometer, which measured longitude, and his sextant, which fixed latitude. According to Angel, Bartlett never changed the chronometer; instead, he would "note how many seconds it was off, and seconds, not minutes, seconds."[112] Dismissing the easy way out of a problem was just one of Bartlett's many eccentricities.

Peary had failed to reach the Pole after discovering too much open water to cross, but on 21 April 1906, he had reached 87'06" North, only 174 nautical miles south of the North Pole. The ailing *Roosevelt* had pushed farther north than any ship in history.[113] This achievement was not enough for Peary who, lusting for immortality, planned to return the next summer. Reaching the Pole was his sole focus. Bartlett, meanwhile, had to get the ailing ship back to New York somehow. His latest troubles included a leak in the remaining boiler and steering difficulties because the makeshift rudder was too small; the ice kept pushing through the hole they had covered earlier as best they could and water kept coming in. Bartlett stationed crew members near the hole at all times, and the vessel "limped along as best it could."[114]

Still in northern Greenland, the crew was short of food, which was demoralizing as well as unhealthy; meal times were one of the few things to look forward to during such a long and cold voyage. Before long the ship was stuck in the ice again. Bartlett, a fatalist despite his heroic efforts, "used to go up on deck and decide that [they] would sink in a few minutes and then go down and make a last entry in [his] diary. Then [he]'d come up again and [they]'d still be afloat and [he]'d try to explain how it was possible for a wreck like [theirs] not to sink."[115] For two weeks, the situation continued, "an awful strain," as Bartlett called it, especially as the *Roosevelt*'s bottom was constantly being shredded.[116] It took 75 days to make it back to Cape Sabine in what is now Nunavut, Canada, only a week before the encroaching ice would have trapped the *Roosevelt* for the lengthy and cruel winter.

On 1 September 1906 the crew discovered a cache left by a British expedition in 1876, the year after Bartlett was born, containing a can of boiled beef in good condition.* At Etah, Bartlett beached the *Roosevelt* to assess the damage, which included a broken jury rudder, twisted and cracked propeller blades, and an increase in the size of the hole in the bottom. Bartlett almost laughed when Peary told him they had to hurry home so that he could mount another attempt the next year. Bartlett ordered the crew to work without stopping until the ship was more seaworthy. Because of the damage to the bottom, they could not take the *Roosevelt* inshore to collect the coal they had stored and that they badly needed. Instead, they used an improvised raft, but a sudden blizzard nearly sank it. Another complication was that the coal was frozen into a lump which had to be broken up with dynamite, a dangerous prospect at the best of times.

It was not until 20 September, very late in the season, that they left Etah. Without exaggeration, Bartlett wrote, "I had never cruised around up there so late. The landmarks all looked queer in the strange light ... But we were racing for our lives."[117] They ran aground again at Kookan, but this allowed them to discover that the nuts and bolts on the last propeller blade were loose; they tended to this and other repairs immediately and rapidly, their nerves jangled. They made it across Melville Bay to be met by another blizzard and yet another crisis: the bilge pumps were blocked by ashes, and water poured into the *Roosevelt*. More improvisations followed and

---

* The food was left by the 1875–76 expedition led by Sir George Strong Nares, a Welshman charged with claiming the North Pole for Britain.

the exhausted crew carried on. They lost their third rudder on 4 October and their topmast around the same time, necessitating further improvisations so that they could steer the ship. The job of making and attaching the rudder to the ship all but knocked them out. They had no coal left by the time they reached northern Labrador; according to Bartlett, "the firemen were sweeping the bunkers to fill shovels; We began cutting away beams and loose timbers for fuel."[118] To this, they added wood and blubber they had picked up at the Moravian mission stations at Hebron and Hopedale, Labrador, where no coal was available. At the aptly named Windy Tickle, Bartlett's chart blew away—a potential disaster in unforgiving Labrador waters. Crew members took to a small boat and tried to retrieve the chart but failed. "Providence guided us into Hopedale," Bartlett wrote with relief, referring to the Inuit settlement established by Moravian missionaries.[119] Finally reaching Battle Harbour, southern Labrador's commercial hub, on 22 November, almost two months after they should have been there, the *Roosevelt* lost her anchor. The men were working on their fifth rudder and the trip had long since become a string of calamities, with danger ever present.

Bartlett concluded his account of the 1905–6 expedition: "[T]here is no use prolonging the yarn because it was all exactly the same; just one narrow shave after another, and interminable hours of hard labour ... The poor old *Roosevelt*, as well as ourselves, was ready for the insane asylum or the dump heap."[120] When they landed at New York on Christmas Eve, 1906, Peary turned and gripped Bartlett's hand without uttering a word. Peary had been outwardly optimistic throughout, even as Inuit threatened to desert and crew members fretted to the point of breakdown. He had to have noticed the stress Bartlett was under and the life-saving ingenuity the younger man demonstrated. Perhaps the wordless grip was Peary's way of thanking Bartlett. In Bartlett's case, it was all he required; it was easy for "great men" to please him.

The *Roosevelt* was sent to the shipyard at Staten Island while Peary devised a way to get her properly repaired in preparation for his next attempt on the Pole. Almost 30 years later, when the age of polar exploration was on its last legs in the middle of the Great Depression, the *Roosevelt*'s 1906 return from the Arctic was still considered by the Explorers Club to be "without comparison in the annals of exploration."[121]

The *Roosevelt* in 1909 on her way to Greenland, anchored at Battle Harbour, Labrador. *The Rooms Provincial Archives Division, VA 118-83.9.*

Bartlett's indefatigable efforts were in no small part responsible for this accomplishment.

Since 1909, discussions of Peary have focused on whether or not he made it to the Pole. Little attention is paid to his methods of Arctic exploration, although these are at least as noteworthy and they show Peary to be intelligent, resourceful, and innovative instead of merely a tower of ambitious physical strength and stoicism. Peary's skills and adaptations in Arctic travel are, in fact, his main achievement. Due to Peary's own fixation on 90 degrees, however, the misplaced emphasis on the Pole is the explorer's own fault as much as anyone else's. Bartlett understood Peary's singular abilities, which contributed to his strong attachment to Peary as well as his attraction to Arctic exploration. In his words, "Peary reached the Pole mostly because he spent nearly 25 years of eliminating the obstacles that had prevented other explorers for four centuries from doing what he was trying to do."[122] Key to what Bartlett, among others, saw as Peary's success was his placing of a ship at the north end of Grant

Land, which allowed for direct travel with dog over ice in spring. This decision resulted from Peary's long-term study of several hundred miles of ice conditions from Cape Sabine to Cape Sheridan, which enabled him to understand that sites like Kane Basin were frequently blocked with ice. According to Bartlett, "slow methodological progress is the best way to success."[123] By 1909 and his final push for the Pole, "Peary had learned to use open leads close to land formed by ebb and flow of current tide ... [he] knew more about navigating that important stretch of pack ice [Robeson Channel] more than any man who had ever lived."[124] If nothing else, Peary had demonstrated incredible patience in his study of the Arctic.

The methodological Peary knew the value of adaptation in such a challenging setting and climate. He was not afraid to innovate either. He tested narrow wooden "Norwegian snow-skates," also known as skis, against Canadian Indian snowshoes and found the former to be more useful for his purposes because of the speed they afforded.[125] Peary learned to cope with the psychological depression that sometimes develops during the long dark Arctic winters and to which he was not immune. He soothed himself with books and music, as Bartlett would do during the Canadian Arctic Expedition of 1913–14 when his ship, the *Karluk*, sank, stranding her crew on the ice. Peary protected expedition members from bleak moods as much as possible by introducing a system whereby they kept busy all winter, instead of merely waiting. They broke and maintained trails through the unrelenting polar darkness, their activity non-stop. The practice also had the benefits of ensuring that the trails were ready for travel when darkness broke. Peary's system, wrote Bartlett, prevented "health and spirits [relapsing] into Arctic melancholy so fatal to the success of an expedition."[126] This had been a problem on many Arctic expeditions, Bartlett noted, and he tried to institute a similar system himself after the *Karluk* became stuck in the ice some years later. But it would be a problem again.

For so long a contentious figure—one historian concluded that Peary was a liar and a megalomaniac—it is difficult to imagine that Peary might have had some redeeming features, let alone charisma and integrity.[127] Yet this was likely the case. Bartlett clearly fell under Peary's spell and consistently reported that the Inuit felt the same way about Peary, observations that are impossible to assess since the Inuit voices are silent, at least in western texts. In the patronizing tone so often used by explorers when alluding to Indigenous people, Bartlett wrote, "Each time I went north it was a revelation to me how they [the Inuit] loved the big white man who came to them year after year, treating them like a father and always leaving them gifts of priceless value."[128] Writing well within the boundaries of conventional thinking of the time, Bartlett also provided concrete examples of Inuit devotion. For instance, Peary once resolved a conflict between a young Inuit couple over the care of their baby, winning their enduring friendship, Bartlett claimed. Peary was firm in times of stress and he was strict with the Inuit, according to Bartlett, but also kindly, implying that the Inuit had to be treated like children. Peary was also capable of using humour, even during a crisis. He once risked his own life to rescue two Inuit lost in a blizzard, during which he froze both his legs to the knees and lashed himself to a sledge so that he could travel in rough and windy conditions. (In keeping with the heroic tradition, like many explorers, including Bartlett, Peary consistently minimized his own discomfort; after the loss of his toes, he dismissed medical advice that he rest.)

Bartlett entirely ignored the other dimensions of Peary's relationship with the Greenlandic Inuit; in the view of Genevieve LeMoine, curator of the Peary-MacMillan Arctic Museum at Bowdoin College, the admiral was "racist, sexist, authoritarian and paternalistic."[129] Peary was not unique in this respect; Elisha Kent Kane, the mid-19th-century explorer who had tried to find the two ships and 129 men of Sir John Franklin's lost expedition, described the Inuit as a "declining and obsolete people."[130] Peary, who caused a revolution in Greenlandic Inuit hunting practices by introducing guns and steel traps, was also sly and self-serving. In particular, he used rationing to exert control over the Inuit, upon whom he depended, and his employment of them led to considerable stress due to family separations.[131] These things and their long-term effects escaped the notice of Bartlett.

Also in keeping with explorers' culture, Peary had a well-developed sense of entitlement. It did not occur to him that the lands he explored were Inuit lands and known to the Inuit. He saw the naming of newly "discovered" sites as, in his words, "the explorer's prerogative," and thus christened numerous locales, including Melville Land, Academy Glacier, Daly Land, Independence Bay (after the 4th of July), and Heilprin Land (after the Hungarian-American geologist and paleontologist Angelo Heilprin, who travelled to the Arctic with Peary) on the east coast of Greenland.[132] In so doing, he completely ignored the long-standing Inuit presence in the Arctic. Peary was, above all, ambitious and desperate to be renowned as the discoverer of the North Pole; it is this for which he is remembered, not for the Arctic travel skills and methods he so cleverly acquired and which are so well documented.

Peary's wife, Josephine Diebitsch-Peary, was equally zealous and demonstrated a remarkable ability to compromise when necessary to preserve Peary's reputation and advance his goals. Married to Peary in 1888, Josephine was the daughter of a Smithsonian Institution linguist. She first went north with her husband in 1891 in the Newfoundland sealing ship *Kite*, captained by Harry Bartlett.[133] Then she spent a year at McCormick Bay, halfway between the Arctic Circle and the North Pole, living among 350 Inuit, always referring to them—inaccurately—as a "tribe" in her book. Her understanding of the Inuit was limited by the fact that she rarely entered an Inuit dwelling: "Having heard about the filth and vermin was quite enough for me."[134] *My Arctic Journal*[135] was well received by the public,[136] especially the conventional audience of middle-class women for whom it was intended.[137] Josephine's narrative dwells in the female domains of domestic life, children, and the like, bringing a sense of civilization to the wild and masculine Arctic of her explorer husband.[138] As languge scholar Heidi Hansson explains, by celebrating Thanksgiving and Christmas and marking birthdays with special meals of auk stew, apricot pie, and Liebfraumilch, Josephine effectively responded to the gender codes of the time, despite where she was. In this way, she did not threaten her husband, the men with him, or her readership back home. Accordingly, like her husband, Josephine attracted honours, most notably the National Geographic Society's prestigious Medal of Achievement in 1955, and was buried next to him at Arlington National Cemetery after her death at 92.[139] She outlived her husband by 32 years.

Josephine once showed up in Greenland unannounced, having heard the rumours about her husband's Inuit family. Allakasingwah (Aleqasina), or Ally, a teenager, was allegedly proud of her status as Peary's common-law wife and the mother of his two Inuit sons, one of whom, Kali, was born on board the *Roosevelt* in 1906.[140] Like Peary, Josephine demonstrated striking flexibility and pragmatism; she promptly made friends with Ally and kept quiet about the young woman's relationship with her husband. In one of his books, Peary published a nude photo of Ally, one that very much objectified her, especially as it failed to identify her by name. His shocked financial backer told him never to do such a thing again. Peary's circle never mentioned Ally or her children publicly after that.[141]

In spite of her ability to get along with Ally, Josephine's opinions of Inuit were low. As she wrote, "These Eskimos were the queerest dirtiest-looking individuals I had ever seen. Clad entirely in furs, they reminded me more of monkeys than of human beings."[142] Josephine applied her racist attitudes to individual Inuit she had come to know during her time in the Arctic: "Yesterday Nowdingyah and his picaninny, a little girl about 2½ years old, put in their appearance."[143] She even mocked them in *My Arctic Journal*: "It was amusing to see the queer-looking creatures, dressed entirely in the skins of animals, seated at the table and trying to act like civilized people."[144] What is most notable about her startling writing is that Josephine obviously lived in an atmosphere in which the blunt expression of racist thought was entirely acceptable and normalized; these words appeared in a celebrated book by an author who quickly became famous and revered.

As Bartlett's did in so many ways, Josephine Diebitsch-Peary's views reflected contemporary mores. Her assessment of the Inuit, hardly unique among polar literature, says more about the society in which she lived than about her, except to reveal her conventionality. Paralleling Orientalism—influential western stereotypes of Arabs and Asians—her comments reveal absolutely nothing about the Inuit.[145] Josephine was so in tune with her cultural milieu that, while applauding her contribution to "ethnological learning," her publishers wrote, "These people had never seen a white woman, and some of them had never beheld a civilized being."[146]

The Pearys matched their keen intelligence to their ambition and included their family in this effort. They gave their daughter, Marie, an Inuit middle name—Ahnighito—after she was born in the Arctic in 1893.* Then they successfully publicized and marketed the blond Marie as the

---

* Similarly, the current Danish Crown prince and princess, Frederick and Mary, gave their twins, born in 2011, Greenlandic Inuit middle names for political reasons: Minik for Prince Vincent and Ivalo for his slightly younger sister, Princess Josephine.

"Snow Baby," most notably through a book by the same name published in 1901 and co-authored by Josephine and Marie.[147] In total contrast, Robert Peary neglected to support his Inuit children, acknowledge them publicly, or learn their language.[*][148] Further, he brought six Inuit to the United States, where he handed them over to the American Museum of Natural History so that they could be studied.[149] All the adults died of tuberculosis, leaving an Inuit boy, Minik Wallace, alone in New York. Minik returned to Greenland with Peary's help as an adult, but went back to the US of his own volition, his desperate rootlessness by then entrenched.[150] Minik's life was dominated by unsuccessful attempts to retrieve his father's body from the museum.[†][151] Frederick Cook, too, took Inuit children from the Arctic and brought them on the lecture circuit, which was made all the more lucrative by their presence.[152] Cook and Peary were able to convince themselves that Inuit lacked the normal human attachments to family, community, and place. Or perhaps these questions never occurred to them, although it would have been hard to ignore Minik's long campaign. Josephine Diebitsch-Peary also brought a young Inuit woman back to the United States, where she was mistaken by "Chinamen" as one of their own, which buoyed the unlikely theory of Peary and others that the Inuit originated in Siberia and were driven out by the Tartars.[153]

Race would always be a factor in exploration, but other elements could blunt its importance; the American dream could be achieved even by blacks with the right mix of characteristics. Accordingly, Peary wrote in his short introduction to Matthew Henson's 1912 book, *A Black Explorer at the North Pole*, "race, or color, or bringing up, or environments count nothing against a determined heart, if it backed and aided by intelligence."[154] Interestingly but not surprisingly, the racism exhibited by the Pearys was something they had in common with Henson, the African-American explorer who, with Peary, claimed the Pole, and who began as a colleague and became a fan of Bartlett's. In 1911, Henson described the Inuit as "the best-natured people on earth with no bad habits of their own, but a ready ability to assimilate

---

*   Peary's descendants live in Greenland today and, in 1987, some of them, including his son Kali, travelled to the US to meet Peary relatives, including Peary's son, Robert E. Peary Jr. and Robert E. Peary III. This reunion occurred in spite of the initial objections of the Peary family, who had denied Kali Peary's paternity and tried to dissuade their Inuit relatives from travelling to the US. A banquet in honour of the Greenlandic Pearys was attended by over 200 people, including Harvard University's then president Derek C. Bok (S. Allen Counter, *North Pole Legacy: Black, White and Eskimo* [Montpelier, VT: Invisible Citis Press, 2001], 112, 153).

†   The body was finally returned to Greenland in 1993, largely due to the efforts of Minik's biographer, Kenn Harper.

the vices of civilization," meaning, in this case, tobacco-smoking, which became general among Inuit during Henson's time in Greenland.[155] Henson went beyond benign patronizing when he, a very articulate speaker and writer, stated: "They are very human in their attributes, and in spite of the fact that their diet is practically meat only, their tempers are gentle and mild, and there is a great deal of affection among them."[156] In common with most explorers, Henson failed to individuate Inuit, and seemed to view them as sweet but dumb animals. He correlated the consumption of meat, the archetypical male food,[157] with aggression, reflecting the association between meat and violence and, in turn, vegetarianism and pacifism.[158] Henson's internalized racism—his own view of himself as a human being mirrored that of white society—is obvious.

Matthew Alexander Henson was born in 1866 in Maryland to Lemuel and Helen, tobacco tenant farmers, both of whom died before their son's seventh birthday.[159] As Booker T. Washington wrote in the foreword to Henson's memoir, Henson's first job was cabin boy on an ocean-liner which took him as far away from the United States as China.[160] Henson went from there to work under Peary for 20 years, becoming, finally, in Washington's words, "the most trusted [and] the most useful member of the [1909] expedition."[161] For Washington, Henson was proof that "courage, fidelity and ability are honored and rewarded under a black skin as well as under a white."[162] For Washington, who was born a slave, and Henson, too, born so soon after the abolition of American slavery, it was important to prove the genuine quality of black people, to demonstrate their value as human beings and as Americans. In seeking this basic form of recognition, Henson served as a symbol of inclusion while also acting as a tool through which the pernicious effects of systemic racism, which extended through the United States, could be denied.

Henson saw considerable charisma in Peary, just as Bartlett did, and, crucial to his ability to thrive as a black man in a racist milieu, he discerned that Peary would be a good employer for him. He wrote, "it was with the instinct of my race that I recognized in him the qualities that made me willing to engage myself in his service."[163] Henson could see that his race, as he called it, despised by many whites at that time, would not necessarily impede any social or economic progress he could make working for Peary, as long as he proved himself. Indeed, Henson was able to achieve his goals and some measure of fame and recognition alongside Peary. Because Henson was black, however, his status could never parallel Peary's. Unlike Peary, Henson was not afforded the honour of being buried in Arlington National Cemetery; Henson's grave was in the Bronx at the less prestigious Woodlawn Cemetery until his body was reinterred in Arlington in 1986, the same year a United States postage stamp was issued in his and Peary's honour.[164] Henson often visited Peary's grave, demonstrating the loyalty Peary inspired in those who worked closely with him.

Racism permeated every aspect of Henson's world. He would not have been surprised to learn that the members of an Arctic expedition a few years later, that of the ill-fated *Karluk*, named one of their dogs "Nigger"; this was not an uncommon name for black dogs at the time.[165] The Explorers Club in New York admitted Henson to their honorary ranks, making him the first black member; there is a photo of him at the Club sitting next to Danish explorer Peter Freuchen.* [166] Unlike Peary, Henson led a quiet life after the North Pole claim, working for the New York Custom House as a clerk until he retired in 1936,[167] a job he acquired through an executive order of President Taft.[168] Except for Taft and the Explorers Club, the larger society was slow to acknowledge Henson's importance. African-Americans consistently honoured him, however, and in 1955, Henson's funeral was held at the fabled Abyssinian Baptist Church in Harlem, with which he had long been associated.† This church was where murdered theologian Dietrich Bonhoeffer had taught Sunday school and formulated many of the ideas that propelled him to resist the Nazis; it was where Dr. Martin Luther King Jr. would preach during the turbulent 1960s and it held a singular place in African-American history. The service for Henson was conducted by Rev. Adam Clayton Powell Jr., New York City's first black congressman, who, with some creativity, compared Henson's accomplishments to those of Marco Polo and Ferdinand Magellan.[169] By this time, Henson's friend, Bartlett, had been dead a decade, but a fellow explorer, Peter Freuchen, served as a pallbearer.

---

*   Freuchen fought in the Resistance in World War II and was imprisoned by the Nazis.
†   Anuakaq, Matthew Henson's son, visited this church for a special service in 1987 and was applauded by the congregation (Counter, *North Pole Legacy*, 170).

Bartlett and Henson were central figures in Peary's 1909 expedition but there were others of note. One was Professor Ross Marvin, the Cornell University faculty member and chief scientist and keeper of the ship's log. Among the Inuit who featured prominently were the brothers Ootah and Egingwah, Seegloo and Ooqueah, all of whom took Peary to the Pole—or, more probably, near it.[170] Another Inuk whose role was significant in the expedition was Kudlooktoo, who would gain some infamy, rightly or wrongly.

After Peary's first failed attempt to reach the Pole in 1905–6, his return expedition to Arctic Greenland in 1908 was not easy to mount. Peary was broke and he and Bartlett, not to mention Henson, were glum after their failure and the harrowing incidents with the *Roosevelt*. Further, Peary's book, *Nearest the Pole*, failed to sell but, instead of defeating him, this left him more determined to succeed, and success meant one thing only: reaching the Pole. Although Robert Scott's demise at the South Pole a few years later would prove otherwise, it seemed at the time that people wanted to hear stories of success, not failure, at least not in the United States. Peary's singlemindedness aside, his bad luck mounted; his main financial backer, Morris Ketchum Jesup, president of the American Natural History Museum, had died.[*] Further fundraising did not go well, despite Bartlett's being pressed into service. Bartlett himself had no money and had to return to Newfoundland to go sealing for the winter, which must have been a letdown after his Arctic adventures, which had been reported all over the western world.

At the last minute, however, funds came from General Thomas Hubbard and Zenas Crane, the former a Union Army colonel and the son of the Maine governor who brought in early prohibition legislation in 1871, and the latter, a member of the fine paper manufacturing family of Massachusetts. Peary would memorialize the colonel through his naming of Cape Thomas Hubbard at Grant Land. He would also call a cape after Jesup.[171]

After the ship docked as far north as it could get in 1909, the explorers set out on their sledges and trekked toward the Pole. Bartlett was in for a jolt.

---

[*] Honoured by Nicholas II, the doomed Russian czar, Jesup was a celebrated philanthropist, supporting immigrant settlement initiatives in New York, the city's Women's Hospital, African-American schools, and the Siberian, Canadian, and Alaskan work of Franz Boas, the "Father of American Anthropology." These were all progressive causes with exploration not being seen as anything different during the early 20th century. On the other hand, Jesup was also heavily involved in the New York Society for the Suppression of Vice, pointing to the upholding of morality as, perhaps, his chief motivator in all his causes.

In the exploration tradition, Peary would take at least one white explorer with him to the Pole. Frederick Cook eschewed this practice, taking two Inuit,* with the result that he had no white or western witnesses. Bartlett might have assumed that he would be the chosen one in 1909, but this was by no means a certainty, and it developed into a matter of lasting public discussion. After an impressive pace during the last half of the march north, Bartlett was "very sober and anxious to go further."[172] This implies that it was at least possible that Bartlett would go farther, and that Peary had not yet made up his mind about whom to take to the coveted spot. But then Peary chose Matthew Henson.

Peary later claimed there was a set program, which involved Bartlett's returning to the *Roosevelt*, which is what he asked Bartlett to do while he went on with Henson.[173] Both Bartlett and Henson could not accompany him; there were not enough supplies.[174] As compensation, Peary urged Bartlett to go north to 88 degrees, making anything beyond that "the Farthest North of Bartlett," as Henson put it.[175] This Bartlett did. But he sounded disappointed with his unique experience, saying, upon his return, "Why, Peary, it is just like every day."[176] After his solitary trek of a few miles toward 88 degrees and his short time as the most northerly human being on earth, surpassing the Italian record by a degree and a quarter,[177] Bartlett faced south. He was "ready and anxious to take the back-trail," to return to the ship, leaving Peary, Henson, and their Inuit aides to go north.[178] As leader of the pioneer party, Bartlett was completely exhausted and had to travel a long distance back. It was later discovered that drifting ice meant that he did not even get as far as 88 degrees, his goal. Characteristically, he downplayed his disappointment in his memoirs, writing, with less than complete honesty, "It was a tough blow to my pride, but made no real difference."[179]

For his part, Peary "felt a keen regret as [he] saw the captain's broad shoulders grow smaller in the distance and finally disappear behind the ice hummocks of the white and glittering expanse south."[180] Henson, too, was open about his feelings and he was his usual generous self in his depiction of Bartlett: "this brave man, who had borne the brunt of all of the hardships, like the true-blue, dead-game, unconquerable hero that he was, set out to

---

* These were Ahpellah and Etukishook.

do the work that left for him to do; to knit the broken strands of our upward trail together, so that we who were at his rear could follow in safety."[181]

Bartlett's regret about not being with Peary for his push to the Pole likely set in later, when Bartlett recovered from his arduous work breaking the return trail; it was only then he had time to think and energy to ruminate. Upon his return to Canada, Bartlett told a New York *Herald* reporter that he had felt strong on the top of the world and thought he could have made it to the Pole.[182] The uncharacteristically open account Bartlett gave to the *Herald* in 1909 is filled with regret: "It was a bitter disappointment. I got up early the next morning, and started north alone. I don't know, perhaps I cried a little. I guess perhaps I was just a little crazy then. I thought that perhaps I could walk on the rest of the way [to the Pole] alone. It seemed so near."[183] His later accounts were more tempered, strategic, and reflective—and less truthful. Alluding to Peary's choice of Henson for his well-honed skills at driving dog teams, Bartlett said, "I think Peary's reasoning was sound."[184]

For Horwood, Peary's choice of Henson was "breaking faith," since the explorer had apparently promised Bartlett he would be going all the way, as Bartlett implied to Teddy Roosevelt on the president's Oyster Bay visit. What Bartlett said to Roosevelt, however, was, "Its [sic] ninety or nothing."[185] This does not mean Bartlett would be on the final trek. We cannot know if, as Horwood contended, Peary made the greatest mistake of his life; that would assume that Bartlett's presence on the final trek would have guaranteed the Pole. Horwood claimed that reporters saw Peary and Bartlett quarrelling before starting for Cape Columbia, Ellesmere Island. Horwood, an erstwhile reporter himself, would have been predisposed to take the word of other scribes, but it is doubtful that cautious and ambitious men like Peary and Bartlett would have squabbled in front of the press—or anyone else, especially at such a crucial time. Both were too canny for that.

The celebrated explorer Donald Baxter MacMillan, who was on the expedition, described Henson as Peary's most competent assistant.[186] This may well have been the case. Besides being an excellent dog-driver, Henson was also an American, like Peary, and he shared his leader's keenness to plant their country's flag at the Pole. As a Newfoundlander, Bartlett was a British subject and not yet a naturalized American citizen, as he would later choose to become (largely so that he could have easy access to rich benefactors on the eastern seaboard). Peary was keenly aware of the politics surrounding these facts and summoned every diplomatic skill in his arsenal to address them. In *The North Pole*, he cited three reasons for giving Bartlett "the post of honour in command of [his] last supporting party."[187] These included Bartlett's competence and his positive approach as well as the fact that "it seemed to [him] right that, in view of the noble work of Great Britain in Arctic exploration, a British subject should, next to an American, be able to say that he had stood nearest the North Pole."[188]

Yet other less psychological factors were more important. Given his long-term association with Peary and the odd norms of polar exploration, Henson had almost the status of a white man in the Arctic; in fact, on this trip he carried out the duties of a white man, leading a unit northward. Henson had been with Peary for many years and it is likely that Peary was more loyal to Henson than he was to Bartlett; Peary may even have felt that he owed Henson something. Most importantly, however, Henson was in better shape than Bartlett, especially as he had not led the pioneer party breaking trail. It was imperative to Peary that he reach the Pole. In Peary's words upon landing back in Canada, "This position I have given [Henson] primarily of his adaptability and fitness for the work; and secondly on account of his loyalty. He has shared all the physical hardships of my Arctic work."[189] Given the evidence, these words should be taken at face value.

As Bartlett's remarkable future accomplishments would demonstrate, he was certainly capable of trekking to the Pole. But in March 1909, he had endured the long hard marches of the pioneer party, making Matthew Henson a better choice; Peary was a pragmatist with an all-important goal in mind. It is possible that Peary probably never intended to take Bartlett to the Pole; otherwise he would not have assigned him to the pioneer party. If that is the case, it brings us back to the more suspect sides of the argument, which are harder to decipher.

After his journey, Bartlett rested in his cabin for 10 days; his ankles, knees, and hip joints were swollen, making movement difficult. He would experience this same reaction after the long icy hike that followed the sinking of the *Karluk* in 1914. It is possible that the return journey from nearly 88 degrees did him in, especially if he was deflated at not being chosen for the final attempt at the Pole. If Bartlett was fatigued, Peary would have noticed this and simultaneously seen that Henson was not flagging to the same degree.

According to Bartlett, it was "an easy jaunt to the Pole from where [he] left him [Peary]."[190] This is an incongruous statement about Arctic travel but it reveals the depth of Bartlett's support for Peary and his ambitions. Peary left with 40 dogs, "all prime," undamaged sledges, and rations for 60 days; he was accompanied by four young Inuit—Seegloo, Ooqueah, and the brothers Ootah and Egingwah—as well as Henson.[191] It was hard going, with plenty of falling down and little sleep. Peary was restless. Henson fell into icy water one day and was saved by Ootah, who skilfully retrieved him using only one hand.[192] Bartlett struggled as he headed in the other direction; drifting snow obscured the trail and he fell through the ice, which was beginning to soften and slow him and the Inuit who accompanied him. Henson used this detail as another opportunity to lavish praise on Bartlett, whom he always referred to by his title while patronizing the Inuit: "I have never heard the story of the return of Captain Bartlett in detail; his Eskimo boys were incapable of telling it, and Captain Bartlett is altogether too modest."[193]

The historic moment—and the claim of achieving the Pole makes it a historic moment—was described by the Royal Geographical Society, which steadfastly supported Peary through the controversy that ensued: "Peary reached a point on the drifting floes where an observation of the sun gave lat. 89 57' N.—3 miles from the Pole. A short sledge journey carried him over the coveted spot."[194] Peary wrote in his diary: "The Pole at last. The prize of three centuries. My dream and goal of twenty years. Mine at last. I cannot bring myself to realize it. It seems all so simple and commonplace."[195] He echoes Bartlett's words at travelling farther north than anyone had ever done. There is also a hint of the more eloquent Robert Scott, who was sorely disappointed when he reached the South Pole in 1912. "Great God!" he wrote in his diary, "This is an awful place and terrible enough for us to have laboured to it without the reward of priority."[196] All that could be seen at both poles was, of course, more snow and more ice. The explorers encountered only the same monotonously bleak landscape they had been travelling in for weeks. There was nothing to mark either the South or the North Pole, although, before travelling there, both Scott and Peary may have convinced themselves that there was. After all their efforts, they probably expected a powerful feeling of triumph or elation, such as Everest climbers expect. As so often happens, anticipation is more rewarding and meaningful than the desired experience itself.

The party spent about 30 hours at a camp at or near the Pole. Despite his inferior social and political status in the early 20th-century United States, Henson was almost overcome with patriotism at the flag-raising. He and Peary planted the national flag, which, with Utah's 1896 entry into the Union, had 45 stars, as well as the flags of the Daughters of the Revolution Peace Society, the Navy Leagues, and various college fraternities from New England. It was only after securing the flags in place that Peary made his navigational observations. Peary said nothing, but the "resolute squaring of his jaws" meant he was "satisfied."[197] Henson noted that Peary turned aside when Henson congratulated him and covered his eyes with both hands. This might have been caused by a gust of wind blowing snow in his eye or it might have been eye pain, Henson wrote a few years later. But perhaps Peary was uncharacteristically emotional and did not want Henson to see any tears. It is also possible that he had begun a general or self-deception in the face of failure to achieve his life's goal. As the flags flapped in the polar wind, it was a nasty -29°F.[198]

Henson did not question that they were standing at the Pole. In his 1912 account, he put his internalized racism on full display, writing, "From the building of the pyramids and the journey to the Cross, to the discovery of the new world and the discovery of the North Pole, the Negro had been the faithful and constant companion of the Caucasian, and I felt all that it was possible for me to feel, that it was I, a lowly member of my race, who had been chosen by fate to represent it, at this, almost the last of the world's great *work*."[199] As legal racial segregation, known as Jim Crow, persisted in the United States, Matthew Henson could never be just an individual; he had to stand for the entire African-American population without the freedom of the individual that should have been his.

Peary and Bartlett were reunited at the *Roosevelt* on 27 April and Bartlett rushed forward to greet the explorer. Peary was not ebullient as might be expected, but a little subdued, as he had been with Henson at—or near—the Pole. Bartlett spoke first, exclaiming, "I congratulate you, sir, on the discovery of the pole!" Peary answered, "How did you guess it?"[200] Not much else was said. It must have occurred to Bartlett that Peary's claim to have covered the last 220 kilometres to the Pole in five days followed by another 800 kilometres in 16 days to return to the *Roosevelt* was, as one writer noted sarcastically, "a surprising record."[201]

Only fragments of evidence indicate that Peary reached the Pole. Peary was the only person who took any navigational observations. In Peary's defence, Bartlett claimed that navigation in the Arctic was as easy as anywhere else. As Bartlett described it, the navigator lay on a warm muskox fur and used a sextant to make about six measurements, which were then averaged. According to Bartlett, who had taken thousands of navigational observations by this time, a papered mariner could do it in a minute. "There is nothing very complicated or obscure about it," he asserted.[202] Although he was a civil engineer, Peary was not a qualified mariner. Further, magnetic variations in the Arctic were not well understood in 1909. In Horwood's words, 90 degrees North was "one of the most difficult spots on earth to locate by instruments."[203] Bartlett argued that Inuit never keep secrets, implying that they would have ratted on Peary if he had staged a deception. Besides making a generalization that is not worthy of much attention, Bartlett forgot the alleged Inuit loyalty to Peary of which he often spoke. Bartlett also vowed that Peary was very fit, a questionable claim given the damage to the explorer's feet, and the fact that, according to Henson, Peary had to ride a sledge most of the way to the Pole.

One of Horwood's theories—that Peary did not want a competent navigator at the Pole, presumably so he could deceive the public if he needed to—assumes that Peary was dishonest. If Peary was dishonest, however, it would have been mostly to himself. He may have convinced himself that he had reached the Pole, while he did not. Or he may have caved to pressure, from himself and from the waiting public and the Peary Clubs that were dotted all over the United States, to pretend he had accomplished his goal when, in fact, he had not. No less a personage than President Roosevelt, after all, had seen them off. But Horwood's theory also requires that Peary would have planned a deception, which is unlikely; Peary badly wanted to attain the Pole and, though determined, there is no reason to conclude that he was capable of lies to that degree; over-confident people rarely are. On the other hand, Peary wanted to control the narrative and was in the habit of requiring expedition members like Ross Marvin to sign agreements stating they would never lecture or speak to the media about his expeditions. This may have been an attempt to monopolize the financial rewards of his Arctic forays but it does not cast Peary in a positive light, as he would have been the chief recipient of such financial rewards in any case. One can be capable of selfish ambition without being a liar, however.

Bartlett never criticized Peary and became and remained his most steadfast supporter outside the Peary family. To the day he died, Bartlett was adamant that Peary had attained the Pole. To the contention that Peary and other expedition members faked their diaries and figures, he responded, "I think that any man who has been through a polar trip would only laugh at such accusations. It seems quite inconceivable to me that anyone with a knowledge of human nature could study our hard trip over the ice and our simple observations and think for a moment that Peary's record could possibly be anything but what he claimed it to be."[204]

The controversy was propelled further by Frederick Cook's claim, just emerging at that time, that he had gained the North Pole in 1908. Criticism of Peary began almost immediately, but Cook showed the kind of generosity of which Peary was incapable when he said, "There is glory for us all!"[205] Peary produced charts and maps after questioning Cook's Inuit assistants when they visited the *Roosevelt*. He then sent a telegram—that would later become famous—from Battle Harbour, Labrador, on the way back from Greenland. He wrote, "Do not trouble about Cook's story ... He has not been at the pole on April 21, 1908, or at any other time. He has simply handed the people a gold brick."[206] As Peary set pen to paper, Cook, a very charismatic man supported by the ubiquitous Stefansson, was being honoured in Copenhagen for his presumed accomplishment.[207]

Neither side could furnish proof, though at first it looked as if Cook might be the victor.[208] Determined to win what became a propaganda war, Peary marshalled his supporters. The normally generous Henson, who did have a stake in the matter, wrote, "I have reason to be grateful to Dr. Cook for favors received; I lived with his folks while I was suffering with my eyes, due to snow blindness, but I feel that all of the debts of gratitude have been liquidated by my silence in this controversy, and I will have nothing more to say in regard to him or his claims."[209] Bartlett would have loved to have shied away from the argument but, given his pivotal role, it was impossible. Although his support for Peary was unwavering, he allowed that Cook had been at James Sound and had over-wintered on Devon Island, making the physician's claim possible. Indeed, McGhee points out that successful trips to the Pole have been achieved with less resources than Cook had.*[210] Peary was finally afforded victory, albeit a contested one, because Cook was discredited, first, by the University of Copenhagen, which investigated his claims and, later, by his arrest and imprisonment for mail fraud.†[211] Cook was also expelled by the swanky Explorers Club, of which he had been a founding member, but Peary—and Bartlett—were always welcome there. Yet questions surrounding both claims endure. As late as 1934, the Brooklyn *Daily Eagle* asked, "Did Peary or Cook Discover the Pole?"[212] Three decades later, long after Bartlett's death, a book appeared called *Peary at the North Pole: Fact or Fiction?*[213]

This controversy and the return of the *Roosevelt* obscured a real tragedy and another mystery from 1909. This was the death of Ross Marvin, a close friend of both Bartlett and Henson. When Bartlett returned to the *Roosevelt*, he was told by a fireman that Marvin had fallen through the ice and drowned, not an unlikely scenario in Arctic expeditions. But Bartlett reported that "[t]he rest of the crowd were very uneasy. Since Marvin's death they had feared for the rest of us [the whites]."[214] This suggests that suspicions already surrounded the episode, centring on the Inuit who had made up Marvin's unit. As Henson described it, two Inuit came upon Marvin's body floating in frigid sea ice. They did not try to retrieve it; there was no point in the cold temperatures. Henson was not judgmental about the loss of his friend and, as usual, he was condescending toward the Inuit: "No blame can be laid to his [Marvin's] childish companions."[215] Henson did criticize them for leaving the professor's belongings behind; these represented a loss to western science. To the Inuit, however, the personal effects, if brought along, would result in the dead man's spirit following them. Because of this decision, rooted in Inuit spiritual and cultural practice, Henson called them "foolish boys."[216]

---

*   There is, for instance, the 1996 journey of Hans Webber, a Canadian, and Mikhael Malakov, a Russian. Michael F. Robinson, *The Coldest Crucible: Arctic Exploration and American Culture* (Chicago: University of Chicago Press, 2006), 239.

†   Cook was pardoned by President Franklin Delano Roosevelt in 1940, the year the explorer died.

Others were not so generous toward the Inuit in Marvin's unit, and Bartlett joined their ranks. He returned to Greenland multiple times and in 1926 was told that Marvin had been shot by Kudlooktoo, who allegedly confessed to the killing after converting to Christianity. Marvin, the story goes, had his foot badly frostbitten and became angry at the Inuit for not carrying him on the sledge; a fatality ensued. The nervousness Bartlett mentioned upon his return to the *Roosevelt* indicates some turmoil and perhaps wrongdoing but the truth cannot be known, given the passage of time, the absence of witnesses, the racism that coloured every interpretation of Inuit action, and the absence of information from the Inuit involved. There is some evidence that Marvin treated the Inuit like servants, not understanding the importance of independence in Inuit culture and, subsequently, their probable aversion to being viewed as menials.[217] If he had been disrespectful or callous, Marvin was hardly the first explorer to treat Inuit this way. In fact, the entire structure that supported Arctic exploration placed the Inuit in a subservient position and racism underpinned every action taken by, if not every thought of, every member of the expedition. In this light, remarkably few explorers and scientists have been harmed by Inuit and it is unlikely Marvin was killed because he acted superior at times.

It is probable that some Inuit, perhaps Kudlooktoo among them, were unable to tolerate the unjust setup in which they found themselves. It would have been, in fact, highly unpalatable to any Inuk who gave the exploration hierarchy a moment's thought, as many would surely have done. Kudlooktoo may have lost his temper with one remark too many, but all that exist are incomplete accounts of the he said/she said variety. One story is that Marvin, as unit leader, would not allow Kudlooktoo's younger cousin to ride on the sledge. If this is true, it would indeed have irritated Kudlooktoo, for the Inuit cultural norm, extant even today after so much cultural, social, and economic upheaval, is to treat children and young people with kindness and munificence.

A more chilling, and therefore less believable, account emerges from Harvard University neuroscientist S. Allen Counter, who was responsible for the bizarre staged reunion of Peary's elderly Inuit and white descendants in the United States in 1987. Henson, too, fathered a son in the Arctic,

Anaukaq, whose mother was Akatingwah.[*] Like Kali Peary, this boy was born on the *Roosevelt*; in fact, the two children were born within days of each other.[218] According to Counter, who visited the Greenland village of the expedition descendants, Ross Marvin treated Kudlooktoo and Harrigan, another Inuk in Henson's unit, "brutally."[219] Counter says that the version of events current among Greenland Inuit in the late 1980s was that food had run low and Marvin tried to convince one Inuk to leave the other behind.[220] It is hard to imagine such cruelty, unless Marvin had gone mad. It is worth noting that Counter refers to Bartlett as a Nova Scotian, inaccurate reporting of a basic fact. What really happened will remain a mystery; there was no investigation or trial, given the remoteness of the location, the lack of white witnesses, and the absence of western legal traditions in the Arctic at the time.

No one seems to have mourned Marvin more than Henson. Resorting to the vivid and sometimes flowery language that features throughout his book, *A Black Explorer at the North Pole*, he concluded, "In unmarked, unmarbled grave, he sleeps his last long sleep."[221] Bartlett displayed his usual fatalism. Like most Newfoundlanders, he expected nature, especially the unpredictable ocean, to take human life whenever it could. He was only 10 when he witnessed the grim spectacle of the 1885 Eskimo Coast disaster. Closer to home, his uncle Harry had been lost at sea. Bartlett grew up hearing about drowned fishermen, many of whom he knew as neighbours in and around Brigus. By 1909, he was reconciled, if not hardened, to a career that would regularly feature the spectre of death. Of Marvin, Bartlett wrote, "little did we think he would soon be taken from us. I believe that when a man's time has come he will die and that it is useless to worry about the future."[222]

The trip home in 1909 was, thankfully, uneventful compared to the *Roosevelt*'s last return voyage from the Arctic. Bartlett picked up Harry Whitney, who had failed to kill the polar bear he coveted. Whitney was not to be deterred, however. When Captain Sam Bartlett showed up on

---

[*]   Henson's son grew up ashamed of the curly hair he inherited from his father, declaring, "As a child, even as a man, I wanted straight hair, like my mother and later my wife." Kali, Peary's son, was more secure in his identity, asserting as an old man, "I am Eskimo. I was born and raised Eskimo. I think Eskimo. I was an Eskimo hunter" (Counter, *North Pole Legacy*, 97-98). On his now-defunct website, Counter, who died in 2017, stated, "These subjects range from his recent scientific findings on the high lead and mercury exposure levels among Andean children to his discovery of the Amer-Eskimo children of Arctic explorers Matthew A. Henson and Robert E. Peary in Northwest Greenland." The use of the word "discovery" is, to say the least, unfortunate in this context.

Bob Bartlett, second from left, probably at St. Anthony in northern Newfoundland on the way from Greenland in 1909. With Bartlett are Edith Hegan, Lousie Hegan (Edith's sister), John Croucher, and S.M. Carr-Harris. Croucher was the agent for the Newfoundland fish firm Baine Johnston, while the women, all from Canada, volunteered for the International Grenfell Association. *The Rooms Provincial Archives Division, VA 103-161.*

the Greenland coast in the schooner *Jeannie*, Whitney hitched a ride to Labrador, where he would try again. Captain Sam brought mail to Peary's crew along with the news that the Anglo-Irishman Ernest Shackleton had gotten within 111 miles of the South Pole—the closest to that time.[*][223] Sam also brought provisions, which were especially welcome as the crew of the *Roosevelt* had, once again, been on rations. Bartlett stopped in at Turnavik, where he and his crew feasted on fresh vegetables and other most welcome foods.[224] There was no media to greet them in Labrador, lacking rail and

---

[*] Like Bartlett, Shackleton made a rescue journey–from the Antarctic to the Falkland Islands/Malvinas by small boat and trekking–that would catapult him into heroic status on an international scale. Shackleton never reached the South Pole but he was honoured for his explorations, survival skills, and his stunning rescue of his stranded party. More recently, he has been viewed largely as a model in business and organizational leadership, although it is a leap to extrapolate lessons in leadership from his context to that of modern organizations, as Michael Elmes and Bob Frame convincingly explain ("Into Hot Air: A Critical Perspective on Everest," *Human Relations* 61, no. 2 [2008]: 213–41).

Robert Peary, second from left, at Indian Harbour, Labrador on board the *Roosevelt* in October 1909 on the way back from his North Pole attempt. Peary is with International Grenfell Association staff. *The Rooms Provincial Archives Division, VA 118-98.4.*

road connections to the rest of the continent, but at Sydney, Nova Scotia, Peary and Bartlett talked to reporters and encountered schoolgirls who presented Peary with an impressive bouquet of flowers. The streets of the coal mining town were decorated and a holiday proclaimed. If Peary had deceived, it was difficult to turn back at this stage. The expedition members began to disband here, with Peary meeting his family and leaving with them to travel to the United States via train. Henson found the parting difficult.

Peary retired in 1911 as controversy still raged around him, the public, newspapers, and his fellow explorers taking sides. It had certainly taken its toll; according to the Royal Geographical Society, Peary "felt bitterly the hardship of having to prove his common honesty before tribunals of his own countrymen. The verdict was in his favour but the joy of achievement was gone."[225] In the years following his polar claim, Peary suffered ill health but gave lectures throughout the United States when he could. While ill, he would lie on a muskox skin, like those which had kept him warm in the Arctic, in his Eagle Island, Maine, home.[226] He must have turned the events and narrative surrounding the North Pole push over and over in his mind, perhaps feeling regret for the things he might have done differently. He might have wished that he had kept better records or that he had had someone else with him to ascertain 90 degrees with certainty. It was unreasonable to assume that his word alone would be sufficient to stake his claim and have it universally recognized. Bartlett could have been the navigator he needed, though this would have taken considerable planning and a different strategy.

Peary died at 64, triggering a disturbing lack of direction in Bartlett that would last some time and threaten to rob him of any enjoyment of life and a meaningful career. For a while Bartlett considered entering the aviation field; he had a specific desire to fly over the North Pole and did considerable research on the possibility.[227] At the time Peary died, Bartlett was 45 and had achieved hero status himself, as the *Roosevelt* and *Karluk* skipper and for his heroic attempt to rescue the stranded *Karluk* survivors. He would soon have his own vessel, the *Morrissey*, as his father, William, had long hoped for him. He wrote about his dead leader with adoration: "There is no one I revere more than Admiral Peary ..."[228] His obsession with leaders and leadership never left him, though, curiously, he never saw himself as a leader. Not long before his 1946 death, as the world tried to recover from the atrocities of war, he asked anxiously, "Where are the great leaders we need?"[229]

Josephine Diebitsch-Peary wanted to erect a monument in her husband's honour—as per Peary's own instructions—but the family's specifications were too grandiose for Arlington National Cemetery,[230] also the burial place of Adolphus Greely and, later, Admiral Richard Byrd, another contentious polar explorer. Josephine's chosen site for a monument was Cape York in Greenland, which meant that the project would be extremely expensive, not to mention physically challenging. This did not deter Bartlett, who offered his services as well as the use of the *Morrissey*, and began working with Peary's daughter, Marie Peary Stafford, on fundraising and planning. Eventually, in 1932 as the Great Depression climaxed, Josephine's extravagant dream became a reality, and 5 miles from the magnificent cape there stands a massive obelisk, featuring a giant "P," where once stood Bartlett's great man himself. As Marie wrote, "The transporting of the heavy loads of material up the side of the mountain through wind, rain and the heartbreaking drag of slush and melting ice calls for hard work and lots of it."[231] The project had entailed "the loan" of Inughito, an Inuit interpreter and guide, by the Danish governor Hans Nielsen, a gesture which was much appreciated by Marie.[232] She made no mention of the Newfoundland crew who did most of the difficult work, hauling cement by dog team, scaling the 1,500-foot glacier to get to Cape York, where they erected the monument from fragmented igneous rock. In addition to his regular crew members, Bartlett had hired a mason and two experienced woodcutters in their 60s, Gilbert and Reuben Hiscock, from Victoria, Newfoundland, near Brigus, for this daunting mission.[233] Bartlett's nephew Jack Angel, who was a member of the crew, accused Marie of haughtiness, but not, of course, to her face. "She had to have people who would kowtow. And I certainly wouldn't do that," the young engineering student claimed.[234] Meanwhile, Bartlett stayed on board ship while the men slaved away on the ice. Bartlett maintained his friendship with Marie to the end of his life, the two of them determined to shore up and promote Peary's reputation. As wily as her parents, Marie sought Bartlett's advice in this regard when she was asked to broadcast to the McGregor

Expedition in 1938; one of the expedition's aims was to clarify the status of Crockerland, a vision of Peary's.[235] Marie told Bartlett that if he thought it unwise, she could use the illness of her uncle Emil Diebitsch, Peary's former astronomer and photographer, as an excuse for not taking part.[236]

One of the last letters written to Bartlett was from the Explorers Club, just 12 days before he died in the spring of 1946: "You will be pleased to know that we have again exhibited in the Club Rooms the picture of admiral Robert E. Peary, painted by Operti."[237] Apparently Bartlett had requested that the painting be shown; to the end of his life, Peary remained uppermost in his mind, ever his hero. Bartlett longed for heroes, measuring heroism by endurance, bravery, and granite-like stoicism. He never got over this boyish propensity. He need not have looked far to find hyper-masculine godlike figures. As Peary himself wrote, "Captain Bob, as we affectionately call him, comes from a family of hardy Newfoundland navigators, long associated with Arctic work."[238] This is an understatement for, in the days of sail, the Bartletts were celebrated for their seagoing exploits, some of them gaining mythic status on the island of Newfoundland to New York and beyond. The Bartlett women, too, were colourful and striking in their attitudes and achievements. These people, most of whom it could be said had steel for backbones, would have demanded that their son and grandson Bob be nothing less than the way Peary described him: "brave, indomitable ... tireless, faithful, enthusiastic, and true as the compass."[239] Bartlett had none of Pytheas's natural fear of the unknown Arctic and plenty of the romanticism that surrounds it.

CHAPTER TWO
A COTTAGE HEARTH
AND OPEN WATERS:
AN EXPECTANT CHILDHOOD

Such a clamor of voices, and such
a rattle of glasses and applause!

– Frances Hodgson Burnett, *Little Lord Fauntleroy*

Women were not welcome on voyages with Bartlett, as with other captains; it was not until World War II that Bartlett sailed with a professional woman, Louise Arner Boyd, whom he loathed and who felt the same way about him. For explorers, the Arctic had become an exclusively male sphere in which white men could demonstrate and push their masculinity—masculinity, like femininity, a social idea reinforced through performative acts.[1] The Arctic allowed elite men to display the kind of heroism that was lauded without question. Referring to the 1934 Ellesmere Island expedition, one of a string of similar ventures by the Oxford University Exploration Club, Scottish geographer Hugh Robert Mill proclaimed, "We have grown accustomed to bright descriptions of the achievements of the young men from the universities of Oxford and Cambridge."[2] Free of western women, the Arctic also became, at least in theory, a safe haven for men whose sexuality was ambiguous, uncertain, or considered deviant by the prejudices of the era. This may have been the case with Bartlett.[*] Ernest Shackleton once refused three female applicants to a polar expedition by bluntly stating there "[were] no vacancies for the opposite sex on the Expedition."[3] The women were "strong healthy girls, and also gay and bright and willing to undergo any hardships."[4] They argued, "we do not see why men should have the glory and

---

[*] This is true of other solely male venues, as recent church history shows in Canada, the United States, Ireland, Australia, Germany, and other countries.

women none, especially when there are women just as brave and capable as there are men."[5] Yet Shackleton dismissed them without hesitation, for these women were going off script and attempting to shatter gendered boundaries erected by male explorers and their many supporters. Given these strictures, the women's applications were absurd. Margaret Atwood understood this when she wrote, "even though the North itself, or herself, is a cold and savage female, the drama enacted in it—or her—is a man's drama, and those who play it out are men."[6]

But male hegemony was being threatened. After long and difficult struggles, women in much of Western Europe and North America would soon gain the vote, and some would be elected to high office. In Bartlett's native Newfoundland, in 1930 Lady Helena Strong Squires became the first woman elected to the House of Assembly. She managed this although Sir Richard Anderson Squires (her husband, a Bartlett family friend, and the prime minister of Newfoundland) consistently opposed female suffrage. The masculinity of the late Victorian and early Edwardian eras was "harder and more violent" than the manliness of a few decades before.[7] With its carnage and shell shock, World War I dealt a death blow to "the image of the rock-hard hero."[8] Yet for as long as explorers could maintain it, the isolated Arctic was a site of "white male leadership."[9] It was, then, the stage on which masculinity could continue to be performed, its worth proven, its exalted status maintained.

The effect of this on Inuit women has rarely been considered. But in combination with middle and upper class over-confidence, the hyper-masculinity of Arctic exploration made Inuit women vulnerable targets. One act of gendered violence involved Elisha Kent Kane, winner of medals from the United States Congress and the Royal Geographical Society. Kane once suspected a group of Inuit women of theft for which he had them stripped, tied, and marched 30 miles.[10] Peary seemed to reflect the general views of explorers when he claimed that an Inuit woman was "as much a part of the man's property as his dog or sledge."[11] He allowed that it was otherwise in rare cases. In terms of relations with explorers, some Inuit women, perhaps among them Allakasingwah, Peary's common-law wife, may have enjoyed a degree of agency, but others likely did not and were left pregnant with explorers' and crew members' children. It would be naive to conclude that no Inuit women were sexually abused or raped in the polar exploration era, given the gender and racial power imbalances inherent in exploration. Peary wrote that Inuit women married as early as the age of 12,[12] and Allakasingwah was very young when Peary impregnated her. Inuit women were objectified, not dissimilar to the collected Arctic bird and plant specimens.

Little attention has been paid to the western women in the lives of Arctic explorers. With carefully constructed images, the Peary women, Josephine and Marie, were the exception. These women are viewed as having provided vital support in the manner of women behind great men. They have been described as "polar wives,"[13] but also involved were sisters and daughters like Cecily Shackleton, who ably masterminded her brother Edward's trip to Ellesmere Island. Bartlett had no wife but he had two grandmothers, a mother, sisters, and nieces, one of whom— his sister Beatrice's daughter, Hilda Dove*—he took to the Arctic. And, despite the machismo threading through his life, it was these women who shaped Bartlett.

Chief among these influential women was Bartlett's maternal grandmother, Mary Norman Leamon, who was small in stature but a striking figure. Blond and immaculately polished, she kept a fine horse and gig, the leatherwork spotless, and the brass bell always shiny. She had, the locals said, a stately sort of air. She was cultured, a keen piano player, an accomplished dancer, and a talented singer—she excelled in all the fine arts imparted to Victorian girls of the upper classes. She had been educated partly in Clifton, Kent, England, where T.S. Eliot wrote at least some of "The Wasteland," and sent her daughter, Mary Jemima Bartlett, Bartlett's mother, across the Atlantic for schooling.[14] She bequeathed her fine home to this daughter, bypassing her only surviving son—this in a society that was rigidly patriarchal. In addition, she added an unconventional stipulation to her will that could have torn the family in two forever.[15]

Despite her imposing nature, Mary Norman Leamon was more than capable of playing the indulgent grandmother, with a focus on her eldest grandson, Bob Bartlett. As a result, she was immortalized by Bartlett, who

---

*   This Hilda was named after Bartlett's sister, Hilda Northway Bartlett Wills, who died in 1905.

compared himself as a child to Little Lord Fauntleroy, listening to his grandmother's weekly renditions of Bible stories:

> Ah, but those were golden Sunday afternoons with Grandmother Leamon! The western sun shining in through the windows of that fine old place, a little lad in velvet clothes and Eton collar sitting up in a chair before the open fireplace, with its crackling logs and the kettle on the hob. Then came the singing of the kettle, the fast fading daylight, the drawing over of the curtains, and Grandmother Leamon busy over the tea things. There were the big silver urn and teapot, the wonderful thin real Chinese teacups with pale pink flowers all over them; and finally all the good things to eat that a hungry boy would like.[16]

This paragraph could have been written by any of Queen Victoria's privileged offspring or their children on a visit to Windsor Castle.

Bartlett clearly adored Mary Norman Leamon and asserted that, while he was fond of both his grandmothers, she was his favourite.[17] An avid reader himself, Bartlett wrote that Grandmother Leamon was "great in literature as well as in music."[18] Adulation was the sum total of Bartlett's feelings for the woman who showered attention on him; at least, characteristically, this is all he would reveal. Conflict-averse and intensely devoted to his family, he would never speak of any doings that reflected ill on Grandmother Leamon, or on any of his relatives or ancestors. An introvert, he was far too private for that and, as a Bartlett, much too proud. To Bartlett, Grandmother Leamon was "vivacious, full of fun, almost always on the go." Bartlett admitted that she had "a will of iron" and he hinted at her imperiousness, noting that she had eyes like a hawk and that she would never tolerate, say, a horse not well curried. Although she lived in a time when women's roles were circumscribed and their movements often controlled, Bartlett proclaimed of his grandmother, "Anywhere she wanted to go, go she would."[19] This was all he would say of her, although there was more to say.

Grandmother Leamon's late son Robert Leamon Jr. died a bachelor, as would his namesake nephew, Bob Bartlett. Robert Leamon Jr. left his portion of the family home to his sister, Mary Jemima Bartlett, Bob's mother, and not to his surviving brother, John, who had a quarter share in the house. Despite the grief she must have felt at Robert's death, Grandmother Leamon responded swiftly to her son's last will and testament by deeding her own portion of the home, Hawthorn Cottage,* to Mary Jemima, sidelining her son John again. But she did not leave it at that. She went on to create potential, and potentially embarrassing, complications in the life of her grandson and other descendants. She barred Bartlett from marrying any member of the Butler family of Brigus if he wanted to inherit the house. The same stipulation applied to his younger sister Emma, too, whom she named as heir in the event of Bartlett's dying without issue (as he, in fact, did many years later—or at least without legitmate issue).

Grandmother Leamon's will read:

> for and in consideration of the sum of one dollar ... I have given, granted, bargained, conveyed and confirmed unto my said daughter Mary [Mary Jemima, Mrs. Captain William Bartlett] for and during the term of her natural life, and after her decease unto my grandson Robert Abram Bartlett, eldest son of my said daughter, and his lawful issue ... [and] in that case my said grandson Robert Abram Bartlett should die unmarried and without lawful issue or that he shall or will marry with any member, descendant or connection of the family of Constable Butler of Brigus ... the said share or portion of house and premises therein conveyed shall go and is hereby given, granted and confirmed unto my granddaughter Emma Gertrude Bartlett, third daughter of said daughter Mary ... or in case of her marriage with any member of the Butler family here before mentioned ... the aforesaid house, land and property shall go to the surviving children of my said daughter Mary.[20]

Grandmother Leamon's machinations left Mary Jemima Bartlett with three-quarters of Hawthorn Cottage, with the final coveted quarter in the

---

* The spelling would be changed to Hawthorne Cottage at a later date. As Bob Bartlett's childhood home, the building is now a National Historic Site of Canada.

hands of Mary Jemima's brother John Leamon. A year after his brother Robert Leamon Jr. died, John sold his portion to Mary Jemima and her husband, William Bartlett. With that, Bob's parents completely owned Hawthorn Cottage and the substantial holdings attached to it: the land it sat on, its shop, barn, cattle, carriages, and carts and sledge. John Leamon's motivations for selling are unclear and unusual. His loss of property and inheritance flies in the face of the patriarchal traditions which ensured that tangible legacies went primarily or even solely to eldest sons. John was the only living Leamon son and presented the only possibility of the Leamon name surviving in Brigus, where it was colourfully pronounced "lemon." He must have been under terrible pressure to turn his remaining quarter over to Mary Jemima and the Bartletts to sell it off.[21]

As an old man in 1987, John's namesake grandson, John Northway Leamon, was at pains to avoid revealing his great-grandmother's motivation. "Well, I could give you the story," he said to a Parks Canada interviewer. "I was a little bit surprised when it got printed in the newspaper at all. There is a little something right there and probably I am the only person who knows it ..."[22] The eccentric John Northway Leamon was a graduate of Trinity College, London, and taught music in Brigus and Carbonear.

What were Grandmother Leamon's motivations? Her concern was not the potential for inbreeding and ill health in subsequent offspring; there was no known blood relationship between the Butlers and the Leamons or Bartletts and none in the respective family genealogies. Even if there were, members of the royal families of Europe regularly married their first cousins, as the well-read and English-educated Grandmother Leamon would have known. In Newfoundland, as in other largely rural societies, there was little prohibition on marrying relatives in the 19th century. Such alliances were sometimes necessary because of tiny populations and remoteness.

It seems that her desire to prevent marriage with a Butler was more specific than any such broad concerns. One of Grandmother Leamon's descendants had already married a Butler. Her son John Leamon's bride of two years was Mary Eliza Butler, the daughter of Benjamin Butler, a farmer but also the constable and jailer at the Brigus Court House, and the man named in the unusual will. Perhaps Grandmother Leamon did not like her new daughter-in-law. She also had no affinity for the young woman's family—Butlers past, present, and future—and she used her considerable power to demonstrate this in a vindictive manner. In revealing her preferences so publicly, Grandmother Leamon went against the norms of her elevated class; this was out of character for her and points to her strong feelings in the matter.

Meanwhile, in spite of her attitude, the Butlers of Conception Bay can claim to be one of the oldest settler families on the island of Newfoundland; censuses from the 17th century list a Thomas Butler as a Port Grave (Port de Grave) planter.[23] Although not unique in his extensive holdings, Thomas Butler was "a substantial planter" who employed 20 servants and owned 30 head of cattle, 20 sheep, two fishing rooms, and five fishing boats, making him "one of the leading inhabitants of the island."[24] Given local geography and the sparse population, Thomas Butler may well be the founder, with some unnamed woman, of the Butler clan of Brigus.

Years later Grandmother Leamon's great-grandson John Leamon told an interviewer, "You see, if you will look on the family genealogy there, you will find that my grandfather John married Mary Eliza Butler. I am not sure really whether I should tell this or ... It's not something that we are ashamed of. It is something that ... My father passed it along to me and he got it from his Grandfather Butler. There are some things that I can tell you but I wouldn't like to see it in print. I think it would be better not to carry it any further."[25] As tantalizing as these statements were, Leamon's interviewer kindly did not press the matter with the old man, although Leamon said he planned to write a book, "so, I suppose it will be public knowledge anyway."[26]

John Leamon's book, *Brigus: Past Glory, Present Splendour*, is a richly detailed account of Brigus history but it contains no hoped-for revelation, not even a hint.[27] In the text, Leamon implies that the estrangement between the Butlers and the Leamons resulted from Grandmother Leamon's will, that bitterness between the families grew out of the old lady's pointed exclusion of the Butlers through the document. With Hawthorn Cottage in Bartlett hands, Constable Butler maintained his position that the Hawthorn property should belong to his son-in-law, the only male descendant of the Leamon line—and in this he voiced his opinion "in no uncertain terms at every opportunity."[28] Although they maintained ownership of Hawthorn Cottage, the Bartletts were upset by Constable Butler's ongoing disapproval. Grandmother Leamon, in particular, would have been annoyed by Butler's willingness to pursue the issue in public, though she could have predicted it if she had been able to engage in sober reflection. According to Leamon's book, "[this upset was] ... in all probability, why the will of Mary [Grandmother Leamon] reads as it does and why it comes down so hard on Robert Abram Bartlett who was growing up around the town right at the time when Constable Butler's several [known to be attractive] granddaughters were among the most popular young people of their day. We can, of course, be certain that if young Bob happened to express even the slightest interest in them, the thought was no doubt swiftly and effectively 'nipped in the bud.'"[29]

But the explanation in Leamon's book makes no temporal sense. Leamon claims that friction occurred because of Constable Butler's vociferous objection to the will, but this does not shed any light on why Grandmother Leamon wrote the will as she did. Was it an illegitimate birth or a series of them that offended Grandmother Leamon with her well-known attachment to propriety? Perhaps, but Bob Bartlett was conceived before his parents walked down the aisle, in violation of the religious principles to which the family adhered. Was there a murky or dark, perhaps petty criminal, background that made her loathe them so? This is unlikely given Benjamin Butler's status as an officer of the law. Perhaps Grandmother Leamon had run afoul of Butler in his official capacity, although that, too, is difficult to imagine in view of her preference for order and her high social status in Brigus. There may have been an illicit affair that she could not forgive. Or maybe foreign or Indigenous blood in the Butler veins, suspicious blood she did not want to enter her own blue line. Historically, there was an Indigenous presence in Brigus; Marge or Marg, "an Indian woman," was buried in the town between 1810 and 1813, having been baptized two days before her death.[30] Marge's son Thomas, likely a newborn, was baptized on the day of her death, indicating that she may have died in childbirth. Marge or other Beothuk, Mi'kmaq, or Inuit—given the region's connections with Labrador—may well have had descendants in Brigus and the stigma of Indigenous blood would have been quite real in such a lofty town, as it was even in less illustrious Newfoundland settlements.

John Leamon hinted that Grandmother Leamon was trying to prevent a union between Bob and a certain Butler girl. There would not likely have been such a girl in Bob's sights; Bob was only 11 years old when Grandmother Leamon wrote the will. Besides, Grandmother Leamon's will prohibited her granddaughter Emma Bartlett, too, from marrying a Butler on pain of disinheritance. At the time Emma was only five. It may simply be that Grandmother Leamon thought the Butlers were not good enough for her progeny and that she regretted the fact that one had already married into her family. Bob admired Grandmother Leamon regardless of this, displaying his lifelong habit of overlooking the flaws in those he loved. He may have developed this capacity on the cusp of adolescence as he witnessed his formidable grandmother isolate her son and his family. This might have inculcated a fear in him, fear that he would be punished similarly for one action or another, which may have had the unintended effect of stifling him as a person. Bartlett was an able leader, as he would prove in the western Arctic, but he was also, at heart, a conformist.

With Grandmother Leamon's unusual will, relations between the Butlers and the Leamon/Bartletts were severed as surely as a sharp blade cuts through softened sealskin. Writing in the 1990s, John Leamon said the rift "to a certain degree has lasted to this very day."[31] That was all he said on that matter, choosing not to dwell on his troubled family relationships and exhibiting a penchant for privacy, if not secrecy, that he shared with Bartlett. Some evidence exists that Grandmother Leamon's relatives were able to repair the rift; in 1904, long after Grandmother Leamon's will was written, Constable Butler named Captain William Bartlett as one of two executors of his will.[32] Despite cutting them out of her will, Grandmother Leamon seems to have had good relationships with her Butler/Leamon grandchildren, if John Leamon's published recollections are reliable.[33]

Grandmother Leamon had been born Mary Norman, the niece of the famous Captain Nathan Norman who entertained titled men in his grand hilltop home in Brigus. Grandmother Leamon's brother, Captain William Norman, had rescued the Greely Party in 1884, the seven survivors who had been shipwrecked, stranded, and starving on Ellesmere Island and then Pim Island, where they had walked in hopes of salvation.[34] While Adolphus Greely's contribution to science was vast, he is mostly remembered for this episode and his near death. According to *The Rescue of Greely*, the wasting expedition leader's words of greeting were: "seven of us left—here we are—

dying—like men. Did what I came to do—beat the best record."[35] Greely's team of 25 had started its Arctic mission as the pride of the United States military and ended it, it was said, by literally eating each other. One young member had been executed by gunshot on Greely's order. Those still alive owed their lives to the intrepidness and persistence of Captain Norman, who made international headlines by the rescue and wove the family into compelling and heroic, if exaggerated, Arctic lore.[36] Just as Grandmother Leamon did, the association between the Arctic and heroism would have a major effect on Bartlett's formation.

Grandmother Leamon's daughter Mary Jemima would become Bartlett's mother. Born on 18 August 1852,[37] she was a content and active child and very musical, as would be her daughters. She played a melodeon that had been in her family for two generations and, in 1876, when Bob was an infant, had a pipe brought in from London on the schooner *Hydrantha*.[38] She was dainty as a child and remained petite throughout her life, despite bearing many children. Bartlett estimated she weighed no more than 100 pounds, about half the size of her eldest son's considerable frame.[39] Beloved by Bartlett, she lived to 91, dying on 16 January 1943.[40]

Mary Jemima Leamon married William, son of Abram Jr. and Elizabeth Bartlett, on 9 December 1874 in Brigus. She was 22, her groom a year older.[41] Grandmother Leamon was delighted with her new son-in-law, the accomplished Captain William Bartlett, and allied herself with the Bartletts the rest of her days. Grandmother Leamon died at 79 in 1909 as her much loved grandson over-wintered in Greenland in the company of Admiral Peary. In the grandmother he venerated, Bartlett had an early and influential example of a shrewd politician who would go to great lengths to protect her interests, as she saw them. The Pearys, also the subjects of Bartlett's awe, fit this mould and Bartlett was never less than comfortable with them.

Grandmother Leamon had the expectations any gentlewoman would have for her offspring and their offspring. She cultivated a love of high art and reading in Bob, that struck deep in his soul. This seems to have been a deliberate program of hers with literary Sunday afternoons in her parlour. As his ship, the *Karluk*, sank in the Arctic many years later, Bob Bartlett sat in his cabin, playing Chopin's "Funeral March" on the Victrola.[42]

This was an unforgettable scene that even Grandmother Leamon with her dramatic flair probably would not have envisioned, although she would have been quite proud of it.

Like his grandmother, Bartlett became a thoughtful and critical reader. He frequently mused about writers, once remarking perceptively to a friend that Burns would have been a better poet than Wordsworth if the Scot had had willpower.[43] But Grandmother Leamon was not all about high art; she was conventional in some respects. Form meant a great deal to her. In true aristocratic fashion, she valued correctness, cleanliness, and presentation at least as much as she cared about Shakespearean sonnets. These values, too, were imbibed by Bartlett who had, outside the Arctic, a carefully crafted image that he guarded.

The Bartlett women tended to produce many children, with most surviving to adulthood, defying the odds of the time. Susannah Leamon, Grandmother Leamon's mother, was not as lucky, in that only two of her children made it past childhood. Susannah's son Robert Leamon Sr. grew up to marry Mary Norman (Grandmother Leamon) and they had three children, including Mary Jemima, Bob's mother. Mary Jemima and her brothers were raised at Whitehorn Cottage, later renamed Hawthorn Cottage. Mary Jemima's father, Robert Leamon Sr., was "a general importer and dealer in the British and foreign goods, provisions, etc."[44] He owned two ships, the *Joseph* and the *Nimrod*, but was at heart a merchant rather than a mariner, unlike so many of those with whom he dined.

Mary Jemima and her husband, Captain William Bartlett, lived in several Brigus homes before they moved into Whitehorn Cottage. Bob, their firstborn, was born in the stately home of his Bartlett grandparents, a house filled with expensive furniture imported from England. The house featured French windows, framed by long crimson curtains and heavy mahogany rods; the brass rings that held them in place were always gleaming. Bartlett remembered the rich Brussels carpet, the marble clock on the mantelpiece, and the bold but pretty red and gold wallpaper.* When Bartlett was five years old, his family moved to a duplex at 22–24 North Street, Brigus.[45] "Brookside," as the house was called, was a former grist

---

* Unfortunately, like so many wooden structures in Newfoundland, the house burned to the ground—in March 1916 (*The Log of Bob Bartlett: The True Story of Forty Years of Seafaring and Exploration* [1928; St. John's: Flanker Press, 2006], 40).

Beatrice Bartlett Dove, Bob's sister and the mother of Hilda Dove. Taken in 1914, this photo is attributed to Rupert Bartlett. *The Rooms Provincial Archives Division, VA 150-18.6.*

mill where its original owner had tried his hand—or rather those of his servants'—at milling oats, barley, and corn. North Street was prone to flooding; after heavy rains, the Bartletts and others often went down the street in a rowboat. This happened so often that Bartlett and his sister Beatrice, nicknamed Triss, became almost casual about it. On one such occasion, Mary Jemima quickly rounded up all her children but could not find Bob. She finally discovered him happily sailing about the kitchen in a washtub; the witty Triss dubbed this "Bob's first sea voyage."[46]

In the other side of the North Street duplex lived the large Scotland-rooted Crosbie family. The Crosbies' second youngest child, Jack, was about Bartlett's age and the two boys became fast friends. Bartlett's world was decidedly feminine, surrounded, as he was, by his admiring mother, his devoted grandmothers, petticoat-clad Triss, and a cooing baby girl or two. His father was often at sea. Brookside provided a male peer right next door. Bartlett's playmate Jack Crosbie later founded a business empire of fish, insurance, margarine, and politics. Carrying on family tradition, Jack's namesake grandson, John Crosbie, became Canada's finance minister in 1979, and Jack himself was knighted by the king of England, becoming Sir John Chalker Crosbie; Bartlett, in turn, would be presented with an award by the king of Italy, among his many other accolades.[47] By the time the Bartlett brood consisted of Bob and three little girls, Grandmother Leamon opened up Whitehorn Cottage to accommodate the family. The Bartletts, in return, were to take care of her, as she was now a widow. After her husband's death, Grandmother Leamon had lived mainly with her unmarried son Robert Jr. at the cottage until Robert Jr. died in 1886. The cottage was moved from its original location a few miles away in the country and situated conveniently in the middle of elegant Brigus with its narrow winding streets. The harbour was a stone's throw away, two of the churches looked down from the hills above, and the Bartlett children could sail paper boats in a river around the corner. In the English fashion, the Brigus upper classes were fond of giving their homes names and Captain William and Mary Jemima followed this tradition, both of them never hesitant about putting their stamp on things. Eventually, they rechristened their house Hawthorn Cottage, a name that finally stuck.

Like Mary Jemima, most young women in Brigus would have been delighted to be courted by the handsome Captain William Bartlett. William had a lineage that he might have coasted on; his ancestry and family history gave him advantages—material, cultural, and, most importantly, psychological. But he aimed to live up to the Bartlett legacy and expectations and to earn any privileges he might receive. He studied at the Harbour Grace Grammar School, open only to boys from the elite families of Conception Bay, quickly developing an appetite and an aptitude for navigation. William did well at high school, too, graduating, and then going to the Labrador fishery with his father at 15. The next year, he took to the rolling ice pans in search of seals.

In 1874, he had a new wife and he was captain of the *Panther*, following in the footsteps of his brother, Captain John Bartlett. On this ship William set a record for seal hunting in the Cabot Strait, bringing in an average of more than 10,000 pelts a year.[48] Sealing occupies a singularly important place in the rural culture of Newfoundland's northeast coast. Appearing on ice floes every spring, it was seal that allowed the first European settlers to over-winter in Newfoundland; the rich meat gave them the nutrients they desperately needed as the long winter waned. Seal had served a similar function for the extinct Beothuk. Without the seal hunt, the European settlers of the northeast coast would have starved.[49]

From the early days of European settlement, seal hunting became a rite of passage for Newfoundland boys from St. John's to the Great Northern Peninsula, who risked their lives jumping from one wobbly ice pan to another in bloody pursuit. Seals and sealing were and are emotional subjects for the people of the region, the Bartletts included. Besides bloating his bank account, Captain William's feat in the Gulf of St. Lawrence propelled him to the top of society. William's ancestors would have been delighted and Mary Jemima always derived enormous pleasure from the accomplishments of her husband and sons, dangerous though their professional activities were. Not surprisingly, she suffered great anxiety whenever her husband went sealing. In later years, her daughter Betty Angel would come from St. John's to stay with her during the annual seal hunt, providing comfort and a balm for her legitimate fears.

Dynastic in aims and attitude, the Bartletts were fond of repeating Christian names from one generation to the next. Mary Jemima and William's first child was Bob or Robert Abraham, although Abram was his preference. He was born on 15 August 1875.[50] His name honoured both his grandfathers and his maternal uncle. Four girls came in the next eight years: Beatrice Stentaford Bartlett or Triss, Hilda Northway Bartlett, Emma Gertrude Bartlett, who was chosen for Grandmother Leamon's special attentions in her notorious will, and Mary Elizabeth Bartlett or Betty, all of them conceived over Christmas, one of the few respite periods in the work-driven Newfoundland calendar, and born in late summer or fall. Blanche Eleanor Bartlett, always known by her middle name, came in 1894 when Bartlett was 19. The use of surnames as middle names for some of the girls suggests a strong sense of family history and no fear of doing things a little differently. The girls all lived to adulthood, but Hilda died in childbirth at age 26, taking her newborn with her. Emma, Eleanor, and Betty were close; Triss less so after she married and moved to St. John's.[51] Like Eleanor, Emma enjoyed a special lifelong friendship with her doting older brother, Bob. Grandmother Leamon need not have feared: not only did Emma not marry a Butler, she did not marry anyone. The choice of Emma, the third daughter, as her heir remains part of the mystery of the will. Perhaps Emma resembled Grandmother Leamon or reminded her of a beloved relative. Or she may simply have been her grandmother's favourite. Whatever the reason, Grandmother Leamon had no qualms about revealing her preference for Emma in the most obvious manner.

Mary Jemima and Captain William's second son was born in 1885 but died six months later. Captain William wanted a namesake son, just as he had been named for an ancestor of mythic stature, Captain William Follow-On Bartlett. When the next Bartlett baby was a boy, born on 7 October 1887, his parents christened him William Leamon Norman Bartlett. In his name, this new baby carried the legacies of his father, his grandfather Squire Leamon, his great-grandfather Captain William Norman, and Follow-On. Will, as he was known, lived to be 70. In a pattern that repeats itself in the Bartletts, a family in which couples seem to have been faithful and loving, Will's wife, younger by six years, died the same month—August 1967—as her husband. Will was Bob's junior by 12 years but, brought up in a family that consistently emphasized blood ties, they were best friends their whole lives and made numerous Arctic voyages together.

Two more Bartlett sons came. Lewis Goodison Bartlett arrived in the winter of 1890; he was 76 when he died in 1966, two years before his wife. Rupert Wilfred Bartlett was born a year and a half after Lewis and named after the northern Newfoundland missionary doctor and evangelist Sir Wilfred Grenfell, who, many years later said of Captain William Bartlett, "Of all the men I used to like to meet on the Coast, no one was more helpful to me in his attitude to life than he. He was a very fine man."[52] Meanwhile, Rupert's death on a World War I battlefield scarred his mother, Mary Jemima, while Bartlett's reaction to the tragedy nearly curtailed his own career.

The large family was rounded out with the birth of Winifred Grenfell Bartlett, who was also named in honour of the missionary doctor. Winifred became Mary Jemima's second child not to survive infancy. The family's final child was Blanche Eleanor, known by her middle name. Of their 11 children, nine reached adulthood, although two would perish as young adults. Mary Jemima and Captain William were pious people, especially Mary Jemima, and knew they fared much better than many of their

Captain William Bartlett, Bob's father, lower right, at Turnavik, Labrador, in 1893. This photograph was taken by the missionary doctor Sir Wilfred Grenfell. *The Rooms Provincial Archives Division, VA 91-18.1/W.T. Grenfell.*

neighbours, especially those who scraped the bottom of the flour barrels in February and March.

Education was important to the Bartletts and the children were introduced to formal schooling by the unconventional and demanding but enterprising Percey sisters. The sisters, Ady, Livy, and Susannah Percey, who acted as housekeeper, were dedicated Methodists who ran a small school out of their two-storey Brigus house. As was the practice, the Perceys expected Bartlett, his sisters, and the other students to bring junks of wood to heat both floors of the schoolhouse: the downstairs classroom and the living quarters upstairs. As Bartlett said, "having [wood] with you of a morning was as important as having your homework well done."[53] If the wood ran out, Ady and Livy promptly cancelled classes and sent the oldest children out to fetch it. Bartlett chafed at being confined to a classroom, so he relished "the small adventure of these extracurricular excursions."[54] He was sorry to go to the larger, less intimate Brigus Methodist Academy later.

The Academy was built when Bartlett was a toddler, its construction a community effort; Bartlett's father, whose own father memorably converted to Methodism, donated land at Riverhead worth £28 upon which the school was built.[55]

By all accounts, the Bartlett children were content growing up, but the rigidity in the home mirrored Captain William Bartlett's approach to shipboard life. As committed Wesleyan Methodists, William and Mary Jemima tolerated no liquor, cigarette, or card playing in their home. Neither did Skipper William curse, ever, although his most famous son would take a different approach to verbal expression. Although he was a lifelong Christian, the strict Methodism of his childhood did not stick to Bob Bartlett. His papers at Bowdoin College in Maine contain a copy of the *Book of Common Prayer* in excellent condition, indicating that it was hardly opened. The only evidence of a human hand is Bartlett's signature inside which lists "Schr. Morrissey, New York Harbour" as his address and is dated 13 May 1934. Captain William practically turned the Bartlett house into a church on Sundays, in combination with the obligatory church service and Sunday school; this regimen did not appeal to his eldest son. William regularly read at least five church journals, among them the *Christian Age* and the religious columns in the Montreal *Weekly Witness*, aloud to his children. Bob, on the other hand, had a bit of a liberal or independent streak and was not interested in the sermonizing. His tastes were more poetic, literary, and, as he aged, mystical. His nephew Jack Angel described him as somewhat religious.[56]

At his father's knee, Bartlett heard and particularly enjoyed John Bunyan's Christian allegory from 1678, *The Pilgrim's Progress*. Another of William's choice of authors, interesting for so dour a man, was Thomas à Kempis, the 15th-century German monk who is thought to have penned *The Imitation of Christ*, a work of religious devotion.[57] Thomas à Kempis wrote these compelling lines: "Without the Way / There is no going / Without the Truth / There is no knowing / Without the Life / There is no living."[58] This mystical text is an example of the philosophical poetry for which Bartlett had a lifelong love, often scribbling such quotes in his little black diaries. Another of the monk's teachings—"For man proposes, but God disposes"—would have resonated with the deeply ingrained sense of fate that Bob and William shared as mariners. According to Bartlett, Captain William also read Ernest Renan's *Life of Jesus* to his children, one of the first books to take a critical and biographical view of Christ, positing Jesus as something of a historical figure as well as the son of God and, as such, the target of much public anger.[59] The book was enormously popular and a fascinating choice for an uptight Methodist like Captain William— after all, Renan was a French philosopher of Roman Catholic origins. While Bartlett enjoyed Renan, his favourite of his father's reading picks was Josephus, the early Jewish historian who wrote about Jesus. Given this, it is possible that Captain William might have approved of his eldest son's habit of carrying around with him, in adulthood, Edward Fitzgerald's translation of *The Rubāiyát of Omar Khayyám*. Based on the work of the 11th-century Persian writer, *Omar Khayyám* has been published annually almost every year since 1878 and translated into dozens of languages. Late Victorian society witnessed the establishment of Omar Khayyám Clubs, where people, mainly young men, gathered to read such verses as: "and if the Cup you drink, the Lip you press, End in what All begins and ends in—Yes ..."[60] Bartlett would have ruminated on "Fears and Sorrows that infest the Soul" and taken the text seriously, but, for many, having *Omar Khayyám* on one's person was a fashion trend, like *The Catcher in the Rye* or *On the Road* in other eras.[61] So widespread was the trend that even characters as fiercely pragmatic as Irish nationalist leader Michael Collins fell victim to it.[62]

One memorable scene illustrated the depth of the Bartletts' immovable stance against drink. When Captain William appeared to be dying of grippe, his anxious doctor prescribed brandy for him. Despite the spectre of early widowhood, Mary Jemima would not permit her husband to drink it. Fortunately, William survived without its succour.* In Bartlett's words, "Though both had been raised in homes where there was plenty of liquor, card-playing and dancing, when Mother got a home of her own she had none of it."[63] The Bartletts' love of doctrine and religiosity was seen elsewhere in the extended family. Captain Moses Bartlett, the son of Captain John, noted

---

* In one version of this story, Mary Jemima relented, but her husband pulled through before the brandy could touch his lips (George Putnam, *Mariner of the North: The Life of Captain Bob Bartlett* [New York: Duell, Sloan and Pearce, 1947]). Both versions emphasize the couple's antipathy to alcohol.

Captain Moses Bartlett, centre, son of Captain John Bartlett, with two unidentified men in the 1890s. Moses went to the Arctic in the *Windward* in 1902. *The Rooms Provincial Archives Division, VA 23-42.*

in the 1902 *Windward* log: "This being Good Friday all hands kept holiday," and "This being Sunday no work today."[64] Newfoundlanders in general were religious and most northeast coast Protestants paid respect to the Christian calendar and church commandments as diligently as the Bartletts did. Mary Jemima longed for her firstborn to become a clergyman but, though she drilled this notion into his head from early childhood, it did not take hold and, at some point, she ceased to struggle against the impossible.

If Mary Jemima was the shore boss, in Newfoundland parlance, she had plenty of role models close at hand, including her powerful mother, Grandmother Leamon, and her mother-in-law, Elizabeth Bartlett. Her home differed from theirs, however, in the austere atmosphere she created. Her children got relief from the grimness at home when they visited Grandmother Elizabeth Bartlett's high-ceilinged house; there, one of the girls would play the piano and the children would dance waltzes, mazurkas, reels, polkas, lancers, and quadrilles.[65] Why William and Mary Jemima would abandon such entertainment, yet allow their children to enjoy it elsewhere, is curious.

For much, but not all, of his life, Bartlett continued the family's teetotal tradition with an enthusiasm that sometimes surpassed that of his parents. Captain William's commitment to abstinence was considerable; he viewed the duty to take care of one's body as a commandment from God, a sacred trust. This sanctimoniousness was quite useful in a skipper with the responsibility for many lives, and Bartlett inherited his father's way of thinking in this regard. Captain William had his share and his fill of drunken sailors interfering with the smooth running of his ships, and Bartlett took care to avoid these pitfalls as well.

Although they may never have discussed it, father and son parted company on prohibition in Newfoundland, behind which Captain William was one of the leading figures. Captain William was delighted when Newfoundland "voted dry" and legislation made alcohol illegal.[66] Bob was more practical, however. By 1915, when prohibition took effect, Bob had been to the West Indies and Europe and "knew there'd be trouble."[67] He was right. Under prohibition, Newfoundland, as in Norway, its sister country in fishing and trade, quickly sank into deficit. Ships could not sell fish to Portugal, for example, and come home empty—with no port in their holds—for long. Jack Crosbie,* Bartlett's childhood friend and

Newfoundland's finance minister at the time, pragmatically ensured that Newfoundland returned to "wet" status, and solvency.[68]

The oft-repeated saying that children were to be seen and not heard accurately describes Bartlett's early years. Bartlett and his siblings did not dare initiate conversation with their father or even come into the captain's presence wearing a cap. A stern look from Captain William was all it took to clear a room and Bartlett was more than willing to scurry out. Bartlett's younger cousin, John Leamon, said simply of Captain William: "I was fearful of him."[69] As a boy John Leamon longed for a little wooden boat that was tucked away in the Bartletts' shop. He could not muster the courage to ask for it as long as Captain William was present, as he was every day in the off-season sitting by the pot-bellied stove. John told his uncle he "just came to watch the cuckoo clock" and then he would stay until it struck the hour.[70] Finally, the day came when Captain William was absent from the shop, and John hurriedly asked young Will, a jolly sort of fellow, for the boat. "Yes, my son, take it!" Will answered. "It was Bob's but he won't need it anymore."[71] John scurried off with the coveted item, and treasured it throughout his boyhood years. Captain William never mentioned the boat, so it is doubtful he would have missed it or resented his great-nephew's taking it. But he was so unapproachable that children, including his eldest son, shrank from him.

On the other hand, Mary Jemima's stiff ways were tempered by an attractive sweetness and an inviting nature that endeared her to many. Oblivious to class resentment, Bartlett might have been exaggerating when he claimed she was "loved by everyone in Brigus, old and young."[72] He was proud of her multiple talents: knitting, sewing, "fancy work" (embroidery), and managing a store, a farm, and a garden. Reared to be an efficient homemaker, Mary Jemima was steeped in formality, like her mother, and often gave tea to relatives in what was known as the little China room at Hawthorn. Her great-nephew, John Leamon, remembered being admonished for the impropriety of buttering bread in his hand instead of on his plate. "Put that down," Mary Jemima scolded, "That's not the way you behave at table."[73] Leamon adored his great-aunt: "somehow, in spite of the

---

*   Crosbie was misspelled as Crosby in Bartlett's *Log*.

generations that separated us, there always seemed to be an affinity there that enabled us to confide in one another."[74] In saying this, the grandson of the infamous Butler/Leamon union considered Mary Jemima his "other grandmother," demonstrating that Mary Jemima had some grace in victory.

Mary Jemima was always well-groomed, with a curly hairdo described as "magnificent." Like her mother, she cut a striking figure. She wore long black dresses in the fashion of the day, and hats, sometimes attaching small purple flowers as accessories. She expected her young granddaughters to show up for afternoon tea every day at 4 p.m., and they did. "She ruled the house, she really did," said John.[75] The Bartlett men had the strength to confront raging seas. On land in their tidy parlours, however, the women presided over the upper-crust Victorian England atmosphere, Mary Jemima Bartlett leading the way.

As the wife of a wildly successful and celebrated sealing captain, Mary Jemima had sufficient help to run her households. But she did not leave everything to the maids; she gave her children and grandchildren chores galore. In many respects, Victorian children were still viewed as little adults and Mary Jemima knew how to produce independent and self-sufficient children. Autonomy, confidence, and self-reliance were values she had in common with her husband. There was not a lazy bone in a Leamon or Bartlett body, even a mild case of idleness would not have been excused. Indeed, among the early generations of Newfoundland settlers and the Beothuk, Innu, and Mi'kmaq before and after them, idleness could have meant death. Coming from the British Isles, the Channel Islands, France, Portugal, and other European countries, the first settlers were unused to the climate and topography of Newfoundland, its long harsh winters, its rocky, unforgiving soil. They worked or they died. Even when European settlement was long established, the value of hard work remained, the ethic embedded in island culture. Mary Jemima epitomized this and she made sure her children did, too; there was no other way of being.

Mary Jemima passed her strict version of etiquette to her young relatives and was a leader in her own female sphere. In her son's words, "when Father was sealing with three hundred men aboard from March to April and sometimes May, any trouble with the families, Mother saw to it herself."[76] In this, her role paralleled that of titled ladies back in England where she had attended an elite boarding school, as had her mother before her. Mary Jemima's tendency toward rigour and her brand of noblesse oblige did have a sensitive edge. When she sent baskets of bread and jam to needy neighbours, she did so through messengers or under the cover of darkness to spare the recipient embarrassment. This sensitivity and generosity were characteristics she passed on to her children, including Bob, who was equally careful to preserve people's dignity—providing he respected the individuals concerned. During the Great Depression, Emma and Eleanor discreetly took food, often soup and dessert, and sometimes clothing, to families in need.[77] Brigus native Gordon Spracklin, born in 1921, said the Bartlett sisters were often seen walking through the town bearing packages intended for local poor families.[78]

Like most grandmothers, Mary Jemima could be indulgent. In spite of the presence of maids and kitchen help, she baked cookies and cakes every Friday morning. Her granddaughter, Ruperta Angel Murphy, also known as Paddy, recalled Mary Jemima's reaching into her deep apron pockets, fishing for one of her many keys, and opening a cupboard filled with goodies for the children to enjoy.[79]

Hawthorn Cottage was a busy place. On its grounds was a store that supplied the fishermen going to Turnavik in Northern Labrador. Captain William Bartlett employed more than 150 men, women, boys, and girls at Turnavik.[80] In the store window was the cuckoo clock that had attracted young John Leamon. A large barn housed cows, a horse, hens, and chickens. A man called Spracklin, almost surely a relative of Gordon Spracklin's, minded the animals for the Bartletts and drove members of the family the mile to their farm by horse and carriage. This farm was unnamed until the 1930s, when Will Bartlett settled there and christened it Willowon, which strikes the ear as a cute combination of William and Follow-On, the sobriquet of his famous ancestor. From the farm, Will's American wife, Ethel Sargent Hyde Bartlett, served as secretary-treasurer of the Avalon Poultry Association. The couple kept Jersey and Guernsey cows and delivered milk and eggs to Brigus homes. There was a dairy and ice house under the cooling Hawthorn trees, which are long gone. Mary Jemima stored raw cream and scalded cream in the dairy in brown earthenware basins. Her granddaughter Ruperta remembered how Mary always had plenty of fresh butter on hand

and she made ice cream with a hand mixer for special occasions, "ensuring [that] the dairy was always an engaging place."[81]

Mary Jemima kept a riotously coloured flower garden featuring columbines, tiger lilies, rockets, and yellow loosestrife growing as high as the fence. She maintained syringa bushes on either side of the front door, with white waxberry lining the path up to the steps. She wanted Hawthorn Cottage to be a showpiece, and in this she succeeded. In her kitchen garden were raspberries as well as the usual hardy root crops upon which Newfoundlanders relied—potatoes, cabbage, carrots, and turnips. The hay that grew in the front garden fed the cattle. Ruperta, a St. John's girl who spent her summers in Brigus, recalled that a Union Jack was always flying from the flagpole, a poignant reminder of a devastating family loss.

The front steps to Hawthorn Cottage led to a verandah which wrapped around the house, except for the protruding kitchen area. Inside the house was a bagatelle table next to the Bartletts' grandfather clock. The steep staircase leading to the bedrooms was almost out of view. Downstairs were eight rooms of different sizes, most joined to a long hall. During Ruperta's 1920s and 1930s childhood, there was a spare room and a "front room" or parlour, a cupboard-lined pantry where fresh produce was stored, another spare room, a den, a sewing room, and a dining room, which often served as a guest bedroom, opposite the kitchen. The sitting room where the elderly Mary Jemima spent much of her time had a large bay window and a fireplace. The room also held a piano, played by Mary Jemima and her talented daughter Emma. There was also a mahogany dresser table and chairs, and a walk-in closet. Mary Jemima made sure the low brass door knobs in this and other rooms always glistened.

Among the six rooms upstairs was, of course, the master bedroom with its fireplace, dormer window, walk-in closet, bed, highboy, washstand, dresser, and rocking chair. To young Ruperta, this room was beautiful. Next was a large bedroom with a fireplace, a dormer window of the kind Ruperta so loved, and a huge cupboard. Steps led from this room to the verandah; this was a fire escape, but Mary Jemima told her grandchildren it was for anyone quarantined, providing the contagious with his or her own handy exit. This bedroom featured a double bed, a dresser, washstand, chair, and large chaise longue. The final bedroom on the right side of the hallway had been added to the house, presumably as William and Mary Jemima's considerable family grew. It had plainer windows and contained furniture that was Newfoundland-made, unlike that in the other rooms, which was all imported, mainly from England.

The nursery was opposite and sometimes contained as many as four beds. Bartlett's room was alongside the nursery; he slept there when the *Morrissey* called at Brigus in the 1920s and 1930s, which meant he used it only a few nights a year. This room was next to a big bathroom "with all modern conveniences"; according to Ruperta, "[it] was kept beautifully warm from a grill in the ceiling of the kitchen which was immediately underneath."[82] The maid's room was next; it, not unexpectedly, was smaller than the others with no fireplace, meaning the maid could not enjoy the heat so relished by the Bartletts. This chamber did, however, have "a darling dormer window" and a walk-in cupboard or closet, though these would not have kept a young woman warm at night.[83] Nor, most likely, would she have had sufficient possessions to fill the closet. The furniture in this room was Newfoundland-made, with the implication that this furniture was inferior to the imported pieces that featured in the family's bedrooms and throughout the house.

Eleanor's room was at the top of the stairs. Bartlett's youngest sibling, who lived at Hawthorn virtually all her life, slept in a small room with a dormer window and walk-in cupboard. She had a dark wood dresser with washstand and chair, making her room cozy. Like virtually every Hawthorn room, Eleanor's had a crammed bookcase. Wrote Ruperta of the Bartlett home: "14 rooms in all including the scullery, china closet and Pantry (which were all fairly large). That was Hawthorn as I knew it between 1920–1940 and I loved every bit of it."[84]

Throughout the house were paintings by acclaimed American artist Rockwell Kent, who had lived with his wife and children at Landfall, a cottage built in 1786 at Freshwater on the outskirts of Brigus.[85] Known colloquially as Kent Cottage, this was the artist's home from 1914 and 1915 and his daughter's birthplace; it was dilapidated when Kent moved in but, to him, it was always "a sweet little house."[86] Kent was, according to the New York *Times*, "a thoughtful, troublesome, profoundly independent, odd and kind man."[87] That description is an endearing one, but that was not generally how Kent was received in Brigus. He arrived a stranger during wartime with propaganda in full swing and everyone on edge. Kent was fond of speaking German and singing the German songs he had learned as a child from his family's beloved Austrian maid. He could not have been too shocked when rumours began circulating in Brigus that he was an enemy spy. The objections to Kent's allegedly sinister presence broke down along class lines with the less worldly and educated agitating against him while he continued to be most welcome in refined Brigus parlours, including Mary Jemima Bartlett's; there the genteel clapped enthusiastically no matter what language Kent sang in.

The tensions surrounding Kent came to a head when the idiosyncratic artist aggressively built a tennis court on contested land, hoping to secure the land for his new tennis club. The matter landed him before a judge, and Kent used the courtroom as a vehicle for personality display, causing raucous laughter with comments like "Yes, Your Honour, I threatened not only to kill the plaintiff but to eat him!"[88] The liberal judge stifled his own laughter and, while he found the artist guilty as charged, he sentenced Kent to 30 days in jail, giving him the option of paying $5 instead. Kent was free. But he had taken to wearing a moustache like the kaiser's and he posted a sign above his studio that read "BOMB SHOP."[89] This was not all an act; in the words of Kent scholar Frederick Lewis, "Kent was an unabashed lover of German culture [and] freely espoused the merits of the Fatherland."[90] Finally, the Newfoundland government threatened to deport Kent and free Brigus of his provocations. Eight prominent Brigus men signed a testimonial of friendship to Kent, including John C. Cozens, who had a master of arts from Harvard University and taught Latin in Brigus,[91] Captains William and Sam Bartlett, merchant J.W. Hiscock, customs officer S.E. Chafe, and Reverend R.H. Maddock.[92] Despite their considerable combined influence, Kent and his wife and children, including his Newfoundland-born daughter, were unceremoniously shipped back to the United States.*

Unlike those who ostracized Kent, Mary Jemima Bartlett bought some of his paintings and even commissioned a few. Mary Jemima was worldly,

---

*   Some 40 years later, the Newfoundland government would apologize for the deportation, bringing Kent back, happily, for a visit that included a glittery state banquet and a stay at then-premier Joseph Smallwood's expansive ranch home at Roaches Line near Brigus (Ed Roberts, "Rockwell Kent–'The Brigus Spy,'" *The Compass*, 18 January 2012).

not insular, and was comfortable with those deemed to be oddballs by the pedestrian. For her, Rockwell Kent was an opportunity on her doorstep. Having married into the restless and adventure-thirsty Bartlett family, she may have recognized and understood the artist's wanderlust, moving as he did from one remote area to another, including Alaska, Tierra del Fuego, and Greenland, to paint the bold and mystical lands and seascapes that inspired him. Bartlett lacked his mother's ease in the upper echelons of society but, at sea, he would work with Americans, Scots, Norwegians, Danes, Canadians, New Zealanders, and Inuit. Indeed, Bartlett men moved in storied circles. None of the family, not even the women, would have been intimidated by the compelling peculiarity of a character like Kent.*

During her Hawthorn summers, Ruperta watered the flowers and dusted the sitting room, sometimes thrice daily, and the parlour at least once a day. By the 1930s, Mary Jemima had christened this room "the Arctic Room" in homage to Bartlett's career. Through the early 1960s many Bartlett fans came to see it.[93] In July 1982, Parks Canada made Hawthorn Cottage a National Historic Site of Canada. Restored and opened as a museum containing 3,500 items in 1995, Hawthorn Cottage has attracted tourists and Arctic aficionados from around the globe. At the time it was the only remaining intact example of the Newfoundland Picturesque or cottage orné style. With prescience and no small amount of ambition, Mary Jemima had started all this in motion after her son attempted the Pole with Peary. Extremely proud of Bartlett, she wanted his fame to spread and to endure. She was always delighted to welcome visitors to her home, where the Arctic Room featured beautiful furniture, attractive china and silver, and numerous pictures, including family portraits, which served to cement Bob Bartlett's accomplishments as a family, rather than individual, legacy.[94] Mary Jemima purposefully contextualized Bartlett's achievements and status. She spent considerable energy collecting and caring for items from his career, from New York *Times* articles to letters from President Theodore Roosevelt, who had seen Peary and his *Roosevelt* crew off.

---

* When Kent left Brigus and Newfoundland, Albert Edward Harris, a British engineer who immigrated to Newfoundland to work in the island's burgeoning lumber industry, bought and restored Landfall, renaming it Kent Cottage. Harris, too, was an artist and one of the founders of the Newfoundland Society of Art. Mary Jemima befriended him as well and he, in turn, painted for her. Harris remained at Kent Cottage until his death four years later. Newfoundland Supreme Court Justice Rupert Bartlett, Bob's nephew named for Bob's late brother, eventually purchased Landfall. Today, Landfall is an artist's retreat. Judge Rupert Bartlett also inherited Hawthorne Cottage and, in 1987, donated it to the people of Canada.

Rupert Bartlett, Bob's younger brother, in 1914, not long before he enlisted. *The Rooms Provincial Archives, VA 150-20.2.*

In the Arctic Room she put Bartlett's medals and letters from dignitaries on display, almost obscuring the costly wallpaper. She hung pictures of Roosevelt, George Putnam (Bartlett's passenger, friend, and biographer and, for a while, the husband of aviator Amelia Earhart), as well as Harry Whitney, Peary, and other explorers like Richard Bird and Stefansson, all famous men known—if not necessarily admired—by her son.

Rupert Bartlett was killed in action in Marcoing in Northern France. Two of Rupert's siblings, Betty Angel, mother of Ruperta, and Lewis, named children after him. Baby Rupert Bartlett was born three years after his uncle died and would later sail with Bartlett to the Arctic, assisting with collecting and pressing Arctic flora samples for universities and museums.[95] Baby Rupert became Judge Bartlett; his father, Lewis, Bob's brother, had been a soldier in the Royal Newfoundland Regiment. Lewis caught anthrax in Mesopotamia but miraculously survived.

The naming of these grandchildren—Rupert and Ruperta—meant a lot to the grieving Mary Jemima. It would have touched Captain William as well but, with her children grown, Mary Jemima had more time to mourn her

Lewis Bartlett, Bob's younger brother, in 1914. This photo was probably taken by their brother Rupert, who died two years later. *The Rooms Provincial Archives, VA 150-19.3.*

terrible loss. Her son Rupert's death differed in degree from the deaths of her babies, since she had known and loved Rupert for almost three decades.

Pride in and love of family, sometimes verging on tribalism, were characteristics that came from Grandmother Leamon as well as from the Bartlett side of the family. Mary Jemima was even more religious than her own mother and she took her children and grandchildren to the Methodist cemetery every Saturday to leave flowers. By this practice, she also wanted to solidify her children's, and later her grandchildren's, identity as Bartletts. Ruperta continued these cemetery visits through her life.[*]

Bartlett's sister Emma Gertrude Bartlett inherited her mother's drive. A skilled musician, Emma played the church organ in Brigus for over 50 years. Energetic like Mary Jemima, Emma also had the confidence of a woman from society's higher reaches. With her younger sister, Eleanor, who had qualified as a nurse in New York, Emma operated the Benville Tea Rooms through the Great Depression and beyond. Financed by

---

[*] Ruperta died in 1991; in keeping with Bartlett tradition, her death occurred only a year before her husband's, the noted oncologist Harry Bliss Murphy, from whom a cancer centre in St. John's is named.

Bartlett in 1929, the enterprise stood on the site where their grandfather Abram Bartlett Jr.'s house had long ago burned down. Local carpenter Percy Roberts built the restaurant using materials from one of the Bartlett sheds and Emma and Eleanor filled it with antiques.[96] The plan was to give the tea rooms a rustic, homey feel, one that would be particularly attractive to affluent guests from St. John's, the island's capital city. The word "tea room" does not do the women's establishment justice. No fewer than 4,600 patrons dined there in one year[97] and in 1934, despite the Great Depression, Emma and Eleanor prospered.[98] As Brigus native Gordon Spracklin put it, "The sisters used to make a barrel of money down there at the tea rooms."[99]

The Benville Tea Rooms, John Leamon recalled, offered "high class meals catering to the elite, made by appointment."[100] Emma's and Eleanor's guests feasted off fresh vegetables from Will Bartlett's farm and eggs from the Kennedys in nearby Frog Marsh. There was such traffic at the Benville that John Kennedy kept chickens solely to supply the restaurant. Frog Marsh lacked electricity but Kennedy innovated, constructing incubators for hatching eggs. His son, Bernard, was tasked with candling the eggs to see they were acceptable to the Bartlett sisters and their high-end customers. Bernard explained, "I can recall checking the eggs and if there was anything unusual, I would lay them aside to be checked by my father later."[101] As a teenager, Bernard made deliveries to the tea room and remembered Emma and Eleanor as "aloof and reserved," although they always offered him a piece of cake and reminded him to tell his father that more chickens would be required the next week.[102] John Kennedy once had a frightening encounter while making a delivery; another son, Leo, said "he thought he'd be killed by the fifteen or sixteen huskies in the house … they went right for him."[103] These would have been dogs Bartlett was transporting from or to an Arctic voyage. Gordon Spracklin recalled how the Bartlett sisters met his father in Brigus one day and asked him to do some cleaning. "They gave him ten cents after working all day," Spracklin told me, "He was some happy to get it."[104]

Undoubtedly influenced by Mary Jemima's green thumb and attention to detail, the Bartlett sisters paid special attention to the Benville grounds. "Ye Olde Tea Rooms" and "Here Caste Ye Anchors" read the signs near the parking lot.[105] On the trimmed lawn was a sweet-smelling flower-filled canoe and primitive wooden benches wrapped around tree trunks. During the warm summer months, diners ate fresh chicken and new potatoes and drank tea under the sun. As dusk crept in, Eleanor switched on the electric hanging lanterns that dropped from the lilac trees. When a ship's bell rang for dinner, mouths watered. Emma recruited her nieces as uniformed waitresses and it was not unusual for the sisters to create a three-course meal for 40 people. Inside, guests ate in one of three dining rooms: a red one, a blue one, and a gold one, each with china and stoneware in the appropriate colour. Diners might linger in the fireplace-adorned lounge before eating, gazing at the copper kettles, powder horns, hooked rugs, and brass candlesticks. Even more atmospheric were the hardwood floors and walls and ceilings of aged and stained pine. Patrons saw exposed joists and beams, adding to the atmosphere Emma and Eleanor so carefully and successfully cultivated. As one guest remembered some years later: "The warm greetings, the polished brass, the bric-a-brac, the crisp starched curtains, the delicious meals, the gracious service—a true treat ... [a visit to the Benville Tea Rooms] was the grand expedition—to be anticipated, experienced and forever remembered."[106]

Not everyone felt nostalgia for this latest Bartlett achievement. Cynicism about the Bartletts was entrenched in Brigus society. There were rumours that Bob siphoned supplies off his ship, the *Morrissey*, for use by his sisters at the Benville Tea Rooms, implying that the captain was pilfering from the museums, universities, and large American food companies that at least partly funded his Arctic voyages.[107] Gordon Spracklin remembered his father hauling food, including coveted grapefruit, and coal from the *Morrissey* to the tea rooms, but he saw this as business, not theft.[108] It is doubtful that either Eleanor or Emma would engage in anything that bordered on skulduggery, much less thievery—but some people in Brigus thought they would. The Bartlett sisters were insulated from the realities that many of their neighbours faced and were capable of sounding patronizing, as when Eleanor wrote that her sister-in-law "could not manage without a little maid."[109] In her old age, after a lifetime of having live-in maids, Eleanor claimed that "in Newfoundland as in other places it is difficult to get help."[110] From the town's earliest days, people in Brigus knew their place and Emma and Eleanor's posh tea rooms with its important clientele served, for some at least, as a reminder of this.

Everyone called Emma "the boss," and she was certainly the elder sister in charge. In the days before government-provided medical services, Emma and Eleanor spent every spare minute caring for the sick and needy of Brigus and, despite being a qualified nurse, Eleanor never charged for her services. In their constant concern for their neighbours, the sisters carried on a tradition that Mary Jemima had institutionalized. While laudable from some perspectives, this noblesse oblige was, of course, afforded by their status and it grew out of their keen awareness of their social station. Not everyone around them could afford to be generous. Accordingly, class-based antagonism manifested itself through gossip, slurs, snide remarks, and innuendo. One man recalled that when he complained about the food at home, his mother would stop what she was doing, turn around to face him, and say, "Why don't you go up to the tea room?"[111] His mother's words dripped with sarcasm and were aimed at the Bartlett sisters as much as at her children's whining. Such comments were and are often made—usually quietly—toward the loathed Newfoundland merchant class by those from the "lower orders." The tendency of Newfoundlanders to avoid conflict meant that Eleanor and Emma probably lived their entire lives without becoming aware of such bitterness.

Bob Bartlett also seemed oblivious to class divisions, or at least to their impact. In his view, all was well and his fishermen-farmer neighbours were content with their lot. The main thing was to have their needs met, he wrote in the *National Geographic*, forgetting that for his own family, such insignificant aspirations would never have sufficed. He wrote: "The Newfoundland fisherman is a pretty independent individual. He owns his own home—every nail in it. Usually he has money in the bank. He has a horse, a cow, and a boat. He raises his own potatoes and turnips, catches his own fish. Each family has a sheep or two and the women spin and weave their wool. If the share of the sealing trip covers the family's few needs, then what they get in the cod fishery during the summer is profit."[112]

This idealized description homogenizes the society Bartlett came from. Many families in Newfoundland did not have money in the bank or had to cope with poor catches or losses in the seal hunt or the fishery. Many fishermen never saw an end to their debts. Some years were hungry and dire poverty was hardly unknown. Newfoundland society was a stratified one in which some people had more than others. Perhaps the standard of living was higher in Brigus, but the Bartlett women's charitable activity and Gordon Spracklin's recollections make it clear that there were many needy people in Brigus, too. Given its broad readership, Bartlett generalized for *National Geographic* but his article also leaves the impression that he had never suffered the hardships known to many Newfoundland fishermen. It is almost as if he saw them, his fishing, farming, and sealing island neighbours, as a faceless mass rather than individuals with varying stories. This ability to detach from others' less attractive realities is typical of a natural self-contained observer, and a lifelong member of the privileged classes, although he would fall from his position for a time.

Bartlett did admit that the seal hunt, in which he had taken part so many times, made for "a hard life," noting that the men, who slept in the hold and on bloody sealskins on deck, were "jammed as tight as sardines in a box."[113] The shares they earned from the hunt could be as high as $238, he wrote, but the average was closer to $60. Still, the seal hunt came at a difficult time of year—at the end of a long winter and, in spring, at the time of year that is most distant from the rewards of the cod fishery, uncertain though they were. Sealers and their families were hungry enough to eat the entire seal: the liver, lungs, heart, brains, and flipper. Ever the optimist, at least publicly, Bartlett stated that his preferred way of eating seal was the same as the sealers'—with plenty of onions and butter, boiled or fried—and he noted that in the north, seal prevents scurvy.* He added that a seal flipper dinner in the "swagger clubs" of St. John's was "a great event, as great as an ambassadorial function in Washington."[114] Bartlett thus pretended he was a typical Newfoundland fisherman, but he never was; he had a financial safety net that the vast majority lacked and, as a papered mariner, he had a formal education that was advanced for the time. For the

---

* Interestingly, in 1917 an American surgeon, John M. Little, noted the nutritional value of seal meat, something most Inuit would verify. Working for the International Grenfell Association, Little observed few deficiency diseases among the Inuit of Labrador, with *kallak*–pustule-like skin lesions, intense itching, and secondary infection–a rare exception. The appearance of *kallak* was attributed to the increasing Inuit dependence on cod: "if they have plenty of seal flesh to eat, they don't have *kallak*" ("An Eskimo Deficiency Disease," *Boston Medical and Surgical Journal* 176, no. 18 [1917]: 642-43, quotation at 643).

women, the dangerous seal hunt presented the possibility of widowhood. Mary Jemima Bartlett never fully adjusted to having her husband and sons at sea; as late as 1928, she felt lonely and worried that her son Lewis, then living in St. John's, was going to the front, as Newfoundlanders called the sealing grounds.[115]

The most significant reality check of Bartlett's early adult life was his experience as an apprentice on the *Corisande*, a large square-rigged ship that he described in his *Log of Bob Bartlett*, a homespun ghost-written memoir published in 1926. Fights broke out almost as he boarded the ship and by the time they dropped cargo in Brazil, the mate was not on speaking terms with the captain. Bartlett was a nobody on board among the tough crew of the *Corisande* and its possibly alcoholic skipper. The trip to Brazil from Newfoundland took twice as long as it should have and there were odd happenings, such as the unexplained disappearance of the ship's cat, that disturbed Bartlett. When the ship sank near Cape Race, Newfoundland, just before Christmas, under the clifftops known as the Devil's Chimney, Bartlett and the rest of the crew made it to shore but then faced the prospect of freezing to death or being drowned by the rising tide. They were fortunate and skilled enough to scale the cliffs and find shelter in a fishing shed.

But the drama affected Bartlett in a way that was new to him. Upon his return home to Brigus, he was depressed, not for the only time in his life. He was not surprised when his mother did not hesitate to show her relief at his return, but he did not expect the consistent kindness shown by his father, Captain William. His stern and ambitious father did not demonstrate any of the disapproval that Bob might have have anticipated. Captain William gave Bob time to recover quietly at Hawthorn, suggesting tactfully after some weeks that his son go on the spring seal hunt with a family friend. The near tragedy gave Captain William the opportunity to show empathy, which would have meant a great deal to Bartlett and probably acted as a salve. Captain William's approach helped Bartlett recover but it also meant that the son would be firmly under his father's thumb the rest of his life; such is one's overreaction when a normally remote parent shows a little evidence of caring. Meanwhile, Captain William's psychology worked; the seal hunt did allow Bartlett to move on. That hunt was followed by time in the West Indian trade which, as in the slavery era, saw low-grade Labrador fish exchanged for Jamaican fruit, such as bananas (with higher-grade fish going elsewhere).*

During Ruperta's childhood and adolescence, her grandfather Captain William Bartlett was phasing out the once successful Turnavik, Labrador, fishing station founded by his father, Abram Jr. For myriad reasons, the Labrador fishery was in general decline, with fewer and fewer Newfoundland ships and stationers travelling there each summer. In 1930, virtually the entire town of Battle Harbour, long considered Labrador's capital, burned to the ground.† The replacement of saltfish products by frozen fish, around 1950, was the nail in the coffin for the Labrador fishery of the floaters and stationers but, like many, Captain William had geared down years before then.‡

Like most Newfoundlanders, the Bartletts frequented Labrador only in summer when the coast was kinder, the winds gentler, and the sea less treacherous. All Ruperta remembered of the Labrador fishery was posting the Newfoundland newspapers, the *Evening Telegram* and the *Morning News*, to Turnavik's year-round minders, the Evans family, of mixed Inuit and British descent. The Bartletts never experienced the winter hardships known so well by the Evans family and other Labradorians. This may be the reason Evans and others employees of Newfoundland merchants like the Bartletts were not paid through the winter and the occasionally frightening scarcities of the Labrador spring. Profits were paramount in the social contract of the day and the Bartletts were accustomed to privilege.

By the time the Turnavik station fell silent, Bartlett was a world-renowned explorer headquartered in New York. He had abandoned the business of sealing and fishing in the unforgiving ice and waters of Newfoundland and Labrador. He did not have to take advantage of the likes of Tom Evans, and he moved in entirely different circles. By the

---

* The trade between Newfoundland and Jamaica was so extensive that Jamaica's national dish is saltfish and ackee (fish from Newfoundland and ackee fruit from Jamaica). Poor-quality Labrador or Newfoundland cod fed Caribbean slaves for decades, serving as an essential pillar in plantation capitalism dependent on slave labour.

† According to the knighted missionary doctor Wilfred Grenfell, even the Marconi pole atop the hill in Battle Harbour was destroyed. Battle Harbour would never be a fish capital again; rebuilding took place at nearby Mary's Harbour.

‡ Ironically, the technique of freezing foods, brought to the world and patented by Clarence Byrdseye, had its start in Labrador; there Byrdseye observed that fish caught by Inuit around Cartwright froze instantly in winter yet remained fresh (E.W. Williams, *Frozen Foods: Biography of an Industry* [Boston: Cahners Publishing, 1963]), although the Inuit did not share in the profits the patent generated.

1930s, he was charging the college-educated sons of iconic American industrialists to come sail with him and his winter days were filled with letters to and fro between these boys, their parents, and Bartlett at the Murray Hill Hotel in midtown Manhattan. He depended on the New York and New England elite for his income. This meant currying favour with them and playing the part of a salty dog, a rough and ready sailor. This was against his introverted nature. Like most of his concerns, however, he kept this one to himself. He had learned to keep a stiff upper lip and his own counsel at the hands of Captain William and his renowned uncles. As sealing skippers, they reigned supreme, and some of them had gone north to the Arctic, leading the way for Bartlett.

CHAPTER THREE
SCULPTING A LIFE: GAFFS, COMPASSES, AND FOLLOWING ON

I will show him what a man can do
and what a man endures.

– Ernest Hemingway, *The Old Man and the Sea*

In Brigus, on the Labrador Sea, and on the ice—definitely on the ice—men doffed their caps to Captain William Bartlett. Even his children addressed him as Skipper or Captain, rather than Father or Papa. Bob Bartlett, Captain William's eldest son, developed nervous habits, including Bob's bedwetting, which he could not control and which persisted well into his teenage years.[1] Bedwetting, which was highly embarrassing during his adolescence, might have resulted from Captain William's severity, which set the tone for life at home and at sea. In this regard, Bartlett identified with the fishermen who scurried away when they caught sight of Captain William. As an adult and a skipper, Bob had affection and respect for his father, but he did not have Captain William's naturally authoritative and commanding presence. The larger-than-life characters that surrounded him—Captain William, Grandmother Leamon, and the high-achieving Bartlett uncles—left little room for Bob to find his own way.

One of "the Black Bartletts" of Brigus, Captain William was stocky and burly and had the swarthy skin and inky black hair of mysterious ancestors never mentioned and probably, perhaps deliberately, forgotten. His shoulder-length hair increased his exotic aura.[2] Bartlett claimed that these ancestors may have been Basque. Fishermen from Euskal Herria, especially the Bay of Biscay, had been coming to Newfoundland shores for hundreds of years; hence the existence of place names like Port aux Basques on the

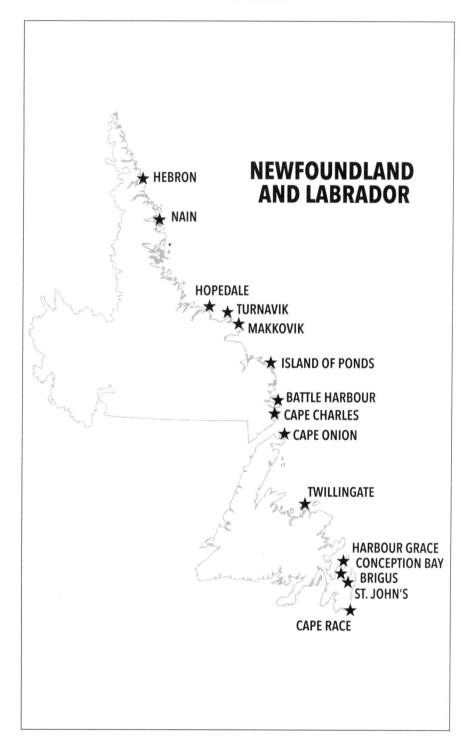

island's southwest coast.[3] Like the English, the French, the Portuguese, and the Spanish, the Basques came west across the remorseless Atlantic Ocean to Newfoundland in search of the prized codfish, *Gadus morhua*, King Cod.[4]

On the other hand, Captain William's dark skin, brows, and hair may have been a legacy of Indigenous ancestors, the Beothuk of Newfoundland—the original "Red Indians" of North America, with their ochre-dyed faces—now extinct. With European incursion, the Beothuk lost access to the coastal waters that offered them seals and salmon. The entire population starved and/or succumbed to tuberculosis and other imported diseases.[5] In 1829, the presumed last of their number, the young Beothuk woman Shanawdithit, died in St. John's.[6] But before that tragedy more than one Beothuk begat children with the settlers whose lives centred around small open wooden boats, rickety fishing stages, "rooms" to store fish, and cold little dwellings. John August, for example, a Beothuk man captured as a four-year-old, assimilated into settler society and became a ship's master.[7]

Or Captain William may have been part-Mi'kmaq. Until this century, Mi'kmaq ancestry was commonly hidden; after all, every Newfoundland school child was taught in Grade 5 that the Mi'kmaq were brought by the French from Nova Scotia to slaughter the beleaguered Beothuk, cruelly chopping off their heads and collecting scalps;[8] the oddly named Noel Boss,[*] it was claimed, had 99 such trophies and was aiming for 100.[9] Despite these nonsense claims, the Mi'kmaq were scapegoated in Newfoundland rather than romanticized like their Beothuk cousins—so much so that Mi'kmaq women with braided black hair halfway down their backs told their children they were Spanish. It is possible that Captain William Bartlett's dark face showed some of this heritage, but nobody wanted to be Mi'kmaq in 19th-century Newfoundland. William and the other sallow-skinned Bartlett men, like his brother Captain Harry, gladly took their places at the Jubilee Club in Brigus, where Brigus's merchant princes met.

Bob Bartlett was lighter-skinned than many of his relatives. Like other Newfoundlanders with sallow skin in the family, he referenced Spanish ancestry, as if suspect phenotypes had to be accounted for. With no small dash of romance, *The Log of Bob Bartlett* states:

---

[*] Boss is probably derived from the Mi'kmaq surname Basque.

> In 1588 the Spanish Armada ... cruised north to make all England Spanish ... a great storm arose and the proud fleet was dashed to pieces on the rock-ribbed coast of England and Scotland, from Land's End to John o' Groats. From these ships hundreds of Spanish soldiers and sailors were washed ashore, dead and alive. Many were so well treated by the coast folk that there they stayed. Thus came to the Nordic Bartletts a strain of somber Spanish blood, accounting not only for their complexion and their hair but ... for the independence and the airs still found among them.[10]

Perhaps.

At least some of Bartlett's paternal ancestors came to Newfoundland from Bridport, Dorset, between 1725 and 1750. In his English West Country links, Bartlett has something in common with more than two-thirds of Newfoundlanders.[11] Although Bartlett wrote about his Newfoundland origins, and these were well known in the United States, where he spent much of his life, his ethnicity and nationality seemed to cause some confusion. Besides S. Allen Counter's assertion that Bartlett was a Nova Scotian,[12] there was knighted British journalist Philip Gibbs's 1923 reference to Bartlett as "the British seaman."[13] This might have been an imperial claim of the kind that was common at the time, at least in Britain. The British claimed as their own the New Zealander who scaled Everest, Sir Edmund Hillary (who reached the summit along with the lesser celebrated Sherpa Tenzing Norgay). Such was the emotional reach of the Empire that Hillary (and Ernest Shackleton, who was raised in Ireland) happily went along with such claims. Newfoundland was, at that time, a self-governing Dominion, like Canada and the other "white" former British colonies of Australia and New Zealand.[14] But at his death in 1946, Bartlett was viewed by the American press as an American; their assertion had some legitimacy given Bartlett's long-term residency in New York as well as his decision to become a United States citizen.

Bartlett looked nothing like his father. He told his friend Daniel Henderson that he was not strong as a child. It was the challenges and risks of seal hunting and cod fishing, especially in Labrador, Bartlett reckoned, that enabled him to become "husky,"[15] and, as an explorer, he spent his life expounding the virtues of hyper-masculinity. Bartlett's young cousin Sam, who sailed with him in the *Morrissey* in the 1930s, said that Bartlett expected his crew members "to display, what shall we say, manly traits, [and] seamanship."[16] In Peary's words, Bartlett was "stocky and steel-muscled."[17] The prolific Newfoundland essayist Henry Shortis wrote in 1917 that Bartlett was thickly set and deep-chested.[18] Bartlett stood at 5 feet 8 inches, not terribly tall by North American standards but about average for a Newfoundland man born in 1875. Bartlett was, wrote Shortis, "as solid as an iceberg," adding, "[h]is frame is so sturdy that he might be compared with the ancient Norsemen."[19]

By the 1910s, Bob had made international headlines with his role in the Arctic rescue of the *Karluk*; he was ensconced in the era as a man's man, a true hero, an icon to be admired and emulated. Philip Gibbs wrote of him in *The Graphic*: "And Captain Bartlett, with his hat pushed to the back of his head, with the sun shining full on his bronzed face and into his grey-blue eyes, strode on slowly, as through there were no hurry at all in life, and spat over the kerbstone with a sublime contempt for all this civilisation."[20] This theme—of Bartlett as a sort of higher being, as beyond the "herd," in Nietzsche's words—appeared after the Peary trips, and stuck. In 1911, a New York *Times* headline announced that Bartlett was "Tired of Civilization,"[21] thereby associating the Arctic with the savage and with man's deliberate turning his back on modernity. Bartlett did nothing to disabuse Gibbs and the public of this idea. He was, wrote the adoring Gibbs, tall, square-shouldered, tanned, and—it could not be otherwise—weather-worn. The captain had a strong jaw and "a fair little moustache" as well as "eyes that seemed to look 1000 miles away."[22] Bartlett disappeared further into a cliché as Gibbs concluded his article: "[His] large strong hands that had gripped the life out of polar bears ... could choke a City clerk between thumb and forefinger."[23] Such robust misrepresentation would be repeatedly applied to Bartlett; he could never escape it. In fact, he encouraged it, knowing how his career rested on this image.

Another legacy obsessed and pushed Captain William and Bob: William was the namesake of his great-grandfather, the orginal William—or Billy, the legendary Follow-On Bartlett. Billy Bartlett was daring, brave to the point of foolhardiness, but with an uncanny ability to judge the line and never cross it. According to Newfoundland legend, he had the strength of two ordinary men, though, like Kaiser Wilhelm, he had a useless hand from birth, a constant reminder of his mortality. Like the ultimately doomed kaiser, Billy felt a need to prove himself, and he compensated for his deficiency through outrageous acts.

One year, the story goes, Billy left Brigus to go sealing with a crew of 10 or 12 men in a 30-ton shallop, an open boat with a cuddy (a small compartment) at each end. When there were no seals within sight of Brigus and none farther up the shore, he went as far as Baccalieu, an island in the outer reaches of Conception Bay. He acquired his nickname with the constant phrase, "Boys, we must follow on." The sealers kept going, reflecting the rigid at-sea hierarchy which they were well used to, not questioning him. They reached the Funk Islands, way off the island's northeast coast, north of a frigid straight shore. Here, the smell of the auks would, as they say, raise the dead, and Follow-On expected plenty of ice and seals. He found neither.

Confounded, Billy's response was to order his crew to keep going. In their shallop, they passed Cape Onion at the tip of Newfoundland's Great Northern Peninsula, and it was such a clear day that they saw the Mewstone high atop the ledge there. But as there was still no ice and no seals, they kept going. They eventually reached the Labrador coast, determined to carry on until they hit a patch of seals. There were none at Cape Charles in the south, so they kept northwest along the coast. Billy Bartlett pursued, never doubting they would have the bloody bow for which he lusted. They reached Spotted Islands, where they struck a heavy jamb of ice and, at last, got at the abundant seals. When they were done, they drifted south with the ice, taking their time and sheltering in the bow of the shallop. Finally, they saw Baccalieu and knew they were safe and nearly home.

Some in Brigus and environs thought the sealers were dead. But the Bartletts claimed that they were never less than certain that Follow-On would return. He had never lost a man in all his years in charge of ships and he would end his life without having done so—unlike Bob, his most famous descendant, whose record was in contrast. Follow-On got as far as sealers ever got in an open boat in Newfoundland, and Captain William was named in his honour.

Years afterward, the story of Follow-On was not subject to veracity, but it had spread through the whole country of Newfoundland and seeped deep into the collective consciousness. Thus, the heroic flavour that would characterize Arctic exploration was foreshadowed by the uber-masculine exploits of Bartlett's celebrated ancestor, his feat all the more striking because of his disability. The story of Follow-On was the root of many of the unspoken assumptions with which Bartlett grew up; in his immediate environment, men completely ignored ailments and injuries, pushed themselves, took significant risks, aimed high, and expected their crews to ape them without question. This was the only way things were done.

Captain William might have been thinking of the noted acts of his namesake in 1885 as he stood at the wheel of the *Panther*, recently given to him by his father, Captain Abram Bartlett Jr. William was quick, as Abram Jr. put it to the rest of the family. Indeed, William was a high school graduate who began fishing "on the Labrador," as Newfoundlanders called it, with his father at 15. When Captain William set a record for seal hunting in the Cabot Strait, he felt relief rather than joy, given that, as Follow-On's namesake, such achievements were expected.

Captain Abram Jr. had done well financially. Like Follow-On, his grandfather, Abram Jr. was not afraid to take chances and regarded risks as integral to the life of a seaman and an entrepreneur, and he was both to the core. He had confidence in abundance and would tolerate no nonsense. In a scene that recalls Jesus of Nazareth's only recorded temper tantrum, Abram once marched to the chancel of the Anglican Church in Brigus and angrily took the altar apart, piece by piece, flinging candlesticks and crosses to the floor. He had decided that these items were, at best, distracting totems that ought to be destroyed. After this shocking performance, he left the Church of England and became a Methodist.[24] His wife later collected £23 to purchase a pipe organ for the Old Wesleyan Chapel. Bought from the award-winning organ builders Henry Bevington & Sons, the instrument had 437 speaking pipes in nine ranks.[25] Bartlett once described his grandfather as a well-known sealing captain, meekly put since Abram Jr. was nothing less than a star at the ice, ground zero of Newfoundland's masculinized maritime culture. In the *Panther*, Abram Jr. averaged about

8,500 pelts every spring.[26] About this he was pleased but never boastful; that was not the Methodist way, the Brigus way, or the Bartlett way.

But ambition was their way. In the early 1870s, when he was in his 50s, Abram Jr. sailed into the sheltered harbour of West Turnavik, Labrador, surveyed the land from the bridge of his ship, and proclaimed, "This is the place"—he would build his fishing premises and base his schooners there.[27] For some decades, the fishery on Newfoundland's northeast coast had been getting crowded and there was opportunity, Bartlett realized, in Labrador's far north. Like others who had decided to fish in Labrador, he had to bypass Newfoundland's French Shore, where France had rights and skirmishes were not uncommon. There was no need of conflict to Abram Jr.'s mind, however. He was innovative and desirous of expansion and did not mind dealing with the moods of the sea. Disagreements with people, however, were to be avoided; in this, he shared the social risk-aversion of Newfoundlanders and, perhaps, islanders the world over. Nor was Abram Jr. deterred by a painfully short fishing season in Labrador and a surly sub-Arctic sun that might or might not appear long enough for fish to dry onshore. He was not put off by the increased distance from markets or the need to start from scratch with fishing rooms and the like.

Abram Jr. did not think of Labrador as unceded Indigenous land, the age-old home of the Inuit or the Innu, the more elusive "Indians" of the Quebec-Labrador Peninsula. When Bartlett went north, there was little resistance to the arrival of Newfoundland, British, American, and Canadian floater ships and the fishermen who lived on and fished from these larger vessels. The Newfoundland stationers, who lived on land through the summer, had a free pass, too. The Inuit of Makkovik, Hopedale, Nain, and the other north coast villages had long been under the thumb of the strait-laced Moravian missionaries from Germany and England. The *kablungajuit*, the half-white Inuit cousins in Rigolet and other communities on the lower end of the north coast, were a little wilder in the missionaries' view.[28] With their feet in both worlds, the *kablungajuit* would automatically have less reason to oppose the newcomers. Below the gaping mouth of Hamilton Inlet was Labrador's south coast, home to hundreds of "breeds," "half-breeds," or "natives," like the *kablungajuits*, their ancestry an admixture of Inuit, Welsh, Scottish, Irish, French, and, in some cases, Innu. They had grand-sounding British names like Russell, Montague, Cadwell, and Turnbull and spoke only "pieces of Inuktitut," the language of their mothers and grandmothers. It would be a long time—well into the 20th century—before the Indigenous people of Labrador registered any public dissatisfaction with Newfoundland fishermen and the pillaging of Labrador seas. This is not to say that the Labradorians wanted outsiders on their land and sea, taking the fish they needed to sustain themselves. But their resentments and grudges were quiet, their passiveness toward and their ignorance of their rights quite marked. And, demonstrating the complexities of colonial impacts, at least some of them likely saw economic opportunity in the summer arrivals as well.

The Inuit and settlers' summer shacks constructed on Turnavik were dwarfed by Abram Jr.'s ever-expanding premises, which came to include a fine two-storey house, a large salt house, and a bunkhouse for the company's fishing crews. By 1885 West Turnavik was one of the largest summer fishing stations in Labrador and a notable mark of Abram Jr.'s success.[29] Eventually, save the big St. John's merchants and the Scottish Munn family of Harbour Grace, who also had Turnavik premises, Abram Jr. would be almost singular in the success he experienced in Labrador. Despite its relative isolation, Turnavik saw fishing ships come from Spain, Portugal, Wales, and the distant continents of South America and Africa. Later, of course, Peary visited on his way to Greenland.

The Labrador fishery might have yielded a certain amount of profit and status for the likes of Abram Jr., but it was taxing for the stationers and their families who travelled from the island with their pots and pans and windowpanes for the shacks that gave them a modicum of shelter. Never mind the unceasing labour that greeted them in Labrador. Even getting there was a hellish experience: "all this immense traffic was carried on by sailing vessels, mostly small schooners; there was overcrowding, and a great want of proper accommodation for the women," wrote Judge Daniel Prowse.[30] The below-decks scenes of the Labrador fishery were so unforgettable they were condemned by at least two foreign newspapers, including the New York *Times*, which referred to the fishery as trafficking.[31] Echoing local newspapers, like the St. John's *Mercury*, which called the fishery "a blot on Christianity and civilization," the concerns of the *Gazette*'s editors were primarily moral rather than focused on safety.[32] Editors primly fretted about the proximity of men and women in these circumstances and voiced distress at the constant opportunities for lapses into immorality.[33] One wonders how the temple-wrecking Abram Jr. was able to tolerate these possibilities, but, in the manner of businessmen everywhere whose main objective is to generate profit, he did so.

Besides unimaginable discomfort, the Newfoundland fishing families also faced constant danger.[*] Fishing in Labrador's cold, turbulent waters was at least as menacing as fishing in Newfoundland's. The 1886 Tinker Harbour gale, in which 26 vessels were thrown ashore, was one of a string of storms that took the lives of men, women, and children, at least eight in this case.[34] Accidents were not uncommon and many fishermen lost a finger, some an arm. It was said that if a man fell overboard the skippers kept on going, chasing the fish that had brought them there in the first place. Forbidding though he was, Abram Jr.'s son, Captain William, was not callous and he played a crucial role in rescue efforts for the worst gale ever, the Eskimo Coast disaster of 1885.[35]

In the late 1860s, Abram Jr. decided he needed more mooring facilities in Brigus's crowded harbour. The thick granite that curved around the harbour posed a challenge; grey cliffs rose high out of the water and there was simply nowhere to tie up one's boats. Abram Jr. decided to tunnel through it. He brought miners over from Cornwall, England, to drill through the rock cliff. They removed 100 feet of granite so that Abram Jr. and his crews could tie up on the cliff and walk through it, 5 feet of space on either side of them and 4 or 5 above them.[36] Abram Jr.'s tunnel, which is extant, gives mute testimony to the captain's firm belief that nothing was impossible in the face of human determination, a belief that he had inherited from Follow-On and then hammered into his children's heads.

---

[*] In November 1868, the *Hunter*, a brig commanded by William Rabbitts, a Bartlett in-law, was presumed lost on her return from Labrador, a not uncommon occurrence in the northern fishery. The *Hunter* had left Labrador in early October. Finally, one November morning, the *Hunter* sailed into Brigus, weather-beaten and ragged with only her topsails intact. Judge Prowse went on board: "I shall never forget the scene–the women and children, goats, pigs, and dogs crowded in her hold. After seeing and smelling, I believe I can now form an idea of the horrors of the middle passage, and the odours and sufferings of the chained negroes in the slaver's hold" (*A History of Newfoundland from the English, Colonial, and Foreign Records* [London: Eyre and Spottiswoode, 1896], 603).

The tunnel in Brigus built by Captain Abram Bartlett Jr., Bob's grandfather, to expand his mooring facilities. *The Rooms Provincial Archives Division, VA 15A-8.1.*

A modern photo of the Brigus tunnel. Note the graffiti paint. *Marianne King.*

Abram Jr. was born in 1819 and married 20-year-old Elizabeth Bellamy Wilmot on 4 December 1841 in the Brigus United Methodist Church.[37] Like so many Newfoundland weddings, theirs took place in winter because there was no time or energy for festivities during the test of stamina and courage that was the fishing season. Abram Jr.'s slightly older brother, John, had married the delightfully named teenager Patience Rabbitts on 27 February 1839.[38] Sadly, Patience died a day after she gave birth to her and John's only child in 1841, a daughter called Selina Patience, who lived only four years.[39] Abram Jr.'s wife, Elizabeth Bellamy Wilmot Bartlett, had at least five children, including William, Bob Bartlett's father, but three of them died as toddlers, two of whom had been called after their father.[40] They called their next boy Henry Bellamy Bartlett and nicknamed him Harry. This child would survive to adulthood, but he would become the only Bartlett to die at sea.[41]

Elizabeth was a product of a place where men were absent half the year, off in schooners chasing fish or seals; the gendered division of labour was rigid in the earliest days of European settlement but women were able to better negotiate their roles after this time.[42] Like many rural Newfoundland women, Elizabeth's job was to manage home responsibilities, and she did not hesitate to assume all available authority in this respect; she clearly and loudly demarcated her territory, her husband's ending at the beach.[43] Burly sailors might be intimidated by Captain Abram Bartlett Jr., who was known for raging on deck as he had in church, but his wife was not. "Abram, while I live, I reign," she announced one day. She was, in her grandson Bob's view, "the boss of our tribe ... as full of authority as ever a skipper at sea."[44] Elizabeth's imperiousness was tempered with an inherent kindness but, like that of his father and Grandmother Leamon, it would make its mark on the naturally timid and somewhat diffident Bartlett.

Abram Jr. was the third child of Abraham (or Abram) Bartlett Sr., born in 1788, and Nova Scotian Ann Richards, who, at only 14, was about 11 years younger than her husband when they wed. They married at the height of the 12-day Christmas season in 1813, amidst mummering* and religious

---

* Mummering (or janneying) is the Christmas tradition of getting disguised in costume (men frequently cross-dressing) to call on neighbours who are expected to guess the mummers' identity. Afterwards, mummers and their hosts dance and drink. The custom is long associated with rural Newfoundland but it has roots in the British Isles and appears elsewhere, such as Philadelphia, where there is an annual mummers parade. Herbert Halpert and George Morley Story, *Christmas Mumming in Newfoundland: Essays in Anthropology, Folklore, and History* (University of Toronto Press, 1969) and Charles E. Welch, *Oh! Dem Golden Slippers: The Story of the Philadelphia Mummers* (Philadelphia: Book Street Press, 1991).

services; Ann's first child was born 10 months later. Ann had 14 children, eight girls and six boys. By the time she finished child-bearing, 10 of her children were still living, although 12-year-old Amy was not long for this world. Infant and toddler mortality remained high until the 20th century in Newfoundland.[45] As in much of the western world, physicians and medical services were rare on the island; even the hospitals in St. John's belonged to the British military until 1814 and were not always available to the general public.[46] Medical services were only part of the puzzle of life and death for children around the globe during this era. Ignorance of sanitation practices, hygiene, and infectious diseases contributed to high infant mortality rates—in the United States, for instance, they reached 25 per cent.[47] Poverty was a factor in many cases, but the Bartletts were not poor, at least not compared to many of their neighbours. Ann and Abraham Sr.'s descendants, in fact, would rank among the wealthy of their town and their small country.

All the children of Ann and Abraham Bartlett Sr. were born at Brigus. Brigus was favoured by European fishermen because of its wide harbour mouth, high lands, and deep waters that went right to the cliffs. The harbour's shape gave ships an easy passage in and out. Through the 19th century, the harbour was packed with vessels on their way to Britain, South America, and the Mediterranean. The town's prosperity came from an entrenched and unquestioned work ethic, propelled by the Protestant impetus to work for the glory of God. The people of Brigus enjoyed their wealth, filling their homes with mahogany dressers, beautiful lamps, plush carpets, and luxurious settees, as the Bartletts and Leamons did. The common view was that they had earned it, forgetting that luck also played a part in their good fortune. The Brigus women had a reputation for pretentiousness: it was said throughout Conception Bay that they were as high-minded as the goats.

Ann and Abraham Sr. fed ambition along with porridge to their children, this trait being the natural inheritance of Billy, more often known as Follow-On, Bob's great-great-grandfather. Together with his brother, Billy bought land on the edge of the water at Riverhead, Brigus, in 1780; this became known as "the oil beach."[48] The name is unpleasant to the modern mind, evoking images of pelicans drowned in slick greasy oil. But in Billy's time, the oil beach was a place to accrue wealth; it was there that seal fat and cod livers were kept in huge vats or "boilers" to be rendered into lucrative oil. According to Brigus natives, the area is still called "Around the Boilers."[49]

Follow-On married a woman named Ann. Not much is known about her, except that Follow-On and Ann died in old age within a year of each other, in 1829 and 1830. It is tempting to conclude that their 50-year-plus marriage was a match of the kind in which mates begin to resemble each other, their features and mannerisms gelling like their love for each other. Indeed, in his will, Follow-On referred to Ann as his "loving wife."

Follow-On's last will and testament reveals a singular man who, despite a noteworthy disability, was a success in a very physical profession and was quite conscious of that fact. Two of his three sons* were each left the house they lived in, while the third was given the family house "after his mother's decease," as well as the middle part of the fishing stage. The easternmost part of the stage and the flake went to one son, with a schooner to be shared by the other two. Follow-On referred to "money kept in England"—an unknown amount held in an unknown location—which was to be divided equally among his three sons. The fact that Follow-On, who signed his will with an X—an indication of illiteracy—had money in England is notable. Actual cash was not something the average Newfoundland fisherman possessed in the early 1800s; only the most successful merchants had money for bank accounts abroad.[50] For most, money was not readily at hand and, as in England, social mobility was restricted in Newfoundland. It was difficult enough to earn a living, the winter months and the hungry month of March being especially dicey. Many rural people lived by the truck system, in which fishermen were supplied with fishing gear and then food for the winter in exchange for their catches. Within this system, most—but not all—fishermen spent their entire lives in credit, which is at least partly responsible for the class resentment that has marked Newfoundland life.[51]

Impressively, Billy managed to pull himself above the truck system and accrue at least some money for his children and heirs. It had come

---

* The sons were called, confusingly, William Jr., Abraham, and Joseph. Bob Bartlett was descended from Abraham, who became Abram Sr., the father of Abram Jr., Captain William's father. Thus, the paternal line is Billy/Follow-On, Abram Sr., Abram Jr., William, and Bob.

through a life of hard work. The seal hunt, with which he is inexorably associated, was prosecuted from stormy March until the nippy month of June in ice-skiffs and decked boats or schooners. Working in the iceberg-chilled waters, fishermen flung nets from their boats, their wrists blistering with "water pups."[52]

"[I]n the northern posts there is most certainty of [sealing] success," wrote John Bland of Bonavista in a 26 September 1802 letter to the island's Governor Gambier.[53] Sealing was a risky business, and, like the early cod fishery, rarely profitable for the majority who took part in it. Yet Follow-On, who lived this life, withered arm and all, was able to deposit money in a British bank. It was not until 1834, a year after the House of Assembly held its first sitting in St. John's, ushering in Responsible Government, that members passed a bill to establish the island's first bank, the Newfoundland Savings Bank.[54] The British Bank of North America opened in 1836 and other banks followed.[55] These banks would be used by succeeding generations of Bartletts, but Follow-On died in 1829, before the first of them opened.

Follow-On's myth and his image figured large in the life and mind of his great-great-grandson, Bob Bartlett. In 1929, Bob wrote about him in *National Geographic*, having told the story in shorter form in his 1928 autobiography.[56] In 1800, said Bob, Follow-On built the first boat to explore beyond Brigus Bay, the waters leading from Brigus Harbour to Conception Bay. Describing Follow-On's most famous trip, Bob creatively contrasted his ancestor's courage with the caution of Follow-On's crew, understandable though their hesitation would have been: "His men said, 'No use to go farther!' But he bade them Follow on!"

Follow-On might have been a first-generation Newfoundland settler but it is likely he was not; there was no significant European settlement in Conception Bay, including Brigus, before his birth. English fishermen-farmers came to the island in the early 1600s not long after John Guy set up a colony in Cupers Cove, or Cupids, adjacent to Brigus, on behalf of the Society of Merchant Venturers in Bristol, England. Around 1612, Guy sold about half of Brigus to the Spracklin family, whose descendants live in the town to this day.[57] In its early years, the town's name was variously spelled Brigue, Breckhouse, Brighouse, Breegas, and even Baracas North.[58]

It had difficult days. In 1695, the French warrior Lieutenant Boisbriand was ordered by his superiors to burn Brigus to the ground.[59] This they did. The fact that Brigus was targeted by the French meant they regarded it as a force to be reckoned with, a place that had to be reduced to rubble. Sixty men lived there at the time, noted a French priest—enough to worry the enemy.[60] By 1775, Brigus was "the most progressive and prosperous settlement in Conception Bay," said Roland Wells, a onetime Brigus resident, who may well have been right.[61] In 1819, Captain William Munden built the *Four Brothers*,* the first 100-ton schooner in Newfoundland to go sealing, in Brigus.[62] One of the brothers for whom the ship was named was Azariah Munden, the son of an Englishman, and one of Bob's maternal great-great-great-grandfathers. Follow-On and Azariah were among the first sealing captains, Azariah as early as 1768.[63] By mid-century, at least 66 ships left Newfoundland in search of seals, half of them skippered by Brigus masters.[64] Many thought the *Four Brothers* a folly, too massive to turn around in heavy ice, but Follow-On would have shared Captain Munden's enthusiasm for the new and different. Progress meant something to these restless, goal-oriented men and their equally aspirational wives. Bob inherited this inclination.

Reverend Philip Tocque wrote of Brigus during this, the town's heyday: "Brigus is well cultivated and for the extent of population has a large number of good residences."[65] Charles Lench, also a clergyman, referred to the 1830–80 period as "the piping time of prosperity."[66] Indeed, the local Bartletts, Mundens, Normans, Percys, Whelans, Roberts, and Wilcoxes were among Newfoundland's "richest planters."[67] For Bartlett, reflecting many years later in his memoir, this was the island's "Golden Age."[68] He overlooked the kinds of social inequalities in Brigus and elsewhere that might merit our attention more today when he wrote: "Conditions there were then the same as in New Bedford, New London, Mystic, Stonington, and other New England places in their eras of prosperity. There was plenty of money in Brigus at the time; no unemployment; ten children to a family; and everywhere a great pervading happiness."[69]

If anyone had cared to look and as Bartlett himself, with his sharp

---

*   The ship was later renamed *The Four Sisters*.

mind and talent for insight, should have realized, Brigus was a stratified community, with people on both ends of the socio-economic spectrum. The decline of Brigus as a great port was already well within view in Bartlett's lifetime. Newfoundland's argosies did indeed "whiten every sea," as parliamentarian Robert Parsons had roared in the House of Assembly in St. John's.[70] But the age of sail was closing and the thunderclap of schooner sails through the deepness of the night would soon become a thing of the past. Steam was the culprit,[71] triggering the long road to the ultimately tragic industrialization of the Newfoundland fisheries in the mid-20th century[72] and the near disappearance of the once-abundant cod, the island's lifeblood, in the late 20th century.[73]

Captain Abram Bartlett Sr., Bob's great-grandfather, was Follow-On's third son. By the end of Abram Sr.'s life in August 1852, the family's holdings were substantial. On his death Abram Sr. left "plantations" (waterfront premises), fishing rooms, dwelling houses, vessels, household furniture, and "ready money."[74] Abraham Sr. had purchased his first ship in 1823, a 62-ton schooner called the *John*. Other vessels, ranging in size from 29 tons to 107 tons, followed: among them the *Mary*, the *Brothers*, and the *Cordelia*. One of Abraham Sr.'s executors was his friend John Leamon; their descendants, Mary Jemima and Captain William, married and produced Bob. At Abraham Sr.'s death, Ann, with 17 years still ahead of her, was almost alone in the family's vast 23-room house, chockablock with imported Georgian and Victorian furniture. Abraham Sr. left everything to Ann and instructed that all their sons and daughters and heirs would be "equally entitled" at her death.[75] Most of their sons signed their names to the document, while their sisters' husbands did not, indicating that at mid-19th century, the Bartletts were more formally educated than some of their neighbours and in-laws. Indeed, Abraham Sr.'s eldest son, John, had been educated at Harbour Grace Grammar School alongside the headmaster's son, who would become Sir Thomas Roddick, the founder of the Medical Council of Canada.[76] John's academic success did not go unnoticed by his father, who presented him with a brig, the *Henrietta Grieve*. In this ship, young Captain John traded between Canadian and American ports as the bloody American Civil War raged and, when the cool northern spring came, headed to the ice floes to hunt seals.

There may have been toing and froing about Abraham Sr.'s legacy but the outcome of that was that everyone in the family was looked after. Ann Richards Bartlett received the impressive sum of £250 annually "during her life for her maintenance and support."[77] Also going to Ann were pews in the Episcopal Church, which had been consecrated in 1845, and others in the Wesleyan Meeting House "to do with as she pleases."[78] The marital home and all its contents remained Ann's, after whose death these would pass to Moses, the couple's youngest son, who, at about 21, appears to have been still living at home. A horse named Dick went to Moses, while all the cattle and farming implements went to Ann. Captain Abram Sr. left his daughters the hefty sum of £500 each and gave the family piano to a daughter who was musically inclined and loved to play it.[79] Abram Sr. included the girls in his last will at a time when patriarchal tradition might easily have left them with nothing. For Abram Sr., and the rest of the Bartletts, family meant even more than gender. Bob Bartlett would adhere to this philosophy his whole life.

The boys were also given £500 each.[80] But, more significantly, Abram Sr.'s sons were the inheritors of his considerable business assets, in keeping with the long-held patriarchal notion that women's husbands were their legitimate support. The Bartlett daughters did indeed inherit well but, in contrast to those of their brothers, their inheritances from their father were one-time gifts. In business terms, Captain Abram Sr. had schooners and fishing premises to pass on to his sons.[*] He seems to have given a great deal of thought to the distribution of his property, because the arrangements he made were complex. Three sons were to share the Bartlett ground in the Wesleyan Meeting House Yard and two of them got a church pew each: one in the gallery of the Meeting House and one in the Episcopal Church.[81]

Clearly, the Bartletts were involved in both of the most subscribed Protestant denominations in Brigus and along the coast. A strain of inter-denominational cooperation in Brigus continued through the 20th century; when Bob Bartlett was buried there in 1946, the bells of all the town's churches tolled in his honour.[82] Abram Sr. and Ann belonged to

---

[*]   Abram Sr.'s sons were John, Abram Jr. (from whom Bob descended), and Moses.

different churches, but this meant little to the couple—Ann inherited pews in both and Abram Sr. urged her to do as she liked with them. It would have been good politics to be in with the Wesleyans as well as the Episcopalians and Abram Sr. was nothing if not shrewd and pragmatic, another trait he passed on. Although much has been made of sectarianism in Newfoundland, the phenomenon was arguably confined to certain parts of the island, notably St. John's, where anti-Catholicism had a foothold, and at Harbour Grace, the scene of a fatal fracas. Elsewhere, such as the south coast of the island, where the total population was small, "mixed marriages"—between members of different Protestant denominations and even between Catholics and Protestants—were fairly common. Even in St. John's, the lofty goals of Irish-born Bishop Michael Anthony Fleming, who built the Roman Catholic Basilica of St. John the Baptist, were spurred in part by the ecumenism Fleming observed with some horror. Fleming, concerned about the limited rights of Catholics, could not abide the weekly shared religious services of the Protestants and Catholics and felt moved to act against this sort of fraternization and collegiality by building a giant edifice that members of his flock could not resist.[83]

Brigus was home to a substantial Roman Catholic community and an Irishtown. Tensions were certainly not unknown and, at least in the settlement's early history, religion, and ethnicity—which were one and the same in this relatively homogenous setting—placed one in the inelastic local class system. In 1697, when the invading French captured prisoners from Brigus, they found "eight Irishmen, whom the English treat[ed] as slaves."[84] Happily, Newfoundland would never become Northern Ireland. The settlers were smart enough to put stopgaps in place, including alternating positions of importance between Catholics and Protestants, such as chief of police and, later, the prestigious Rhodes Scholarship (which was, for decades, open only to men). The people of Brigus were too practical to care too much about religious differences. Hard work mattered, so did ambition and pride. The Sisters of Mercy, four women from Ireland, were welcomed in 1861, when they founded St. Joseph's Convent and began teaching the local Catholic children.[85] Only a version of Calvinism and, later, the Salvation Army did not succeed in getting a foothold in the town, despite an early attempt at building a base there.[86]

It is likely that the Army's boisterous drums and tambourines held no appeal for so taciturn a people. (Elsewhere on the island, however, the new religious movement thrived.)

Like his father, Abram Bartlett Sr. was clever and diligent in accumulating assets. He made it a point to buy land when he could, continuing the practice until just a few years before his death, knowing he was building his sons' futures and, to a lesser degree, that of his daughters and their heirs. A purchase made in 1848, when the captain was 60, is interesting; Abram Bartlett Sr. became the owner of land at Domino Run, Labrador, next to one of the most lucrative fishing grounds in the Atlantic Ocean and a reliable place for seals, as the Inuit knew. For a mere £50, he acquired the Big Room Plantation, as it was called, from James Glendon, who signed with an X, as he could not read and write. The plantation consisted of houses, stores, stages, flakes, a wharf, wheelbarrows, scales, boats, and myriad other fishing equipment and Abram Sr. left it in the care of a local Inuk. Like the Bartletts who followed, Abram Sr. had no qualms about doing business with or hiring Indigenous people. Bob would follow him in this. In the manner of explorer Charles Francis Hall, he would even demonstrate some respect for Indigenous skills and values, titling one of his lectures "The Kind Eskimo."[87] Although this title sounds condescending to the modern ear, it was outside the explorers' mould in its recognition of Inuit.

The Bartletts who survived infancy had solid genes, and many lived long lives, most into old age. Bob Bartlett came from at least four generations of strong stock on his paternal side, people who escaped the deadly infectious illnesses of their times and the accidents of their profession, people like Abram Jr., who had worked on board fishing boats well into his 60s. Bartlett would inherit some—but not all—of the remarkable Bartlett constitution.

His maternal Brigus roots went back back three generations, beginning with the arrival of Mary Jemima's grandfather John Leamon from the beautiful Georgian town of Blandford, England, where Leamon had been born in 1802.[88] As was the habit of the time, Christian names were, confusingly, repeated in every generation. John was the son of Robert and Mary Leamon and the executor of more than one Bartlett will, including Abram Sr.'s. He had deep-set eyes, a square face, and a large rounded nose.

He started his career in England as an agent for Charles Cozens, also of Blandford, Dorset, and a relative, as Leamon's mother had been a Cozens.*

By 1828, John Leamon was Cozens's partner, but the firm went belly up in 1833, the year after the island finally achieved Representative Government. Like his kinsman, John Leamon likely came to Newfoundland to make his own fortune, and he reached his goal. He set up a store in Brigus and was soon a major supplier; he acquired a fishing station at Indian Harbour, Labrador, and other Labrador properties at Holton, Ice Tickles, Batteau, and Rogers Harbour.[89] Most Newfoundland merchants, especially those who were native to England or Scotland, made the leap into politics, and John Leamon was no exception. As a Conservative, he won the seat for Port de Grave, which included Brigus, in 1859 and was re-elected twice.[90] Given the incestuous nature of rural Newfoundland politics, it is no shock that this was the seat his friend, former partner, and kinsman Charles Cozens had held before him. The seat would later be held by another maternal ancestor of Bob Bartlett's, Captain Nathan Norman, who lost it to Bob's paternal uncle Captain John Bartlett.[91] Thus, in the latter part of the 19th century, Bartlett's forebears practically had a lock on the Port de Grave seat in the Newfoundland legislature. Captain John Bartlett was known for his famous grindstone campaign, through which he promised a grindstone in every community so that everyone could grind their axes at public expense. After he was elected, grindstones were placed in Brigus, Bareneed, Port de Grave, Clarke's Beach, and PickEyes, an illustration of the patronage-type politics that endures in Newfoundland. Yet Captain John earned the nickname Honest John[92] "by his sturdy independence and biting condemnation of all matters of a shady or unpatriotic nature."[93]

On 17 February 1828, 26-year-old John Leamon married 20-year-old Susannah Norman, the youngest daughter of James Norman and Mary Munden.[94] Practicing a sort of endogamous marriage, Mary Munden was a local woman, a member of the affluent and prestigious Munden clan.

---

*   Charles Cozens himself was what was then called "base born"–the child of an unmarried woman who was forced to scrape by on poor relief to the tune of 1 shilling. a week (John Leamon, *Brigus: Past Glory, Present Splendour* [St. John's: Harry Cuff Publications, 1998], 373). But, after arriving in Newfoundland as an adventurous teenager, Cozens became one of the wealthiest merchants Brigus had ever seen. He had extensive lands, all freehold, which was unusual at the time, and a fleet of schooners, brigs, brigantines, barques, and sloops–until he went bankrupt in 1833, an event that also curtailed his budding political career, though he landed on his feet and served a 30-year term as a stipendiary magistrate (Sean Cadigan, *Newfoundland and Labrador: A History* [Toronto: University of Toronto Press, 2009], 120).

Susannah's father, James Norman, came to Brigus from Jersey in the Channel Islands and built on a piece of land at the Battery in Brigus because the land so resembled the homestead he had left behind and seemed to have longed for.[95] Susannah Norman grew up in a home "like an English castle," a long Victorian house with dormer windows and a glass front porch of the kind that was so favoured by the Brigus elite.[96] The building was demolished in 1956, but before that, it was said to be haunted by Johnny Cole, an eternally restless servant who had lived in the back wing and spent the afterlife clicking his heels throughout the three-storey house.[97] John Norman's 1801 gravestone managed to combine sobriety and colour: "My wife and children left behind, with aching hearts and troubled minds, I hope in Heaven their souls to see, prepared for Christ to follow me."[98]

Susannah's immigrant father and grandfather were roaring successes in their new world. In contrast, her mother's people, the Dorsetshire Mundens, including Captain Azariah Munden of *The Four Brothers*, were established by the time the Normans arrived, and had already scaled the heights of Brigus and Conception Bay society. The Mundens were among the few who posed for oil portraits, some 3 feet high—large enough to dominate their well-appointed parlours and often gaily crowded dining rooms.[99] In a highly masculine environment, Susannah's grandmother was one of the few local women to make it into the historical record on her own account. One hundred years after her death, Ann Percey Munden was described by Charles Lench as "the Peace-Maker" of Brigus.[100] Susannah Norman was 17 when she walked, black-clad, in Grandmother Ann's funeral procession. The girl would have known Ann well and perhaps been under her influence, learning diplomatic and negotiating skills of the kind necessary for serenity in a small town where conflicts are many and barely below the surface.

As the sister of the celebrated sealing skipper and shipowner Nathan Norman, Susannah Norman brought some glamour into the Leamon family. Captain Nathan Norman ranks as one of the greatest sealing skippers of all time, giving him, like Follow-On Bartlett, mythic status in Newfoundland.[101] Even before his sealing record garnered accolades, Nathan Norman had performed an astonishing feat during the savage winter of 1829. It normally took a vessel like the *Bickley*, his brother's ship which he commanded, a week or so to sail from Halifax, Nova Scotia, to Brigus. One year the *Bickley* left Halifax harbour in January and, by the end of the month, Brigus residents figured that she was lost. They began mourning her loss and that of 21-year-old Captain Norman and his crew. As February, March, and April passed, the bereaved widows, children, fathers, and mothers tried to get on with their lives. Then someone sighted the *Bickley* at North Point tentatively turning into Brigus harbour. The ship was battered and beaten, a ragged sight indeed, and onlookers held their breath as she limped into port. But Captain Nathan Norman and all hands were alive after four months of warring with almost unimaginable waves, wind, and ice to get back home.

The young skipper went on to build his own fleet of nine ships, with catchy—and dated—names like the *Indian Chief*, the *Lively*, and, ominously, the *Trial*.[102] Embracing progress in the usual manner of the Brigus aristocrats, Norman was the first to use the cod trap in Labrador; this was a new piece of fishing gear invented by an American in 1865 to increase catches.[103] Captain Nathan Norman made even more of a mark in politics, serving as the Conservative member of the House of Assembly from 1878 to 1882.[104] There he successfully pressed for the construction of a railway across Newfoundland; this was aimed at opening up the island's interior, the domain of the Mi'kmaq, for industrial development. In this campaign, he was no doubt influenced by his good friend Lord Strathcona, the former Scottish fur trader who rose to the top of the Hudson's Bay Company, served as the Member of Parliament for Selkirk, Manitoba, and was a frequent guest in Norman's elegant house atop Battery Hill in Brigus.[105] A multi-millionaire, Strathcona helped to finance the Canadian Pacific Railway. But Norman and others were unwise to follow Strathcona's lead when it came to railways; the construction of the line nearly bankrupted Newfoundland.

The Mi'kmaq who hunted throughout central Newfoundland would have been invisible to Norman and the Reids who constructed the railway; there was simply no thought that the lands acquired belonged to others. This was also true of Nathan Norman's fishing station at Groswater Bay, Labrador, where he employed 250 fishermen[106] and, of course, Abram Bartlett's properties farther north at Turnavik. Norman also became the justice of the peace for Labrador. While he would have dealt mainly with

Newfoundland summer stationers, his position represented yet another foothold for Newfoundland in the still-contested territory of Labrador, a region legitimately claimed by Indigenous peoples as well as, more dubiously, by the adjacent Canadian province of Quebec. Meanwhile, Strathcona ceded Hudson Bay lands to Canada; these represented the ancient home of the Inuit, the Dene, the Cree, the Innu, and other Indigenous peoples, some of whom had made treaties with the Crown, while others had not. For Norman, Strathcona, and the other entrepreneurs of the 19th century, the wild Canadian and Labrador north were *terra nullius*, and thus theirs for the taking. This paralleled the Arctic exploration project in which Norman's great-great nephew, Bob Bartlett, would become so prominent. And as if in response to the daunting feats of the Amazon-like Bartletts, Nathan Norman's figure provided yet another looming childhood hero, this time on the maternal side of Bartlett's family.

The wedding of John Leamon and Susannah Norman took place a few days after Valentine's Day in the dead of a Newfoundland winter. Fittingly, their first child, Robert John Cozens Leamon, was born in Labrador in 1829.[107] John acquired the nickname Squire Leamon and this has been memorialized in a 41-verse recitation that was a popular lover's lament in Brigus and the area around Valentine's Day. In their early married life, John and Susannah lived at Cottage Pond, on what is now called Goulds Road, located about 5 lonely miles from bustling Brigus—at least that was the young bride's take on the matter. Besides the quiet and relative remoteness of the setting, Susannah was practical; she wanted her children to be formally educated and there was no school near her home. In contrast, there had been a school in Brigus since the very early 1800s. Susannah urged her husband to move his family to Brigus, demonstrating the high value placed on formal education that would run through the family for generations, especially on the Leamon side. Susannah was a modern woman, in tune with the trends and thinking of her time. As she planned her return to Brigus, the House of Assembly in St. John's was preparing an education act which would establish nine school boards on the island, one in each electoral district. The act was passed two years later and, with it, the MHAs allotted £300 each for Church of England schools and Roman Catholic schools.[108] Thus Newfoundland's denominational school system came about, in a way that was seemingly just to all, for the separation of religion and education was unthinkable. Susannah's children, one of whom would become Bob Bartlett's grandfather, attended the Church of England school, founded by the Society for the Propagation of the Gospel. By 1845, less than a decade after the act was passed, there were three schools with a total of 226 students in Brigus.[*][109]

Motivated by Susannah, John agreed to move into town. In the winter of 1834 a group of men placed the Leamon house on skids and wooden rollers and, using their horses and their own impressive strength, moved the house over frozen roads, ponds, and bogs.[110] They hauled it to a prepared foundation on Charles Cozens's property in Brigus. (The Cottage Pond location was owned by Cozens as well.) "House hauling" was a Newfoundland tradition; like Amish barn raisings, it was communal, with ample food as a reward. The Leamons provided their guests with a memorable feast of port wine, roast beef, tame and wild ducks, a side of mutton, a large turkey cock, stuffed roast pig, boiled tongue, potatoes with a baked crust, pudding, custard, pastry, and pies. Because of this move, Squire John Leamon, one of Bartlett's maternal great-grandfathers, lived on in the consciousness of modern-day Newfoundlanders well past his lifetime. The recitation "Squire Leamon's Housewarming" first appeared in the *Harbour Grace Standard* in 1841.[111] The recitation is about the house party that followed the challenging move and the ruckus that was inevitable after an excruciating hard day's work, a large hours-long gathering, and plenty of drink:

> Squire Leamon has his pretty cottage removed,
> By the advice of his friend and her whom he loved,
> Three miles is the distance, perhaps it is more,
> Such a great undertaking was not known before.
> The building was finished, and all was complete,
> The bedrooms and parlour and kitchen were neat;
> He said to his partner, his dear loving wife,
> Come see the sweet residence intended for life.

---

[*] In 2018, reflecting general population decline in rural Newfoundland, there is no school in Brigus, with the few remaining local children bused to schools in other communities.

So far so good, but then Robert Brown and Dr. Doby (or Dobie) almost came to blows over Julia Danson, for whom both men carried a torch. A planned duel in the cottage garden was halted only by the clergyman and the "crippled" Church of England schoolteacher J.N. Harris. Inspired by an event that did not take place—a fight that almost happened but didn't— the recitation testifies to the lack of violence inherent in Newfoundland social intercourse and the island culture's ingrained conflict aversion. There is, of course, nowhere to hide on an island, even one as large as Newfoundland. In addition to this, Newfoundland men had plenty of physical outlets for their frustrations and daring, most notably jumping from moving ice pan to moving ice pan wielding a gaff over frantic seals.

When John and Susannah's house stood at Cottage Pond, it was known simply as "Leamon's House." It contained such treasures as more than 100 engravings, silverware dated 1830, and a three-volume Stratford edition of Matthew Henry's *Family Bible*, published in 1707 (only three of which survive in 2018).[112] Upon the move to Brigus, the Leamons renamed it Whitehorn Cottage, although people often mispronounced it as White Thorns Cottage and, of course, it later became Hawthorn(e) Cottage. Penned by Scotsman John Sharpe, the High Constable at Harbour Grace, who must have been a little bored, the recitation continues:

> Reader, I'd fain to thee impart,
> What was of this the ending;
> Where love of maid filled full each heart,
> And made each will unbending.
> Did Harris crutch cut short the fight,
> And shook they hands across it;
> Or did the maid allay the heat,
> That rose from wine's hot faucet.
> The lines are lost that did record,
> The details of that story;
> Enough that Doby saved the maid,
> That both saved life and glory.[113]

Julia became Mrs. Doby, leaving poor Robert Brown to achieve success in other endeavours as one of the founders of the Commercial Bank of Newfoundland and as a Member of the House of Assembly for Port de Grave (perhaps the only Port de Grave MHA that century who was not related to Bartlett). Julia's story ended in tragedy; her doctor-husband hanged himself in or near the famous stone barn in Brigus, just a few months after the couple's first child was born, in 1837. Doby was mourned in the Scottish fashion with men walking two by two, wearing black crepe around their hat brims and white "weepers" on their cuffs. The widow died later that year, orphaning their baby.[114] Romantically inclined, young Bob Bartlett loved to hear this recitation, which he learned by heart as he did with many of the verses he loved.

In 2018, Brigus is pretty rather than grand. Though there are signs of a glorious past on its narrow streets, it has lost its status as one of the island's premiere settlements and, as in much of rural Newfoundland, commerce is minimal. The town relies on tourism, summer homes, and commuting to St. John's or nearby Bay Roberts. No sealing ships leave its port in spring and no highliners like Captain William live in the town. What became of the extraordinary wealth of Brigus accumulated through the 1880s? Some of Brigus's riches were lost in the bank crashes, one in 1894 and, of course, the global crash in 1929. Captain Harold Sinclair Bartlett, a cousin of Bartlett's, once gave a brutal assessment of Brigus's decline: "More was taken in legalized theft by some lawyers and merchants who were unscrupulous in their dealings with estates and a large portion squandered on boozing and gambling."[115] Harold Bartlett recalled ancient Rome when he explained, "An educated observer who had lived in Brigus during part of its palmy days told me that the main cause of its downfall was drunkenness, not so much the cost of liquor as the fact that it unfitted some of the sons of the old Captains of industry to take their fathers' places."[116] He went on to provide one sorry example of downfall, recounting how a Brigus merchant's son lost all his seal hunt returns in a drunken brawl at Portugal Cove near St. John's on the way back from the front. Not surprisingly, the money was never recovered.[117] Anecdotes like this do not provide much in the way of economic history but the harkening to a Sodom-and-Gomorrah-type scenario is in keeping with local Brigus narratives and their focus on heights no longer reached. Bob Bartlett would have his own dark days, with apparent alcoholism one manifestation of them, and this bleak time began in 1914 with the tragedy of the *Karluk*.

CHAPTER FOUR
THE MAKING OF A LEGEND: THE *KARLUK* AND SIBERIA IN 1914

As historian Margaret MacMillan cautions, people cannot be expected to think things that have not yet been articulated.[1] Some people do think such things, however, or there would be no prophets, no innovative thinkers, no inventors. Bartlett, however, was none of these. He was attracted to the new, especially new technology, but he largely operated within the conventional explorer framework. Like most, he did not question the norms of his time. Nor was he necessarily progressive; he was not as just to the Inuit as had been the explorer Charles Francis Hall, who died just before Bartlett was born. Yet Bartlett was not rigid in the way of Peary, and on at least one occasion, Bartlett forged a personal relationship with a young Inupiaq in 1914, which, if only briefly, allowed him to move beyond the standard explorer's view of Indigenous people. The Inupiat were one of the people indigenous to coastal Alaska from Norton Sound on the Bering Sea to what is now the Canadian border. The young Inupiaq in question, Claude Kataktovik, was a teenager and a skilled hunter when he encountered Bartlett; Bartlett was already a seasoned mariner.

Bartlett took command of his first vessel at 17. That year, 1892, he took one of Captain William's vessels to the seal hunt. He spent several springs after that also sealing—in the *Kite*, the *Nimrod*, the *Algerine*, and, in 1907, the *Leopard*,[2] but he lacked Captain William's craving for bloody decks and, unlike most of the Bartlett men, he did not distinguish himself

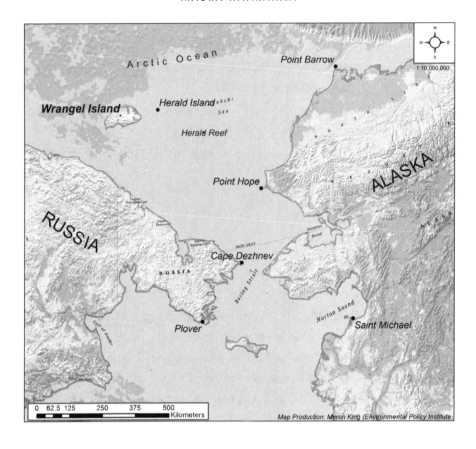

Map of Siberia developed by Myron King, Environmental Policy Institute, Grenfell Campus, Memorial University.

as a sealing skipper. Worse, he was skipper of the *Leopard* when she was dashed on the rocks off Cape Race, Newfoundland, lost before she even got to the seal patch. Bartlett never publicly examined his own failures as a captain—and, like his uncle John, whose style he emulated, he did have some. In what would become a pattern, he put the loss of the *Leopard* down to hard luck. To his credit, Bartlett refrained from criticizing other skippers. He would not hesitate, however, to direct disdain at Vilhjalmur Stefansson, whom he, and others, would come to view as treacherous.

Failures aside, Bartlett's time at the front contributed to his impressive store of sea and ice knowledge and to his embracing of the fearless improvisation that would benefit him the rest of his career. His favourite sealing trip was on the *Bonaventure*, carrying 270 men.[3] Despite her extra heavy beams and thick shell plating, the ship got stuck in the ice. Not to be deterred, the crew made trenches with axes and, when that failed, used dynamite on both the port and starboard sides, setting off six shots at a time.[4] After doing this all day, they finally freed the *Bonaventure*. This was the kind of *Boy's Own* activity Bartlett relished.

As agile seals are not easy to catch, nimbleness on the ice was vital for sealers. Bartlett claimed of himself and his fellow sealers, "to get light, we take off everything except our underwear and boots."[5] His experience as a sealer, which included clubbing baby whitecoats, seemed to harden him; in an article on sealing written for *National Geographic* in 1929, he glossed over the loss of 48 men from the SS *Greenland* in 1898 and the deaths of 77 men from the SS *Newfoundland* in 1914.[6] When the *Greenland* disaster occurred, Bartlett was in the *Hope* in the Gulf of St. Lawrence with Captain William. These events were national tragedies for Newfoundland, but Bartlett's brief descriptions of them are bloodlessly factual, and, as became his habit, blameless.

Yet Bartlett did have dramatic flair, demonstrated when he recounted the story of the *Leopard* to the *Newfoundland Quarterly* in 1910. In a scene that was practically a dress rehearsal for events on the *Karluk*, Bartlett was the last to leave the sinking ship and he did so in some style: "Entering the cabin he set up a small stove which had been overturned and proceeded to refresh himself with hot coffee and 'hard tack'" which

---

*   A hard biscuit eaten by sailors historically and incorporated into the Newfoundland diet.

he claims to have enjoyed heartily."[7] This took place while gelid salt water flooded the doomed ship. As captain, he was, of course, the last to leave the sinking ship and deftly made his way over unstable ice pans to shore. Wrote Allan Nurse, "The sight of the waters closing over his ship a few minutes after he had made his escape did not disturb him in the least."[8] Bartlett knew his reputation was secure; he had gotten the *Roosevelt* safely home from Greenland to great acclaim in 1909. He had also come to appreciate the public's respect for calm in a disaster and he would keep this in mind as he wrote of his escape from the *Karluk* later. He understood the centrality of reputation and bravado in polar exploration and, in his day, in sealing; he had picked up advanced skills in image-making from Peary, a master.

In 1929, Bartlett decided to return to Greenland, using the same route he and Peary had used in their attempt to reach the Pole. He said that his purpose was to perpetuate the memory of Peary, who died in 1920. But then he added, somewhat unusually, "and his Eskimo helpers."[9] As he explained, "I feel that men like Ootark, Seegloo and Enughitok should have their pictures and stories put in permanent form ... They suffered and toiled in the name of exploration just as much as we white men did."[10] Bartlett was a great deal more liberal than some other explorers, and certainly more than Peary. Unlike most explorers, he had been around Indigenous people since having been introduced to Inuit as a boy during the Labrador fishery. In a 1932 reunion with the Greenland Inuit who had worked for Peary, Bartlett showed his affection for Enughitok (or Inughito) when "the two men flung their arms about each other in a welcome that came from their hearts."[11] It is hard to imagine, for instance, Sir Edward Shackleton, for whom polar exploration was a rite of passage, given his pedigree as Ernest's son, hugging an Inuk. It is just as difficult to think of the charismatic Stefansson embracing one. In wanting to memorialize Inuit contributions, Bartlett demonstrated a degree of appreciation for the Greenland Inuit that was unexpected in someone of his station. He named and acknowledged outright some of the Indigenous people who had been key to Peary's and his own achievements. He would never completely step outside the exploration hierarchy, however.

Peary's relationships with Indigenous people were more complex than both Matthew Henson's and Bartlett's. Henson had entered not one but two marriages that were accepted by the Inuit;[12] he also fathered a son.

Peary, though undeniably racist and dictatorial, was also capable of fully participating in an Inuit funeral and associated practices such as taking care to eschew the use of his knife during the mourning period and sitting up for three days as per Inuit custom.[13] Though Peary encouraged sexual relations between expedition members and Inuit, there is no firm evidence that Bartlett responded accordingly; there remains only the odd rumour, while the liaisons of others like Henson and Peary are well documented. There is, however, some support for the contention that Bartlett developed, for a man of time and origins, the beginnings of genuine respect for Indigenous people. Bartlett would not have been able to develop such regard, inadequate though it may be by today's standards, were it not for Claude Kataktovik. Bartlett and Kataktovik shared a singular experience that moved them away from the traditional explorer-Inuit relationship to something slightly more complicated, genuine, and human.

Their story began in 1913 when the *Karluk* sailed out of Victoria, British Columbia, as part of the Canadian Arctic Expedition. At the time, the Expedition was the largest ever scientific mission to the Arctic,[14] with members from Australia, Estonia, Portugal, Norway, the Netherlands, Scotland, Canada, and the United States.[15] It was also the Canadian government's first such expedition to the western Arctic[16] and one of its aims was the advancement of Canadian sovereignty in the Arctic. Canadian prime minister Robert Borden spoke of "protecting these northern lands and having the British flag fly over them."[17] The British and their deputies in Canada aimed to claim land—and ice—before the United States could do so. The eastern Arctic had been claimed by the British when Bob's uncle, Captain Sam Bartlett, brought the *Neptune* and, subsequently, Canadian law, there in 1903–4. The Minister of Naval Service gave the Canadian Arctic Expedition leader "authority to take possession of and annex to His Majesty's Dominions any lands lying to the north of Canadian territory which are not within the jurisdiction of any civilized Power."[18] Thus the expedition represented an early chapter in the history of Canada's national ambitions in the north.

As plans for the Canadian Arctic Expedition were being laid, journalists referred to it as "one of the most sensational, as well as one of the most important, exploring expeditions of modern times. For [it] is going to penetrate as far as possible into an enormous area never before visited by civilized man; probably the last unexplored region on the surface of the earth."[19] The wooden-hulled *Karluk* was the ship selected for the voyage by Theodore Pedersen, a Danish-American whaling skipper,[20] who served as the ship's master as she sailed from San Francisco to Victoria.

The expedition included prominent and emerging scientists from several academic disciplines, including assistant topographer Bjarne Mamen, 22, who was born in Halden, Østfold, Norway, and was the son of an Oslo funeral director. Mamen was the youngest member of the expedition and the last to join it in Victoria.[21] Canadian-born ecologist George Malloch, 33, was a graduate of Queen's and Yale universities.[22] New Zealand-born anthropologist Stuart "Diamond" Jenness had graduated from Oxford in classics and had contracted malaria during a one-year stay in New Guinea.*[23] He would become a famous anthropologist, but at 27, Jenness was "soft-spoken, modest, always courteous, and almost diffident" with no Arctic experience.[24] Meteorologist William Laird McKinley, 24, was a graduate of the University of Glasgow and an expert in terrestrial magnetism. McKinley would become a lifelong friend of Bartlett's and wrote extensively of the sad events of 1914. Anthropologist Henri Beuchat was the 34-year-old son of Swiss parents, although he was French-born.[25] Beuchat graduated from the Sorbonne after writing a thesis entitled "The Religion and Social Ceremonies of the Kwakiutl Indians,"[26] relying exclusively on secondary sources since he had never been to North America (a research process that was not unusual at the time). Not long before he joined the Canadian Arctic Expedition, Beuchat won the Prix Loubat, worth $600 US (about $15,000 in 2018), for his splendid 800-page *Manual of American Archaeology*.[27] Edinburgh-born Alistair Forbes Mackay was a Royal Navy surgeon who had served with Sir Ernest Shackleton.[28] Stefansson's secretary and assistant, Burt Morton McConnell, was a New Jersey

---

*   Jenness would become fluent in Inuktitut and famous as an anthropologist but he was "no husky, outdoor adventurer"; in fact, he was small, never weighing more than 125 pounds (Stuart Edward Jenness, ed., *Arctic Odyssey: The Diary of Diamond Jenness, Ethnologist with the Canadian Arctic Expedition in Northern Alaska and Canada, 1913-1916* [Gatineau, QC: Canadian Museum of Civilization, 1991], xv). Before his 1969 death, he was influential in shaping Canadian Arctic anthropology through such texts as *The Life of the Copper Eskimo* (1922) and *People of the Twilight* (1928). As Renée Hulan explains in *Northern Experience and the Myths of Canadian Culture*, Jenness's unexamined notions of gender, his lack of scholarly interest in Inuit women, and his position as a subjective western man all inform enduring understandings–or misunderstandings–of Inuit and Inuit culture (Montreal & Kingston: McGill-Queen's University Press, 2002).

Vilhjalmur Stefansson, ca. 1915. *George Grantham Bain collection, United States Library of Congress.*

native and the son of a civil war veteran.[29] McConnell had suffered from tuberculosis, going west for a cure, and briefly studying medicine before doing various business courses and joining the Expedition.[30]

Some of these young men would not survive the trip, which meant that the expedition resulted in significant losses to western science as well as to the men's families and friends. Canadian Arctic Expedition scientists and crew were assigned to either the Northern or the Southern Party; those on the *Karluk* were part of the former. Besides scientists, there were 13 crew members on the *Karluk* as well as Kuralek, an "indefatigable hunter,"[31] his wife, Kiruk, a seamstress, their young daughters Helen, about 11, and Mugpi, 3, and, Claude Kataktovik, 19, who was hired for his hunting skills.[32] The Indigenous people were referred to as "local assistants," a term that did not reflect how vital their services were to the endeavour.

The expedition was organized by Stefansson, who brought along English cinematographer George Wilkins to make educational "moving pictures of the natives."[33] Stefansson believed there was a northern continent yet to be discovered and he was far from alone in this belief;[34] two years after the *Karluk* sank, Bartlett spoke of the possibility of "unexplored [northern] land" to the New York *Times*.[35] R.G. Harris, a longtime mathematician with the United States Coast and Geodetic Survey, called this land "Theoretical Land" and was convinced it "must exist."[36] This mysterious land mass might, it was believed, be home to vegetation as well as animals, mineral wealth, and "even new families of the human race with habits, customs and beliefs that will be of exceeding interest to everyone."[37] In the first half of the 20th century, the media and the public devoured these stories; they were as eager to hold on to the romanticism of the age of exploration as were the explorers themselves.

Each of the expedition's two groups had its own mandate. The Southern Party in the *Alaska* would search for this mysterious land mass; the Northern Party in the *Karluk* would roam the Canadian Arctic islands to conduct scientific work.* Built in 1884 the *Karluk* was 247 tons. As the North American media had faith in him, so Stefansson had confidence in the *Karluk*, although he admitted that she lacked the powerful engines of

---

*   Led by Stefansson, the Northern Party was responsible for the "discovery" of Borden and Mackenzie King islands (named after Canadian prime ministers), the low-lying Brock Island, and others.

the *Roosevelt*. This was also a concern of Bartlett's, as was the *Karluk*'s weaker hull.[38] Young Mamen, the assistant topographer, observed that the *Karluk* was a poor icebreaker; instead of breaking ice, she pushed it ahead of her and could not gain momentum, with her tendency to roll back and forth.[39] Yet Stefansson told the Ottawa *Evening Journal*, "I know the Karluk well and I have cruised her when she was breaking ice in the Arctic. By the time she comes out of the Esquimault [British Columbia] navy yard, she will be ready for almost anything. She is plenty strong enough to run at full speed—6½ knots in heavy ice; and she has a slating bow so she will climb up on the ice and weigh it down, crushing it under her. But I don't think she would stand a nip—that is, a tremendous pressure between ice masses in summer time."[40] In this last assertion, Stefansson was, unfortunately, correct. He was also right to note that the *Karluk* was carrying more than she should below decks as well as on deck; this would not have been allowed if the inspectors at Nome, Alaska, had been more concerned with adhering to regulations and to common sense. Said Stefansson, "[The *Karluk*] was so deep in the water with heavy cargo that her decks were nearly awash."[41] None of this portended well.

The *Karluk* was skippered by 39-year-old Bartlett. He had replaced Captain Sam when his uncle declined to accompany Peary to the Arctic in 1904 and he subsequently became the first captain to take a ship north of 88 degrees.[42] Theodore Pedersen was Stefansson's first choice of captain for the *Karluk* but the experienced Dane doubted Stefansson's methods and wisely bowed out. Despite his own misgivings, Bartlett was not yet as risk-averse as he would become—although risk-aversion at sea was never his practice. On land, it was another matter. Peary told Stefansson, "[Bartlett is] a marvel at handling sailors or stowing a ship, and (is) a man to take responsibility of every detail off your shoulders."[43] This turned out to be accurate as far as Stefansson was concerned; in his words, "[Bartlett] won the admiration and confidence of everybody. And he obeyed every order effectively and without quibbling."[44] But Stefansson's admiration of Bartlett was never unequivocal, as Bartlett was to learn a decade later. Stefansson was concerned from the beginning that, despite Peary's recommendation, the only Arctic region then known to Bartlett was Greenland and the eastern Arctic, not the western Arctic, where the expedition would head.

Bartlett could not hide his lack of western Arctic experience, nor did he try. He also knew he was Stefansson's second choice, but, desperate to return to northern exploration, he agreed to go. And he was, as ever, ambitious, writing to a friend in Boston, "This will have the north pole trip beaten to a frazzle."[45] He was not far wrong.

At least on board the ship, the voyage started well. In June 1913 McConnell and Makay created a single page typewritten newssheet called "The *Karluk* Chronicle," which featured autobiographies of expedition members, updates on the ship's position, and general news of the *Karluk*'s goings-on. Expedition members drew lots for berths, with everyone satisfied with their assignments.[46] To relieve the monotony on the voyage north, they took bets, with prizes going to whoever gave the best estimate of when the ship would enter Unimak Pass.[47] But soon some expedition members rubbed each other the wrong way, unfortunate for the men stuck together in small quarters for a very long time. To cope, George Malloch took to sleeping in the chart room, although he emerged every morning shivering with cold.[48] "Poor boy he is so vain," Mamen wrote uncharitably.[49] Mamen called Beuchat "a pup" to his face, which greatly offended the young Frenchman.[50] Mamen did little to hide his feelings, concluding in his diary that Beuchat was "the laziest man I have ever seen in my life."[51] The young Norwegian's complaints about Beuchat were unrelenting; Beuchat's alleged penchant for sleep annoyed Mamen and he accused the anthropologist of expecting other people to do everything for him.[52] Mamen's notes about the Inupiat indicate a huge gap in understanding and respect that outdid even Josephine Diebitsch-Peary's: "These Eskimos we have on board are some lazy swine, one has to urge them continually—very bad."[53]

Inupiat reaction to these attitudes is hard to gauge. Kuralek, Kiruk, and Kataktovik* kept no diaries and the European and Canadian expedition members rarely recorded statements uttered by Inupiat. It is quite possible that Inupiat today have inherited stories from their great-grandparents about the members of the Canadian Arctic Expedition but, if so, these are not easily accessible to outsiders. Mamen did become more

---

* The name is spelled variously in historical accounts.

reasonable about the Inupiat, whose expertise and work were crucial to the expedition,[54] but, like most explorers and scientists, he failed to refer to them by name even after they had been together for months. Later, McKinley described the camaraderie he experienced as a Canadian Arctic Expedition member: "friendship bred under such conditions as ours, so remote from civilization was not ordinary friendship. Men get down to the reality of things there, where the ordinary conventions find no place; and friendship has a greater significance."[55] In the context of polar exploration, however, none of this extended to the Indigenous people.

Of greater concern than shipboard tensions was an early snowstorm on 1 August 1913, while the *Karluk* was in Alaskan waters, south of Point Barrow, unable to "lay her course."[56] Bartlett and his crew sighted sea ice near the cape, which turned into a solid ice pack to the east. Immediately Bartlett saw the danger and suggested a return to the south, but Stefansson insisted on pushing on.[57] Bartlett had also seen a polar bear, which, like a Newfoundland fisherman, he superstitiously regarded it as "a beacon toward future disaster": "I am more than ever a believer in signs," he wrote,[58] a sentiment that Kataktovik and the Indigenous Siberians the two later encountered would have understood.

As she made for Nome, the *Karluk* lost a whale boat in strong winds.[59] Conditions were not in their favour and, by 13 August, the *Karluk* was well and truly "fast in ice."[60] This was, Bartlett wrote later, the "most tragic and ill-fated cruise of my whole career."[61] Pushed by the Japanese Current, the *Karluk* drifted until she was north of Alaska.[62] Initially, she was within sight of land, which lent a happy air to the on-board atmosphere, but the ice carried her along and she eventually ended up north of uninhabited Wrangel Island. Also known as Ostrov Vrangelya, Wrangel Island is, at 78 miles wide, the largest island in the eastern Russian Arctic and, although it has been called Kellett Land, Plover Land, and New Columbia, it has been indisputably part of Russia since 1924.[63] Gales blew almost continuously. Bartlett recalled, "The drift of the *Karluk* was a much worse experience than the voyage of the *Roosevelt* through Kennedy Channel from Kane Basin into the Arctic Ocean."[64] The *Roosevelt*'s crew knew where they were headed, "whereas in the *Karluk* [they] might drift in the ice even to destruction, unable to do anything to save the ship."[65]

The expedition had been led by Stefansson, but he famously left the ship at about 1:30 p.m. on 20 September 1913. As Bartlett noted at the time, "Stephenson [Stefansson] with two Esquimo[,] McConnell, Wilkins, Geness [Jenness], and twelve dogs, two sledges ... left for the land."[*] Stefansson left Bartlett in charge and triggered a controversy that has never truly been resolved. Stefansson said he hoped to make landfall on Thetis Island and then to hunt caribou and buy fish from the local people.[66] He took with him two Inupiaq hunters from Port Hope known as Jimmy and Jerry, Diamond Jenness, George Wilkins, and Burt McConnell, his 24-year-old secretary and assistant. Before leaving, Stefansson advised Bartlett: "Should the Karluk during our absence be driven from her present position it will be well for you so soon as she has come to a stop again, and as soon as it appears safe to send a party ashore, to erect one or more beacons, giving information of the ship's location ... It is likely that we shall be back to the ship in ten days, if no accident happens."[67] McKinley noted that Stefansson gave different reasons for his departure; first, to hunt caribou, as Bartlett noted, and second, to begin studying the Inuit. This did not impress McKinley, who said, "I have never ceased to wonder why he did not include [anthropologist] Beuchat for the same reason."[68]

The leader's departure left a profound impact on McKinley, who claimed those left behind now felt "like lambs to the slaughter."[69] And he detected a change in Bartlett, describing him as "a very lonely man [with] responsibility, not of his choosing, for the lives of us scientists as well as his crew, and the Eskimos and their children, weighing heavily on him."[70] Bartlett spent a lot of time in his cabin, alone, as the ship drifted; this had been his habit until then but now it had another dimension as he tried to figure out how best to cope with looming danger and the seemingly impossible task of getting everyone rescued.

By 11 November 1913 it was dark day and night and the *Karluk* was still drifting helplessly.[71] In addition to hunting seal and Arctic foxes, the Inuit spent 11 days cutting snow blocks and banking up the sides of the ship.[72]

---

[*] The supplies included two Burberry tents, a stove and piping, two axes, a dozen candles, four gallons of alcohol, one box of dog biscuits, six tins of tea, 10 pounds of sugar, three sleeping bags (with sheepskins for sleeping robes), four slabs of bacon, 10 pounds of lard, 120 pounds of fish, 20 pounds of rice, one box of tin beef, 5 pounds of salt, one case of Underwood man pemmican, 15 pounds of chocolates, one box of biscuits, matches, a rifle, a shotgun, ammunition, six seal floats, and one camp cooking set (Diary of R.A. Bartlett, MIKAN 1641255, Canadian Arctic Expedition-Stefansson Arctic Expedition, Library and Archives Canada, Ottawa, 20 September 1913, 10).

Bartlettt was optimistic, writing on 16 December, "We have seal meat on the table both in the dining room and forecastle once a day. We will, therefore, have plenty of fresh meat until the sun returns."[73] Bartlett had learned much from Peary, who knew that everyone should be kept busy through the winter, instead of having them wait endlessly for daylight to appear. Bartlett tried to maintain shipboard discipline by keeping daily routines intact, including set times for exercise and recreation, and by marking special occasions, but adverse weather brought many days of forced idleness.[74] They planned a sports program for Christmas Day, consisting of 12 events, beginning with the 100-yard dash and ending with wrestling. In his diary from the time, Bartlett noted only the calm and clearing weather that day[75] but he drew up a notice that provided the schedule and stated that "dogs and bookmakers not allowed on the field."[76] Wearing a paper rosette, the ship's doctor acted as umpire. Bartlett described the atmosphere as "merry,"[77] explaining that "the spirits of the whole party were excellent; now that they were in the neighbourhood of the place where Santa Claus came from they seemed determined to observe the day in a manner worthy of the jolly old saint."[78] Leading up to Christmas, there had been a chess tournament, with Mamen winning the first prize of 50 cigars and first officer Alexander "Sandy" Anderson winning the second prize of half that amount.[79] On New Year's they laid out a regulation-size football field and made a ball of seal gut encased in sealskin for a Scotland versus All-Nations game. Bartlett tried to use a whistle but his lips froze to the metal and he settled for hand signals. The result was Scotland three, All-Nations eight.[80] There was lots of singing. "Loch Lomond," "The Wearing of the Green," and "Jingle Bells" were favourites, while Helen, the elder Inupiaq child, and her mother, Kiruk, liked to sing "Twinkle, Twinkle Little Star."

"It may be hard to believe," Bartlett recalled with no trace of irony, "but we were really enjoying ourselves these days. We were comfortable in our quarters with plenty to eat and no lack of fuel. There was work to be done and all hands kept busily at it, with no time to mope or indulge in vain regrets; sleep came easily ..."[81] Bartlett's faith in the work ethic of his Methodist ancestors never wavered; as far as he was concerned, work did not just facilitate the accumulation of wealth, it also prevented idleness, depression, and devilry, all of which needed to be kept at bay. He was partly right in this, but only partly, and it did not apply to everyone.

Bartlett retained his natural optimism as well, from which the scientists and crew benefitted, but storms were brewing among the men on board. Many of them were scientists with inflated egos, privileged backgrounds, and little experience of shipboard life. Mamen continued to pour vitriol into his diary as he and others aired petty grievances against each other.[82] Bartlett seemed oblivious to these worrying developments. His almost jolly recollection of this period on the *Karluk* contrasted with Mamen's and even with that of Ernest "Charlie" Chafe, the ship's 19-year-old mess room boy from Newfoundland. Chafe's tone was sober when he wrote of his *Karluk* experience two years later: "We had been drifting so long without any unusual incident that our ship became a veritable home to us. We had comfort and plenty on board, and—in a measure—forgot the helplessness of our situation."[83] Chafe credited Bartlett with keeping calm and for the captain's unrelenting efforts to keep up morale. Bartlett told Chafe never to say anything discouraging to his fellow crew members, as was his own unwavering practice. "Captain Bartlett was very thoughtful in that respect," he wrote, "he would never say or do anything that would discourage them, although he knew we were in great danger. He would try hard to laugh, saying, 'Why, there is nothing to it,' and that he had met with the same thing dozens of times on his trip with Peary to the Pole."[84] But Bartlett's constant references to Peary, who remained controversial, and the Pole may have rankled some among the scientists and crew. In addition, he might have sounded dismissive of genuine concerns, which would have been clear to educated people committed to facts and the evidence in front of them. Crew members might have been assured by pats on the back but this approach was unlikely to have appealed to the scientists.

Their luck began to change for the worse on New Year's Day when the ice tightened around the ship. According to Bartlett's log notes, 10 January 1914 was a dramatic day, beginning with

> ... a tremor all through the ship. Up until 7:30 P.M. the ship received no pressure, only slight shocks ... During the afternoon, [the wind] hauled to the N.W. increasing and

in force, followed with blinding snowdrift. Began making preparations to leave ship should occasion arise ... Had the snow house on the floe fixed up all ready for persons to go in.

The night intensely dark. The sheet of ice passing on starboard side lifted ship, heeling her to port when the point of this sheet on port side penetrated the planking and timbers in engine room ripping off all the pump fixtures and putting the pumping out of commission ...[85]

After having the crew unload 10,000 pounds of pemmican, furs, clothing, rifles, and cartridges, Bartlett gave the order to abandon ship.[86] This process was completed with what McKinley called "remarkable calmness and efficiency."[87] Harm came only to Dr. Mackay, who fell into the icy water up to his neck[88] and was "in a fighting mood" the whole evening.[89] Mackay and Mamen fought, with the doctor eventually asking the Norwegian's forgiveness, which he promptly received—an act that redeemed Mamen as well.[90] Afterwards, the two sat down together and "talked about [their] chances to get back to civilization without loss of human life."[91] Stuck on an Arctic ice floe watching a ship that was about to sink, they were weighed down by stress. The loss of life that would ensue makes this scene all the more poignant.

Bartlett later wrote, "At 10:45 o'clock that night eleven feet of water had got into the engine room. The ice was holding the ship up for a time and little water came in. By midnight all the supplies had been placed on solid ice. The coffee kettle was boiling constantly in the galley. At this time I sent the men to the shelter house."*[92] By 9:30 a.m., the *Karluk* was listing 30 degrees to port.[93] As the hours ticked by, Bartlett sat in his cabin, drinking tea and coffee, playing his full stock of records on the Victrola and then throwing them into the fire. According to McKinley, "The list to port caused the port side of the deck to be under water, but the skipper was high and dry in the galley and could walk along the deck on the starboard side to check for any change in the ice and keep an eye on the water-level in the engine room."[94] Bartlett stayed on board alone all day while, in their ice houses nearby, his scientists and crew ate roast

---

* This was one of several structures the crew had built, using mainly ice but also some wood, on the icefield to provide shelter for when the ship sank, as they knew it would.

beef, mutton, salt pork, cheese and bread, finishing up with cigars.[95] They no longer had tobacco, though, as Bartlett had not allowed them to save "luxuries, souvenirs, or useless things" that would add to the weight they would have to carry on sledges.[96]

By mid-afternoon, it was clear the inevitable was about to happen. Bartlett demonstrated his dramatic flair by playing Chopin's "Funeral March" on the Victrola.[97] Then, as water poured down all the hatches, he stood at the rail until it sank to the level of the ice. At that moment he stepped off the doomed ship. The *Karluk* sank gracefully and slowly with the Canadian Blue Ensign fluttering in the Arctic wind until it hit the water. Bartlett recalled: "I stood on the ice, surrounded by the officers and crew of the expedition, who lifted their hats, saying one and all 'Adios Karluk!' We watched the final plunge, with the blue ensign at her main topmast cutting the water as she disappeared beneath."[98] Bartlett's notes from the time are less dramatic: "4 P.M. With the blue ensign at the main topmast head the Karluk disappeared ..."[99] The *Karluk* was soon in 38 fathoms of water[100] and the people she had carried were now stranded on the Arctic ice. A few weeks earlier, Mamen had written, "it is best to be prepared for the worst."[101] He had been right.

Bartlett quickly cast off all theatricality. His first strategic move was to develop a plan that would get the whole group to Siberia. Meanwhile, dissatisfaction was spreading among the independent-minded scientists like a cancer. Alistair Mackay was particularly unhappy and longed to escape from the Arctic, which had become a disappointment and a prison. Beuchat, Scottish biologist and oceanographer James Murray,[*] and 26-year-old seaman Stanley Morris were impatient to get away, too. Though they lacked Arctic experience, Mamen frequently wrote in his diary that these men disagreed with Bartlett's plans.[102] It "grieved" McKinley that his fellow Scots were "so much at variance" with the captain,[103] to whom he was consistently loyal. As the dark days passed, Mackay, Beuchat, Murray, and Morris grew more determined to trek to safety in spite of the foolhardiness of such a venture.

Finally, after a series of surreptitious meetings with Mackay and the others, Murray asked Bartlett for a sledge and supplies for 50 days. Murray

---

[*]   Like Mackay, Murray had worked with Sir Ernest Shackleton in the Antarctic.

grew belligerent when Bartlett told them they should stay and travel with the whole party. Mackay would not budge from his position either; he was determined to walk to safety on land. Bartlett knew when he was defeated and noted, "I told them if they signed an agreement to absolve me from all blame later on and to cut themselves loose from our party, I would give them the supplies they wanted, and, further, told them if at any time they wanted to come back to camp they were perfectly welcome here. Also if they required assistance later on and it was possible I would render the assistance they would deem necessary."[104] Once in receipt of the letter and the signatures of all four men, Bartlett gave the group the supplies they requested. They refused to take any dogs, insisting on hauling the sledge themselves. Just two years before, Robert Falcon Scott's decision to man-haul sledges in the Antarctic had been a primary factor in his death. Bartlett would have seen Scott's action as a mistake, but, clearly, the departing men did not. Circumpolar inhabitants from Russia to Canada used dogs for ice travel but these lettered men, fuelled by hubris, eschewed them as Scott had done. They all signed the letter to Bartlett, which concluded, "we declare that we undertake the journey on our own initiative and absolve you from any responsibility whatever in the matter."[105] In a letter penned later that year, Grace Malloch, the wife of George Malloch, quoted Bartlett as saying that the four "were dead when they left the camp."[106]

Four crew members, including the *Karluk*'s first and second officers, Sandy Anderson and Charles Barker, were sent out to do advance work for the journey to safety and did not return, causing great distress to all, including, if not especially, Bartlett. Anderson was a capable Scot, already a master mariner at 22; Bartlett was so impressed with him that he had quickly made him first mate.[107] Bartlett sent several search parties out for the lost men and found it exceedingly difficult to turn his attention away from their probable fate to a rescue of the remaining survivors. But in keeping with his stoic nature and in the interest of salvaging his own reputation, he did not dwell much on this tragedy in his 1916 account of the *Karluk* or in his later memoirs. Yet the disappearance of these men had to have shocked him. He knew their chances of survival on the ice were minimal and he would have been worried that others would meet a similar fate. He faced a genuine predicament. He knew, however, that he had to continue sending men out to hunt and blaze trails. He understood that he had to get as many people home as he possibly could and that the outside world would want to hear every detail of what had happened. He was also worried about his career as a mariner and Arctic explorer.

After abandoning the *Karluk*, the crew, remaining scientists, and the Inupiaq family were reasonably comfortable on the ice, where they had stored no less than 10,000 pounds of provisions and built two shelters during the weeks that preceded the ship's sinking. Although their tobacco sank with the ship, Bartlett knew the importance of creature comforts at what came to be called Camp Shipwreck and later wrote in the New York *Times*, "There was a stove in each [ice] house, and plenty of coal to keep things warm. We had a comfortably constructed galley, with a large stove, regular meals, and good food."[108] Nevertheless, Bartlett worried about his men: "Further the men have been living on the ship and were not inured to the cold and the privations that they would have to undergo. They were also not conversant with the ways of taking care of themselves in travelling over the Arctic ice during the small amount of light during the low temperature that for at least a month we will have to contend with ... Travelling on sea-ice is altogether different from land travelling."[109] Further, they were handicapped by not having enough dogs. These facts had to be set aside, given their circumstances. Bartlett sent men from Camp Shipwreck to Wrangel Island to break trail, determine ice conditions, and look for driftwood. For their journey, he taught them something he had learned from Peary: to attach red and blue sheets of tin to ice pinnacles—these signals could be seen up to 2 miles. Others, especially the Inupiat, he sent out on regular hunting trips. He did advance work himself, sometimes with Bjarne Mamen, with whom he became close.

When, some weeks later, light returned for a grand total of five hours a day, they began breaking a trail and carting their supplies to Wrangel Island with the intention of moving everyone there. It was not easy: "Building a road across (ice rafters) was like making the Overland Trail through the Rockies," he later wrote. The scene reminded him of a picture called *Chaos before Creation* in the first volume of Ridpath's *History of the World*, in which polar bears destroyed cached coal oil and biscuits of tins, bluntly signalling their vulnerability and dampening morale. Along the way they had to contend with stragglers getting temporarily lost, polar bears destroying supplies, and feet getting soaked in icy water. In addition, one of the Inuit[*] had a bad back that ice travel aggravated. Fortunately, the weather was "continuously fine," although temperatures dipped to -40°F.[110] On 13 February, after walking 100 miles, the remaining 17 people, including the two little girls, one of whom walked and one of whom was carried on her mother's back, could see Wrangel Island. Recalled Bartlett, "It is perhaps easier to imagine than to describe our feelings of relief at being once again on terra firma, after months of drifting and traveling on the ice."[111] On 18 March, with Kataktovik and a Peary sledge, Bartlett left again on a mission to Siberia that must have been daunting even for him. Before departing, he told the men to write short notes to their friends, which they did. He knew "[t]he great essence was time."[112]

He was still haunted by the departure of the rebel group and the loss of mate Sandy Anderson's party. Upon leaving Wrangel Island, Bartlett left explicit instructions for searches for Mackay's party and Anderson's group but he knew that they would never be found. Anderson's party was believed to have been lost after the first mate decided to try for Herald Island; ice prevented him from making an attempt to reach Wrangel Island. As Bartlett had written in February, "Herald Island is no place for a party to land upon. It is inaccessible and, further no driftwood on its shore, owing to the precipitous cliffs all around the island. It is only three and a half miles long, half a mile wide, twelve hundred feet high."[113] He must have seen images of frozen corpses as he slept at night. He also realized the urgency of getting help for the people left on the island. They had full rations for 80 to 86 days and Kuralek was a talented hunter; there was some comfort in that. Further, Wrangel Island was bigger and better resourced than Herald Island. Bartlett ordered them to split into three parties and live apart to ensure sufficient hunting territory and, therefore, sustenance; this tactic was gleaned from the Inuit environmental knowledge about the dispersion of animal resources that Bartlett had been accumulating for years. He left chief engineer John Munro, "well fitted for the post," in general charge and ordered Munro to go to Herald Island,[†] a small and rocky piece of land, to search for Anderson's party.[114]

---

[*]   This was probably Kurulek as Kataktovik remained healthy up to this period and Bartlett usually referred to Kiruk as the Inuit woman.

[†]   Like Wrangel Island, Herald Island is now part of Russia.

Stefansson had long reached safety—perhaps his greatest crime. On 30 October 1914, Stefansson sent a dispatch via Point Barrow, then some 420 miles on sledge to Candle, also in Alaska, where it was relayed to Boundary, Alaska, Skegway, Seattle, and, finally, New York.[115] Stefansson's news was widely reported, appearing in newspapers from the Indianapolis *Sunday Star* to the New York *Times*.[116] In his much-anticipated communication, Stefansson's words made little sense in view of the drift of and danger to the ship; "let me say that none of the plans of the expedition have been abandoned. They have merely been delayed."[117] When Stefansson disappeared, Bartlett had turned his attention to those who were still with him as if he knew that the erstwhile expedition leader was gone for good. Some claimed there was "no great effort" to find him: "there is a growing feeling that the ship's party were none too anxious to get Stefansson back on board again."[118]

Long after Stefansson's departure, as the first glimmers of spring light appeared, Bartlett's mind turned almost exclusively to Wrangel Island, named for Ferdinand von Wrangel, who led a Russian expedition there in the 1820s.[119] The island is bereft of vegetation and marked by mountain ridges stretching over its 80-kilometre length; coastal lowlands lie at the south of the island, tundra to the north.[120] Some of the peaks reach 2,500 feet. The island was frequented by polar bears in the winter and birds in the spring and summer.[121] Although no human beings lived there, plenty of driftwood was found, fortunately for the *Karluk* Party.[122] Bartlett originally intended to walk the entire group to Siberia but realized this was impossible given the inexperience of most of the crew and scientists still with him. In addition, some were in poor condition, having been injured; they could not have travelled very far.

When Bartlett chose Claude Kataktovik to accompany him, Bjarne Mamen was extremely disappointed. Mamen wrote disparagingly of Bartlett in his diary for the first time, painting the captain as selfish and self-centred and referring churlishly to Kataktovik as the captain's "nursemaid."[123] This was in striking contrast to his earlier assessments of Bartlett, to whom he seemed to have been quite attached. Mamen likely resented Kataktovik because Kataktovik was Inupiaq, strong, healthy, and capable, all attributes which were now being so significantly recognized by

Bartlett. Mamen's kneecap had been badly dislocated on one of his searches for the lost Anderson party and showed little sign of improvement a month later.[124] On 16 March, two days before he left for Siberia, Bartlett noted that Mamen's leg was causing him "a good deal of suffering."[125] Mamen was loathe to admit it, but his presence on the trek, even if it were possible, would have endangered himself and Bartlett. Those still on the island knew that any chance they had of leaving Wrangel Island alive depended solely on Bartlett and Kataktovik.[126]

The journey to Siberia was arduous, requiring unfailing physical strength and alertness. Most days the light was bad. Neither Bartlett nor Kataktovik knew the way and did not know when they would come across open water, which posed a challenge for travel but also offered possibilities for seal and bear hunting. As they struggled along, the ice moved incessantly and there were blinding snowdrifts. As Bartlett noted a week into the journey, "A good deal of criss-cross traveling was done today."[127] The next day they managed to cover only 4 miles.[128] Much of the snow was deep and soft, making it difficult for the dogs and sledges as well as the two men on their snowshoes. Sledges—of the sort favoured by Peary and by Bartlett—broke down often, due to the rough ice and the pinnacles that dotted the white landscape. Repairs ate up precious time. The dogs kept chewing the harnesses and running away, and Bartlett and Kataktovik lost more time and energy trying to catch them. The men had no time to cook, so they ate raw polar bear caught by Kataktovik. The dangers of the trip necessitated constant decision-making; the dogs' diets had to be carefully monitored, for instance, lest they overeat and become lethargic; the men were required to make hourly judgments about ice and water. At times the dogs were frightened of the open water, especially after the sledge broke through the ice, soaking everything, including the animals.

Bartlett and Kataktovik built igloos almost every night. One night the wind tore the canvas top off their igloo, exposing them to the frigid air. On 26 March, "the weather [was] beastly."[129] Bartlett had a nagging pain in his left eye, which sometimes became acute. "It was a slow job," Bartlett later wrote laconically, as he often did when recalling times of stress.[130] Kataktovik got depressed at times, telling Bartlett, "We see no land. We no get to land; my mother, my father tell me long time ago Eskimo get out on ice and drive away from Point Barrow never come back."[131] The young man was a committed Christian, his people having been converted through the 1890s, and this may have steadied him somewhat through the desperate journey. "I like to believe to God and Jesus very much," he had written from the *Karluk* in 1913.[132]

There were memorable moments. One occurred, probably on 29 March,[133] when the two men tried to retrieve a seal they had just killed: "Braced against a hummock, Kataktovik held my feet to keep me from sliding down into the water and I caught hold of the seal by the flipper and held it. The seal was not quite dead and made some resistance. On account of my position I could get no purchase on the ice to pull up with my arms and the seal weighed about 100 pounds. I managed to lift it out of the water far enough to get its hind flipper in my teeth, and then Kataktovik hauled us back. When I got up a little way he passed me a rope and I grabbed a hole in the flipper and passed the rope through. I was then able to let go with my teeth, sprang up with the rope in my hand and dragged the seal up to the level ice."[134]

Bartlett freely admitted that he "knew as much about Siberia as he knew about Mars" but had faith that "the natives" there would help.[135] He also had Kataktovik, who was "a good walker" and could go without rest day after day, worn down and suffering from pain in his hands and feet.[136] Besides eye pain, Bartlett suffered snow blindness, as he frequently did in the Arctic, necessitating the almost constant use of snow goggles. He described the affliction as "like having sand thrown in the eyeballs."[137] As he later explained their journey, "Kataktovik was with me and built our igloos and killed seal and bear ... [an] Eskimo and a white man could live indefinitely on the ice."[138] On 30 March, Bartlett wrote, "Just before Sunset saw land."[139] Later he described his relief when Kataktovik suddenly called, "Me see him, me see him, *noona** [land]!"[140] The following day they could see the land more clearly, in spite of their persistent eye trouble. But for the next several days they had to deal with moving ice, very bad light, and dogs that were feeling poorly. Finally, after three weeks doing battle with the Arctic, they reached land on 5 April. Thick snow limited their vision but they found the Chukchi dwellings and, at long last, spent a comfortable

---

* Spelled Nuna today, as in Nunavut, Nunatsiavut, Nunavik, and NunatuKavut, all Inuit regions in Canada.

night.[141] Eventually, the two reached Siberia's East Cape 37 days after they had left their companions. They had travelled 700 miles, most of it on foot.

Kataktovik was indispensable to Bartlett. Yet, perhaps not surprisingly, most accounts of the *Karluk* and indeed much of polar literature give little credit to the role of "local [Indigenous] assistants."* Bartlett's account of the Canadian Arctic Expedition and the *Karluk* pays some attention to Kataktovik, with the story of the young man's participation in the rescue attempt woven in. But the spotlight has never been on Kataktovik and he was almost unknown outside the western Arctic, rarely appearing in the newspaper accounts and lectures that followed the *Karluk*'s sinking.

Claude Kataktovik was a native of Point Hope, Alaska, a community in North Slope Borough, Alaska. Like other Inuit groups, who are all descended from the Thule,[142] the Inupiat constructed driftwood and sod houses, which were partly subterranean;[143] Kataktovik would have spent much of his life in such structures. These houses, home to one or two families totalling eight to 12 people, were built around another larger building, a *qargi*, which served as the council house.[144] The Inupiat built their economy and society around the bowhead whale—the yearlings they often hunted weighed about 10,000 kilograms.[145] Whalers were organized into crews that hunted from *umiaks*, relatively large boats, lead by *umialiks*, who owned the boats and the equipment, directed the rituals that governed hunting, and wielded substantial social and economic power in the community through the distribution of resources, including whale meat and trade goods.[146] There was, then, a well-developed social hierarchy in Inupiat society, which had been relatively stable for almost a millennium.[147] This rigid structure and the knowledge of one's place in it would serve Kataktovik well during the *Karluk* crisis when heeding Bartlett's orders was vital. The racialized power imbalance inherent in polar exploration added another dimension to Kataktovik's experience and comfort with inflexible social structures, but it would not have shocked or even discomfited him.

Kataktovik was born about 1895 in a time of great transition for the Inupiat. The mainstay bowhead whale economy was in precipitous decline in that era because of rapacious American whaling, which was showing

---

* An exception is Jennifer Niven's 2003 book *Ada Blackjack: A True Story of Survival in the Arctic* (New York: Hyperion, 2003).

its effects as early as the 1850s.[148] The Inupiat faced other crises as well. At the same time the whaling economy was disappearing, the caribou population was "all but exterminated by the Inupiat themselves."[149] Thus, the Canadian Arctic Expedition's local assistants, including Kataktovik, would have needed the work the expedition offered. McKinley observed that, although he was an excellent hunter, Kataktovik lacked the skills to build a solid igloo[150]—yet Bartlett did not complain about those the young man erected on the way to Siberia.

Beginning in the early 19th century,[151] European diseases arrived, soaring to epidemic proportions among the Inupiat.[152] Along with the decline of the caribou and whale populations in the late 1800s, this led to the decimation of the people themselves.[153] By the 1880s, the writing was on the wall for the cultural continuity and stability the Inupiat had long enjoyed. Christianity was on the rise, resulting in the conversion of most Inupiat, although, like Indigenous people elsewhere, they were able to adapt their new belief system to their own ideas.[154] Kataktovik would have been raised with Inupiat values and stories as well as those related to what has been called "Eskimoized Christianity."[155] The first Christian missions began appearing among the Inupiat in the 1880s, for example, the Mission Covenant of Sweden established a station at Unalakleet in Norton Sound in 1887.[156] Given the emergencies facing the Inupiat, Christianity with its notions of heaven and salvation had appeal. Elsewhere, Inuit conversions were responses to crises of an unfamiliar nature; this was the case with the northern Labrador Inuit, known to Bartlett from his Turnavik days, who converted to Moravianism in the late 1700s following epidemics. Kataktovik's childhood would have been stressful—unlike Bartlett's, which featured leisurely afternoons with the cultured Grandmother Leamon as well as the unthreatened affluence of Captain William, his highliner father.

From Bartlett, whose accounts contain many casual and sometimes touching references to Kataktovik, we know that Kataktovik was a widower at 19; he had left his daughter in the care of his mother so that he could work for the Canadian Arctic Expedition. Kataktovik had experienced personal tragedy and trauma, and he certainly had his endurance tested with Bartlett as the two of them attempted to save the *Karluk* crew. Kataktovik could read and write, and Bartlett, who often loaned him books and magazines, taught him to decipher nautical charts as well. Bartlett also gave him blank books to write in, and mused, "What would Peary say?" in reference to Peary's belief that Inuit should not become "dependent on the white man's methods of life."[157] Bartlett did not hold to Peary's way of thinking in this regard and realized that social change was inevitable for the Inuit, as well he might, given his role—and that of his uncles, not to mention Peary's—in bringing it about. He did not view such changes as necessarily negative, although perhaps he could have: as Canada slowly established itself in Inuit lands in Bartlett's lifetime, Inuit populations suffered a great deal of trauma; from the 1950s, after Bartlett's death, these traumas escalated with forced community relocations and residential schooling.[158] Inuit populations were also affected by the erosion of their economies, with the cumulative effects of a widespread decline in Inuit health today with, for instance, suicide occurring at alarmingly high rates,[159] including among the Inupiat.[160]

Bartlett's Inupiaq language skills were as rudimentary as Kataktovik's English and it seems they spoke a basic mixture of both tongues to each other. Many instances demonstrated Kataktovik's resourcefulness and budding leadership skills. It is unfortunate that we only have his voice in his second language; this tends to mask a speaker's intelligence and obscure his or her personality. After the *Karluk* first floundered and Bartlett began executing rescue plans, he and Kataktovik spent weeks laying trails and making roads, sometimes just the two of them together, these experiences feeding the captain's confidence in the younger man. After this work, Bartlett decided how rescue would be achieved: "I would take Kataktovik with me. He was sufficiently experienced in ice travel and inured to the hardships of life in the Arctic to know how to take care of himself in the constantly recurring emergencies that menace the traveler on the ever-shifting surface of the sea ice."[161] In the short and sometimes terse entries in his *Karluk* journal, Bartlett often referred to Kataktovik as "the Esquimo." His tone changed by the time he had digested his experience and written *The Last Voyage of the Karluk*. Chapter 19 is titled "Kataktovik and I Start for Siberia," an intimation of the respect Bartlett had for Kataktovik and an indicator of the relationship between them, their bonds showing hints of relative egalitarianism, at least for the time and place. This relationship could never be one of equals, of course; Bartlett was a seasoned 39-year-old, twice Kataktovik's age and old enough to be his father, he was the captain, he was a famous explorer who had navigated for Peary, and he was white. Reverting to the conventions of polar exploration, he frequently told Kataktovik what to do, including telling him, with no trace of courtesy, to fetch his mug from the sledge to bring into a Chukchi dwelling after they had finally reached Siberia.

Kataktovik feared the Indigenous peoples of Siberia; as Bartlett recalled, he "was sure they were going to kill him. He told me it was a tradition of his own people that the Siberian Eskimos were a bloodthirsty outfit."[162] When they had first sighted land, Kataktovik was afraid to advance, such was his fear of the Chukchi. Bartlett worked hard to persuade him to continue on to meet them. Bartlett knew he needed the young man's cooperation and presence; not lending Kataktovik's misgivings any credence, he tried to ignore them. He also tried to capitalize on Kataktovik's smoking habit, telling him he would be able to secure tobacco from "the natives." Still, they stood on the Arctic ice, while Kataktovik worried and weighed his options. His hesitation was based on conventional Inupiaq wisdom, engrained in him, that held that Siberians were dangerous and violent; this resulted from the history of warfare in the Bering Strait region, with many cases, motivated by economics, recorded in the 18th and early 19th centuries;[163] the two peoples "cherish[ed] a mutual contempt," as one western scholar wrote in 1881.[164] Kataktovik was oppressed by such thoughts, but he was also cold, hungry, and sore and in his mind were visions of the men, women, and children left behind on frosty Wrangel Island as well as his own baby daughter. He bravely took a step forward and did not stop until they finally saw signs of human life.

Bartlett began the encounter Kataktovik so dreaded by confidently approaching the Chukchi. Communication was difficult for, as Bartlett put it, it appeared at first that "they were as ignorant of my language as I was of theirs."[165] Thankfully, Kataktovik's fears were completely unfounded; the two visitors were received with kindness and remarkable generosity. As Bartlett described their initial meeting, "I put out my hand and walked towards them, saying in English, 'How do you do?' They immediately rushed towards us and grasped us each warmly by the hand, jabbering away in great excitement."[166] One "native" used the mariner's term "old man," confounding Bartlett at first: "His question puzzled me at first; presently it dawned on me that he was speaking in nautical parlance and wanted to know if I was a captain. 'Yes,' I replied. 'You come below in my cabin, old man,' he said, meaning that I was to go into his aranga."[167] It turned out that the Indigenous man knew other rudimentary terms in English; in fact, he understood much of what Bartlett told him. In addition, he knew some of Kataktovik's mother tongue, which would have been reassuring for Kataktovik. Bartlett and Kataktovik spent their first day on land drying out their clothes and eating deer meat. Bartlett wanted carbohydrates, though, and lamented, "Of course, these people have no flour, or biscuit."[168]

The Chukchi seemed to take their visitors for granted, although Kataktovik was a bit of a mystery to them; as Bartlett wrote, "I could see that the Siberians were puzzled about Kataktovik. They talked about him and to him; at first, I am quite sure, they did not think that he was an Eskimo. They evidently took me for a trader, though they had not seen me go up the coast. The sledge was all bundled up, so that they could not see what I had, and rather lightly loaded, so that apparently I had sold my goods and was now working down the coast on my homeward journey. They were in evident doubt about Kataktovik, because he and they could not understand each other's speech. He would talk to them in the language of the Alaskan Eskimo and they would put up their hands and touch their faces to show that they did not understand. Then they would talk to him and he, in turn, would throw up his hands and say, 'Me no savvy.'"[169] Despite questions about Kataktovik, the Chukchi shared food with the interlopers, mended their clothes (with one old woman eagerly helping Bartlett out of his coat), and provided them with shelter, *arrangas*, dwellings fashioned from driftwood and skins. There, Bartlett and Kataktovik slept on deerskin on platform beds which provided a welcome divergence from the rough beds of ice they had endured for many weeks. As Bartlett described it, "About eleven o'clock that night we all lay down together on the bed-platform, men, women and children; the youngsters had all remained outside the curtain until that time."[170]

Once in Siberia, Bartlett "studied" the people, perhaps influenced by the anthropologists he had gotten to know on the *Karluk*: "I did not, of course, acquire all my information about the natives from the first ones I met, though to be sure they were a typical group and exemplified, the more I studied them, all the customs of the country, especially that of continual feasting of the stranger within their gates."[171] The Chukchi were curious to know where their visitors had come from and indicated this with hand signals. Bartlett's response was to take out his charts and show them Wrangel Island, explaining, as best he could, his concern for the *Karluk* party that remained there. Because of his extensive experience with Greenlandic and Labrador Inuit, he was not intimidated by the language barrier and managed to achieve the necessary communication: "By drawing pictures of trees and reindeer on the chart I found that I could make them understand what I wanted to know; then by marking on the chart they showed me that they made journeys of fifteen sleeps' duration before they reached the reindeer country."[172]

Bartlett provided a comprehensive picture of *arrangas*, although, like many visitors to the region, he confused the Chukchi with the Siberian Eskimo. Still, he made useful observations that would have impressed Diamond Jenness and Henri Beuchat: "The Siberian Eskimo or Chukches, as these natives are called, know nothing of snow igloos or how to build them. Their house, as I was presently to learn, is called an arranga. There is a framework of heavy driftwood, with a dome-shaped roof made of young saplings. Over all are stretched walrus skins, secured by ropes that pass over the roof and are fastened to heavy stones along the ground on opposite sides. The inner inclosure, which is the living apartment, is about ten feet by seven; it is separated by a curtain from the outer inclosure where sledges and equipment are kept."[173] According to Bartlett, an arranga he stayed in had three lamps, fuelled by seal or walrus oil, and were not ventilated, with the result that it was hot inside, about 100°F, while it was -50°F outside. He wrote: "Cold as it was outside, the air inside was very warm, too warm for comfort ..."[174] Bartlett later published in several academic journals, such as the *Journal of Mammalogy*,[175] and this diary may have been the serious beginning of his intermittent and sometimes successful attempts at scholarly writing.

The *arranga* was crowded and tobacco smoke clouded the air, which Bartlett, with his abstentious background, found hard to cope with. Adding to this was the constant tubercular coughing of the Chukchi. Of another *arranga*, Bartlett wrote, "The air was hot and ill smelling, and filled with smoke from the Russian pipes which the Chukches used, pipes with little bowls and long stems, good for only a few puffs. When they were not drinking tea they were smoking Russian tobacco. All the time, with hardly a moment's cessation, they were coughing violently; tuberculosis had them in its grip. When they lay down to sleep they left the lamps burning. There was no ventilation; the coughing continued and the air was if anything worse and worse as the night wore on."[176] Between 2 and 3 a.m., he woke up and the substandard air prevented him from returning to sleep: "The air was indescribably bad. The lamps had gone out and when I struck a match it would not light. The Chukches were all apparently broad awake, coughing incessantly."[177]

In some ways, Bartlett found shelter in Siberia as arduous as the desperate struggle from Wrangel Island. Despite his life on board ship, Bartlett was an introvert and disliked crowds, especially in small spaces; making his way along the Siberian coast, he lacked the captain's cabin which had always served as a retreat and a buffer from shipboard social life. But, having reached safety and with rescue on his mind, he coped. The Chukchi offered him and Kataktovik rancid walrus meat, pemmican, and deer meat and allowed Bartlett to make strong Russian tea, a favourite of theirs. Bartlett noted that young children ate decayed walrus meat and drank tea sweetened with a great deal of sugar.

Bartlett and Kataktovik moved on from the hospitality of the first Chukchi group they met and stayed in other *arrangas* as they travelled toward the ports of the East Cape from where they hoped to access Alaska. Bartlett noted with pleasure that the owner of one *arranga*, at Cape Wankeram, was a music fan like himself and like Grandmother Leamon. This man "treated us to an extended concert, numbering forty-two selections, starting off with 'My Hero' from 'The Chocolate Soldier' ... Like the true music-lover, he kept on playing until he had finished all of his forty-two records."[178] That night Bartlett had the best sleep he had had since leaving Camp Shipwreck on the ice. The Chukchi music-lover had a wife and two "fine-looking daughters" (as well as a son) and copies of the *London Illustrated News*, *National Geographic*, and *The Literary Digest*.[179] Bartlett gave the family snow-knives, steel drills, a skein of fish line, a gill net, and a yard of ribbon for the daughters. He was particularly taken with this family, especially by the man's action of silently harnessing up his own dogs for the two travellers, writing, "Our treatment at the kind hands of this Chukch [sic] family will always remain in my memory."[180]

Bartlett was full of admiration for all the Chukchi he encountered; it went beyond the relief and appreciation that were inevitable after his dangerous journey and it was down to the people themselves. The Chukchi let Bartlett take one of their dogs. They traded in a just manner, offering the visitors a much-needed dog in exchange for a gun, and one man went out of his way to return a dog he had traded with Bartlett but that had run back home. Bartlett came to appreciate the complexities of Chukchi culture. He figured out that his behaviour did not always meet their standards—such as when he used a less than gentle tone of voice—even though the Chukchi chose not to point out his transgressions. This was the first time Bartlett truly grasped the nuances of Indigenous ways and, in the main, he did so respectfully. But he could be patronizing and, like most explorers, failed to use the names of the Indigenous people he encountered. Of the Chukchi, he said effusively, "Never have I been entertained in a finer spirit of true hospitality and never have I been more thankful for the cordiality of my welcome. It was, as I was afterwards to learn, merely typical of the true humanity of these simple, kindly people."[181] His time in Siberia was a balm after a great deal of trauma and he realized that the Chukchi had made it so.

Through the weeks in Siberia, Kataktovik matured and became relaxed around the Chukchi. He traded with them, on his own, procuring flour on one occasion. He spent time alone with them, without Bartlett, to whom he sometimes relayed messages from them. He had come to recognize elements of Chukchi culture or he had at least become comfortable in an unfamiliar milieu. Kataktovik's wariness never quite disappeared, however, and, at times, he seemed to be on guard. Kataktovik worried about the captain's excitement and enthusiasm in conversation, even before Bartlett recognized it was a problem. "You must not talk that way," he told Bartlett, fearing, wrongly, that the Siberians would take offence and perhaps exact revenge on the visitors.[182] In this, he was telling Bartlett what to do, and not do, and it appeared that the captain took Kataktovik's advice seriously.

Like Kataktovik's people, the Inupiat of Alaska, the Indigenous people of Siberia were in a time of transition. Since the Russian Orthodox Church had established missions in the region in the early 1800s, the Russian presence was being felt in other arenas, including food practices; the tea so loved by Bartlett's and Kataktovik's hosts, for instance, had replaced the once-favoured and more nutritious Chukchi soup made from the contents of reindeer stomachs.[183] Bartlett was a quick study and, despite his initial confusion, realized that there were Indigenous peoples distinct from each other in this part of Siberia; his observations were elaborated on by scholars many years later. As he wrote, "[there were] two kinds of natives, the coast Eskimo and the deer men, the latter a hardier type of man than the former. The coast natives get their living by hunting, their chief game being walrus, seal and bear. Some of them have large skin-boats for travelling from settlement to settlement, covering in this way considerable stretches of coast. They do not go out upon the drift ice."[184] Baron Kleist, the supervisor of northeastern Siberia, told Bartlett of two renowned deer men who owned no fewer than 4,000 reindeer in two camps; they spent so much time outdoors without shelter that their faces were black from windburn. Reindeer have been hunted in Siberia for as long as 10,000 years and the Chukchi and other Indigenous people have developed methods of protecting domestic and wild herds,[185] as did the Saami of Scandinavia. By the time Bartlett visited Siberia, there were many more domestic herds than there were wild herds.[186] The Chukchi killed privately owned reindeer with a quick stab to the heart; every part of the animal, except the contents of the stomach and intestines, was used and governed the disposal of the animal's bones.[187] In the manner of Indigenous people virtually everywhere, the Chukchi of Siberia had long been in the habit of preventing the production of waste.

As Bartlett and Kataktovik trudged through the snow drifts, there were growing fears in the outside world that the *Karluk* would "never be heard from again."[188] Indeed, the people left on Wrangel Island had run out of food on 5 June and were scavenging for birds' eggs or, more accurately, bird fetuses.[189] The Canadian government would not admit it, of course, but there was a widespread assumption that all on board were dead—"including the men of science."[190] The story of the *Fram*, a vessel which was thought to have been lost in the Arctic for three years before re-surfacing, was brought up in order to inspire hope. The London *Times* tried to encourage:

"What chiefly inspires optimism is that Captain Bartlett, commander of the *Karluk*, was with Peary on his last North Pole expedition and is one of the most experienced sailors living."[191] The long months of not knowing Bartlett's fate pained his mother, Mary Jemima, and the rest of the family in Brigus.

The London *Times* had been keeping vigil for months, noting in early July that Bartlett had not been heard from and that nothing had been heard of the eight men missing from the *Karluk* since 5 February—Beuchat, Mackay, Murray, the two ship's officers, and the three seamen.[192] Then, still in the winter deeps but less than two weeks after they had left Camp Shipwreck, Ernest Chafe encountered Beuchat's party while out testing the ice on Bartlett's orders. Beuchat was feeling poorly but he foolishly refused offers of help.[193] Chafe poignantly described their condition and their unfortunate stubbornness: "They had been on the trail for ten days, and looked a most pitiful sight. Their clothes were all frozen and stiff as boards. Morris had driven a hunting-knife through his hand while opening a can of pemmican, and blood-poisoning had set in, leaving him in a bad way. Beuchat, who was half a mile in the rear, had both feet badly frozen ... He was in such a state that the doctor said he would not live another night ... They had no dogs, and as there were only two of them fit to pull the sledge, I advised them to return to Shipwreck [Camp]. This I pleaded, but all in vain; they said they had made their bed and were going to lie on it."[194] Bartlett's prose from the time was more spare: "Chafe offered assistance; they refused and said they were bound for Wrangell [sic] Island."[195]

On 22 April, Bartlett reached Cape Serdtse-Kamen, Russia, to the northwest of East Cape, and got treatment for his ailing legs.[196] Over 37 days, he and Kataktovik had travelled 400 miles along the Siberian Coast. Now they were, as Bartlett put it, "in touch with the world again."[197] Bartlett left East Cape, Siberia, on the *Herman*, skippered by Theodore Pedersen, who had been Stefansson's first choice as *Karluk* skipper and who now supplied him with "American clothing" to replace his raggedy furs. Bartlett's first attempt to send a cable to Ottawa from an American military station ended in calamity when the sergeant there insisted on payment, which Bartlett, with his empty pockets, could not provide. Usually slow to anger, Bartlett nearly lost his patience and, given the circumstances, it is remarkable that he did not. His perennial good luck held out, however, when he bumped into United States marshal Hugh J. Lee at the station. Not only had Lee sailed with Peary in 1892 but, he had also visited Turnavik, the Bartletts' Labrador fishing station, in 1896.[198] Lee came to the rescue and Bartlett's cable finally got sent. Almost right away, many others poured in, including an especially pragmatic one from an American magazine regarding the use of Bartlett's image for a tobacco ad campaign. They asked, "What brand do you smoke?"[199]

"My own special task was done," Bartlett later wrote,[200] forgetting Kataktovik, who had been so essential to their success, for the moment. When Ottawa asked for advice on how to proceed, Bartlett suggested that the *Bear* coordinate a rescue effort with two Russian icebreakers, the *Taimir* and the *Vaigatch*, which were leaving for Vladivostock. Another Newfoundland connection surfaced; now part of the US Coast Guard, the *Bear* had been built for the Newfoundland seal hunt and, from the *Bear*, Bartlett's great-uncle, Captain William Norman, had rescued the Greely survivors. He had complete faith in the ship, calling her "a crack sealer."[201] "I want go on relief ship," he cabled, the truncated language of the wireless rendering his plea touchingly childlike. Bartlett felt his own powerlessness keenly: "these days had been nightmares to me."[202]

Onshore in Alaska, Bartlett recovered from severe swelling in his legs, which virtually paralyzed him, while seeking a rescue ship. The world was regularly following news of the *Karluk*. The Nome *Daily Nugget* gave the *Karluk* almost equal billing with the *Empress of Ireland*'s sinking in the St. Lawrence River: "1000 Go Down on Boat" was followed by a more triumphant article titled "Exploring Ship *Karluk* Sinks—Captain Bartlett Returns."[203]

Bartlett was cheered by a friend he made while waiting in Alaska—Lord William Percy, one of the seventh Duke of Northumberland's 13 children and a dedicated ornithologist, who went on to write the impressive study *Three Studies in Bird Character: Bitterns, Heron and Water Rail.*[*] The dukedom going to Alan, his elder brother, William Percy was free to pursue his chosen interests and was going north in the *Bear* to study Arctic ducks. Bartlett was fascinated by Percy and his collection of knives, scissors, and

---

[*]   More recently, Percy's family seat, the sprawling Alnwick Castle, has hosted film crews for "Downton Abbey," two Harry Potter movies, and "Star Trek: The Next Generation."

other tools with which to mount the ducks he collected. The aristocrat could identify the sex and species of birds at a glance, Bartlett noted admiringly. Through his association with Percy, Bartlett hovered on the edges of a small elite Anglo-American male world and it turned out that he and Percy had friends in common in Boston and New York. This would not have surprised either of them.

After the trauma of the *Karluk*, the seemingly disparate spheres that made up Bartlett's life were coming together. Percy was something of a kindred spirit and here he was in the Arctic, bringing news of New England and listening to Bartlett's stories and fears for the people left on Wrangel Island. Another distraction for Bartlett onshore in Alaska was a new acquaintance, the wealthy gold mines owner, John Linderberg. Typically, Bartlett quickly developed a sense of affinity verging on veneration for Linderberg, favourably comparing him to one of the best known and increasingly controversial imperialists, Cecil Rhodes, and the two of them went horseback-riding and trout-fishing together. These activities were therapeutic for Bartlett, who was wracked with anguish about the fate of the scientists, the crew, and the Inupiat left on Wrangel Island. By this time, the stranded survivors were in a state of semi-starvation; while Bartlett could not know this for certain, he would have inferred it—or worse. Linderberg personally financed an additional rescue vessel to go to Wrangel Island. "There was no limit to his kindness and generosity to me," Bartlett wrote.[204]

It would not be easy to reach Wrangel Island where, by 1 September, when help had still not come, the survivors had "practically given up all hope of being rescued."[205] They had eaten nothing but seal blubber for 10 days in August and the weather was turning colder. They had only 40 rounds of ammunition left, severely limiting their hunting abilities. Chafe wrote with an admirable degree of understatement, "The idea of spending another winter on Wrangell [sic] Island was not a pleasant one."[206] William McKinley had suffered terribly from snow blindness with eye pain so acute he could not sleep.[207] He wrote, "The temptation to rub the eyes in an endeavor to clear them of the grit of which they seemed to be full was very great; but rubbing merely aggravated the trouble."[208] The survivors were starving and tried mightily to resist their small store of dried meat in case they were forced to spend another winter on the island. They ate or tried to eat sealskins and consumed seal flippers "and other indescribable scraps,"* supplemented by inadequate rations of blood soup and roots, which were hard on their weakened digestive systems.[209] Some relief came on 4 September when they feasted on seal meat and blubber and three dozen tomcods caught by Kiruk, whom they called Auntie, and her children.[210] This meal was a far cry from that of the previous Christmas when they had had dined on oyster soup, lobster, bear steaks, ox tongue, potatoes, green peas, asparagus in cream sauce, mince pies, plum pudding, mixed nuts, cake, shortbread supplied by the women of Victoria, British Columbia, and strawberry preserves.[211] Memories of such lavish meals taunted the survivors now. Poor morale, tinged with fear, had been a problem for a long time.[212] Morale plummeted again when crew member John Hadley's pregnant dog, Mollie, went missing in August. She had eaten her last two litters and now she was gone, triggering a frantic search by Hadley and McKinley. They found her with eight new pups, digging at the grave of *Karluk* fireman George Breddy, who had died late in the spring. She was "bent on rearing her family from Breddy's body, as it showed signs of her having commenced to eat it."[213] Since there was no way to feed so many pups, the men drowned five of them; this left them with a team of six dogs in case they had to overwinter again, a truly frightening prospect.[214]

Bartlett and his new chum Lord Percy sailed in the *Bear* on 13 July 1914. Bartlett knew that the survivors on Wrangel Island did not know if he and Kataktovik had made it to Siberia. At Point Barrow, he encountered several shipwrecked crews and thought: "It [is] getting late ..."[215] On 4 August, news of the outbreak of war between Britain, Germany, and France reached the *Bear* and resulted in Percy's quick departure to London, as the gentleman was an officer in the British army. On 25 August, the *Bear* was only "ten or fifteen miles" from Wrangel Island but "thick weather" and a lack of coal forced her to return to Nome.[216]

Then on the morning of 7 September 1914 Kuralek stood at the beach on Wrangel Island and shouted "Umiakpuk kunno"—"ship maybe."[217] Hadley and McKinley tumbled out of their tent to fix their eyes on a ship 2 miles

---

*   Seal flippers, however, were long considered a delicacy in Newfoundland, with annual celebratory flipper dinners a common occurrence for many decades.

away at the edge of the ice. As McKinley recollected it, "We raised a shout that must have scared all the seals in the Arctic Ocean; we fired a volley with rifle and revolver; and then we sent the native [Kuralek] out on the ice to the ship."[218] They then saw men leaving the ship, the *King and Winge*, to head toward them. This ship, an American schooner on a walrus-hunting and trading expedition, had sailed to Wrangel Island at Bartlett's request, but Bartlett himself was on board the *Bear* after her return to Nome.

After several months with Stefansson, the anthropologist's secretary, Burt McConnell, was on board the *King and Winge* when it reached Wrangel Island. From the ship McConnell sighted a small tent, a lonely flagpole and, ominously, a cross. No one, not even dogs, responded to the ship's whistle, which the crew blasted repeatedly. Just as the men on the *King and Winge* concluded there were no survivors, someone emerged from the tent. McConnell wrote, "without even so much as waving his hand in welcome, he returned to the tent, brought out a British flag and raised it to half-mast. He was then joined by two others, neither of whom seemed to be half as excited as we were."[219] The emaciated men were chief engineer John Munro, fireman Frederick Maurer, and cook Robert Templeman, but with their faces grimy, their hair matted, and their clothes reduced to rags, they were unrecognizable. Said McConnell, "Their sunken eyes and emaciated cheeks told of suffering and want."[220] Olaf Svensen of the *King and Winge* reached the survivors first, followed by at least six Inupiat and several crew members. Kuralek, Kiruk, and their two children were now safe, as were Munro, Williamson, Templeman, Hadley, McKinley, Williams, Chafe, and Maurer.* The *Karluk*'s cat, inky all over, had survived, cared for by the elder Inupiaq child, Helen, who carried the animal onto the *King and Winge*. Two "motion-picture men" began shooting film of the survivors, who did not mind this intrusiveness in the least, according to Chafe.[221] Said McKinley, "As soon as the ubiquitous cinematographer had been satisfied, we were hurried aboard and set down to a great feed. Then we had a wash, and adorned ourselves in borrowed plumage, after which we felt much better."[222] They were safe now and could finally eat as they wished: "We turned in and tried to sleep, but no, we were too happy and overjoyed to even shut our eyes; so after lying down for about

---

*   Fred Maurer would die in the Arctic in 1922 on another of Stefansson's expeditions, this one ill-conceived and poorly resourced. He had spent a second desperate interlude on Wrangel Island (Niven, *Ada Blackjack*).

an hour, we turned out again, and spent the night making tea and coffee and eating."[223] The *King and Winge* hastily left the scene of the men's long torment and then tried to stop at Herald Island in search of any sign of the lost parties, but ice prevented them from getting close. They had long known there was no hope anyway.

Chafe was frostbitten. Robert Templeman was the sickest of the lot. John Munro, who had been left in charge, McKinley, and Hadley were in relatively good shape in spite of their ordeal. Stefansson asserted that Hadley's had the longest and deepest Arctic experience of all the polar explorers in history and that he might well have made it through another winter if there had been no rescue;[224] this conclusion was a stretch, however, given other circumstances such as the lack of ammunition. Ironically, it was not the cruelly frigid Arctic that did Hadley in but Spanish influenza, contracted in the relative comfort of San Francisco a few years later.[225]

Bartlett soon joined the survivors and was treated to "three hearty cheers." As Chafe wrote, "we knew that it was his hazardous trip to Siberia that had saved our lives. He had been faithful to his trust, and for us and our safety he would have braved any danger."[226] Following the polar exploration tradition of rendering Indigenous people invisible, the survivors' accounts make no mention of Kataktovik, though he had been so central to the rescue narrative. Bartlett's thoughts turned quickly to the mate's party, lost months before near Herald Island. An attempt by the *Bear* to reach the Island failed; the ship could get no closer than 12 miles due to heavy ice.[227]

Bartlett's first question to the men still living was a simple but urgent "Are you all here?" McKinley told him that Malloch, Mamen, and Breddy were dead.[228] "There was nothing to be said," Bartlett later wrote, "it was an especially sad and bitter blow to learn that three of the men whom I had seen arrive at Wrangel Island had thus reached safety only to die."[229] His reference to Wrangel Island as "safety" is jarring—Bartlett had believed that they might all survive or at least he had convinced himself that this was possible. His assessment implies that he was blameless and had done all he could for them, although he had made a crucial mistake at the beginning of the Canadian Arctic Expedition in agreeing to go north in the doubtful little *Karluk*.

Bartlett arranged for the survivors' transfer to the *Bear*. When the ship reached Nome, he kept them on board, arguing that, in their fragile condition, they would be susceptible to contagious diseases. They might, he later wrote, "fall victim to some ailment of the civilization to which they had so longed to return."[230] Perhaps this was a risk, although two days in isolation would hardly have made a difference. It is more likely that Bartlett wanted to gather as much information as he could before the world's press descended on the survivors, as he knew they would. Outstanding questions had to be resolved, at least in Bartlett's mind. Having lived through the controversy following Peary's claim of the Pole, he knew that most tragedies attract scapegoats and he needed to be reassured that his behaviour had been seen as exemplary by those effectively imprisoned on Wrangel Island. He had been clever enough to secure letters from the departing scientists and crew members absolving him of responsibility for their fate. He was still young and ambitious and had a long career ahead of him; he had to look after his interests, as he had seen his father and uncles do, and he knew that information is a useful weapon that can afford protection when nothing else can.

At the same time, Bartlett mourned and some time was required to process what had happened; the presence of the survivors would have helped with that. He felt terribly for Bjarne Mamen, for whom he had had a special affection. In his account of the *Karluk*, Bartlett immortalized Mamen as "a great companion, indoors or out" and "a devoted and helpful associate."[231] Chafe gave a full reckoning of Mamen's horrific death, which would have pained Bartlett. The dying man had written in his diary: "My body looks horrible. It has swollen up now so that I am frightened about myself. Is it death for all of us? No, with God's help we will get out of it."[232] Mamen's last entry read, "I for my part cannot stand it staying here." Tragically, his late entry consists only of the date, 22 May, for he could write no more.[233] The death of George Malloch, too, was tough to absorb and Bartlett seemed shocked by it. Malloch had been "one of the most self-sacrificing men with whom it has ever been [his] lot to be thrown into intimate contact."[234] Malloch was happy to sweep the floor if it needed to be done and his egalitarian nature appealed to the captain. Malloch died a few days after Mamen.

The third death on the island is mysterious. George Breddy was described by Bartlett, who was generous with praise for the other dead men, as "a careful and efficient worker."[235] Breddy was found dead in his tent one morning; his demise had followed an argument over rations. John Hadley, the oldest expedition member at 57, claimed he heard the second engineer call out, "Oh, call Mr. Hadley; Breddy has shot himself!" Hadley then went to the nearby tent and saw a bullet hole in Breddy's right eyelid.[236] McKinley observed that the bullet had emerged from the left side of Breddy's brain, just above the ear.[237] Years later, he wrote, "Was it an accident? Did he commit suicide? If he did, then what had gone on in the other tent to drive him to such a desperate action? Or was it just that he could not face the prospect of many more weeks, perhaps another winter on the island? We would never know the answers."[238] Although McKinley didn't mention it, another possibility was murder.

Both Stefansson and Bartlett were deluding themselves if they seriously entertained the thought that another lonely winter on Wrangel Island was possible. McKinley, the only scientist to survive, started feeling low after July, especially as he had no animal skins suitable for making clothing and he was cold; before this, he had been philosophical about his dilemma.[239] By the time they boarded the *Bear*, the survivors were at the end of their tethers, starving and demoralized. Dictating his account to writer Ralph T. Hale two years later, Bartlett could not bring himself to admit how close to death so many of the expedition his members really were. Eleven of those of the *Karluk* party of 31 had died—almost a third of the total. It was a great deal to have on one's conscience and Bartlett was genuinely troubled, while Stefansson, the expedition leader, was apparently far less concerned.[240]

Bartlett's suffering paled in comparison to that of the men who had been stuck on Wrangel Island, some of whom had lost their lives while still young. Seven months after his rescue, McKinley had not recovered from the effects of his stressful time in the Arctic.[241] Besides lingering physical ailments and what would now be described as survivor guilt, McKinley also fretted about not getting to war in Europe, where so many of his compatriots had gone.

As to the lost parties, various ships looked for them but they were not to be found; Bartlett found it "very hard to give them up."[242] His efforts were inspired, if not haunted, by the memory of Commander George Washington De Long, who had searched for a route to the North Pole via the Bering Strait in 1879, having watched his ship, the USS *Jeannette*, sink near Wrangel Island. De Long led his crew to Siberia but most perished, and he died of starvation in Russia. Twelve expedition members were lost in addition to others who attempted their rescue.[243] Bartlett wanted to better De Long's tragic record and his place in history. He greatly admired De Long and, upon meeting the commander's widow later, told her, "My dear lady, I want to tell you that your husband has been one of the inspirations of my life."[244]

There was great interest in the story of the *Karluk* in 1914, despite momentous events happening in Europe, and this interest was sustained. In November 1916, the New York *Times* published an account by Bartlett and a chart showing the ship's progress until it was crushed.[245] Meanwhile, Bartlett expressed his appreciation for the skills and companionship offered by Kataktovik and sent the young man's pay to him as soon as was possible. Of their leave-taking at the East Cape, Bartlett wrote, "we were parting here. I thanked him as I bade him good bye, for all that he had done, and told him how greatly I was indebted to him for his constant help and for his faith and trust in me."[246] In an almost fatherly tone, Bartlett added, "I asked Mr. Carpendale [a trader] to tell the Chukches what a good boy Kataktovik was. I gave him the rifle we had carried on our journey and some other things we had with us, and then we shook hands warmly and parted."[247] By the time Bartlett wrote his book about the *Karluk*, he had, for the second time in his life, made international headlines. As the central figure in the dominant narrative of the disaster, Bartlett was ensconced in popular consciousness as a man's man, a true hero, an icon to be admired and emulated. The crucial roles of Kataktovik and the Chukchi of Siberia in the *Karluk* rescue, meanwhile, faded into oblivion.

The history of Arctic exploration has, on the one side, the Indigenous, and, on the other, the white men who were frequently the recipients of international accolades—Bartlett and Peary among them. Omitting Indigenous perspectives, Bartlett uncritically used language that reflected the prejudiced thinking of his profession and peers; he wondered, for instance, if Siberian natives were "afflicted with tuberculosis, to which so many primitive races have succumbed after contact with the beneficent influences of civilization."[248] Yet Bartlett's telling of the *Karluk* events shows that he, while still very much entrenched in western-Indigenous power relations, had progressed enough to be able to individualize, respect, and credit at least one Indigenous person, Claude Kataktovik. Nor did Bartlett romanticize the Inupiat or the Chukchis, writing of an *arranga* with his usual bluntness, "It smelled worse than any Greenland igloo I have ever been in, which is saying a good deal."[249] This, in combination with his habit of seeking advice from Kataktovik and freely writing about this practice, suggests that Bartlett had some respect for the Chukchi and the Inupiat. Bartlett also tried to be courteous in Siberia and he had fulsome praise for the hospitality that probably saved his life. This is but a small debt repaid to the Indigenous people who were so vital to Arctic exploration—and to whom exploration cost so much, but, given its relative uniqueness, it merits some attention. Bartlett's views of and relationship with Indigenous people occurred within a colonial context; after all, the Canadian Arctic Expedition aimed to extend Canadian sovereignty in the western Arctic, which was consistent with goals throughout the era of polar exploration. Bartlett's account, however, demonstrates that, even in this sort of power-riddled and unjust scenario, genuine humanity can assert itself from all sides.

Bartlett also contributed something of a window into the life of the Chukchis after whaling had declined and before they were radically changed by Soviet-era policies which would begin a few short bloody wartime years after the *Karluk* drama. Although there was evidence of trade and sickness, Chukchi society and culture seemed relatively intact in 1914 from an outsider's perspective. It is impossible for outsiders to know if the Chukchi felt their culture and economy were threatened when Bartlett and Kataktovik stepped onto their land. Neither can it be known if they had the sense that their ministrations and generosity likely saved the lives of their two visitors and, indirectly, the lives of the *Karluk* survivors. Today the landscape through which Bartlett and Kataktovik travelled is part of the Chukotka Autonomous Orkug (region) of the Russian Federation.

Kataktovik cannot be overlooked. This young man is an example of a skilful Inupiaq, who was largely responsible for the rescue of the stranded Canadian Arctic Expedition crew members and scientists. Kataktovik was resilient, a young widower who would remarry not long after parting ways with Bartlett. He was able to begin again, after a life of considerable turmoil and an amazing accomplishment in walking from north of Wrangel Island to Siberia and the East Cape.

Carrying on after the *Karluk* presented huge psychological challenges for Bartlett and Kataktovik but also for the relatives of the men who had died. In some cases, death was not official for seven years.[250] Well into 1915, some *Karluk* family members would not believe that their husbands, fathers, or brothers were gone forever. McKinley, who struggled with his own recovery, wrote a lengthy, sensitive, and detailed letter to first mate Sandy Anderson's brother trying to convince his fellow Scot that there was no hope of rescue. Anderson's brother wanted to send planes to search for Sandy, who had been last seen 13 months before, an interminable time in the Arctic;[251] the juxtaposition of the surviving Anderson's wish with the impracticality of his plan was tragic. McKinley realized that the mate's party had likely met their fate in the blizzard toward the end of February in 1914.[252] He explained how the *Karluk* crew had tried to find Anderson and the other lost men; "I feel only too strongly that there is no hope of any [kind] ... Nothing would give me greater pleasure than to think that we could still restore our lost companions, but I am only too painfully aware of what must have been endured by them ever to think that possible."[253]

McKinley suffered terribly and tried to find relief from his nightmarish memories of the *Karluk* by enlisting in World War I as soon as he could. The time on Wrangel Island had been particularly brutal; there had been fracas and ongoing tension between Mamen and Kuralek, Mamen and Malloch, Williamson and McKinley, and Munro and McKinley.[254] McKinley wrote bitterly of his last days stranded in the Arctic: "The misery and desperation of our situation multiplied every weakness, every quirk of personality, every flaw in character a thousandfold." After tidying up Malloch's grave, McKinley wrote of the dead man's "staring eyes continuously before [him]."[255] To be sure, squalor, protein poisoning, and starvation made up the bulk of their suffering, but these things could have been made much more tolerable if there had been some sense of camaraderie among those stranded. Instead, there was a *Lord of the Flies*-type atmosphere of "every man for himself,"[256] in addition to which the crew pitted themselves against the scholars with criticisms of "them scientists."[257] McKinley found the muddy battlefields of Europe more bearable because the soldiers supported each other. In contrast, the individual and collective doom of the Wrangel Island survivors had been all but guaranteed months before as the *Karluk* was trapped in the ice. Mamen summed up the views of too many of them when he had written, "I have decided to fight for my life as much as I can, one has sufficient to do to take care of one's self, one cannot take his fellow-men into consideration, it surely sounds awful to civilized ears but it is the only right thing here in the Arctic."[258] Despite his football games, Christmas dinners, and the winter busyness he instituted, Bartlett had not managed to knit these men together. Perhaps no one could have.

On a sunny day 10 years after the *Karluk* tragedy, a ship's captain was exploring Herald Island and came across bones wrapped in torn reindeer skin sleeping bags, shreds of tent canvas, a sledge, ammunition, a 30-30 Winchester rifle, a primus stove, snow glasses, an axe, tea, and pemmican.[259] The rifle's barrel was rusted and its cartridges were green with time; the gun bore the initials B.M. and the items lay among the tracks of Arctic foxes and polar bears.[260] Captain Louis Lane was in the *Herman* and in the process of claiming the "small and savage island" for the United States.[261] Lane concluded that the dead had been trapped in a blizzard as they lay sleeping in the tent, sharing a fate with Scott and his colleagues in the Antarctic. They "took fate in their own hands," the Winnipeg *Evening Tribune* opined,[262] trying to lend some semblance of honour to the dead. Lane's crew members took articles that could be linked to their owners—the Winchester belonged to Burt McConnell, who was then living in New York—and laid stones on top of the rest.[263] The dead left no written record but they were the *Karluk*'s first officer, Sandy Anderson, whose brother had appealed to McKinley for relief from his despair, Charles Barker, the second officer, and John Brady and Edmund L. Golightly, both seamen.* Lane's discovery ended speculation about what was "until today, regarded as one of the most mysterious tragedies in the Arctic."[264] Ironically, the *Herman*, which carried Lane to Herald Island, had searched for the lost *Karluk* in 1914, skippered by Theodore Pedersen, but she had been hampered by terrible weather.[265]

---

*   Golightly's real surname was King; he may have been hiding from or trying to put something behind him, or he may have adopted a new surname for more frivolous reasons.

The discovery of the sorry detritus on Herald Island provided a window into the experiences of the mate's party. Sandy Anderson and his colleagues had known they were in trouble and had erected a shelter as best they could—in this case, a tent that would have offered only minimal protection from an Arctic blizzard. In trying to advance the entire party of *Karluk* expedition members by locating a viable trail, they had gotten stuck on Herald Island, which is devoid of resources, although Bartlett did not know that. Bartlett had hoped Herald Island would be a stopping place on the way to Wrangel Island, which at least had driftwood and the possibility of game. Anderson's group set up camp but had only a Primus stove that did not work and they had run out of oil. Mamen, Kuralek, and Kataktovik accompanied them as a support party but they turned back, taking the dogs and leaving Anderson and three others on an ice pan near Herald Island. Anderson should have gone back with them. The four left behind were surrounded by fast-running open water, which made Bartlett frantic when he heard Mamen's report of it. Yet somehow the men got to Herald Island, and it is hard to say how long they survived there. It is not too much of a stretch to conclude that Anderson, Barker, Brady, and Golightly died from starvation, stuck in a flapping tent, miles from any source of sustenance. It was heartbreaking; Anderson had not turned 21. As McKinley concluded 60 years later, "They were ... four young men with no grand ideas about exploring the Arctic, or finding new land, just four sailors trying to follow orders."[266] Bartlett knew this, too, and was desperate when his attempts to find the lost men failed; he had thought so highly of young Anderson and he must have known that he had given the young Scot responsibility that exceeded his experience level.

Although no one wanted it, there was plenty of blame to go around. Bartlett still stung from the Peary-Cook controversy and he was well aware of the criticisms aimed at Stefansson. In keeping with his homegrown preference for peace—or least the appearance of it—he tried to tamp down discussion in his 1916 account of the *Karluk* disaster. Stefansson was most vulnerable to criticism because he had left the expedition, despite his status as leader, without ever looking for the lost parties himself. Worse, he had survived, unlike most of the scientists, and he had done so without a scratch, unlike Bartlett. Yet Bartlett's description of Stefansson's leave-taking was casual: "We had luncheon together as usual. There was nothing out of the ordinary about the trip that was about to take place .... We all went out on the ice ... to see the shore party off ... Stefansson expected to be back in about ten days and there seemed no reason to suppose that the ship would not remain where she was until next summer brought a genuine smashing-up of the ice and freed her."[267] This certainty about the ship's position is incongruous, given Bartlett's initial concerns about her Arctic-worthiness, his knowledge of ice conditions and drift, his superstitious nature, and his awareness of the unpredictability of the Arctic, as drummed into him from an early age by his seagoing uncles and his father. An ambitious man himself, Bartlett also understood Stefansson's ambitions and determination; it surely would have occurred to him that the anthropologist would not be back if he could help it. Stefansson claimed he did not return to the *Karluk* as he could not find her; the *Karluk* had indeed drifted. The two of them would return to the topic many years later, for both Bartlett and Stefansson were capable of holding grudges.

Although Stefansson's reputation continues to be sullied by the *Karluk* catastrophe, not all this criticism is merited. One of the most common accusations has been that Stefansson snuck away from the ship in the darkness, indicating a fundamentally dishonest nature. But, as anthropologist Niels Einarsson has pointed out, it was dark virtually all the time in the autumnal Arctic, so darkness can hardly be considered evidence of subterfuge. Further, the detailed letter Stefansson left with Bartlett contained precise instructions for the erection of the aforementioned beacons should the *Karluk* drift from her present position.[268] Stefansson also left instructions for "the Eskimo woman" (Kiruk) to keep sewing winter boots and for Malloch and Mamen to continue their survey work.[269] Wise or not, these directives show he was not being furtive. Stefansson's claim that he hoped to be back in 10 days was probably genuine, given that the list of stores taken seems about right for a journey of less than two weeks. Stefansson sinned, yes, but perhaps not in the manner people seem to think. Unlike Bartlett, he settled for sending out a notice of the *Karluk* calamity,[270] thus exhibiting minimal regard for the people of the Canadian Arctic Expedition's Northern Party. After leaving the stricken ship, Stefansson sledged over the Beaufort Sea, eschewing adequate supplies in an experiment to test the ability of the land to support human life. He was to spend four years in the Arctic, living off the land and sea, and he was, deliberately, out of touch with the world for many months. The result was his most famous book, *The Friendly Arctic*, a lengthy but compelling tome that garnered critical acclaim at the time.[271] Thus, Stefansson had all too publicly merely carried on, while Bartlett trekked across the icefields and Siberia with Kataktovik and then returned to Wrangel Island. In so doing, Bartlett amply snatched a measure of victory from the jaws of defeat, although it cost him in terms of his health, his reputation, and, struggle against it as he did, his conscience.

The *Karluk* tragedy would not necessarily have happened even a few years later, thanks to radio and other new technologies. Bartlett understood this. When he went home to Newfoundland after the Canadian Arctic Expedition, his small country was in angry mourning. Earlier that year, the decision of Harvey and Company to pull the wireless from the sealing ship the *Newfoundland* was among the most prominent factors in the stranding on ice for two days and nights of most of her crew and the subsequent deaths of 78 of them.* With the *Karluk* and the *Newfoundland* uppermost in his mind, at the end of 1914 Bartlett was even more committed to innovation than he had been before. In the immediate aftermath of the 11 *Karluk* fatalities, however, he would admit only that it was "hard to settle down."[272] In this, he hinted at the lingering effects of a tragedy that would trigger the descent he experienced over the next few years.

---

* Driven by the profit motive, as Newfoundland fish firms were, the Harveys wanted to cut costs, in this case with horrific results.

CHAPTER FIVE
THE HAUNTED AND THE HEALED: AFTER THE *KARLUK*

Every moment and every event of every man's life
on earth plants something in his soul.

– Thomas Merton, *New Seeds of Contemplation*

As the *Karluk* headed north in 1913, Donald Baxter MacMillan journeyed to the Arctic in search of the hypothetical continent of Crockerland. Peary had developed a conviction that there was another continent about 130 miles north of Ellesmere Island, which he named after George Crocker, a fellow member of the New-York-based Explorers Club and a financial supporter of polar exploration. MacMillan came to share this conviction. MacMillan's expedition, like that of the *Karluk*, ended in disaster. MacMillan and Bartlett had been together on Peary's final North Pole expedition and knew each other well. MacMillan had turned back from the Pole before Bartlett,[1] suffering from frozen feet; the Crockerland expedition would bring them together again.

Crockerland may have been a mirage or the result of Peary's unrelenting ambition and his overactive imagination, but belief in its existence was almost general among early-20th-century explorers, the public, and even scholars. There were, as always, a few doubters, including the astute archaeologist and museum curator Junius B. Bird, who could see no evidence for Crockerland.[2] But MacMillan's 1913 expedition was a serious venture, sponsored by prestigious organizations such as the American Museum of Natural History, the American Geographical Society, and the University of Illinois. Of course, Peary and MacMillan were both wrong— there is no mysterious Arctic continent.

MacMillan's search for Crockerland went drastically wrong. In anthropologist Stanley Freed's words, "A sea of troubles dogged [the expedition] like an evil spell ... not only brushes with frostbite and starvation, but also a murder."[3] Freed did not exaggerate. The expedition ship, the *Diana*, struck rocks off the coast of Labrador as a result of the captain's drunkenness.[4] A transfer to the *Erik* was hastily arranged. Then Piugaattoq, an experienced Inuk who tried to convince MacMillan that Crockerland did not exist and one of seven Inuit on the expedition, was murdered by Fitzhugh Green, a United States naval ensign and the expedition's civil engineer.[5] Demonstrating poor leadership, MacMillan lied to the Inuit, claiming that Piugaattoq died in a blizzard.[6] But the Inuit suspected the truth and they saw jealousy as a factor in the murder—they figured Green was having an affair with Aleqasina, the mother of Peary's Inuit children.[7]

From Bjarne Mamen's moody yet poignant *Karluk* diary to Josephine Diebitsch-Peary's sudden appearance in Greenland following her husband's adultery, Arctic exploration had its share of soap operas, and the MacMillan expedition perhaps had more than most. Although Green admitted to killing Piugaattoq, he was never prosecuted, paralleling the alleged murder of Ross Marvin by Kudlooktoo in 1909. Polar exploration circles were small, at least among white expedition members; years later, the alleged murderer Fitzhugh Green wrote a biography of Bartlett called *Bob Bartlett: Master Mariner*.[8] This worked as a companion to his *Peary: The Man Who Refused to Fail*,[9] for those with a weakness for swashbuckling tales of heroism in the high Arctic, as so many did.

Weather trapped the MacMillan Party in Greenland for four horrible years. Two relief ships tried but could not get to Etah no matter what they did. Finally, the University of Illinois hired Bartlett and "spared no expense."[10] Bartlett took the *Neptune** north to the Arctic to rescue them. He found the ice in Baffin Bay rough going and it took him 12 days to cross the 200 miles of Melville Bay. To Bartlett's immense relief, he reached the despairing party on 31 July 1917.[11]

In her mighty struggle to reach Etah, the *Neptune* had been damaged and canvas covered a hole in her bow. Perhaps it was not surprising—especially after the *Roosevelt*, Bartlett was well used to sailing in battered ships. Upon

---

*   This was the Newfoundland sealing vessel Captain Sam Bartlett brought through the Eastern Arctic for Canada in 1903-4.

seeing the *Neptune*, MacMillan is said to have called, "Is that you, Bob?" with Bartlett responding, "Of course! Who in hell do you think it is?"[12] By 24 August 1917, with the war nearly over, the *Neptune* sailed into Sydney, Nova Scotia.[13] Once again, a member of the Bartlett family had rescued a major Arctic expedition and, once again, Bartlett emerged as the acclaimed hero, as he had with the *Karluk*. Bartlett should have been proud and his opportunities should have been ever expanding. But this was far from the case.

Instead, a dark period of inactivity and a worrying lack of direction followed. Bartlett was assaulted by desolation. He had spent most springs since the *Karluk* sealing, mainly as mate for his father or uncles but now, astonishingly, he could not find a ship to command. He might have been a hero to the readers of the New York *Times* and the Vancouver *Daily World* but to Newfoundland mariners and shipowners, he had lost two vessels, the *Karluk* and the *Leopard*, and was a business risk. Thus, he distinguished himself as the only Bartlett who did not excel as a sealing skipper. He had spent most of the war doing transportation work for the United States, which he found stultifying and boring, and, with few other opportunities, he feared being trapped in such confining work. The unpredictability and stunning beauty of the Arctic offered Bartlett release from the demons he had accumulated before, during, and since the horrors of the *Karluk*. The labour-intensive preparations for Arctic voyages had provided succour but these, too, were absent as international peace treaties were signed. Relative inactivity, always viewed with suspicion by the Leamons and the Bartletts, brought Bartlett's demons to the fore: the harsh punishments and disapproval that had marked his childhood as Captain William's son, the bodies that littered Herald and Wrangel islands, and the untimely battlefield death of his brother Rupert and its crushing effect on his mother.

Rupert Wilfred Bartlett died on 30 November 1917 in Marcoing, France.[14] According to an unattributed handwritten note in his service record which appears to have been written by an eyewitness, Rupert was "killed ... instantaneously ... by a sniper's bullet through the forehead."[15] The letter writer claimed that Rupert's last words were a reference to the emblem of the Newfoundland Regiment to which he belonged: "Come on Caribous."[16] It is more than likely that this represented creative licence. Many families were assured that their sons died instantly, without suffering—this was implied, if not stated outright. In addition, it is difficult to imagine a dying man's words to be encouragement for his regiment.

When he was killed at Monchy-le-Preux, France, Rupert was 26, and his status as younger brother by 16 years increased the depth of the Bartletts' grief. Rupert had had a difficult last year, having been shot in the leg and hospitalized for three months.[17] He had also been wounded by mustard gas, from which he never fully recovered. And, in the fall of 1916, Rupert had been falsely reported as dead. The news reached Mount Allison University in New Brunswick, where Rupert had been studying engineering, and the Bartletts were probably aware of it, too. It took 10 days for the military to determine that Rupert, a second lieutenant, was still alive and even longer for the good news to reach the other side of the Atlantic Ocean. Seven months later Rupert really was dead. A telegram addressed to "Miss Edith Bartlett"—likely intended for Emma—reported that Rupert, by then a captain, had been killed in action; "please inform relatives," it instructed.[18] To add to the Bartletts' grief, Rupert's body was never found, so he lay in an unmarked grave in faraway Europe.

Rupert was highly decorated, although some of his medals were awarded posthumously. The list included the Victory Medal, the Military Cross, the 1914–1915 Star, and the British War Medal. The Italian government gave him the Order of the Crown of Italy in 1918, making him the only Newfoundlander to receive this citation during the war.[19] These honours were little comfort to the grieving Bartletts in Brigus. Emma wrote, with an understandable hint of bitterness, "It seems hard Rupert was not spared to enjoy his decorations. The sacrifices for Honour and Liberty are great and we wonder when it will all end."[20] Rupert left no will and, while undoubtedly saddened at the loss of his son, Captain William Bartlett was practical enough to enquire whether Rupert left any money in British banks; he was subsequently sent a cheque for $12.62.[21]

Rupert had been in the *Jeannie* when his uncle, Captain Sam Bartlett, headed to Greenland with provisions for the Peary expedition in 1909. Unlike most of the men of his family, Rupert was not a sailor at heart and had planned on becoming an engineer, like his brother-in-law Frederick Angel, who had married Betty.* As the oldest male child,

---

* Fred and Betty were the parents of Jack Angel, who accompanied Bob Bartlett on Arctic expeditions and often acted as photographer. In 1918 they named their newborn daughter Ruperta after the child's dead uncle.

Bartlett was protective of all his siblings. By his own standards, which were stereotypically masculine and old-fashioned even for the day, he was close to his brothers and sisters. Feeling Rupert's loss keenly, Bartlett was especially concerned for his mother. Although he had served at sea, he felt guilty that his younger brothers were on the battlefields, and he was not. Lewis, Bartlett's surviving brother, had contracted anthrax in Mesopotamia but miraculously lived. Bartlett's version of survivor guilt was acute after Lewis's illness and especially after Rupert's death and it added to the survivor guilt that already dogged him.

Embracing the role of firstborn son in a patriarchal society, Bartlett played a central role in memorializing Rupert. By then a longtime resident of New York, he travelled to Brigus in 1921 to help unveil a cenotaph made of Newfoundland granite in the Bartlett family plot. The monument was Bartlett's tribute to his younger brother and it was surely Bartlett, with his literary bent, who chose Rupert's epitaph from the "Song of Solomon": "Until the day breaks and the shadows flee away." Verses from the Tennyson poem "Crossing the Bar" carved into the stone were undoubtedly Bartlett's choice as well:

Twilight and evening bell,
And after that the dark!
And may there be no sadness of farewell,
When I embark;

For tho' from out our bourne of Time and Place
The flood may bear me far,
I hope to see my Pilot face to face
When I have crost the bar.

Tennyson was a lifelong favourite of Bartlett's and these same words would ring through Brigus Methodist Church during his own funeral.

Rupert's death would have filled Bartlett with a sense of his own mortality as well as niggling thoughts about the futility of life. He might have been born to rigid Methodists but he also read poetry and loved classical music. Entering mid-life, he tried to make meaning of his life thus far and he tried to function with his pain repressed; Freud, psychoanalysis, and notions of bringing the conscious into the unconscious were brand new and contentious and had little appeal to stoics like Bartlett. Bartlett succeeded on board ship where rules were all that mattered. But life was not to be lived in compartments and, try as he might, Bartlett could never live it this way. Rupert's death was a terrible blow but, on its own, it might not have been enough to discourage Bartlett. The aftermath of the *Karluk*'s sinking was also at work. Besides the two lost parties of four men, Bartlett mourned the geologist George Malloch and the young topographer Bjarne Mamen, both of whom he had favoured. He mulled over the mystery of George Breddy's sudden death.

Other things compounded Bartlett's misery about the *Karluk* disaster. He had had grave doubts about the ability of the *Karluk* to withstand Arctic ice, yet, as Captain John Bartlett's risk-taking nephew and as Captain William's ambitious son, he dismissed his own instincts and took a chance. He had ample cause to regret it. To top it all off, an admiralty commission that conducted a routine investigation into the loss of life associated with the expedition was highly critical of Bartlett. The commission found him guilty of getting the *Karluk* jammed in the ice, pointing out, correctly, that Bartlett could have predicted the ship's fate. It also criticized him for allowing Mackay and his companions to go off on their own, with fatal results. Bartlett dreaded being blamed for the demise of these men; he had anticipated and tried to circumvent it when he asked Mackay to write a letter absolving him. But as far as the admiralty commission was concerned, the letter was not enough. The commission's conclusion in this regard was unfair—Bartlett had done all he could to stop Mackay and the others from leaving. Although he had been to sea before, Mackay was not a crew member; as a physician he did not accept on-board discipline and the rigid hierarchy that the dangers of the sea necessitated. He was also overconfident and effectively persuaded others of his own ability to get them to safety. The fault for Mackay's demise lies mainly with Mackay, who paid the highest price for his hubris.

Although he denied it at first, Bartlett also felt terribly betrayed by Vilhjalmur Stefansson. After the 1921 publication of Stefansson's book with its unexpected and obviously dishonest title *The Friendly Arctic*,

Bartlett's resentment simmered constantly and occasionally exploded. The book promoted the idea that the Arctic environment was easily conducive to human survival and health, a notion that is debatable, at the very least. Stefansson was widely criticized for his views; the Toronto *Globe* noted that "he placed an estimate on Wrangel Island much above that of the Canadian people"[22] and, after an expedition there left four young Canadians dead, the Montreal *Standard* asserted a wish to wash its hands of the explorer.[23] Bartlett was irate at Stefansson's conclusion that the entire *Karluk* party, a total of 17 people at that juncture, should have travelled to Siberia with him and Kataktovik. By Stefansson's reasoning, "it is well known that coast is thickly settled with people who have an abundance of native food in addition to stores of groceries brought in by traders and could care adequately for almost any number of shipwrecked men that might arrive. A hundred miles over ordinary arctic ice is not too far to walk."[24]

McKinley, who had been rescued from Wrangel Island, begged to differ. The ice over which Bartlett and Kataktovik travelled, however, was not ordinary but jagged, uneven, rough, and pinnacled. Such a journey, with a relatively large number of men, women, and children, was impossible given the substandard condition of the entire party, save the Inupiat; some suffered frostbite, Hadley had rheumatism, and Mamen had a badly damaged knee.[25] "Carrying on [to Siberia en masse] would have been to risk wholesale disaster," McKinley asserted, accusing Stefansson of speaking out of "ignorance and prejudice."[26]

Stefansson never wavered from his belief that Bartlett could have taken the whole party to land with him. He also criticized Bartlett for not following advice concerning travel to and from Shipwreck Camp from John Hadley, the 58-year-old expedition member whose hunting prowess Stefansson greatly admired. In the view of Bartlett supporters like McKinley, Stefansson implied that it was Hadley, not Bartlett, who controlled affairs; statements in this direction were fabrications, McKinley maintained.[27] In addition to these mistakes, Bartlett and company relied too much on pemmican, Stefansson claimed, which led to protein poisoning and, potentially, kidney damage and death. Better to consume fatty meat like Hadley, Stefansson argued, noting that Bartlett had symptoms of protein poisoning, including swelling in his ankles.[28] Stefansson rightly concluded that the men on Wrangel Island had been profligate with ammunition, often firing at birds on the wing. This meant they would not have had enough bullets for much more time on the island and that if a ship had not have saved them, they would have all perished. Yet, although Stefansson did so, it is hard to fault those on Wrangel Island for their foolhardiness, given the terrible situation they were in and the obvious psychological torture they were suffering.

Many criticisms of Bartlett run through an abridged account by Hadley, with commentary by Stefansson, included in *The Friendly Arctic.** Some of Hadley's statements did not portray Bartlett as he wished to be portrayed. Bartlett came across as callous, for instance, when he allegedly refused to give Mackay's departing group any dogs: "if you go off and leave us, you play dog yourself."[29] This, of course, directly contradicts Bartlett's recollection, which is that Mackay refused to take dogs. Bartlett almost certainly would have made some sort of offer of dogs, if only because he was aware of the need to absolve himself from the almost certain fate of the departing scientists. Hadley was not unequivocally critical of Bartlett, however; he agreed with the captain's decision not to take the ailing George Malloch on a trip from camp. But Bartlett saw only condemnation, which he could not tolerate.

Bartlett's various accounts of the *Karluk* differed in some crucial respects. As per his usual approach, his narratives, whether oral or written, lay blame on no one, certainly not himself. He had more than a kernel of insecurity, carried from his childhood and triggered by Stefansson, and he did not have the hard skin necessary for public self-criticism. As Horwood wrote, Bartlett had never criticized a superior in his life and, as expedition leader, Stefansson was his superior—at least until he disappeared. As Bartlett said, "I kept my mouth shut when asked by people about [Stefansson and] made no comment."[30] In fact, despite the inner turmoil caused by Stefansson's assertions, Bartlett would never call Stefansson to account publicly.

Bartlett never moved past his diffident nature; he had spent his childhood watching fishermen doff their caps to his father and it was the fishermen he identified with, not the remote and sometimes harsh Captain

---

* Hadley was deceased by the time this account was made public.

William. But Bartlett's hatred of Stefansson ate him from the inside out. His strong words on the topic are worth quoting at length because they reveal his oft-hidden genuine feelings and something of his nature, which he tried so carefully to conceal. He wrote a six-page letter to McKinley in 1922—ink stains, crossings out, and appalling penmanship (as Bartlett himself put it) were all evidence of his anger. He had come across the United States from San Francisco to New York, where a friend told him about *The Friendly Arctic*. He may or may not have read it for himself; at least initially, he would have been too incandescent with rage having heard about the book's contents to do so. As he wrote: "I was so damned mad that I went over to the Harvard Club where Stefansson was staying, fortunately for me he was not in. Had we met I believe that I could have killed him. When I think of that damn old [chief?] his foolish boys, and utter lack of leadership and him trying to make the best of everything and [John] Hadley, Good God, a man who wouldn't turn his hand unless he had to, a typical Englishman ... but he is dead and he can't defend himself. I am going to tell you I seldom asked his advice on anything or anyone."[31]

The sad *Karluk* episode over, the Canadian Arctic Expedition continued its work until 1918. The Southern Party collected thousands of animal, plant, fossil, and rock specimens, took just as many photos, and shot more than 50 minutes of film. Stefansson and the Northern Party identified several "new" Arctic islands. Canadian Arctic Expedition scientists produced 14 reports on topics from Inuit folklore to botany. The Canadian Arctic Expedition was also successful in its mission of advancing Canadian sovereignty. But there were many hangovers. Besides Stefansson and Hadley, a "hunter" who had been taken along on the expedition for reasons few could discern, Bartlett was also furious with Dr. Rudolph Martin Anderson, leader of the Southern Party. Ironically, Anderson had something in common with Bartlett in that he, too, felt bitterly toward Stefansson. Bartlett wrote, "I intended going up to Ottawa [where Anderson worked for the Biology Division of the National Museum of Canada] and get in the ring with Anderson but it was hard for me to get away, and mixed up with the Government [of Canada], It wouldn't be good for me, but I wrote and visited many of Stefansson's friends, and who are my friends ... he [Stefansson] might lose some good friends over it."[32] Bartlett's campaign against Stefansson extended to the Explorers

Club, from which he wanted the former Canadian Arctic Expedition leader expelled. But, as his usual caution overcome his fury, he told McKinley he was too busy to follow up, explaining that other members who might help him would be similarly pressed for time. He continued the absurdly childish assertion: "my day will come if I ever get him alone. I will beat him to within an inch of his life."[33]

In the same letter, Bartlett described a 1922 encounter with Stefansson at a Washington Club tea after the unveiling of the Peary monument at Arlington National Cemetery. He admitted sighting but avoiding Stefansson at the unveiling. Then Bartlett displayed his lifelong insecurity by name-dropping, noting that he was in conversation with museum officials and other explorers who were "very good friends of mine," implying that he was too preoccupied to talk to the former leader of the Canadian Arctic Expedition. Stefansson, however, had no such shortage of confidence, and approached Bartlett, as the captain recounted: "'Why Bartlett, didn't you see me at the ...' was as far as he got, I could just hold myself long enough to say, 'No, nor do I want to see you' and moved away—now when he returned from the Andes I went over to see him at the Harvard Club. I [had] Mamen's diary [which was written in Norwegian, a language Stefansson could read] locked up in a safety deposit box and gave it to him thinking ... Mamen would have said a lot to make it bad for Stefansson. From that time until he came toward me in the Washington Club, he never spoke to me, unless he had to ... 'the king can do no wrong.'"[34] To add to Bartlett's umbrage, he had recently heard that Stefansson had said that Bartlett should be jailed for the loss of the *Karluk*.

Stefansson may or may not have made the inflammatory remark, but Bartlett was convinced he did. Bartlett manically poured out venom in his letter to McKinley, "He [Stefansson] is of that other Breed, he wasn't raised in the right school. You can't make a silk purse out of [a] Sow's Ear ... He is as lively and cute as a fox. But many have his number ... He thinks that no person can see through his devilry ... You know that he is such a slick man that he has even the Americans buffaloed but when his stock begins to fall believe me it will come down pretty damn quick."[35] In this last comment, Bartlett was right; even today Stefansson's reputation is tarnished. Stefansson had made too many enemies after his association with two expeditions that led to the loss of young lives. Further, he raised the ire of Canadian government officials with regards to the Canadian Arctic Expedition through his assertion that Ottawa's refusal to conduct an enquiry indicated support for him.[36] He irritated anthropologist Diamond Jenness with apparent exaggerations and assertions about events in the Arctic.[37]

Bartlett was apoplectic whenever Stefansson's achievements were compared to Peary's. He hated the debate about Peary, which refused to die: "for the Exploration Game has had lots of black eyes ... poor old Peary did get treated so awfully bad for he was the great man no better ever lived. He was 100% in Everything. I hate to think that Stefansson's name can be coupled with Pearys [sic] as an explorer. For they are [as] unlike as Paste and the Diamond ... I think what a damn ass Stefansson must be to publish that in a Book."[38] Given this, it is not hard to imagine Bartlett's reaction to a letter from a New Zealander who innocently asked years later, "And Sir, is it so, that it has been proved that Peary did <u>not</u> reach the Pole?"[39] When his mood was more temperate, Bartlett rationalized his undiluted allegiance to Peary in terms that were too weak to be convincing. Peary, he said, built his expertise on experience and was supported by excellent personnel and a well-equipped organization. In addition, he claimed, Peary was an American naval officer, his faulty assumption being that this guaranteed competence as well as integrity. Even after Peary was dead, Bartlett often lost his grip on his emotions when discussing his mentor. "Don't let them fill you up with those dammed lies!" he exclaimed to a former Indian missionary who had come to one of his lectures and, like the unsuspecting New Zealander, asked one too many questions about Peary.[40]

In the main, the public agreed with Bartlett. Bartlett had long been ensconced as the hero of the *Karluk* story—and Claude Kataktovik was all but ignored, remaindered in the Arctic, as was to be expected. The public disregarded the admiralty commission's findings and focused almost exclusively on Bartlett's remarkable trek over Arctic ice and across Siberia. They paid little attention to Stefansson's comments that Bartlett should have taken the whole party to Siberia, rather than going for help himself.[41] Stefansson has gone down in history as blameworthy for deserting the ship and the expedition, although his actions were more complex than is generally allowed. Stefansson viewed Bartlett's rescue attempt as a try for the spotlight, but this was more a reflection of Stefansson's goal-oriented approach than Bartlett's. Bartlett hardly avoided media attention but for him the press was a means to an end, a way to boost his image and, in turn, propel his Arctic career. Stefansson was much more extroverted and wanted fame for its own sake. Boastful and blind to the effect of his grandiosity, Stefansson rankled a lot of people.

Bartlett was just as flawed. Circumstances forced him to be a political strategist but he generally kept his own counsel and had few enemies and many friends and fans. He got along with some explorers and even won the admiration of the acclaimed Knud Rasmussen, who sent him a telegram in 1931 that stated: "Congratulation Robert Bartletts splendid brilliantly accomplished expedition East Greenland seized opportunity behalf Danish polar explorers send centurys greatest boldest most experienced arctic skipper our greetings and enthusiastic homage."[42] This should have been enough compensation for Bartlett, but he could never escape the torment he felt regarding Stefansson—he paid a lot less attention to Rasmussen's support than he did to Stefansson's disapproval.

The conclusions of the admiralty commission quietly gathering dust on a shelf, Bartlett was celebrated for his herculean work. The Royal Geographical Society, always a strong supporter of both Peary and Bartlett, honoured Bartlett for his bravery. Accolades were not enough for the captain, who had the frailty of the failed perfectionist; he could not undo the loss of the *Karluk* and 11 men. The images of Malloch and Mamen dying in their tents on Wrangel Island haunted him. Rupert's death was an additional weight he could not shake.

Peary's sinking into invalidity and his death in 1920 hit Bartlett extremely hard; his attachment to the admiral had never waned. As a result, in the years after the tragedy of the *Karluk*, its public hero, based in New York, became a drunk. As prohibition was in effect in the United States, Bartlett began buying whiskey from a midtown bootlegger to drown his sorrows. His private and public personas were more sharply divided than ever. An extremely private person, Bartlett glossed over his downfall in the books he wrote. In fact, he consistently pretended to be a lifelong teetotaller, as his father Captain William had been. But Bartlett

The Murray Hill Hotel in New York City, Bob Bartlett's longtime home. The hotel no longer exists.

made a well-oiled fool of himself more than once in the Explorers Club and elsewhere; accordingly, in the small world of explorers, his personal reputation was in tatters and it looked as though his career might be over.

In the early 1920s, the stockbrokers who had backed Peary turned down Bartlett's applications for financial assistance to go north.[43] During this grey period, a broke Bartlett got free meals from the New York Yacht Club and the Harvard Club.[44] He was so unreliable that the Murray Hill Hotel, which he had called home for several years, insisted that he pay weekly instead of monthly. His family was far away and it seems that Bartlett did not rely on them for help—or even ask for it, too entrenched was he in the role of firstborn son and older brother. In addition, the formidable Captain William was still very much alive and head of the family; Bob could not lay his shame at his father's feet. There was no precedent for a Bartlett falling to pieces. Something had to happen to save him from complete ruin.

And something did. But, as so often happens in life, Bartlett's deliverance initially took the form of a disaster. In 1924, well into the most desperate phase of his life, a laundry wagon hurtling down 44th Street knocked Bartlett down, possibly while he was drinking. Bartlett broke a leg and some ribs and spent a protracted three months in hospital where, in an indication of a continuing inner struggle, he sometimes refused food and drink. He did not have access to liquor and went through painful withdrawal from his substance of choice. Lauded so widely just a few years before, Bartlett rarely had visitors during his long weeks as an invalid.

But this time of incapacitation served as a pivotal point for Bartlett. He was able to regain his health. Lying in a hospital bed for weeks on end, with no external source of solace, he was forced to face himself and figure out a way to live with himself and his life thus far. He made a vow to lifelong temperance, of which his teetotalling parents would have approved. He used his accident and its aftermath to lend credence to his oft-stated public contention that true civilization was found in the Arctic, not in cities, and he resolved to spend the rest of his life among the people he claimed to love the most: the Inuit. With some humour, he referred to the 1776 book by Edward Gibbon, railing, "How can anyone wade through *The Rise and Fall of the Roman Empire* and still stay sober?"[45] He thus equated modernity and the urban with civilization and, not unexpectedly, did so in a manner that smacked of paternalism and romanticism toward the Inuit. Yet there was great appetite for this kind of thinking throughout the United States, and Bartlett would be able to take advantage of it.

After his release from hospital, Bartlett fell in love with an "old girl [whose] topside sparkled in the summer sun like a wedding gown of purest white."[46] This was not a woman; instead, the *Effie Morrissey*, the object of his affections, was a two-masted schooner, almost 100 feet long with a 22-foot beam.[47] Grossing 120 tons, she was launched at Essex River, Massachusetts, in the winter of 1894 and named after her first owner's daughter.[48] With her pine deck, oak planking, and fastenings of Swedish wrought iron, she was "built to last,"[49] and, more importantly, given Bartlett's past and his future plans, she was ice-ready.

The *Morrissey* was the property of Bartlett's younger cousin, Captain Harold (Harry) Sinclair Bartlett, who had inherited her from his father.

The *Effie Morrissey*. Photo by George W. Little, courtesy of Denise Riddell.

Harry estimated the value of the ship at $25,000. Bartlett, however, took the position that she was a bit of a wreck and, after an argument that lasted three days, he convinced Harry to sell the ship to him for a mere $6,000; this was, Bartlett said, "the best bargain I ever made."[50] In fact, it was not Bartlett who paid for the vessel but the vastly wealthy Commodore James B. Ford, one of Bartlett's many affluent American friends who would come to his rescue time and time again. Ford felt sorry for the rudderless Bartlett, who appeared to him to be "a lost soul,"[51] and offered to buy him a ship on condition that he make it profitable. In purchasing the *Morrissey*, Ford gave Bartlett "the gift of salvation," as Bartlett biographer Harold Horwood put it;[52] this description would have resonated with the religious Bartlett parents.

Bartlett had the *Morrissey* refitted at Brigus under the direction of his brother Will.[53] He began scouting for opportunities to take her to the Arctic. He knew that scientific research was the best route and it was something he was interested in, especially after getting to know the scientists on the *Karluk*. He wrote to the United States Department of Agriculture and received a favourable response: "it is of exceedingly great interest to determine the route over which so much of the important mammal life of North America came from its original home in Asia."[54] Further, government officials assured Bartlett that he would have the full cooperation of the department's Biological Survey branch. After the long lonely years, Bartlett had a boat and a bite and he could begin to see a way forward.

In 1925 Bartlett took the *Morrissey* to Labrador for the fishing season, but this was a financial failure, as it often was, given the unpredictable weather and the short season. It is reasonable to assume that Bartlett's heart was not in the fishing expedition, considering how he longed for Arctic adventure. There was a bit of a calamity involving William James "Jim" Dove, the son of Bartlett's sister Triss and her husband, Wilfred, who had come along as a cabin boy. To keep young Jim safe during a gale, Bartlett locked him in the after cabin but a wave crashed through the cabin window and frigid sea water poured in. In fear of drowning, Jim screamed and banged on the cabin door until his uncle rescued him. Relieved to have saved his nephew, Bartlett also realized that if Jim had not raised the alarm, water would have flooded the *Morrissey*, as her ballast shifted, and sank her.

Bartlett's nephews Robert[55] and Jim Dove became regular crew members of the *Morrissey*, with Jim rising to the rank of chief engineer. On their 1930 voyage a photo taken of Jim cutting Bartlett's hair was later published in the New York *Times*.[56] Jim's adventurous sister, Hilda Bartlett Dove, was also on the 1930 Arctic voyage. Hilda was pictured in the same newspaper article in full Greenlandic Inuit dress.[57] Thus, in violation of the age-old gendered code to which he enthusiastically subscribed, Bartlett had allowed a woman on his ship.* This change of heart could have come only via Hilda for she and Bartlett were extremely close and shared the same wanderlust.

No one would have accused Hilda of being ordinary. Unmarried at 28, she made a lengthy solo voyage from Newfoundland to the English countryside, then on to Lisbon, the Canary Islands, and then west again to South America where she journeyed through Rio de Janeiro, Montevideo, and "the great city of Beunas Aires."[58] "I have had one hell of a fine trip since leaving Newfoundland," she wrote jauntily to Bartlett, "that does not sound very ladylike but you will admit it is descriptive—and to relate it in

---

*   Inupiaq women, like Kiruk, were the exception since their sewing skills were so necessary to Arctic exploration and since, perhaps, they did not have the status of white women. (Kiruk also proved herself to be skilled in food acquisition on Wrangel Island.)

detail would fill a volume the size of Gone with the Wind."[59] She relished the three-week crossing of the South Atlantic as "the abundance of sea air [was] better than any tonic." In spite of the 107 degree temperatures in South America, she was "A1."[60]

Hilda also shared Bartlett's curiosity and his talent for observation. She was fascinated by life in the foothills of the Andes, writing that "the agriculture and produce of the very fertile land, the cattle ranches, the mining of limestone, the growing of the sugar cane, and the manufacturing, the numerous species of birds, insects, animals, flowers and trees, the people themselves and their very primitive modes of living are all so very interesting and provide ample food for thought."[61] Hilda was a graduate of the Methodist College in St. John's,[*] where Lady Middleton, fresh from London, attended basketball games and Lady Crosbie[†] presented the trophies. Acdemic, athletic, and confident, Hilda would not have been intimidated by Bartlett's college boy sailors. It is not a stretch to imagine her alongside Bartlett's side as an explorer had she not been born female. But, as Ernest Shackleton made clear in his curt response to female applicants, roles in Arctic and Antarctic exploration were, with the exception of Matthew Henson, the purview of white men. That Hilda Dove got herself to Greenland via the *Morrissey* speaks not only to her obvious connections but also to her determined and adventurous spirit, which, to his credit, Bartlett recognized and nurtured.

Bartlett annually sent Christmas cheques to all his nieces and nephews, no matter where they were. He even sent $1 a year to young Sammy Bartlett, born in 1924, and the grandson of Bob's Arctic-going inspiration, Captain Samuel Bartlett.[62] In 1938, Emma Angel Crichton, the daughter of Bartlett's sister Mary Elizabeth, wrote a four-page thank-you letter from a small town near Liverpool, where she lived with her British husband and child. The next year she alluded to the threatening atmosphere in Europe, asserting that "[t]his awful feeling of jealousy and distrust among nations is degrading civilization. All we hear is the cry for more armaments ..."[63] Less than three years later, Emma was a war widow, left with two children. She did not remarry for 30 years.

---

*   Dr. Cluny Macpherson, who developed the gas mask, was a Methodist College graduate and served on the school's executive.
†   Lady Crosbie had married into the Crosbie family, Bartlett's neighbours in childhood.

Emma's and Ruperta's brother was Jack Angel. Jack learned of the young American men sailing with his famous uncle, so he wrote "the Skipper" to ask for a place on the *Morrissey*. Bartlett readily agreed, explaining that his nephew could not come along for a free ride: "I'll expect you to collect flowers for the Botanical Gardens. I'll expect you to skin birds and so on for the American Museum of Natural History. I'll expect you to be second engineer. I'll expect you to take some pictures for me and make yourself generally useful."[64] Angel "took all this seriously and learned how to press flowers as best [he] could"; he also bought a camera and studied photography.[65] Although he prepared diligently for the first of his several Arctic voyages, Jack was stricken with seasickness before the *Morrissey* left Brigus harbour.[66] But he recovered and did well at sea and in the Arctic. The flowers he collected and pressed that trip were in prime condition in the New York Botanical Garden well into the mid-1980s.[67] After several trips north, Jack decided to stay on land and work as an engineer. As an old man, he explained, "there was a time when I felt I could have spent ... my whole future, my whole lifetime up in the Arctic. I was very fond of it. But ah, it's hard to mix the two you know. You can't mix the two. You can either lead that kind of life or be a normal ... It's not very normal, that kind of life you know. It's very abnormal. So I came back then and came back here [to St. John's] with my father."[68]

Bartlett, who was never accused of being normal, corresponded with Jack "all the time."[69] While an engineering student at McGill University, Jack frequently travelled to New York to visit his uncle, staying with Bartlett in the latter's two cluttered rooms at the Murray Hill Hotel.[*] "I couldn't even see the bed, [packed with] cases and books and everything like that," Jack Angel recalled. "I couldn't even see a bed. And, oh yes, he said, there's a bed in there somewhere."[70] As was his custom at sea, Bartlett slept on the floor at the Murray Hill, his messy bed testimony to his devotion to reading. No longer extant, the hotel was known for its abiding dedication to formal service and decor as well as its excellent food. According to photographs, it was large and imposing, featuring a heavy colonnade at the entrance and elegant curved balconies. Its list of guests was impressive: Mark Twain,

---

[*]   Bartlett was back on good terms with hotel management after the dark days when they did not know when he would sober up and pay his rent.

Grover Cleveland, railway magnate Jay Gould, and the financier J.P. Morgan all rested their heads there or hung out in the lobby inhaling cigar smoke. Yet Bartlett's rooms were drafty and cold; typically, he complained only to his mother and not to the proprietors.[71]

Bartlett's New York routine denotes his love of solitude. His habit, Jack Angel reported, was to show up at the hotel restaurant before it opened at 7 a.m., eat his breakfast alone, and leave before other patrons arrived. This solitary routine was so important to him that he had "a certain knock" that he and the restaurant staff had agreed on.[72] Bartlett was occasionally recognized while out and about. Angel remembered a man in the city's President Restaurant whispering to him "in a voice of awe," saying, "Isn't that Captain Bartlett?"[73] Bartlett once scored free tickets at the Ethel Barrymore Theatre. After the show he sent Angel to his publisher to get a copy of *The Log of Captain Bob Bartlett* and bring it back to Bartlett's hotel for his signature. Then Angel had to return to the theatre, find the benefactor, and give him the book with thanks. Bartlett would "never slip up on anything, any deed of kindness that was done to him, he'd never forget it."[74] This habit of repayment points to what was called good breeding in Bartlett's day but also signifies an over-developed sense of gratitude. The hunger that Bartlett carried with him through his life, his loneliness, and his nagging sense of inferiority all seemed to make him feel that he did not deserve to be on the receiving end of generosity.

As Angel correctly asserted, celebrity-type encounters involving Bartlett might also occur in Newfoundland, but they never happened in Canada. Canadians were not averse to Arctic exploration and its attendant heroics— Captain Joseph E. Bernier, for instance, was a lionized Canadian explorer.* Bernier, however, had never run afoul of the Canadian government, unlike Bartlett who had the *Karluk* deaths blotting his copybook. Bartlett's liberal interpretation of wildlife regulations would later vex authorities in Ottawa. In addition, Bernier was born in Canada, at L'Islet, Quebec,[75] whereas Bartlett was born in Newfoundland, not then part of Canada, and then spent

---

* Bernier, Bartlett's senior by 23 years, had an appointment with Ottawa's Department of the Interior, which supplied ships and equipment for him ("Captain Bernier Dies. Arctic Explorer," *The Polar Times* [June 1935]: 15) and had once proposed a trip to the North Pole (Gordon Smith, *A Historical and Legal Study of Sovereignty in the Canadian North. Terrestrial Sovereignty. 1870-1939* [Calgary: University of Calgary Press, 2014], 146).

Bob Bartlett, ca. 1925. *International Grenfell Association Photograph Collection, The Rooms Provincial Archives Division, IGA 1-196.*

the bulk of his adult life in the United States. Bartlett never actually lived on Canadian soil. Circumstances and Bartlett's choices made it difficult for Canadians to claim him, although this has happened retroactively; in 2009, Canada Post issued a stamp in his honour.[76] In 1978, Hawthorne Cottage, his childhood home, became a National Historic Site.[77]

Bartlett's trips north had begun again in 1926. He had secured a contract with the American Museum of Natural History, who sent taxidermist Fred Limekiller to the Arctic with him. He also had deals with filmmaker Maurice Kellerman, fellow explorer Knud Rasmussen, the University of Michigan, the United States Hydrographic Office, and the Bronx Zoo. Most of these clients wanted samples, the Hydrographic Office wanted research data, and Rasmussen wanted reliable transportation.[*]

Also on board the *Morrissey* in 1926 was 13-year-old David Binney Putnam, fresh from a trip to the Galapagos Islands. Young Putnam was the son of George Palmer Putnam, the New York publisher who oversaw the production of David's book *David Goes to Greenland*, about the boy's first Arctic voyage. David was the product of his father's first marriage. Putnam married four times in total, including to Amelia Earhart,[†] who was lost over the Pacific in 1937; her death made Putnam a widower.[‡] For David, the trip must have been a welcome respite from the turmoil of his parents' failing marriage, the saga of which would include the long sojourn of his Crayola heiress mother in South America with her much older lover. David's book is filled with boyish wonder at the Arctic, admiration for the Inuit, and awe of Bartlett. *David Goes to Greenland* was the boy's second book[§] and was followed by two similar publications, *David Goes to Baffinland* and *David Goes to Iceland*.[78] The other book that resulted from that summer was *The Log of Captain Bob Bartlett*, ghost written by the man who had done the same job for Peary,[79] and published by Putnam.

---

[*]   Considered the father of Eskimology, that dubiously named branch of anthropology, Rasmussen had wanted to be an opera singer and actor before turning to a career in the Arctic. Interestingly, he was one of the few Arctic explorers with Inuit ancestry, in his case, from his mother.

[†]   Earhart provided Putnam with another Newfoundland connection (besides Bartlett), her first transatlantic flights having left from Newfoundland.

[‡]   Earhart likely influenced David Putnam in his decision to fly a stunt plane at 17 and his subsequent piloting experiences.

[§]   *David Goes to Greenland* was a follow-up to *David Goes Voyaging*, about young Putnam's travels to the Galapagos the previous summer.

Putnam's support for the *Morrissey* was critical. After a lengthy period of forced idleness, Bartlett was broke. Putnam invested over $40,000 in the vessel, much more than he had originally anticipated.[80] Despite Harold Bartlett's original asking price, the dilapidated *Morrissey* needed new engines, sails, blocks, ropes, lifeboats, galley equipment, and a sounding machine.[81] From donors, Putnam acquired outboard motors, paint, radio equipment, food, and tobacco,[82] which was considered a necessity for an Arctic voyage, especially as so many Inuit were partial to it. Putnam intended to recoup at least some of his funds. He wrote, "in view of my actual investment in the vessel herself, I am henceforth to be considered as participating in her ownership to the extent of $15,000."[83] He hoped, as well, to make some money from the Arctic films that would be made on *Morrissey* trips and through publications, such as, presumably, his son's. Bartlett made sufficient cash from this first trip to buy his family's Turnavik premises which, in his first experience of failure, Captain William had lost to creditors. It would have been interesting to see inside Bartlett's mind as he wrote the large cheque required; he went from being whipped by his stern father to correcting the exalted Captain William's mistakes and reversing his bad luck, for luck is always a factor in business, especially fishing enterprises. Bartlett's purchase turned the father-son relationship on its head, at least notionally and temporarily.

From the beginning, Bartlett favoured Newfoundlanders, especially Brigus men, for his crew members; among them were his brother Will, who served as first mate, bosun Thomas Gushue, who had been with Bartlett and Peary in 1909, cook Billy Pritchard, another Arctic veteran, and seaman Ralph Spracklin.[84] In Bartlett's view, these men were "English-trained, austere but sign on the dotted line types," meaning they were determined and hard-working—and compliant, a trait every captain valued in his crew.[85] These men were, Bartlett thought, capable of achieving the almost impossible. If letters from Brigus natives like Jim Hearn are any indication, Bartlett enjoyed an easy relationship with them.[86] They always called him "Captain Bob," a combination of the formal and the informal, which indicated that Bartlett was not as remote from the working classes as his sisters were. The only non-Newfoundland crew member in 1926 was Robert Peary Jr., an engineering student at Lehigh University in

Thomas Gushue, mate on the *Roosevelt* in 1908–1909. Gushue was one of Bartlett's hand-picked Newfoundland crew members. *The Rooms Provincial Archives Division, VA 6-91/Brooks.*

Bethlehem, Pennsylvania. Peary Sr. had been dead for seven years but Bartlett remained close to Josephine, her daughter Marie Peary Stafford (the former Snow Baby), and, clearly, Robert Jr.[*]

It was an eventful trip and paints a picture of a time that seems even longer ago than it actually was. In 1926, the *Morrissey* was a floating boys' club, a plaything of the wealthy, an edge-of-empire outpost in which elite men drank port, and a place where personal gain and cruelty to animals were amusing sport. This rarified atmosphere was due to Bartlett's success as a salesman who proffered the ship, the Arctic, and himself. He needed the wealth of the affluent to take him north and the affluent wanted a party with a little science and plenty of blood on deck. The description of the killing and capture of polar bears is incompatible with 21st-century sensibilities.[†] One jarring narrative comes from David Putnam, still a child, and it reveals the deeply embedded hyper-masculine ethos of the explorer's Arctic. To fulfill a contractual obligation, Bartlett needed a dead adult polar bear. Using a bow and arrow, crew member Art Young shot at a female bear as she swam with her twin cubs. Putnam wrote, "It was a hard mark, just the neck and a bit of body showing in the water, and ... the boat rolling a good deal. The bear turned around and roared and sort of cuffed at one of the cubs who was close. On the next circle Art used two more arrows and I guess one went into her pretty deep. She bled a lot and her head went under the water. Then she came up and kind of rubbed noses with the cubs and then her head dropped again. She was dead."[87]

Putnam continued, "The cubs stayed around the body until Carl [a crew member] in the dory came up close. Then they swam off, barking like a whole kennel of dogs. We hoisted the big bear on board and covered her with a tarp. Then we started after the cubs, and it was the most exciting thing I think I have ever seen and an awful lot of fun."[88] In "a great show,"[89] they captured the orphaned cubs using a noose. The first one put up a fight, chewing at the rope that ensnared him, scratching the boat, trying to bite

---

[*] The Pearys' middle child, Francine, died in infancy (Counter, *North Pole Legacy*, 41).

[†] Inconsistent national regulations and insufficient international regulations mean that some countries still capture animals such as whales, dolphins, and polar bears. Zoos, aquariums, and like facilities in many countries, including the US and Canada, continue to display these animals. According to the US-based Animal Welfare Institute, Costa Rica prohibited the capture and captive display of marine mammals in 2005; Cyprus, Hungary, Mexico, and Switzerland have banned live imports; in 2013 India banned dolphin captures (Capture of Marine Life, 2015, Animal Welfare Institute, Washington, DC, https://awionline.org/content/capture-marine-life, accessed 19 June 2015).

crew members and tear the sails, and knocking over the galley stovepipe. The young animal's distress did not register with David and it seems safe to assume that this was true of the adults as well. "It was a great party," David wrote.[90] They managed to get the first, and then the second, cub caged and gave them a duck to eat. George Putnam christened them "Cowboy" and "Cap'n Bob."[91] This bear capture was far from the first on a Bartlett voyage; there had been one as early as 1910—of a bear called Silver King, who was still alive in an American zoo 16 years later.[92]

All this was part of the manliness promoted by Bartlett's summer expeditions and legitimized and glamourized by ongoing polar exploration. Echoing his father's way of thinking, Bartlett wrote in his short foreword to David Putnam's book,* "It's good tonic for youngsters who are lounging away their youth and getting bad starts fussing around dances and nightclubs and autos and all that sort of thing, when they ought to be out getting their hands dirty, their muscles hard and their minds cleaned out with the honest experiences of the sea and far places."[93] Many of the parents who sent their sons on one of Bartlett's voyages concurred.

Presumably being shipwrecked was a good tonic for idle youth as well, for that is what happened, albeit briefly, to David in the *Morrissey* in the middle of the summer. The schooner struck a rock about 10 feet below the surface in Whale Sound on the east side of Baffin Bay.[94] It was, thankfully, windless and, wrote David with artistic licence, brilliantly sunny when the incident occurred around midnight. For the irrepressible David Putnam, "It was very, very exciting. I was almost thrown out of my bunk when we hit. There was a jar and a jolt and then everything stopped."[95] When the tide went out, the *Morrissey* was stranded, listing 45 degrees to port. Several oil drums leaked, greasing the deck and causing injuries, including a cut to Bartlett's hand. Over 1,000 miles from the nearest Danish settlement, though Inuit communities were closer, Bartlett ordered the conveyance of stores and the galley stove to shore. The first couple of attempts to get the ship afloat failed and she soon filled with water; in addition, the wind started to rise ominously. But they worked hard to empty the *Morrissey* of water and work with her sails and engines to get her going. After a false

---

*   A boardgame based on the book is available from the Zulu Toy Manufacturing Company.

start, a large wave combined with the wind to slide her free. After the *Corisande*, the *Leopard*, the *Roosevelt*, and the *Karluk*, it was yet another close call for Bartlett.

David, his father, and one of the crew went ashore to fetch the stores, but thick fog separated them from the ship. They established "Shipwreck Camp," using virtually the same name that had featured in the *Karluk* saga, and, while they had plenty to eat, their wireless failed and David became ill. On the third day of their exile, a small Inuit party met them and gave them the happy news that the *Morrissey* was at anchor only a few miles away. When David's father asked him if he'd like to go on another Arctic trip, the boy could hardly contain his enthusiasm. "I'd like to go anywhere with Cap'n Bob," he said,[96] displaying hero-worship characteristic of Bartlett himself.

After his recovery from alcoholism and his initial successes in the *Morrissey*, Bartlett envisioned a niche he could carve out and he aimed to take his ship north every year to continue his Arctic explorations. In 1930 he stopped at Reykjavik to take part in the millennial celebration of Iceland's parliament, the Althing, after which he dropped his rich pal Harry Whitney in Scoresby Sound, Greenland, for another spot of Arctic hunting. He also left archaeologists in the Sound in search of Inuit relics. The *Morrissey*'s next trip was to the Bering Strait and to Wrangel Island, of all places, to collect Inuit "mummies" for the American Museum of Natural History in New York. This sort of grave-robbing was conducted without so much as the blink of an eye, although it should not have been: Minik Wallace, the young Inuk brought from Greenland to New York by Peary, had spent most of his life trying to retrieve his father's body from the same museum, his ongoing anguish plain to see. Minik, who had also participated in MacMillan's failed Crockerland expedition,[97] died in 1918 and was quickly forgotten. Minik's was a lone voice, so it was easy for the museum and its supporters to ignore him, although he obviously spoke from painful experience. Bartlett knew Minik and would have been familiar with his lifelong quest but he, too, was able to forget him.

Minik was in fact a forerunner of the 21st-century Indigenous-led movement to have Indigenous remains and burial artifacts returned to their original sites and communities. Like Minik's father's body, Inuit bodies were regularly taken without permission and subject to scientific study, put on display for the museum-going public, or both, before and through the 20th century. Twenty-first-century Indigenous protests and campaigns have resulted in the return of Inuit bodies from many museums, including the Canadian Museum of Civilization and the Field Museum of Chicago, whose staff had excavated bodies from marked graves in Northern Labrador.

Bartlett seemed oblivious to Minik's quest for justice. Yet he understood the importance of commemoration, having played a critical role in the erection of a monument to Peary, who already had an honoured resting place at Arlington National Cemetery. He had also tried to advance the recognition of the Inuit who accompanied Peary nearest the Pole and he had developed a relationship with Claude Kataktovik which was as intimate as circumstances would allow. Minik, though, had the bad luck to be associated with Peary, almost as a loose end attached to a project that did not go quite right. Because any interpretation of Minik's story might cast a shadow over Peary, Bartlett could not truly humanize the young Inuit man and respond to his pain.

After the publication of one of his books, Bartlett was asked where he would like to be buried. He answered, somewhat improbably given where he spent the bulk of his time, "Under a tree ... on a side of a hill ... some place. I've always loved trees."[98] He could rest assured that his grave would never be disturbed or his body put on display in a distant museum. His all too human ability to compartmentalize in this way demonstrates that justice was not a concern for him. At this stage in his life, Bartlett's gods were not like the loving god of Jesus, who called the deity *Abba* or Papa, rather than Father; that would come later. In the first half of his life, the forces that guided him more resembled the powerful, string-pulling, and vengeful Greek deities, who favoured some people but not others, and thus were entirely responsible for events on earth, including disasters and tragedies. The Greek gods controlled fate; human beings, then, were absolved from blame. Thus, Bartlett could remain blameless, as could Peary, while the ongoing conflict with Stefansson was personal in nature, a clash of egos, and not concerned with justice, a concept Bartlett did not appreciate.

Bartlett's career took an unusual turn when he decided to try his hand at acting, if his amateurish performance can be called acting. He starred in the first sound-synchronized film made in what is now Canada and one of the earliest films made on location.[99] The film was tentatively titled *White Thunder* and, before that, *Vikings of the Icefield*. A weakly written love story set against the backdrop of the Newfoundland seal hunt, the project was the brainchild of Varrick Frissell, a wealthy young New Yorker, Yale University graduate, and a former Choate boy, having graduated from one of the elite prep schools from which Bartlett recruited his paying guests for his summer Arctic voyages. In 1921, Frissell attended a fundraising lecture by northern Newfoundland missionary-doctor Wilfred Grenfell.* Like so many, Frissell was captivated by Grenfell and immediately volunteered for the International Grenfell Association, delivering medical supplies by dog team in winter and helping to crew Grenfell's medical ship in summers.[100] Frissell also helped establish Yale, the residential school in North West River, Labrador, which was the subject of a 21st-century class action lawsuit brought by its Indigenous former students and a subsequent apology by Canadian prime minister Justin Trudeau. Frissell also keenly assisted Grenfell in his fundraising trips to the United States, showing film footage shot in Labrador, and he acted as a camera operator for Robert Flaherty's 1922 film *Nanook of the North*.[101]

Bartlett was one of Grenfell's supporters; Captain William and Mary Jemima Bartlett were long-time friends of Grenfell's and had named two of their children in his honour. With his speaking tours, books, and personality cult, Grenfell was very much in the mould of Peary—a type Bartlett could never resist. It was likely Grenfell who brought Frissell and Bartlett together. Bartlett starred in what catastrophically became Frissell's last film, and he opened the film's St. John's debut showing with a lively lecture about the ice floes.[102] After the showing, it was painfully obvious to Frissell that the poorly conceived and executed love story had to move from the film's foreground to the background. Frissell had secured a distribution deal with Paramount, but the company reneged. The young filmmaker headed back to the ice in March 1931 on the *Viking* to film new on-location scenes. Filming had to take place in winter, but ice jams blocked the ship's

---

* A staunchly Victorian Briton and a Christian evangelist in the style of Salvation Army founder General Booth, whom he had encountered back in London's East End, Grenfell has long been vigorously celebrated on Newfoundland's Great Northern Peninsula, where the tourism industry still revolves around him. More recently, however, Grenfell has also been characterized as an overconfident self-promoter (see Paul Butler, *The Good Doctor* [St. John's: Pennywell, 2014]); Ronald Rompkey, *Grenfell of Labrador: A Biography* [Montreal: McGill-Queen's University Press, 2009]).

movements and she was trapped. The captain resorted to dynamite to blow up the jams but instead blew up the ship, killing 27 of the 103 people on board.[103] Recalling myriad disasters in the Newfoundland seal hunt, notably the *Greenland, Newfoundland*, and *Southern Cross* tragedies, the *New York Times Magazine* lamented, "Loss of the *Viking* adds another chapter to the story of an industry that has taken many men's lives."[104] Varrick Frissell was among the dead and his body was never found.[105]

Luckily for Bartlett, he was not on the *Viking* at the time of the tragedy. Ironically, all his scenes had been shot on land in Quidi Vidi, a small fishing village then on the outskirts of St. John's. Frissell was skilled, smart, and ambitious and only 28 when he died. Bartlett sounded tinny and shrill in the film, and his performance was an amateurish combination of stiffness and exaggeration. Knowing his talents undoubtedly lay elsewhere and with yet another maritime tragedy behind him, Bartlett never acted onscreen again. While watching the film, however, one senses that Bartlett had a bit of fun making it.

Not everyone admired Bartlett or followed his Arctic career rapturously. In Brigus, episodes like the failed film provided an opportunity for criticism that reflected the undercurrents of resentment toward the Bartletts. The list of the *Viking*'s dead was posted on the train station wall in Brigus and it was announced that Bartlett was coming from St. John's. Of the occasion, one Brigus native told me, "Not much odds. Bartlett was no goddamned good anyway."[106] Some of the locals noticed with cynicism Bartlett's plays for attention. "There was always a lot of excitement when the *Morrissey* arrived; you couldn't help but know [Bartlett] was famous," one Brigus resident coolly remarked, refusing to say more.[107] Said another townsperson, "When he was bringing the *Morrissey* back to Brigus, Bartlett would wait til Sunday at 11:30 when everyone was getting out of church. That way, he'd get the most fanfare."[108] Even 60 years after Bartlett's death, there remains some bitterness surrounding his status and career. The rigid class system put firmly in place by Bartlett's ancestors and their contemporaries survived well into the 20th century. And not everyone in Bartlett's family was thrilled about the attention-grabbing nature of his annual homecomings. Bartlett's sister Triss taught Sunday school and, hearing her brother curse at a stubborn anchor, muttered, "I hope my

Sunday School kids don't hear this."[109] In common with others, Bartlett's young cousin, Sam Bartlett, who sailed with the captain, saw Bartlett's swearing as playing the part of a salty old sea captain.[110]

After his single stint as a thespian, Bartlett looked elsewhere for income, notably through advertising and lecturing. But there were obstacles. As a result of the Peary-Cook controversy, the image of explorers was tarnished; no longer noble adventurers, they were now seen as "greedy" and "corporate mascots."[111] As historian Michael Robinson has demonstrated, when newspapers took a side in the controversy, they cast a negative light on the other explorer.[112] Of course, explorers had often made money; 150,000 copies of Elisha Kent Kane's book sold after his death and Adolphus Greely was offered the huge sum of $40,000 for a lecture tour.[113] But the New York *Herald*'s payment of $25,000 to Frederick Cook for a story struck a wrong note with the public, until then so supportive of explorers. Many still were—but the Great Depression had hit.

At times, Bartlett was short of money, his anxiety reflected in pleas to lecture managers such as Briant Sando, who had been recommended to Bartlett by one of the first motivational speakers, Dale Carnegie.[114] When Sando had not advertised Bartlett's availability for the winter circuit by early December, the captain wrote, "time is now getting pretty short."[115] Bartlett's worries reached fever pitch at times. In a letter that would have been very punishing for him to write, he begged the Charles Daniel Frey Advertising agency for a return train ticket to Chicago for a lecture; in his 60s, he had no money to buy the ticket for which later reimbursement was guaranteed.[116] Bartlett had suffered the indignity and injustice of advertisers failing to pay him "a damn cent."[117] "Lecturing on my summer trips in the *Morrissey* is almost all that I have to keep me going after the trip is over," he wrote. "The New Deal* doesn't keep me either; it's hell now ... If you can help me out I'll appreciate it and I'll not abuse the privilege."[118]

Bartlett's career as a lecturer had not started out well and it never stabilized. At least at first, this was his fault. He failed to reply promptly to letters and to confirm arrangements[119] and his agents found him

---

* President Franklin Delano Roosevelt's New Deal was a program to alleviate some of the financial hardships caused by the Great Depression.

hard to reach; this caused them a great deal of stress, tied as they were to the schedules and deadlines demanded by clients.[120] Bartlett also had the annoying habit of making bookings himself, instead of honouring his exclusive contract with agents like James Pond. Although rooted in Bartlett's unceasing financial worries, this practice predictably maddened the normally articulate Pond. The agent wrote despairingly in a telegram: "Am informed by someone probably Zetts Robert offering you for lecture engagements at ridiculously low prices this contrary to contract giving me exclusive lecture radio rights must be some misunderstanding stop."[121] That was not the first time Bartlett was guilty of this practice.[122] Bartlett had even less control over the fees on offer—only $50 in the case of the Finch School for Girls, where he presented his "Land of the Lost Eskimos" lecture.[123] Bartlett keenly believed in the axiom "nothing ventured, nothing gained" and rarely wobbled in his marketing efforts. He had settled permanently in New York and become a United States citizen, which gave him access to markets that were far from Newfoundland.* He made sure to send attractive pictures of his Arctic trip to Nestlé upon his return to Manhattan. His books brought in some money but not much; in June 1938 he got $13.50 from the sale of 45 copies of *Sails over Ice*, which had been published four years earlier[124] and turned out to be something of a dud.[125] Six months later, Bartlett got $29.10 from the sale of a further 97 copies.[126] Even as the Great Depression waned, the book trade was not an easy one; as a Newfoundland distributor put it, "sales of books are hellish slow: more especially in St. John's."[127] When he wrote this, the distributor had managed to sell only half of his 600 copies of *Sails over Ice*.[128] He had had more success in Conception Bay, especially around Brigus, where he had sold 374 of the 400 copies he had, although many of these were not paid for right away.[129]

Bartlett had the insignificant sum of $47.78 in his savings account at the Royal Bank of Canada in St. John's in 1939,[130] although he probably had some money in New York banks. Despite his perennial financial woes, Bartlett made donations to his family's church in Brigus; in 1928 he sent $25.[131] This was not a feeble offering—the church's annual tea and sale that

---

* If Bartlett had applied for United States citizenship before 1909, it is just possible that Peary would have taken him, instead of Henson, on the final stretch of the attempt to reach the Pole.

same year, presided over by Emma and Eleanor Bartlett, had proceeds of $167.[132] Bartlett gave his time in the form of a lecture to the Nantucket Fishermen's Association after a hurricane had destroyed their gear, boats, houses, and docks[133] and he made similar presentations for other causes.[134] He sent the lesser sum of $5 to the Mariners' Family Asylum for Aged Women of the Sea on Staten Island;[135] the size of this donation may have reflected his awkward relationship to women, save those to whom he was related, or his rather dire financial situation. He did, however, correspond regularly with a Newfoundland-based Roman Catholic nun, Sister M. Rita, who once thanked him for a gift by expressing her fear that his kind heart would lead him to the poorhouse.[136]

Bartlett responded positively to requests from fans for pictures or letters; he sent one such letter to Myrtle Hefferton, a nurse working at St. John's Hospital in Brooklyn, whom he had never met.[137] Brigus native Gordon Spracklin, who worked for Bartlett as a youth, recalled how the explorer was walking home to Hawthorn one night when he met a poor man: "Bob Bartlett looked at the man's old boots with the toes out. What size are you, he asked? Eight? He took off his shoes and [gave them to him] and walked on in his socks."[138] Jack Angel received many generous monetary gifts from his uncle which allowed him to complete his engineering degree at McGill.[139] Bartlett gave money to Angel casually and spontaneously, once handing him one of his own cheques from the Smithsonian; other times, taking him to bookstores and telling him to choose any book he wanted.[140] For the young man's trips to New York, "he'd send me twice as much money as was necessary," Angel said.[141] Sam Bartlett, Bob's young cousin, was given an annual gift, such as a fishing rod or a knife.[142] Bartlett paid for a "first class" headstone for a former crew member, a bosun named George Richards of Port de Grave, Newfoundland.[143] Sam Bartlett said that the explorer was "concerned for the crew, more so than you would believe, you know, deep down."[144] He was loyal, but not effusive or demonstrative. He could be frugal, though, especially in the face of pettiness, such as when he refused to pay to use toilets in New York because he thought the practice of charging to be an unjustified money-grab.[145]

While lectures brought in some money, the amount could never be predicted. According to one ad, Bartlett was "a stirring speaker, combining adventure, pathos and humor in an inimical manner which is a gift of his Newfoundland ancestry and boyhood."[146] Accordingly, lecture invitations came from such diverse organizations as the North Orange Baptist Church in Orange, New Jersey,[147] the Dickens-Irving Fellowship Centenary Committee in New York, whose program featured "Sea Music and an appearance by Charles Dickens' granddaughter, Enid."[148] The Philadelphia Club of Advertising Women,[149] the International Grenfell Association Alumni, whose dinners Bartlett regularly attended,[150] and the Norfolk Hunt Club also sent invitations.[151] Bartlett also entertained the New York's Tri-Ship Boys' Club, which had enjoyed lectures by Will Rogers, Admiral Byrd, and Count von Luckner, the German sailor known as "the Sea-Devil,"[152] the Cornell United Religious Work of Ithaca,[153] the New England Museum of Natural History in Boston,[154] and Johns Hopkins University, where he presented to the entire undergraduate body.[155] There were others as diverse as the Travel Club of Lancaster,[156] the Hebrew Orphan Home,[157] the St. George's Men's Church Club and the Adventurers Club, both of New York,[158] Cleveland's Canadian Camp Fire Club,[159] and the Graduates Club in New Haven.[160] Howard Denbo of South Bend, Indiana, wrote encouragingly on behalf of an organization he did not name in this letter: "We just closed our season, had some fine programs, including one or two sea pictures, but the kids want Capt. Bob Bartlett again. You certainly made a big hit with the youngsters, and the adults, too."[161]

In 1937, Bartlett earned between $150 and $200 per presentation with a quarter of this going to his agent at this time, Llewella Kitchell of World Adventure Series, Inc. in Ohio.[162] Kitchell was among the most enthusiastic and daring of Bartlett's agents. She took risks, booking large auditoria and trying Saturday matinees, which put Bartlett in competition with the ever-popular cinemas. She used humour to keep Bartlett motivated, using the word "pulchritudinous"—which means possessing great beauty—ironically to describe his face while claiming she did not need a dictionary to do so.[163] With reference to Bartlett's Cleveland friends, the Nutt family, attending a lecture, she joked, "Since there are a good many nuts who attend the lectures, a few Nutts will do no harm"; she added, "I'll grant them the privilege of paying their proportion of your fee."[164] While working with Kitchell, Bartlett also had Edward F. Tabbert Concert Management seeking engagements but this company was less successful; Tabbert was able to get bookings in rural North Dakota, Charleston, North Carolina, and Milwaukee but nothing more, for which the agent apologized.[165] "I guess I just struck it wrong," he wrote mournfully.[166] The lecture circuit was, in some ways, like pushing a boulder uphill, but Bartlett did not achieve the meaningfulness Camus attributes to Sisyphus; he merely wanted to be somewhere else—in the Arctic stillness. He never forgot the nagging horror of an empty stomach with no prospects; he once told Jack Angel that, in the days when he was Peary's lieutenant, he "had walked the pavement of New York ... [and] didn't know where the next meal was going to come from."[167]

Product endorsements were another source of revenue. This area called for the pragmatism Bartlett had demonstrated all his life, though he did bring some principles to these endeavours (he refused to endorse Coopers long johns before wearing them, for example).[168] His endorsement of Remington guns read: "For years I've stocked the arms chest of the *Morrissey* with Remington guns. They get a lot of use—hard use. Only a gun that measures up to the highest standards in materials and workmanship will stand up under the kind of treatment it's bound to get in the Far North."[169] This statement was printed on a tag attached to every Remington gun sold in the United States and was part of a large-scale campaign that included print ads in popular magazines.

Bartlett cultivated and polished his image so that he held the pose of the ideal man's man. As historian Willeen Keough put it, through his clothes, the intensity of his gaze, and his decision to swap his salt and pepper caps for berets, Bartlett broke away from his homespun image and tried to convey mastery and heroism.[170] Bartlett tried, rather successfully, to move from the ordinary to the extraordinary. Bartlett's manly image even appeared on boxes of Wheaties breakfast cereal in the 1930s and 1940s, the cereal's heyday. His endorsement described the frigid Arctic weather with temperatures often dipping to -40°F or even lower. Wheaties, it was claimed, provided "the kind of breakfast a fellow appreciates when he finds himself surrounded by mile after mile of ice and snow ... The truth is that whether I'm exploring the Arctic, or resting up at home after a long trip up there, I prefer WHEATIES, 'Breakfast of Champions.'"[171] In 1935, the cereal company sponsored a "Captain Bob Bartlett pirate contest," with a Mickey Mouse watch as the grand prize.

Bartlett got in the habit of treating the company that produced the cereal as his personal pantry. "The cook on the Morrissey said 5 cases wasn't enough of Wheaties, The Boys and Eskimos and the Crew like them so much that we were out of them before coming home," he wrote.[172] He then proceeded to rather imperiously give directions to the company for getting the Wheaties, and flour, to the *Morrissey* at McWilliams Shipyard on Staten Island, his larger-than-usual handwriting making the letter even more commanding. He also asked the company to send his mother a fountain pen with her name stamped on the case. Presumably they had experience of mailing things to Mary Jemima because Bartlett did not include her address.

Bartlett's demands for more foodstuffs also speaks to the question that Brigus natives had about the Benville Tea Rooms; were the *Morrissey*'s supplies being given to his sisters to increase their profit margins? Given the closeness of the Bartlett family, it is not beyond the realm of possibility, and this galled some in Brigus. It is also possible that, if American food companies were unknowingly subsidizing the tea rooms, Emma and Eleanor did not know about it and believed their brother bought these supplies for them. It is unlikely that the sisters would engage in anything underhanded, although Bartlett might well have viewed extra foodstuffs as a perk he had earned.

The use of Bartlett's face on a Wheaties cereal box, a household item of such prominence, testifies to his fame and stature in American culture at the time and to the lasting prestige attached to polar exploration. Lou Gehrig and Jesse Owens were also among the Wheaties "Champs of the USA" featured on the boxes. Bartlett appeared with wild animal tamer Terrell Jacobs and navy pilot R.G. Hanson. Bartlett's caption read: "Famed explorer, hero of countless arctic expeditions. Born in Brigus, Newfoundland. Learned exploring under Peary. Captained Coast Guard Ship Karluk in 1914, escaped with 17 men to an island off Siberia after ice crushed the Karluk! Crossed the ice to Siberia for aid. Reached Nome, Alaska with 13 survivors a year later. Holds dozens of medals, has authored three books."[173] The fact that this description of Bartlett's career was replete with errors and striking omissions seems not to have bothered anyone, including Bartlett. The tone of the cereal box text is representative of the way Bartlett was depicted in many media throughout his life and after his death. But his life, naturally, was more complicated than that.

Bartlett also did business with the pharmaceuticals giant Eli Lilly. Physician Richard Van Dyck Knight requested a number of drugs on behalf of the 1937 Morrissey Arctic expedition and was successful in receiving them.[174] Eli Lilly provided potassium tablets, ephedrine (used to treat asthma), merthiolate (a germ killer), 1,000 ASA tablets, Aspirol Amyl Nitrate (which relieved angina), strychnine (a pesticide used for killing small birds and rodents), and many other drugs.[175] Some of these medications were intended for human use but others would have been used in collecting, killing, and preserving animals so that specimens could be prepared for museums, always an important source of revenue for Bartlett. In 1935, for instance, the Field Museum of Natural History in Chicago commissioned the retrieval of two walrus carcasses, one male and one female; the museum also wanted him to fetch three narwhals for $400.[176]

Sometimes the provision of medical supplies came with a price that would have seemed heavy to Bartlett, especially as he aged. Imagine his reaction when faced with the possibility of entertaining a gaggle of little boys on the *Morrissey*, birthday-party-style, with Bartlett's presence making "their cup of joy replete."[177] Such a request came on behalf of young Edward Ross Jr., the son of medical suppliers, and his playmates. There is no indication of whether Bartlett agreed to the little party but he probably felt obliged to do so. He knew the importance of corporate relations and managed to acquire free supplies for his annual Arctic trips from Brillo, Welch's, Kraft (then Kraft-Phenix) Cheese Corporation, the Columbian Rope Company, Pilot Packing, and Nestlé. He used all sorts of techniques to secure these items, including getting two Inuit dolls for the daughters of a Columbian Rope Company executive.[178] These dolls were a huge hit with the children; they were, wrote their father, "by far the finest they possess and the story of them makes them doubly valuable."[179]

Bartlett had long ceased drinking and his lasting sobriety was an important accomplishment for which he is rarely credited. But he was addicted to the Arctic and the adventure she offered. For Bartlett, adventure meant danger and just the right level of risk. He did not want to get into any spots from which he could not extract a ship but, in the manner of Captain John Bartlett and Follow-On before him, he continued to go close to the line. These near misses gave him something to celebrate and extol; they were the fuel for his lectures and newspaper articles. His skill in overcoming calamities was renowned and served to attract guest crew members who paid his bills and allowed him to keep going north. He lurched from thrill to thrill in this manner, settling into an annual routine. In winter, that routine involved lectures, publicity, making contracts, overseeing ship's repairs, and recruiting paying guests who wrote large cheques for each trip. In summer, he headed to the Arctic as an explorer-scientist-captain. But the veil of danger he craved eluded him throughout his *Morrissey* career. The high stakes drama of the *Karluk* and even the *Roosevelt* was behind him and he never lost a man again. In fact, not one of the young men who sailed as paying crew members was even injured.[180]

Besides Bartlett's reputation, his safety record on the *Morrissey* was a draw for the boys and their parents, who usually, but not always, paid for passage. Bartlett charged $1,000 per child through the 1930s,[181] although he once entertained ambitions of charging the even grander amount of $1,500.[182] For this tidy sum, young men, most of whom had had privileged, if not pampered, lives, spent their summer scrubbing decks, learning to hunt seals and polar bears, and sleeping on thin mattresses on the ship's saloon decks.[183] They would "get a fine training in teamwork, fair play, and thoroughness which [was] of the highest value in building sturdy American characters."[184] Bartlett argued that the hefty bill he sent their parents was necessary as he paid his regular crew well;[185] he also gave them bonuses such as tickets to events such as an Admiral Byrd lecture in Brooklyn, at his discretion, of course.[186]

These boys would not have gone north with Bartlett had it not been for their parents' largesse and enthusiasm. Some parents applied on their son's behalf; the mother of the unforgettably named Pemberton Drinker was one such correspondent.[187] Other potential recruits contacted Bartlett directly, including a George Moffett, who wrote, "My mother and father are both for me."[188] The boys adopted various tones in their letters. Moffett revealed a profound but not unexpected ignorance of Bartlett's passions when he proclaimed, "I saw your picture in the N.Y. Times last Sunday taking tea and I guess it must have seemed a little different than having a mug up on the 'Morrissey' especially when pretty girls were feeding it to you."[189] Alfred G. Reid of Duke University was appealingly modest in his statement: "I have not much recommendation of myself to make but that I am interested, intensely interested in the work you are doing."[190] Hugh K. Myers, an Eagle Scout and another Duke student, offered, "I hope sometime to be a great naturalist and camper."[191] Unlike most of the aspiring polar explorers, Myers was paying his way through Duke through part-time jobs and for this reason wanted to know "the least possible amount of money necessary for the trip."[192] Unfortunately, no record of Bartlett's reply to Myers survives, though one cannot help but suspect that he had to be mercenary when it came to finances on this scale. Thomas K. McIntyre, a 21-year-old Pennsylvanian, told Bartlett he was 6 feet tall and 180 pounds, clearly viewing his size as an asset. He had made several trips to sea but had lost his job with the railroad and was "unemployed at present"; in common with Myers, he could not raise Bartlett's sizable fee,[193] and, unlike most of those who wanted a summer on the *Morrissey* and could seriously entertain the prospect, McIntyre was not a student.

Some applicants found it impossible to take no for an answer. A standout in this regard is the relentless William Quinn of Boston, another correspondent who could not afford to pay Bartlett. Quinn received curt notes from Bartlett that read "I'll keep you in mind" followed by "I'll let you know if I want you," all of which he framed. He wrote to Bartlett again, rather desperately, "The motive behind this, my third letter since Feb. second is not easily explained. It is not that I am unduly impatient, or wish to disdain friends['] advice and haunt you with frequent missals proclaiming my worthiness and exhausting your patience, but that I am tortured by the possibility that you may believe I have lost interest through neglecting to write, or even forget that I am interested. As spring gains my fears are increased and I cannot forbear penning this one last letter before receiving the ultimate reply which I both crave and dread ..."[194] Quinn wrote his letter on 19 April; he should have twigged after not having not heard from Bartlett by that late date. Quinn had assembled an impressive list of references, including museum curators, professors, and teachers, including Dr. Laurence La Forge, a geologist who once went to Greenland with Peary, and Dr. Adelbert Fernald, a mineral collector and physician who ministered to the Inuit on two of Peary's expeditions.[195] Quinn was only in the first year of high school, which mitigated against him, but it is entirely possible that one of the references he listed might have not have been sufficiently loyal to Peary, in Bartlett's skewed view, which would have sealed the deal against him. Whatever the reason, it seems clear that Bartlett did not give the persistent William Quinn the opportunity he so desired.

In some cases, Bartlett's acquaintances interceded on behalf of would-be sailors. Dr. Richard Van Dyck Knight wrote to Bartlett asking him to consider taking as a "paying guest" David Mittendorf, who, though having suffered a head injury two years previous, was now in good health and came from an "excellent" family background with "very substantial means."[196] Yet recruiting these young paying guests was not always easy; in 1935, for instance, the *Morrissey* could not leave New York until the middle of June because Bartlett had not yet recruited enough professional sailors, whose pay was subsidized by the boys.[197] Recruitment was certainly laborious, with a great deal of correspondence, which frustrated Bartlett. New Yorker Geoffrey O'Hara, the father of one potential recruit, wrote to Bartlett, reflecting the sentiments of many parents, "Speaking with our mutual friend today Hal Peat regarding something manly for my 18 year old boy to do this summer. He suggested I write to you about the possibility of an Arctic trip."[198] Harold Reginald Peat, to whom O'Hara referred, was a noted Jamaican-born Canadian soldier and best-selling author who ran a speakers' bureau in New York in the 1930s and 1940s. His roster was impressive, including, besides Bartlett, Winston Churchill, novelists H.G. Wells and Thomas Mann, and Robert Peary Jr., who continued to promote his father's legacy.[199] Bartlett was still looking for two more paying crew members on 7 May 1938 and wrote the president of the Men's Dinner Club of Wichita, Kansas, using language that would raise eyebrows in 2018: "Many thanks for trying to get some boys for me."[200] Bartlett was obviously getting worried. A few days later on 12 May, he sent a flurry of letters—to the editors of *Vanity Fair*, the *Sun Dial*, and the *New York Sun*, and to Helen Miles Reid, then the influential vice-president of the *New York Herald-Tribune*.[201]

Then, student Arnold Knauth telegraphed Bartlett on 3 June, confirming his participation in the cruise.[202] This was a late date for anyone planning a summer Arctic voyage and Bartlett was concerned, especially when one boy cancelled due to illness. Five days later, Bob Wurz, a student at Springfield College in Springfield, Massachusetts, finally confirmed that he, too, would join the ship.[203] That year Bartlett was "left short" two boys, which was a financial problem only. He did not need the lads as crew members and must actually have had some difficulty coming up with things for the boys he had to do. Even more irritating were the parents, or some of them, such as Gladys Tartière, the wife of a French banker and the future landlady of John F. and Jacqueline Kennedy,[204] who wrote to Bartlett regarding her son Hugh Byfield, "This is the first adventure for my son and needless to say I am more anxious about it than he is … will you please try to have him keep in touch with me whenever it is possible." It is hard to imagine that such notes endeared Bartlett to their authors.[205]

Bartlett befriended some of the boys and some of their families, though; David Munsell, a student at Milton Academy in Massachusetts, was one such young sailor. Munsell was comfortable enough with Bartlett to sign his letters to the explorer, "Your friend, David Munsell."[206] He was confident enough to ask Bartlett to fetch him a sealskin "because it might make a swell jacket,"[207] and Bartlett complied.[208] Bob Wurz wrote that "[the] last two summers have been the happiest of my life and the most educational."[209] Another paying passenger, Arthur Manice, expressed the same sentiments and made a point the often foul-mouthed Bartlett would have enjoyed when he said he had learned more on the *Morrissey* than in "this ~~goddam~~ dam place [Phillips Academy in Andover, Massachusetts]."[210] Some of the boys invited Bartlett to their weddings and he attended at least some of these events.[211]

Bartlett developed a particularly strong relationship with David Clark Nutt, who would go on to make a significant mark in Arctic science and play a role in triggering significant climate change research. In the 1950s, Nutt's research team made the first measurements of the composition of ancient Greenland air; this became the foundation for the study of climate change.[212] Nutt also measured the age of Arctic ice and began the drilling methods that allow scientists to retrieve complete ice cores down the bedrock.[213] As of 2008, when Nutt died, these cores dated back 110,000 years in Greenland and 740,000 in Antarctica.[214] These ice cores provide information on temperature changes and thus are vital in understanding the pressing problem of climate change. In 2007 the Nobel Peace Prize was awarded to former United States vice-president Al Gore and the Intergovernmental Panel on Climate Change, an honour that laid the groundwork for the 2015 Paris Agreement on climate change.[215] Nutt's early work had paved the way.

Nutt's and Bartlett's friendship is one of the few relationships in Bartlett's life, outside family, for which there is a relative abundance of documentation. Bartlett was very influential in Nutt's life. Without Bartlett's mentorship, Nutt, though talented and affable, would not have developed into the accomplished scholar he became. Nutt was born in Cleveland, Ohio, on the first day of summer in 1919 with the cards stacked in his favour; his father was banker Joseph Randolph ("J.R.") Nutt, the Pennsylvania-born president and board chairman of the Union Trust Company.[216] J.R. Nutt was also treasurer of the Republican National Committee and a friend and supporter of President Herbert Hoover.[217] Accordingly, David Nutt's family was able to send him to the elite Dartmouth College in Hanover, New Hampshire. The family, too, befriended Bartlett, and J.R. Nutt, David's father, wrote to him, "[David] certainly enjoyed his trip to New York and his visit with you. You have been a great influence for good in his life and he is devoted to you. We all appreciate what you have done for him."[218]

At the time of that letter, David had completed two Arctic voyages with Bartlett and wanted to do another, but his father felt it would be "the same thing over again" and urged him to work for the Cleveland Museum of Natural History instead.[219] Bartlett's papers at Bowdoin College contain David's written response to his father, which is unusual, as most letters in the collection are ones Bartlett received. In this letter, David revealed himself to be sensitive and strongly committed to what would turn out to be his vocation: "After much thought I have come to the firm conclusion that I want nothing else more than to make another voyage with Captain Bartlett—and not without good reason.... True, as you say, they are fine people [the museum staff]. It is not that I love them less but that I love the Captain, the Morrissey, and the sea more. My heart will be with the little Morrissey, wherever she goes whether I be aboard or not."[220]

Bartlett was certainly the young man's ally and colluded with him, sending photographs of David in the Arctic to J.R. Nutt. He also played a part in the composition of David's next letter, since the young man had never been to Baffin Island: "the section of Baffinland where we would go is ... flat lowlands with many lakes and ponds, in contrast with the high mountains and glaciers of Greenland. Not too much is known about this territory. Perhaps once on shore we could climb a hill and gaze upon land never before seen by the eye of man. What could be more different, more wonderful."[221] Like so many, David's letter ignored the Inuit presence and Inuit knowledge. He concluded his persuasive letter with another heartfelt passage: "It hurts me to think that the sailing ship is fast fading from the waters ... Captain Bartlett isn't going to make many more voyages to the arctic. And he knows more about the arctic than any man alive today. Oft times throughout the day I think of the sturdy little Morrissey [making not a drop of water] tied up at Staten Island, and with each ebb tide straining at her moorings, anxious to be pointing her prow toward her true home, Brigus, and the north. I live and dream of another voyage on her."[222] He signed his letter "Love, as ever, David."[223]

David Nutt's efforts succeeded[224] and by the late 1930s, he was playing an intermediary role between Bartlett and the Cleveland Museum of Natural History. The museum's 1938 request for a polar bear skin and skeleton, initiated by Nutt, helped boost Bartlett's financial situation, which remained a concern. At first Bartlett wanted Nutt to keep any money they would get from such a sale, but Nutt demurred, writing, "I wouldn't want you to give it to me like that for nothing."[225] It would not be right for him to take the money, he said, and nor did he want to donate it to the museum, as he had already agreed to collect birds for them without remuneration (although they gave him supplies). "I wouldn't want to get a bear for a museum except as a part of the expedition," he concluded firmly, offering to make the necessary arrangements.[226]

Nutt quickly stepped up to the administrative tasks associated with the *Morrissey*'s trips, asking officials in Newfoundland for a permit to collect birds in 1938 and only then running it by Bartlett, who had no objections. In the manner of most explorers, including Bartlett, Nutt quickly acquired the ability to be economical with the truth. In May 1938, Bartlett had agreed to retrieve a live pair of walrus pups from Greenland for the National Zoological Park in Washington, DC,[227] and this he had done—or, rather, this he had supervised, as his Brigus crewmen caught and brought two young walruses on board. The animals arrived in "fine condition," but the tone of a letter from William Mann of the National Zoological Park was frantic, "Please let us know at once what you have been feeding them and how."[228] Perhaps not surprisingly, one of the traumatized orphaned pups died not long after arriving in the United States.

The pup's death presented Nutt with a dilemma, as he had promised to let *Morrissey* crew member Jim Dooling of Brigus know how the animal fared. Dooling, and possibly other crew members, had become attached to the pup.* Some of them were sealers with experience in clubbing seal pups but catching an animal for prolonged captivity would have been foreign to them and was, for one at least, an alienating experience. Seal kills were instantaneous but it was obvious that the suffering of these pups was not. Nutt's word was important to him but he was in science and exploration for the long term and he thought ahead. He wanted to ensure that crew members were not demoralized and that future such retrievals would continue; for both Bartlett and Nutt, the expeditions would always come first. Accordingly, Nutt reported to Bartlett that he had written the following note to Dooling, "Sorry to be so slow in writing you, but I can't seem to be able to find out very much about the walrus. I know that they got to the zoo in fine shape, and from what I hear they must be getting on all O.K. My best wishes to you all in Brigus."[229] Nutt concluded by emphasizing the importance of Bartlett's story remaining consistent with his. "It is a little white lie, so as to speak," he wrote, "but I think it will make things all right."[230]

Working closely with Bartlett, Nutt emulated him, learning to act first and ask forgiveness later; this was a Bartlett family custom as well as an explorer tradition that reflected the sense of entitlement that was part and parcel of exploration. On one occasion Nutt acquired a permit from the Canadian Department of Mines and Resources to take thick-billed murres, which were protected under the Migratory Birds Convention Act,

---

* This contrasts with David Putnam's book, in which such sentiments are absent and the virtues of catching and killing animals are extolled.

for scientific study in the Northwest Territories.[231] Given a limit of 10, he took 57.[232] In addition, Nutt collected eight ivory gulls.[233] He reported that the birds went to an American museum, probably the Smithsonian National Museum of Natural History in Washington, DC, a frequent client of Bartlett's with its varied interests, including the acquisition of iron ore from Disko, Greenland.[234] Bartlett knew that, in bagging so many murres, he and Nutt had gone a little too far and might be in trouble. They had actually taken most of the murres to eat, as the seabird was a favourite food of Newfoundlanders, who call the bird turrs. Bartlett's natural diffidence got the better of him and he wanted to tell the truth, but he had a mole inside the department who urged him not to, writing: "at least you don't have to tell 'all the truth'—and whatever you do, do not tell them that [you] killed 'murres to EAT'—at least the boys could have exceeded the limit in ignorance of the law and in the interests of pure SCIENCE ..."[235] Bartlett stifled his urge to confess and took Erling's advice. On 26 January, F.H.H. Williamson, the department's controller, wrote Bartlett, "it is noted that you accept responsibility for Mr. Nutt exceeding the limit on his 'scientific permit.' Your explanation in this connection is accepted."[236] Bartlett must have been relieved, yet Williamson continued to question him on the ivory gulls and noted in an offended schoolmaster tone, "any error on the part of 'scientific permittees' may be most embarrassing in consequence."[237] Again, because of the exalted status of explorers and, increasingly, their science projects, Bartlett and Nutt got away with a minor reprimand and were free to carry on.

There was no real way for the authorities to know what Bartlett and his expedition members were up to in the Arctic. If Bartlett contravened Canadian law by harvesting so many birds on that voyage, it is plausible that he did it other times. Outside of expedition members, who would have deferred to him, who was to know? This made him a law unto himself, in common with Peary, Stefansson, and many others who took advantage of their reputations. Part of Bartlett's winter routine was to apply for permits, but his applications were sometimes on the scanty side. North Winship, who had a long career with the United States foreign service, wrote very formally of Bartlett's 1937 application to the Danish government, which was responsible for the administration of Greenland: "The Danish authorities request that it be brought to the attention of Captain Bartlett that it would have been preferable had his demand been supported by a declaration from the scientific institutions he represents, and that the authorization is now granted only because the competent authorities are familiar with the arctic researches made during many years by Captain Bartlett. Special note has been made of his care in not contravening any of the regulations prescribed by Denmark in its administration of Greenland, and the said authorities are now confident that he will again give proof of the same regard on this occasion."[238]

Nutt was keenly aware of the strained financial circumstances Bartlett faced; he worked extremely hard through the fall, winter, and spring of 1938–39 to bring Bartlett to Dartmouth College for a professional visit. He finally succeeded in getting $100 funding from the campus administration and a contribution from the Outing Club.[239] When Bartlett arrived for a two-day visit on 2 March 1939, his packed itinerary included a public lecture, a talk to the Outing Club, a lecture to a zoology class, a lecture to an ornithology class, tea with the Natural History Club, and dinner with the Outing Club. As Nutt wrote to Bartlett, "For all this talking and running around they ask you to do a hundred dollars is not too much but I think you will be able to make some good contacts and it might be well worth the time."[240] He signed this letter, "Well, that is all the dope."[241]

By this time, Nutt and Bartlett had a tradition of spending Thanksgiving weekends and part of the Christmas holidays together, usually in New York, where they exchanged gifts. Bartlett thrilled Nutt one Christmas with the loan of his Arctic films. Nutt corresponded with Bartlett relatives, including Bob's brother Will and with crew members in the off-season. Nutt consistently called Bartlett "Captain," ever mindful of the mentoring aspect of their relationship. Many letters from Nutt are included Bartlett's papers at Bowdoin College. While the Bartlett papers contain correspondence with many people, in most cases there are only a few letters from particular individuals. Nutt is an exception and his letters had the chatty tone that friends use with each other.

An astute young man, Nutt may have understood the deep-seated insecurities Bartlett harboured and never really freed himself from. This may be why he often flattered Bartlett, especially when it came to Bartlett's

Arctic status and the stiff competition he had. After MacMillan lectured at Dartmouth College, Nutt wrote, "His pictures of the birds were just wonderful but your walrus and polar bear pictures surpass anything he has."[242]

Nutt's scientific interests were at the forefront from the onset and, in 1939, still an undergraduate, he co-authored, with J.W. Aldrich, a scientific paper on Newfoundland birds, published in Cleveland Museum of Natural History Scientific Publications.[243] This work was based on Nutt's time around Brigus and elsewhere in Newfoundland from the *Morrissey*.

Bartlett was exceedingly keen to teach navigation to the next generation of mariners and in this way, too, he put his stamp on Nutt's career. Because of the relevant skills he acquired during his five Arctic voyages with Bartlett, Nutt qualified for a commission in the United States Navy, which he joined in 1941.[*] When, in 1947, Nutt joined the department of geography at Dartmouth College as a faculty member, Bartlett was dead and Nutt, who fully realized Bartlett's contributions to science, mourned the loss of his friend and teacher. Happily for them both, however, Bartlett's scientific achievements were recognized in his lifetime. Inez Haring reported on 23 genera and 40 species of mosses Bartlett had collected in Labrador and Greenland in 1940 in *The Bryologist*, the journal of the American Bryological and Lichenological Society.[244] With David Nutt, Albert Barnes, and his young cousin, Sam, Bartlett had collected 16 species of moss at the Inuit village of Surat, Crimson Cliffs, in Greenland; they did similar extensive work at other Arctic and sub-Arctic locations, including Turnavik.[245] As early as the 1920s, Bartlett's work had been reported on in peer-reviewed journals written by Ivy League academics.

Nutt's career had only just begun. Like Bartlett, he bought and refitted a schooner—the *Blue Dolphin*—so that he could carry on working in the Arctic. Through the 1940s and 1950s, he surveyed the deep and beautiful fjords and estuaries of Labrador and helped recruit Stefansson to Dartmouth College, a move that would not have pleased Bartlett. Newfoundland and the Arctic stayed a focus of Nutt's work. Research team member Elmer Harp Jr., a Dartmouth anthropologist and, like Nutt, a native of Cleveland,

---

[*] During the war Nutt charted Greenland and the western Pacific, where he saw action. He left the Navy in 1946, after attaining the rank of commander.

found evidence of ancient Maritime Archaic culture on Newfoundland's Great Northern Peninsula, triggering a great deal of research and tourism development in the region.[246] Nutt also served as a politician in the New Hampshire legislature and enjoyed success as a farmer.* In some ways, his life resembled the generations of Brigus Bartletts who combined politics, farming, and work on the sea, becoming the closest thing Bartlett ever had to a son. Having his own family was never really a possibility for Bartlett and, after David Nutt went off to war in 1941, Bartlett's life was marked by loneliness, with some glimmers of comfort.

---

*   He also owned and operated an airport with his wife, Babs, a sailplane and aerobatics pilot instructor (S.A. Morse, "David C. Nutt [1919-2008]," *Arctic* 61, no. 2 [2008]: 222-23).

CHAPTER SIX
TO HOME THROUGH THE ARCTIC

It's all right while you're exploring. You get used to rotten meat, frozen fingers, lice, and dirt. The hard times come when you get back.

– Bob Bartlett, *The Log of Bob Bartlett*

Bartlett made a typical voyage in 1937 when he sailed to the Arctic to collect data and specimens for the Smithsonian Institution.[1] Throughout his career, he gifted the museum with marine invertebrates, echinoderms, mollusks, fishes, insects, algae, and minerals.[2] On this trip, he planned to lay a wreath, not for the first time, at the foot of Peary's remote monument at Cape York, Greenland. On board were nine students from the usual elite boarding schools and colleges on the eastern seaboard of the United States.

A more lucrative trip took place in 1940 as war raged in Europe. Eleven students and several scientists accompanied Bartlett, along with a cow, three turkeys, and six chickens, gifts for Mary Jemima in Brigus.[3] A small crowd of about 30, primarily relatives of the boys, saw them off from New York. Bartlett still used mostly sail; the *Morrissey* was capable of only 6 knots.[4] Bartlett's report from Greenland to the New York *Times* was lyrical, perhaps even purple and fanciful, the writing of a lover of words: "Early in the morning we saw a beautiful rainbow extending from the eastern to the western horizon, and the previous day a marvelous display of northern lights unusual for this time of year ... It was weather that would make a West Indies cruise agent turn green with envy as under tropic-appearing skies, with a smooth sea, we footed our way north while a glorious Apollo cavorted through a sky of cerulean blue ... On the deck of the *Morrissey* we felt like Cortez when he stared at the Pacific and all his men stared at each other in wild surmise; only we, not silent as he and his men, on a peak in Darien, but on the deck of the *Morrissey* were joyful."[5] Here Bartlett located himself, perhaps not quite consciously, as an inheritor of Spanish nobleman and conquistador Hernán Cortés de Monroy y Pizarro, who defeated the Aztecs and whose arrival signalled the colonization of the Americas.

Less than a decade away from his death, Bartlett had no drama to write about—there were not even any seals or polar bears around—but it did not bother him. He was just as content to sink into the spirituality of the Arctic. The passage above, which, unlike his books, was written by Bartlett, shows clearly that he should have been left to write his memoirs himself. If that had been the case—and if he had agreed—the books would have contained another layer of Arctic life which is sadly missing from his chatty and shallow, if entertaining, tomes, *The Log of Bob Bartlett* and *Sails over Ice*.

The Arctic serenity of 1940 aside, Bartlett had not seen the last of his maritime adventures. In 1944 he wrote a thank-you letter to the Explorers Club for featuring his image on the back cover of the club's journal. He could not resist recounting the troubles he had had from 23 October to 12 November 1944 as the *Morrissey* struggled south to Boston; he nearly suffered another tragedy, this one close to home. At Gloucester, Massachusetts, Bartlett wrote, "Gale after gale, hurricane force at times ... the glass, twice down to 28 24.* Lost my sails, smashed my no. 1 launch ... She is a wonderful little schooner. A sea broke over us, and landed the mainsail, breaking the main boom and gaff. My brother Will mate was washed overboard; but his number wasn't up so we got him back."[6] Despite his professional commitment to image-making, Bartlett never lost his penchant for understatement.

Following his 1940 pilgrimage to Cape York, Bartlett wrote of Peary's lofty Arctic monument, "it stands, sublime and majestic."[7] The admiral had been dead for two decades but Bartlett continued to praise him. Peary had ensured that Inuit became more efficient hunters, he proclaimed, by introducing guns to the Cape York Inuit and importing more dogs. "And the improved diet showed in the years during which Peary took observations, a

---

* Sailors frequently checked the barometer to help forecast weather; a rising of falling barometer number indicates a change in weather was imminent. The speed of the change in the number reading also indicates weather developments. In this case, Bartlett was concerned that the weather was deteriorating.

marked decrease in the death rate and a sharp increase in the birth rate," he wrote.[8] Peary was, in a small way, directly responsible for the higher birth rate, but Bartlett did not mention this. Instead he claimed: "All of this Peary noted with pride and a warm heart, for he loved these sturdy and independent men of the North."[9] Peary's motives were not rooted in concern for Greenlandic Inuit, of course, but in his long-standing quest for fame and adulation. Bartlett even credited Peary with increasing life expectancy among the Greenland Inuit and bringing them "miraculous wealth."[10] In this, he assumed the generally accepted causation between income and health,[11] but he overlooked the independence and agency so prized by Inuit that exploration undermined. In fact, some scholars believe that self-determination is the most significant factor in shaping the health of Indigenous peoples.[12] In 2018, Inuit health is poor compared to that of most populations in the developed world, with high suicide rates[13] and other pressing problems.[14] Thus, the Arctic is a haunted landscape, its Indigenous people having been used by long-gone whalers, explorers, and missionaries and harmed by Canadian government policies that relocated entire communities and removed children to the south. Despite their obvious resilience, Inuit continue to live with abusive systems of power that impact their everyday lives, "especially when they are supposedly over and done with ... [and] their oppressive nature ... denied."[15]

By the 1940s, Bartlett had accrued many honours and would continue to do so. Bowdoin College, Peary's alma mater, gave Bartlett an honorary Masters degree in 1920 for, among his other achievements, "reaching the farthest north of any man of the white race except the great explorer himself."[16] Despite his mixed feelings about all things British, such as the *Karluk*'s John Hadley, Bartlett accepted a special medal from the Royal Geographic Society.[17] He appreciated the practical value of honours; they could not help but advance his career. Perhaps the most meaningful award Bartlett received was the rare Hubbard Gold Medal of the National Geographic Society, which he was given in 1909, three years after Peary had been its recipient. At the time only Roald Amundsen, the Norwegian who had beaten Scott to the South Pole, and Peary had received the medal; afterwards it went to Sir Ernest Shackleton, Richard Byrd, Charles and Anne Morrow Lindbergh, Neil Armstrong, and rather belatedly—well after his death—Matthew Henson. Bartlett would have been pleased that scientists like Richard Leakey and Jane Goodall were later recipients, given his love of science. Edward Shackleton, the explorer son of Sir Ernest Shackleton, said of Bartlett, with some truth, "He did, in fact, provide the link between the heroic age of exploration and modern scientific development."[18]

Bartlett did get two influential explorers, Peary and Stefansson, high into the Arctic, where they made their mark by laying the groundwork for contemporary claims of sovereignty by Canada, Denmark, and other countries on the Arctic. Bartlett made sure to locate himself in the history of exploration, referring, in particular, to De Long in his *Karluk* narratives and, in 1934, notifying the media that he was to follow the course taken a century before by Captain William Parry, who had searched for the Northwest Passage, and Commander George Francis Lyon, who had tried to reach the North Pole.[*19]

Awards are at least partly a matter of politics and fashion, which Bartlett understood. Bartlett would have been genuinely delighted, though, that a marine species found in Labrador and Greenland was named after him. *Elphidium Bartletti* has a pretty shell with a spoke and wheel pattern.[20] Bartlett had collected this specimen on one of his 16 Arctic trips in the *Morrissey*. Bartlett's contribution to science is often overlooked, yet it is difficult to overestimate. Science was and is integral to the colonization of non-western locales, in this case, the Arctic. As Edward Said pointed out in *Orientalism* (1978) and, later, Linda Tuhiwai Smith in *Decolonizing Methodologies* (2012), the collection and classification of everything material in "undiscovered" places render these places subordinate to the countries of the West. As Egypt, for instance, was subsumed into the catalogue of European properties through the compilation of the 23-volume *Description d'Égypte*,[21] so the Arctic became a western possession through the ongoing and systematic scientific research that followed "discovery" and exploration. Bartlett, a man of his time who did not question the legitimacy of international goals regarding the Arctic, was responsible for filling numerous American museums with Arctic plant, animal, and mineral specimens. Indeed, "to survey Captain Bartlett's scientific collections is to

---

*   The Fury and Hecla Strait in what is now Nunavut is named for the ships that carried these explorers to the Arctic.

review the biology of the Arctic regions."[22] Understanding the impact of his scientific work and its place in his legacy, Bartlett was meticulous in this work and he made sure that those under him were just as careful. A curator at the National Herbarium described Bartlett's large 1938 collection as "beautifully prepared and selected."[23] Years after the specimens had been collected, none had a trace of mould, an achievement in itself.

With the United States at war after the Japanese attack on Pearl Harbor on 7 December 1941, Bartlett was, once again, in the service of the United States military. President Roosevelt gave him carte blanche to acquire whatever services and materials he needed, "no questions asked."[24] "Servicing Arctic Airbases," one of the last articles attributed to Bartlett, was published in *National Geographic* a month after he died.[25] Bartlett surely wrote the piece; his gruffness and his love of the sardonic, which escalated in his later years, comes through. Of Elizabethan explorer Martin Frobisher, who sought a route to India, Bartlett wrote, "Any one of the native Eskimo natives, who decoyed away five members of his crew, could have told him he was in a blind alley."[26] Like his devotion to Peary, Bartlett's respect for Inuit knowledge, cemented through the cruel journey he shared with Kataktovik, did not flag.

But, like the Victorians, Bartlett located Inuit knowledge in the past. Anthropologists and others believed that Inuit knowledge could not be part of the contemporary world and that it was fixed, rather than adaptable and changing, as most cultures are. Because he was a pragmatist, Bartlett was firmly in favour of the new and the modern, which he saw in opposition to Inuitness. He also rigidly situated Inuit in the north; westerners could go to the Arctic but Inuit were restricted to their own geography. While few narratives explained Indigenous accomplishments, an exception to this is the lavish praise Bartlett heaped on the Chukchi of Siberia, though he treated them as a collective, not individuals.

Bartlett became a guilty bystander vis-à-vis the Inuit as well, most notably in the troubling case of the displacement of Minik Wallace and in neglecting to give full credit for the traumatic hike to Siberia with Kataktovik. Kataktovik was left a fixture of the Arctic; his story did not feature on the world stage as other, western, polar explorers' stories did. He took other Inuit accomplishments for granted; Kiruk, for instance, likely saved lives with her production of completely watertight boots and warm clothing, all featuring "superlative" needlework.[27] These questions would not have troubled or even occurred to Bartlett because he was so shaped by and immersed in the exploration culture of white male privilege and western entitlement.

As World War II—and his own life—drew to a close, Bartlett sang the praises of radar. In 1946, he waxed enthusiastically about radio, recalling that, many years before, the *Windward* had been completely out of touch for a year and a half.[28] In contrast, *Morrissey* crew members received news from home so regularly that a week without a message was an anomaly. During Bartlett's five decades at sea, he embraced numerous new technologies, including the gyrocompass and the fathometer in addition to radio and radar.

He used ghost writers for his books and some articles, including, on one occasion, John Holman, president of the Audubon Society in Connecticut. Bartlett himself wrote on the topics he cared about, such as the scientific articles that appeared in the *National Geographic* and the *Journal of Mammalogy* under his byline.[29] These featured details about walruses, seals, shipboard life, the Inuit, and Arctic history, and they had Bartlett's tone. In "Newfoundland Seals," Bartlett provided an extensive description of harp and hood seals, including their size, behaviour, whelping grounds, and diet.[30] Showing characteristic ardour for anything Arctic, Bartlett wrote, "Imagine an anxious mother after a hard day's fishing, first finding the ice, which may have drifted a few miles since morning, then selecting its own particular hole out of perhaps 250,000 … but the mother invariably knows her own offspring and cannot be deceived."[31] He also reported that, despite their fierce and quarrelsome natures, hood seals surprisingly and conscientiously avoided the docile harps.[32]

Bartlett could not be bothered to write puff pieces, such as a requested story on pipe smoking in the Arctic for the Pipe and Tobacco Guild. He knew the value of these commissions in generating income, however, so he downloaded the work to struggling writers in New York.[33] At times his involvement in publishing and other ventures bordered on the cynical such as when, in 1931, he became assistant editor at Pathé News, the British producer of newsreels, cinema magazines, and documentaries, at $75 a week.[34] Bartlett's agreement with Pathé gave him no fixed responsibilities and promised that his position would not interfere with his other work; the only condition was that, for the one-year duration of the contract, he do no other motion picture work for anyone else. As the company's Courtland Smith wrote to him, "You know my purpose in making this offer and I know your purpose in accepting it ...":[35] the use of Bartlett's name in publicity. Perhaps Bartlett's foray into the film world would have produced more than just *White Thunder* were it not for the Great Depression. More likely, Bartlett had realized the medium did not suit him.

The ghost-written *Sails over Ice* was published in 1934. According to New York *Times* reviewer Henry E. Armstrong, "[Bartlett] makes no pretensions of literary gifts. Still it should be borne in mind that the captain had a high school education and finished at the Methodist College, St. John's, Newfoundland."[36] Not unusual for a writer from New York, the reviewer was particularly interested in the *Morrissey* as a destination for the who's who of the city; he listed many of her famous passengers, including the ubiquitous Harry Whitney, Arthur Dickinson Norcross (the musician-politician who was a first cousin of poet Emily Dickinson), American Museum of Natural History curator Junius Bird (who may have inspired the Indiana Jones movies), archeologist Donald Cadzow (a specialist in Indigenous people's histories), and Lawrence Gould, the geologist who went to Antarctica with Byrd. Bartlett's status as an adjunct of the east coast elite had solidified, which certainly attracted attention to his books and his other exploits.

Bartlett's father, Captain William, a scion of the Newfoundland sealing fleet, died suddenly in the summer of 1931. Bartlett was in Greenland when he got the news in a cable. He turned to form and ritual for comfort, immediately lowering the *Morrissey*'s flag to half-mast and tolling her bell every two minutes. He gathered his brother, Will, and his nephews, Robert Dove and Jack Angel, in his cabin, where they read Psalm 90, a prayer of Moses.[37] A text of lament and resignation, the verse begins, "Lord, thou hast been our dwelling-place in all generations ... thou art God." Captain William was the product of a rigid, if not cold, upbringing and he inhabited a hyper-masculine world at sea his entire life; he was rarely kind to his sons and daughters. Even so, he had been helpful in his way to his children, notably as Bartlett recovered from the shock of the *Corisande*. Because of this, Bartlett's natural diffidence, and the persistent and pervasive tradition of family loyalty, Bartlett never spoke ill of his father and often spoke well of him.

Bartlett and his brother Will were always close but they drew nearer to each other in the aftermath of Captain William's death. Their own mortality was becoming apparent; Bartlett was 56 by this point. Despite Will's owning and running a farm in Brigus, the two spent every summer together on the *Morrissey* and through the 1930s, Will often dashed off several letters to his brother every week. Will used "Willowon Farm" letterhead that noted his Tom Barron leghorns, New Hampshire reds, Toulouse geese, Peking ducks, and Guernsey cows. Will's letters, some as long as seven pages,[38] and those of his American wife, Ethel, were filled with jolly details about cows, ducks, and pigs, including happy news about Willowon's 14 prizes at a single Brigus Agricultural Fair[39] and their fresh pork going to the front on Job Brothers' sealing ships.[40] The couple practiced the noblesse oblige that was considered a family virtue; they married in their 40s and did not have children, but Ethel once threw a party for 20 of her young neighbours, stating, "Poor kids, they don't have any too much."[41] Also in character, both brothers tried to find work for men who had been faithful to their father.[42]

Mary Jemima died in 1943, three years before her eldest son. The mother of 11 children, she was robust despite her petite frame, and she had enjoyed good health all her life. But in 1934, her son-in-law Fred Angel noticed she was "getting a wee bit smaller."[43]* Five years later, her son Lewis, Bartlett's youngest surviving brother, said Mary Jemima loved listening to hockey games on the radio and collecting recipes.[44] And in 1935, her daughter Eleanor claimed she was "as vain over her powder and soap, etc. as a flapper."[45]

Mary Jemima was eulogized as the last representative of the generation that had made Brigus "the peer of any town in our country,"[46] although Brigus was, in fact, well established by the time of her birth and it was in decline as she aged. Her son Bob Bartlett raised her status, very deliberately so, and their relationship was acknowledged in her eulogy in the Methodist

---

*   Presumably Mary Jemima's skeleton was shrinking, as it sometimes does in the elderly as a result of bone loss.

Church as "an affinity of souls."[47] The two wrote to each other almost daily, Bartlett in a large confident script that closely resembled his mother's. At times Mary Jemima's tone was excitable and youthful; one letter began "Here I am! Home again!"[48] Often her writing was gossipy, with tidbits of news about neighbours, the goings-on of the various fishing and sealing firms, and politician friends like Newfoundland's second last prime minister, Sir Richard Anderson Squires, whose actions are credited at least to a degree with the fall of the Dominion's democracy.

Part of Bartlett's adoration of Mary Jemima must be attributed to the contrast between her and her husband, who would never have addressed his son "My Darling Bob," or anything like it, as she did.[49] Mary Jemima also gave Bartlett leeway that Captain William would never have afforded him; she accepted his decision to reject the career she had chosen for him. On her son's 13th birthday in 1888, she wrote with the skill and balance of an experienced diplomat, "You have not as yet any decisive bias with regard to your future. But you already know that deep in your Mother's heart lay the cherished hope that you will be called and trained for the Pulpit. Be a Christian. Study theology and work for God is the sincere wish and prayer of your loving Mother, M.J. Bartlett."[50] In letting go of her long-standing ambition for her firstborn, Mary Jemima made it clear that she accepted him. Bartlett rarely felt such acceptance elsewhere, in part because he allowed so few to get to know him, out of fear of rejection.

At Mary Jemima's funeral, the minister cited Bartlett's career as the reason for their long separations.[51] The explorer's position gave him leeway to be absent from the event, although it is unlikely that less famous sons or daughters would have been excused. Bartlett had seen Mary Jemima not long before her death and wrote afterward in a letter to a friend of Eleanor's, "Everything is allright."[52] He quoted the romantic poet William Cullen Bryant in adding, "She left us while the soft memory of her virtues yet lingered like twilight hues when the bright sun is set."[53] Mary Jemima had suffered ill health for only a few days, all the while attended to by Will and Ethel, before she succumbed. In Bartlett's words, "At Brigus she had what money could not buy; she had true love, devotion, and the cottage, comfortable, all the family were there, I was the only one that was not at her bedside when she left. Eleanor's letter describing that scene is the grandest thing I have ever read."[54] With his mother's death, Emma and Eleanor become Bartlett's sole heirs, although the Great Depression had been tough and there was not much to inherit.[55]

Bartlett never diverged from the sentimentality that imbued his relationship with Mary Jemima and that also marked his memories of Peary. After Mary Jemima died, he expressed regret that she and Peary had never met. He imagined such a scene occurring at Hawthorne Cottage with Mary Jemima putting on display her old silver tea set, her silver tea caddy, and her Wedgewood cups and saucers. The two would have spoken of Mary Jemima's Dorset and Channel Island ancestors, he mused. Peary would have been resplendent in "all his regimentals."[56] Mary Jemima, he reflected, "was to the manor born. A Grand Lady. A Queen in her own right."[57]

With the Arctic and his mother, Mary Jemima, a close second and third, the *Morrissey* remained Bartlett's true love. In 1933, Bartlett demonstrated again that he did not need ghost writers, writing revealingly and allowing a glimpse into his spirituality when he penned these words from the top of the world:

> Tonight, perched ninety feet above the deck of my little Morrissey, I was permitted to see a never-to-be-forgotten sight. The Strait of the Fury and Hecla runs east and west, and Old Sol, stowing himself away for the night, went down behind the many floating pieces of ice in one blaze of glory. If I were able and could paint the land on both sides, especially the coloring, it would be a thing of beauty and a joy forever to the owner.
>
> Not a sign of new snowfall or any from last season. The shadows deepening from scarlet to purple, then fading into the blackness of night. All around was quiet save for the occasional splash of disintegrating and the ha-ha-has of the red-throated loon teaching her young to fly. In the lines of Shelley, "They made stiller with their sound the inviolable quietness."[58]

Bartlett thus laid bare the Wordsworthian nature of his spirituality. As the Lake District of England revealed God to the poet, so the Arctic revealed divinity to Bartlett. He had long since outgrown Captain William's abstentious Methodism and his grandfather Abram's violent puritanism. With prescience and a sensitivity that few would have expected, he wrote to a friend, "Perhaps it's inevitable that the peoples of the Earth should be destroyed. If it did come, the Sun would shine; the Birds would multiply and sing as well as ever; animals would have a grand time; no one killing them with firearms."[59] Yet he did not entirely throw away the beliefs of his forefathers. In his last years, as the theatre of war expanded, he crustily condemned "easy living, selfishness, greed, lack of discipline in homes [and] in Public life."[60] He remained a Christian, and his respect for Jesus grew as he aged, and he opined that humanity had never been further from Christ than it was during the bleak days of World War II.[61]

Bartlett's lyrical observations about Old Man Sol and the red-throated loon sprung from a peacefulness that he rarely felt. Yet most of his friends and acquaintances seemed not to understand that about him. Many considered him an eccentric and perhaps did not think further about his well of emotions. "What a charmed life you have," his friend Sister M. Rita had written him from Newfoundland.[62] Philip Gibbs went further, and ironically wrote of him in 1910 following an interview in London, "When I met Captain Bartlett I thought of 'Chains.' For here was an unchained man. Unfettered and unmanacled, he stood free, body and soul."[63] In truth, Bartlett was never free. He and Gibbs met on Fleet Street, with its crowded pubs and busy newspaper offices and the massive dome of St. Paul's Cathedral in the near distance. As they talked, Bartlett criticized the hurly-burly of civilization. Gibbs interpreted this to mean that Bartlett had liberated himself from the strictures of society. Indeed, Bartlett had once told his friend Daniel Henderson, "I did hate to come back here to 40th Street and Park [Avenue]."[64]

But that is a simplified, one-dimensional version of Bartlett's reality. He was not running away from anywhere; he was running to somewhere: the Arctic. As anyone who has ever spent time in the north will agree, it offers a series of beautiful and compelling sights: scurrying white foxes, loping bears, endless barrens, glistening ice, sparkling snow, huge cloudless skies, bold moons, and, of course, the hypnotic aurora borealis. Bartlett's description of being in the Arctic is worth contemplating: "One feels free, unstifled. Nature is very close to one. It is fine to be natural. Of course, there are things up against one, the things in one's own nature. Passion sometimes leaps up at a man's throat ... You have to get so very close to your own nature that you have to master it or it masters you. But you are a man, not a dummy. Everything in your manhood tells—your strength of body and heart. It is all pretty simple. The world is wide enough for you ... You get a kind of understanding of the things behind life."[65] It was the otherworldliness of the Arctic that drew Bartlett, as it did, ironically, Peary's rival Frederick Cook, who wrote that the Arctic made him realize "the greatest mystery and the greatest unknown is not beyond the frontiers of knowledge but that unknown capacity in the spirit within the inner man of self ... Therein is the greatest field for exploration."[66] Just as Bartlett had had to face himself in the hospital bed and turn away from alcoholism, the Arctic brought him in close proximity with himself, his flaws, his strengths, and his loneliness. This experience, which became ritualized through his annual trips, allowed him to make peace with himself.

Western culture emphasizes the individual, but Indigenous and other collectively oriented cultures recognize that the individual is never enough. Perhaps this emphasis on the individual can lead to feelings of solitariness or isolation, causing those with the means necessary to push themselves and to seek something that is missing but cannot be readily identified. Regardless, Bartlett's and Cook's sentiments about the Arctic were heartfelt. Bartlett was erratic in his servicing of relationships—friends never knew if or when they would hear from him and he often disappeared for long stretches.[67] Frequently a great deal of time passed between correspondences. Numerous notes abound in Bartlett's papers from friends who had been unsuccessfully attempting to contact the explorer.[68] Normally, they would drop by the Murray Hill Hotel or phone to be told that Bartlett was out or "astray," as Reynold Spriggs put it.[69] L.B. Mann used humour to provoke Bartlett into contacting him: "Dear Captain: February came, but no Bob Bartlett; March, April, May & June, the same. And now I suppose he is standing on the bridge with his feet wide apart, picking his way up in the Far North, but we will be here sometime next Fall, when he comes West again."[70] Bartlett shunned company when he could have had it. He was, in the words of Jack Angel, "a lonely man."[71] Bartlett's loneliness was lifted by few things: the Arctic, the company of kin, and puttering about alone on the *Morrissey* in New York

Harbour. Bartlett told Gibbs he never felt lonely on the icefields and in that he would not have been playing up for the press.

Bartlett was an introvert, veering to the extreme end of the scale, virtually unable to derive serenity or genuine pleasure from the comfort of others, save his family; he derived energy from quietness and from his own company. David Nutt was an exception. Like many introverts, Bartlett was given to judgment and prone to feeling easily overwhelmed by noise and chatter. As Angel put it, "You had to remain on the out, you know, you had to, he didn't like anybody to have too much to say, particularly if the person didn't have a real right to say anything. So you would know when to talk and when not to talk. And he respected that and he thought a lot of it. He didn't like anybody who talked too much. He used to get upset about it."[72] He often ignored invitations. At least a few of his acquaintances perceived this crucial aspect of Bartlett's psychology and put a great deal of effort into their invitations. Joseph Robinson's* plea to attend a party is an example of this:

> [Y]ou're a darling, and sweet is the praise of an honest friend. After making you, God must have stood around all day feeling good. Come with me as my guest to the [Explorers] Club's Bean party the 15th instant ... We'll have a whale of a time— men only. Pumpkin pie, fresh cider etc. served with plenty of tasty beans, plenty of coffee, hot biscuits and butter, in the Club rooms decorated with corn stalks and pumpkin lanterns. Do accept please. A house party at the Club would be sorely lacking without you. The entire Club delights in your presence, as do I.[73]

Bartlett's elusiveness was rooted in his appetite for solitude, something that he shared with Thoreau, and that the Arctic afforded him in abundance. Bartlett has status in the narrative arc of Arctic exploration but his qualities as a philosopher of nature are less well known. In contrast to other explorers, the Arctic was never his adversary. He had the keen observational skills of writer Barry Lopez and, like Lopez, was able to articulate a vivid

---

*   Joseph's son, Bradley, met Matthew Henson at Bartlett's funeral and was inspired to write *Dark Companion*, published in 1948 (Rusty Robinson, "Why Matt Is Special," January 2000, http://www.matthewhenson.com/whymatt.htm).

sense of place.[74] He had Annie Dillard's sense of the wonder of nature in spades[75] and was constantly renewed by discoveries, small and large. A tiny Arctic plant could enthrall him, as could the hunting skill of the Inuit or the overwhelming northern sky. As the *Karluk* lay jammed in Arctic ice, Bartlett took comfort in Dean Hole's *A Book of Roses*.[76] McKinley, the expedition's meteorologist, wrote of that tortuous time, "I never made any attempt to invade the privacy of his cabin, but sometimes he invited me along ... we sat, in the midst of limitless ice, with between 60 and 70 degrees Fahrenheit of frost outside, in perpetual darkness, numberless miles from the nearest garden, talking about roses."[77]

Bartlett was a central figure in the history of the Explorers Club in New York. In 2018 its headquarters occupies a building on 46 East 70th Street, erected in 1910 by the co-founder of the Singer Sewing Machine Company.[78] In Bartlett's day it was housed at 345 Amsterdam Avenue,[79] a short stroll from the American Museum of Natural History. The club was founded in 1904, when Bartlett was in the early stages of his polar exploration career.[80] Today the Club's décor and eccentric collections hint at the atmosphere that would have attracted Bartlett: In 2014, a massive painting entitled "Woolly Rhinoceros" dominated the lounge and bar; in the library, a depiction of the Greely rescue would have reminded Bartlett of Captain William Norman of Brigus; a stuffed polar bear and a huge bell from the former sealer and United States Coast Guard cutter *Bear*, in which Bartlett had been a passenger in the *Karluk* rescue attempt, were elsewhere. The library held a collection of some 13,000 books.[81] Bartlett often had his mail sent to the club, he dropped by to meet friends and to dip into one volume or another, and he attended many formal and more informal dinners there.

This was the kind of exclusively male environment in which Bartlett was most comfortable, and he was not alone in that. With over 100 other well-known American men, Bartlett lent his name to a publication called *The Stag Cook Book: A Man's Cook Book for Men*, which featured his fresh Labrador codfish recipe*—even though Bartlett lived in a hotel, where he

---

* Bartlett's recipe appeared on page 42: "Here is my favorite dish. Viz.:–Fresh Labrador codfish caught during the capelin school [scull]. Place a small bake pot upon a wood fire; then take a few strips of pork fat, cut up into small pieces, and put into the bake pot. When the pork fat has melted, you cut the fish into several small pieces and place in the pot. In about twenty minutes the fish is cooked. The fish must be eaten from the pot with a wooden spoon."

could not cook. Other contributors included Warren Harding, the 29th president of the United States, who would serve another year before he died in office; Harry Houdini, who favoured scalloped mushrooms and devilled eggs; Daniel Beard, the founder of the Sons of Daniel Boone (later to become the Boy Scouts of America); Chick Evans, the celebrated amateur golfer, who offered a tomato soup recipe; Charlie Chaplin with steak and kidney pie; and actor Douglas Fairbanks.[82] The book was published in 1922, when Bartlett was at his low point; it shows that he was not yet beyond the pale as far as publishers were concerned, although his recovery would not begin for another two years. The thrust of the cookbook demonstrates the continuing importance of masculinity in society. The book appeared coincidentally with the granting of female suffrage; thus, it may be seen as an attempted hedge against the post-war decline of male hegemony. The Explorers Club, which continued to advance the male-dominated field of exploration, may be seen in the same light.

While the Explorers Club belongs on Bartlett's personal map of New York, he had his troubles with it, too, especially after Peary's death, for not all members shared his devotion to the admiral. Bartlett told one of his biographers how he had argued strongly for Peary's claim to have reached the Pole;[83] all the while Bartlett clung to his long-term habit of managing to ignore the obvious questions about the claim. Bartlett was resentful but did not have a strong retort when Explorer Club members pointed out that he had not been with Peary at the Pole and therefore could not possibly be as certain as he claimed. Bartlett was always esteemed by the club and, seven years after his death, it donated the significant sum of $2,400 to Memorial College, now University, of Newfoundland in his honour.[84]

While Bartlett was more at home with silence and solitude than the social whirl, his career demanded the social skills of an extrovert and he could enjoy the company of others, though most often in one-on-one encounters. His agendas reflect all these conflicting factors. In 1919, at a low point in his life, his sister Eleanor visited him in New York. Together they went to the Explorers Club and, as both were interested in modernity and innovation, the Automobile Club.[85] That year's little black agenda featured sporadic appointments with people such as "Miss Bell," whom he met at the Plaza at 8 p.m. on 2 May, and "Miss Land," but there was also a great deal of math accounting for the cost of food.[86] In December, Bartlett skipped breakfast one day and dinner the next.[87] This was not a good time for him; Peary was dying, he was essentially unemployed, and he was drinking to soothe himself.

Twenty years later, things had vastly improved; Bartlett hobnobbed with the elite and had his choice of dinner invitations. On a November day in 1939, just after war had broken out in Europe, Bartlett had lunch at a coffee house with lecture agent Briant Sando and then dinner with friends Ed and Susie at their home.[88] The next day he lunched with George Moffett and met David Nutt at Grand Central Station.[89] Later in the week, Bartlett and Nutt went to a museum with Warner Hertz and then to Scarsdale and Long Island.[90] A month before, Bartlett had socialized with some of his more famous friends, attending a reception at the Hotel St. Regis with George Putnam, Amelia Earhart's widower, and a horse show with Ruly Carpenter, who would purchase the Philadelphia Phillies in 1943.[91] On 11 and 12 November, he worked all day in his room and pumped out the *Morrissey* on 13 November.[92] December was slower and Bartlett spent Christmas Day at three separate locations, all the homes of friends.[93] His darkest days were behind him. Still, he remained an outsider and an odd sock. He once attended an Explorers Club dinner in his honour without having RSVPed; he spent the first part of the dinner wandering around looking for his seat, although none had been set out for him. "I didn't know you had to write in and say you were coming to your own dinner," he explained, bewildered.[94]

Bartlett's restlessness and the kernel of unhappiness that dogged him may have had roots in his sexuality. A vague and passing claim from one of his biographers, that Bartlett had been engaged to a distant relative, does not ring true.[95] If Bartlett's sexuality was anything but rigidly heterosexual, this would have sat very uneasily with him, as a Bartlett, a seaman, an explorer, and a native of Brigus. But some people suspected he was gay. At least some in Brigus viewed his practice of writing to his mother every day with suspicion. One elderly citizen who remembered Bartlett referred to the letter-writing: "What was that all about? That'd tell you something. His friends said did you hear him say 'all on board!' in his high-pitched voice."[96] This statement was made in Brigus six decades after Bartlett's death, which testifies to the staying power of the local moral code and the enduring nature of gossip and judgment.

Bartlett's best girl was always his mother, said Newfoundland's lieutenant-governor Sir Leonard Outerbridge in 1979. In 2009, the beloved Newfoundland author Paul O'Neill reported that politician Peter Cashin told him Bartlett was homosexual. According to O'Neill, "Peter would know because he was in politics and all that."[97] Daniel Henderson once described Bartlett as a bachelor who could not be captured.[98] Bartlett's papers at Bowdoin College contain several stock Valentine cards. One reads, "Just a story of warm affection / and happy wishes too / For my Valentine Book of Remembrance / Where I keep sweet thoughts of you."[99] Although the card was unsigned, the "I" was crossed out to be replaced by a "We," suggesting that it, like other cards sent to Bartlett, was a token of friendship rather than a romantic gesture. Another card was more personalized and therefore more intriguing, having been signed "From one who thinks a lot of you."[100] Yet Bartlett's claim, made as late as 1945, to have "sent [Valentines] to my Girl Friends"[101] seems disingenuous. Bartlett had to have known that talk about his sexuality circulated, and it no doubt added to the store of insecurity he carried through life.

Philip Gibbs, who was so fascinated with Bartlett, characterized him as Pan, the Greek god of the wild. The irony is that Pan is associated with nymphs, female nature deities, and Bartlett shied away from women his entire life, except his mother, sisters, and grandmothers. He could not and did not entirely avoid women, however. The casual manner Llewella Kitchell used in her letters to Bartlett suggests that the lecture organizer enjoyed an easy relationship with him, although Kitchell was so flamboyant she probably had such relationships with everyone she encountered. The same is true of a typist from Connecticut called Anne who signed one of her letters, "Thank you, You Old Dear ..."[102] Sister Rita, his nun correspondent in Newfoundland, addressed her letters "My dear Capt. Bob" and signed them "V. sincerely yours." These words reflect the women's own relaxed manners, not Bartlett's personality. Though he was no oil painting, as the expression goes, it is not improbable that some women were attracted to Bartlett, including young women. Sara Lee Tuck dropped by the Murray Hill Hotel sometime in 1938 and left a note for him, which read, rather mournfully, "I wish my name has not faded from your memory in the interval since you visited us at Yama Farms."[103] Sara Lee left her new address as West 67th Street, New York. But Bartlett was unattainable. Many women flirted with him, the mothers of some of the boys he took north among them. But he ignored them.

Excepting his favourite niece, Hilda Dove, the only women Bartlett ever sailed with were Marie Peary Stafford, who, as Peary's daughter, got a pass, and explorer Louise Arner Boyd, a California native. Bartlett worked with Boyd when both were employees of the United States government in World War II. Before this, he dismissively referred to her as "a dollar a year woman,"[104] implying that Boyd was a figurehead instead of the accomplished explorer and leader that she was. Like Bartlett, Boyd received international awards, in her case from the governments of France and Norway.[105] The two had much in common; besides their insatiable thirst for the Arctic and adventure, they lived unconventional lives. In addition, they were both writers. Boyd published two books with the American Geographic Society; one, *The Coast of Northeast Greenland with Hydrographic Studies in the Greenland Sea*,[106] reflected her skill as a cartographer. But the two did not get along, their similarities perhaps contributing to the friction between them.

Bartlett's disapproval of Boyd was transparent when he had to be persuaded to attend a dinner in her honour. He turned down an invitation from Ena L. Yonge, who had written on behalf of the Women Geographers section of the American Geographical Society in New York,[107] and it is a challenge to visualize Bartlett's enjoying the least measure of comfort in a roomful of women. Marie Peary Stafford had the measure of him and knew which buttons to push to get him to attend. She implored, "I am to be toastmistress, you know, the first time I've tried it, and I need you there for moral support. Besides, it makes me furious to have people say you won't appear where Stefansson is. He hasn't anything on you; don't let him bluff you out of parties where you really should appear. You are every bit as important as he is and three times as amusing. Do be a sport now and come."[108] It is impossible to know if Bartlett got over his reservations and went to the dinner but if anyone could cajole him to go, it would be the daughter of Robert Peary.

It is doubtful that he could ever have accommodated a female explorer and, because of his sexism, his relationship with Boyd never flourished. During their 1941 Arctic voyage, with Boyd acting as military consultant, Bartlett called her "Miss Boyd" in the early days but this deteriorated to a condescending "Maggie" by the time they were back in port. Boyd's mandate to collect intelligence necessitated secrecy, which "really irked" Bartlett.[109] Very wealthy and respected by the scientific community, Boyd may have been snobbish but she was in an unenviable position as the only woman on board ship for four long months. Afterwards, she and Bartlett disputed costs and armed themselves with lawyers. As geographer Joanna Kafarowski has pointed out, these two never-married well-read Arctic aficionados should have enjoyed each other's company. Yet Bartlett called Boyd "a dammed old hog" and said she "laughed like a crow."[110] In his treatment of Boyd, Bartlett was at his worst.

Other explorers, notably Robert Peary and Matthew Henson, fathered children in Greenland, which was public knowledge. Although Peary encouraged fraternization, and Bartlett was in awe of him, there has been little discussion of whether Bartlett did the same. The long-held assumption is that he did not, being that he was too occupied with his duties to entertain such possibilities. Bartlett's obsession with secrecy might be relevant here, although he would have found it difficult to control the flow of information out of the Arctic. When S. Allen Counter brought the Greenlandic sons of Peary and Henson to the United States for a family reunion, there was no mention of any Bartlett offspring. It seems obvious from Counter's book that if an Inuit son or daughter had existed, this person would have been included in the reunion. No one made a paternity claim during Bartlett's lifetime, or at least none that was pursued or made public. Yet at least one Greenland family has long believed themselves to be Bartlett's descendants.[111] One such person, who approached the Historic Sites Association of Newfoundland and Labrador, lived in one of the northernmost towns in the world and was also the granddaughter of Qaavigarssuaq Kristiansen, an Inuk who hunted with Knud Rasmussen. It is unlikely that Bartlett impregnated any Greenlandic Inuit women; there is no evidence for this. By the time Bartlett was in Greenland with Peary, he was 34 years and had seen plenty of these alliances; by then, he would have seen them as nothing but trouble and that was enough to scare him off, even if he had been tempted.

Farther south, and much earlier, on 30 November 1895, Leah Mary Ings was born somewhere in Labrador, probably on the coast, as there was little settlement inland. Leah went to her death believing she was Bartlett's daughter. She wrote his name in her Bible, listing him as her father in the family tree (the Bible is now lost).[112] Leah's descendants* believed for many years that Leah was the daughter of Bartlett and an Inuit woman who was brought to Kettle Cove on the southern island of Twillingate, Newfoundland, where she was adopted by the Ings family. Recent DNA testing has determined that Leah had settler (or European) ancestry but no Inuit ancestry. The family's belief that she did reflects the fact of ongoing liaisons and relationships between Newfoundland fishermen and Labrador Inuit. Leah had no contact with Bartlett her entire life. Said her great-granddaughter, "Sadly none of us know Leah's mother's name. Unfortunately, [Leah] looks more like Capt. Bob than her mother ... Before she died, my grandmother, Leah's daughter, spoke a lot about Bartlett and how we were related to Judge Rupert Bartlett [Bob's nephew]. That, to her, was prestigious."[113]

At the time of Leah's birth, Bartlett was 21 and in the middle of his time in the West Indies and Mediterranean trade, in the wake of the *Corisande* wreck. His purpose then was to get enough time at sea to qualify for his papers. He took part in the seal hunt each year and in the spring of 1895 he was in the *Panther* with Captain William in the Gulf of St. Lawrence on an unusually unsuccessful quest for seals.[114] It was not until the end of the trip that they secured enough pelts to venture home.[115] It is possible that the seal hunt took Bartlett to the Labrador coast that year, but that was some distance from the Gulf. Still, the *Panther* might have stopped there to deliver mail, as she sometimes did, to pick people up or drop them off, or to get supplies. To sire Leah, Bartlett would have had to have been in Labrador by 1 April, since Leah was born in late November. It was too early for the Labrador fishing season. Another scenario well worth considering is that, like many contemporary Newfoundland and Labrador children, Leah might not have been baptized until quite some while after her birth. The date of her birth was recorded as

---

*   These women are first cousins once removed.

20 November, but it might have been the date of her baptism instead; this was a common occurrence for the time.* Leah could have been born any time in the preceding months, although a spring birth would be easier to reconcile with Bartlett's schedule, if Bartlett was her father.

Bartlett's sexuality—or the lack of it, a possibility which must be admitted—had, of course, no bearing on his physical ability to produce a child. He may have done so either in Labrador or in Greenland or both places, but questions linger about the circumstances as they are known today. Why would Bartlett, or someone else, bring his child to Twillingate, a town to which the Bartletts had no obvious connections? Why would they bring the child anywhere? Would not the baby have stayed with her mother, among her maternal relatives? How could Bartlett have shipped a baby to the island of Newfoundland without attracting a great deal of attention? After all, fishing ships returning home from Labrador were notoriously crowded with men, women, and children, all of whom were essential to the fishing economy, and the progress of these ships was always reported on in the Newfoundland media. Further, in the late 19th century, anything a Bartlett did was of general interest and made news. A crowded ship is not the best place to keep a secret.

On the other hand, Captain William was sufficiently well connected to prevent a story being leaked to the press and he would not have hesitated to exercise whatever sway he had in such a matter. Family reputation and his eldest son's career would have been far more important than a base-born child, who would have been considered a mistake that needed concealing, especially if there was some suspicion she had native ancestry. Leah's family believes she was hidden away in tiny Kettle Cove for these very reasons. After his extensive travels on the coasts of Newfoundland and Labrador, Captain William had contacts everywhere. Although there is no evidence he did so, he had the financial means to buy silence, if it was necessary. From Bartlett's perspective, there was the certain disapproval and, worse, disappointment that Mary Jemima would have felt and expressed if her son had fathered a child or children. If even one of the Greenland or the Labrador stories were true, Bartlett had Grandmother

---

* This was the case with my grandfather, for instance, who was born one year and baptized the next.

Leamon's determined ostracism of the Butlers to remind him of the kind of retribution he could expect.

Although Bartlett showed scarce interest in women later in life, he may have experimented as a youth in Labrador, as other young men from Newfoundland did, accidentally creating a web of family ties between the Labrador coast and Conception Bay on the island. Bartlett would have felt entitled to do so and he would have felt freer in Labrador, far away from any real or metaphorical constraints imposed by his mother and formidable grandmother. Conversely, we cannot conclude with certainty that he did not have a genuine relationship with a particular young woman in Labrador; many love matches occurred during the summer fishery, contributing to the lasting links between the island and Labrador. Perhaps Leah's mother died in childbirth, a not uncommon occurrence which would account for her absence in the child's life. Her remaining, apparently settler, family in Labrador might not have had the means to care for her. And while Bartlett seems not to have had a romantic bone in his body when it came to women, paternity in this case cannot be ruled out. With her long face and in the way she held her head, dark-haired Leah resembled Bartlett and his sister Triss. Her small mouth and her expression recalls theirs as well. Further, a photo (page 261) features Leah as an adult with a small blond girl, whose identity is unknown but is believed to be a relative of Leah's; with her long face, this child looks even more like the light-haired Bartlett.*

Leah's claim remains unresolved. Bartlett's lack of contact with his alleged daughter, though cowardly, if true, is not hard to explain, given the sense of entitlement that accompanied sexual liaisons in the Arctic and subarctic. Henson's and Peary's experience siring Indigenous children and then abandoning them is yet another reflection of the asymmetrical power relationship between explorers and local people, especially women. This relationship was marked by both class and gender imbalances, which were never questioned.

Even in 2018, this topic has been the subject of very little research and some resistance. There is at least one hint, however, that the possibility of sexual liaisons between his crew members and local, likely Inuit, women

---

*   Leah Ings married John Samuel Freake, her elder by four years, of Fogo Island, where the two raised a family.

Leah Mary (left) with an unknown child. Credit: Family of Leah Ings Freake.

caused Bartlett some anxiety. This is particularly true of his paying crew members, the boys from exclusive American colleges and prep schools whose parents would not have wanted to have grandchildren of what they considered dubious ancestry, no matter how far away these children were and how invisible they might be. A scandal of this nature involving one of his paying guests might well have ruined Bartlett and he worried about it, choosing his passengers as carefully as he could. Of one, he wrote, "Pete never gave me a moment[']s anxiety; and did his job faithfully. Perhaps he is not brilliant but he'll never be in jail; nor will he ever seduce any woman."[116] Fearing impropriety and its results, Bartlett hired crew members he knew well, virtually all of whom were, in his view, "clean living and God-fearing family men" from Brigus.[117]

Staying inside the lines was always a priority for Bartlett; he lacked the strong inner core and confidence necessary for social deviance. He might have been tempted, though, to go down what would have been for him and many men in his time a dangerous path. Though still a fuzzy concept for most people, throughout Bartlett's lifetime, homosexuality was illegal in most countries, including Canada and Britain. Sodomy, as it was called, was not decriminalized in all American states until 2003, a half-century after Bartlett's death. Bartlett's sexuality remains something of a mystery— and it might well have been a mystery to him as well—but the figure of LeRoy Gulotta has to be considered.

LeRoy Baker Gulotta was born in Nevada in September 1876, when Bartlett was 13 months old.[118] He was adopted by George and Alexandria Norcross, a couple living in Ward 14, New Orleans,[119] but he kept his birth name. Gulotta, who was white, was working as a cashier in 1900 and a clerk 10 years later.[120] He met Bartlett in New York where he had moved to begin a career as a writer; the two boarded at 292 (or 297*) Madison Avenue with the Davenel family and two other single men.[121] This rooming house was a stone's throw from the New York Public Library, an institution Bartlett cherished, and very close to the raucous 42nd Street. While living there, Gulotta listed his occupation as editor and told census takers he was in the employ of author Henry Woodhouse, who also lived in the house.[122] Woodhouse was

---

*   Gulotta referred to 297 Madison Avenue, while the 1920 Census lists his residence as 292 Madison Avenue; Gulotta was probably right since he mentioned the address repeatedly in his correspondence and he lived there.

born Mario Terenzio Enrico Casalegno in 1884 in Italy.[123] By the time he roomed with Bartlett and Gulotta, Woodhouse had served time for murder and he later carved out a lengthy career as a forger and frequent litigant.[124] Interestingly, Woodhouse's birthplace was Turin, home of another fake, the famous shroud said to have held the body of Jesus. Gulotta and Bartlett were in their 40s during the time they lived with Woodhouse.

Recalling their Madison Avenue days after he had moved to the midwest, Gulotta wrote to Bartlett: "While things were going well there at 297, we did well, you & I, didn't we?"[125] He continued, "It is true that no man ever stops to take stock in the heart of a cyclone—such as living in New York is. From my haven of rest and solitude here I can better measure the vista of hours, days, years passed at 297. They served a purpose, we know, as all things do. Not least of all they gave us most pleasant memories, which, rightly viewed, are as dear a possession as a mere bachelor ought to demand. And who can cherish associations more agreeable, congenial or happier than those you and I shared in our bachelor quarters side-by-side? For myself I propose to keep the memory green with frequent thoughts and smiles—& some day we can hitch up together and live them over again, elsewhere—as you used to suggest."[126]

Gulotta wrote these words from Valparaiso, Indiana, a county seat with the motto "Vale of Paradise," where he spent "heavenly fall days" farming.[127] He loved the purple clover and golden pumpkins and "the little gems of lakes" scattered among Indiana's rolling hills.[128] "Picture me roaming the country round, or lolling in the sun on a bed of sweet peppermint ... the world of 42nd St. in the dim far away."[129] It is tempting to conclude that Bartlett's and Gulotta's friendship was high in the catalogue of sins, as Evelyn Waugh once put it.[130] It is not hard to read Gulotta's words as a rationalization for activities that were generally considered beyond the pale in the early 20th century. In addition, Gulotta's retreat to Indiana was sudden and may have been the actions of a man fleeing an untenable situation, although he would rather have stayed. Once in the Midwest, he wrote tenderly to Bartlett, "One of the nicest feelings in life is to feel that one is missed. When I find an expression like that in your letter, it pleases me mightily, just as you intended it should."[131]

Like Bartlett, Gulotta loved nature; he wrote lyrically of an extended period of stillness as meadowlarks gathered near him and flirted with each other. In another epistle, he expounded at length to Eleanor Bartlett on the chickadee, a species of bird that had, he said, inspired Emerson to write: "This scrap of valor just for play / Fronts the north-wind in waistcoat gray / As if to shame my weak behaviour."[132] This was similar to the kind of literary allusions Bartlett was fond of making. Both Bartlett and Gulotta were reclusive and given to contemplation; Gulotta alluded to his "natural capacity to sit still for a long time."[133] They loved literature and Gulotta quoted Pope's "Ode to Solitude" in this letter to his friend back east: "Happy the man whose wish and care / a few paternal acres bound / content to breath his native air / In his own ground."[134] The irony is that one uprooted man wrote this to another; neither would live in their hometowns again.

And by this point, they had moved on from each other. Gulotta mentioned a nursing student he had met; by 1930, he had married her and they were living in Chicago.[135] Wilhelmina, the Iowa-born daughter of a German immigrant, was 36 when they married and Gulotta was 50.[136] They had no children and Wilhelmina built her nursing career, while Gulotta worked as a statistician in the grain industry,[137] an occupation that seems colourless next to his poetic description of meadowlarks to Bartlett. By 1940 Wilhelmina was assistant anesthetist at Lincoln General Hospital in Nebraska,* the state in which the couple spent the rest of their lives.[138] Gulotta died in 1958, 12 years after Bartlett passed away.[139]

When he wrote his heady letter to Bartlett in 1920, Gulotta said he wanted to tell Eleanor Bartlett about Wilhelmina, whom he had met early in his days in Indiana. "It does one good, in this rather flippant age, to find the fine & noble qualities in man or woman," he wrote Bartlett.[140] Gulotta may have wanted to share his good news with his friend's sister—or he may have wanted to reassure her that he had moved on from a relationship that could not last. Eleanor had visited Bartlett in 1919 and had met Gulotta. The level of intimacy shared by the two men, as evidenced in Gulotta's beautiful letter, is unusual for Bartlett. Further, it is touching and becomes heartbreaking if one reads this letter as the love letter it may well have been. It took great courage to be a gay man in 1920 and Bartlett lacked courage in most matters not involving sea and ice. For this, he cannot be blamed.

---

* She was earning $1,500 a year (about $25,000 in 2018), which was helpful since her husband was now unemployed (Federal Census 1940).

"There were two sides to Bartlett," said Frog Marsh native Leo Kennedy, whose father supplied the Benville Tea Rooms with eggs. "He was rough and ready. You could hear him on deck before you could see him—a mile away. He could be a real gentleman at other times."[141] Perhaps Bartlett kept his rougher side from his posh friends; after all, his connections with the American upper crust paid the bills. Ben Carpenter, the son of Ruly Carpenter, called Bartlett "Uncle Bob," and Ruly once told him, "I know that you don't mind being left alone at [our home], you are just as much at home there as we are."[142] Bartlett and the Carpenters had mutual friends in the Dupont family, a member of which Carpenter married. The Duponts had grown wealthy through their chemicals business. Scientists recognized Bartlett as a friend; among them was scientist Waldo Schmit of the Smithsonian, who looked forward to Bartlett's visits and wrote "you're such a good friend to a fellow."[143]

Leo Kennedy was not alone in his observation about Bartlett's duality. Nautical scientist Gershom Bradford wrote that Bartlett was "alone among seafaring men in the range of his contrasting characteristics."[144] Although Bartlett had proven his ability to lead motley crews in dangerous circumstances, he was given to oddly timed periods of silence, even in company. One gets the feeling that Bartlett's habit of swearing was borne of expectations, as Brigus native Gordon Spracklin implied; men assumed he would be a tough character, like the other skippers they had encountered. He undoubtedly felt genuine anger at times and did not hesitate to express it. But, at least in some cases, Bartlett's fury seems to have part of his act. Canadian Arctic Expedition member William McKinley wrote of Bartlett's "blistering commentary on the crass folly" of *Karluk* crew members, returning from a foray which he feared had led to their deaths: "I have always had a feeling that his anger was simulated. He spoke only two or three sentences and then followed that characteristic gesture when he was deeply moved—a brushing of his right hand across the left side of his mouth, wiping away the slight flow of saliva. As he turned towards me, with his back to the others, his face expanded in a grin and his right eye closed, but I am not prepared to swear it was meant to be a wink."[145] Bartlett had admonished his crew members in relief, as a parent scolds a child who has disappeared in a department store.

As World War II drew to a close, Bartlett was in his late 60s and his curmudgeonly side let itself out more freely. "Why in the name of Christ don't all the women travelling stay home? Youngsters and what not," he wrote to one of his Explorer Club mates, continuing in a slightly more sanguinely, "I suppose they are saying why in hell don't the men stay home?"[146] Bartlett might well have observed that women had entered the wartime workforce in large numbers, as they had during World War I, and that it would be difficult to put the genie back in the bottle. He surely knew that the social order was changing and that his testosterone-driven world might be in its sunset.

In 1942, Paul Sarnoff spent 10 days with Bartlett at the Brooklyn Army Base; Bartlett had just enlisted at age 67. In *Ice Pilot*, published more than two decades later, Sarnoff lamented that Bartlett was all but forgotten after being a household name just two decades before.[147] Thus began again the glorification of Robert Abram Bartlett—"a unique American hero"[148]—and the rending of him into something of a cardboard cut-out, the stuff of schoolboys' dreams. Sarnoff reported that Bartlett's favourite admonition was "[n]o one knows what the day will bring on God's menu"; thus, in the last years of his life, he retained the entrenched fatalism of the Newfoundland fisherman and sealer and the ancient Greek.

In the 1940s, the works of George Eliot—interestingly, a woman who used a man's name—became Bartlett's *vade mecum*. Bartlett wanted to and even longed to join the choir invisible. He admired Eliot's yearning for immortality[149] and wanted, like the poet, "to live again"

> In minds made better by their presence: live
> In pulses stirred to generosity,
> In deeds of daring rectitude, in scorn
> For miserable aims that end with self,
> In thoughts sublime that pierce the night like stars,
> And with their mild persistence urge man's search
> To vaster issues.

Bartlett admired what he saw as Eliot's haste to be part of an afterlife after engendering gladness on this earth.[150] He compared Eliot favourably with Cicero,[151] whose very different concern was longevity and the narrow present. Like Eliot, Bartlett had largely dismissed church doctrine and cast off official notions of heaven; he continued to appreciate Jesus as a teacher and saw Scripture as sacred, but found his own paradise in the stillness of the Arctic. For years he had quoted Byron, especially "Childe Harold's Pilgrimage," which features the kind of self-destructive exile with which Byron's work is so often associated:

> He who ascends to mountain-tops, shall find the loftiest
>   peaks most wrapt in clouds and snow;
> He who surpasses or subdues mankind,
> Must look down on the hate of those below,
> Though high above the stars of glory glow.

Despite his flaws, the hero is engaged in a quest for something more, something great, something *beyond*. This was, for Bartlett, the purpose of Arctic exploration and the goal for which he spent his life striving. Significantly, he once quietly recited this poem as his contribution to a discussion of polar exploration at the United States Hydrographic Office shortly after Byrd flew over the North Pole. Bartlett could never see the Arctic in political terms, although his notions and those of explorers very much shaped the place of the Arctic in international politics. For him, it was all about romance, humanity, and the mystical.

Bartlett did not, indeed could not, become part of the masses. He could never naturally fit it and aimed for that which was difficult, all within the tight constraints set out by his seafaring family and their lofty ambitions. This was, as a fan noted in a letter to him, all part of his "struggles towards the finest and best things in life."[152] At times family ambitions meshed with Bartlett's own inclinations, but when they did not, he was helpless; he could never truly stop being Captain William Bartlett's bedwetting son, despite the ministrations of Grandmother Leamon and the aristocratic but loving Mary Jemima. Nietszche might have been thinking of an unresolved inner struggle like this when he wrote:

> Nobody can construct for you the bridge upon which precisely you must cross the stream of life, no one but you yourself alone. There are to be sure countless paths and bridges and

demi-gods which would bear you through this stream; but only at the cost of yourself: you would put yourself in pawn and lose yourself. There exists in this world a single path along which no one can go except you: whither does it lead? Do not ask, go along it.[153]

Knowing oneself is indeed a dark and mysterious business. Bartlett met his highest self among the Arctic loons and the blue-white ice pans, among the pinnacles and ridges with Kataktovik. He encountered his desperate lowest self when, well to the south, he sold himself over and over to the highest and sometimes the only bidder. There are ironies. One is that in his constant self-promotion, Bartlett was not selling himself but a facile salty dog image. The other irony is that this soulless marketing financed and made possible Bartlett's engagement with his best self, which he had to sail thousands of miles to meet: the man who came closest to his higher man, the man who was both naked and whole in the frigid Arctic.

Bartlett died in a New York hospital, where he had been confined for a few days with pneumonia. He did not always take care of himself, sometimes not dressing properly at sea and frequently neglecting to get enough sleep.[154] He often rushed on deck in bare feet and did not bother to cover them, even as frigid sea water sloshed about, wetting and chilling him.[155] Perhaps surprisingly, Bartlett was in a good mood during his stay on the hospital ward before he sank into unconsciousness. Upon learning his illness had taken a critical turn, his sister Eleanor booked a flight to New York but the perennial fog of St. John's kept planes grounded. Sadly, she did not get to Manhattan, and Bartlett died alone, without the solace of kin at his side.[156]

Bartlett was 70 and thus did not reach the old age of some of his Brigus forebears; his life had been rough, with his sometimes fragile self-image, the absence of family, and the agonies of the *Leopard*, the *Corisande*, and especially the *Karluk*, with its own particular brand of lasting horror never ceasing to torment him. Island and family tribalism meant there was no question that he would be buried in Newfoundland. Jack Angel did not want Bartlett's body to return home unescorted, so he dashed to New York from his home in Montreal. He escorted the coffin down the

Atlantic seaboard by train, then bus, and finally, ship from Sydney, Nova Scotia, to Port aux Basques, Newfoundland. Will Bartlett came across the island of Newfoundland by train, met Jack and his brother's casket in Port aux Basques, and accompanied the body back to Brigus. To his lasting regret, Jack turned around and went back to Montreal, missing Bartlett's funeral.[157] Given Bartlett's unfailing support of him, he might have been in shock.

Meanwhile, according to the New York media,[158] some 700 people attended a service for Bartlett held at the Methodist Christ Church on Park Avenue and 60th Street. Among them was Matthew Henson who, with Peary, had watched Bartlett begin the long lonely trek back to the *Roosevelt* as they attempted the Pole. Also taking part was Vilhjalmur Stefansson, whom Bartlett had bitterly condemned two decades before—and since. Stefansson's skin was thicker than Bartlett's had been and the anthropologist had the maturity to disregard the conflict of the previous years. An eight-member delegation from the Explorers Club came and at least six Newfoundlanders living in New York were present, as were representatives of the newspapers which had followed Bartlett for many years and the museums for whom Bartlett collected. The assembled listened to Bartlett's two favourite Psalms, the 23rd and the 12th, which reads in part:

> Help, Lord; for the godly man ceaseth; for the faithful fail from among the children of men ... who is lord over us? ... for the sighing of the needy, now will I arise, saith the Lord; I will set him in safety from him that puffeth at him ... (Ps. 12:1,4,5)

The despairing tone of this psalm and the relief and comfort offered to the author appealed to Bartlett. He had felt his own share of sorrow, especially in the 1910s when his brother Rupert was slaughtered on the battlefields of World War I and when the *Karluk* expedition had gone so tragically wrong, littering bodies across the Arctic ice. Bartlett valued the text's emphasis on the insincerity of human beings in contrast to the sincerity of God; one of his chief traits was loyalty and he abhorred disloyalty—in this and other things, his thinking was black and white. But he had chosen to pass so much time alone, on the streets of Manhattan and among the icefields of Greenland. He knew himself well and, in spite of his impressive ability to endure loneliness and transcend hardship, he could acknowledge his own smallness and neediness, which is no meagre feat. This man who had spent his life in dangerous Arctic waters openly sought protection from the god who promised to preserve those under threat.

EPILOGUE
THE *EFFIE MORRISSEY*

Bartlett on the *Effie Morrissey* outside Brigus in the early 1940s. *Photo by George W. Little, courtesy of Denise Riddell.*

The *Morrissey* was in poor shape as the war ended, although Bartlett had sailed in her only five months before he died; she had been beaten about with little opportunity for repairs. After Bartlett's death a lawyer and a doctor bought her for a trip to Tahiti, fitting the ship with electrical instruments for the first time.[1] But the luck she enjoyed with Bartlett was running out; she caught fire, somewhat mysteriously, before they left port.[2] Then Louisa Mendes of Egypt, Massachusetts, bought the *Morrissey*; after the necessary repairs, Mendes wanted to use the vessel to bring codfish from New Bedford to the Cape Verde Islands.[3] This plan did not succeed and very quickly Mendes sold her to a Cape Verdean.[4] The *Morrissey* was renamed the *Ernestina* in 1959 and registered in Portugal, from where she was engaged in trade.[5] After she was presented to the United States as a gift from the Republic of Cape Verde, the *Ernestina* became a national historic site and is being refurbished by the state government of Massachusetts.[6] North of the Canada-United States border is another national historic site, Hawthorne Cottage, Bartlett's childhood home in Brigus.

Meanwhile, serious imbalances of political power endure in the haunted Arctic homelands of the Inuit, the Chukchi, the Even, the Saami, and others whose resources are coveted by Russia, Canada, Denmark, and other northern nations. Climate change, already extreme in the Arctic, is but one manifestation of the tight ties between colonialism and industrial capitalism. Bartlett's concerns would have been narrower than this but quite natural from his own perspective. What would have pained Bartlett most is that, though they once covered the seas, there is not a single schooner, like the rickety old *Roosevelt* or his hallowed *Morrissey*, left in Newfoundland.

ACKNOWLEDGEMENTS

I would like to extend my sincere thanks to many people who have contributed to this project. Among them are two anonymous academic reviewers; Gavin Will, Amanda Will, Stephanie Porter, and Iona Bulgin of Boulder Publications; designer Tanya Montini; the faculty and staff of the University of Lethbridge, especially the Department of Indigenous Studies, the Office of the Dean of Arts and Sciences, the Office of Research and Innovation Services, and Women Scholars; Grenfell Campus, Memorial University, especially the Research Office staff and Myron King of the Environmental Policy Institute; the staff of the Caird Library and Archive, the National Maritime Museum, Greenwich, London; Caroline Moseley, Dr. Susan Kaplan, Genevieve LeMoine, Kathleen Petersen, and Daniel Hope of Bowdoin College, Brunswick, Maine; Naomi Boneham and the staff of the Scott Polar Research Institute, University of Cambridge, England; Mette Sonnicks and the staff of the University of Greenland, Nuuk, Greenland; Morgan Swan and staff, Dartmouth College Library, Hanover, New Hampshire; the staff of Library and Archives Canada, Ottawa; Lacey Flint of the Explorers Club, New York; the staff of the Rooms Provincial Archives of Newfoundland and Labrador; the staff of the Centre for Newfoundland Studies, Queen Elizabeth II Library, Memorial University; students Carey Viejou, Ashley Hendrikson, and Ashley Wiebe, University of Letbridge, and Maria Carolina Dussan, Lori-Ann Campbell, Tsai Allen, and Michael Westcott, Memorial University;

Catherine Dempsey, the Historic Sites Association of Newfoundland and Labrador; Joan Ritcey, chair, Exploring Bartlett Symposium Committee, Newfoundland Historical Society; and Dr. Niels Einarsson and Dr. Jón Haukur, Stefansson Institute, Akureyri, Iceland.

I am also very grateful to my weekly University of Lethbridge lunch group, especially Dr. Heidi MacDonald; Laura Cameron, Garry Cranford, and Peter Hanes of Flanker Press, St. John's; Dr. John FitzGerald, formerly of the Government of Newfoundland and Labrador; Darryl Fillier, Government of Newfoundland and Labrador; Ken Simmonds, the St. John's *Telegram*; Burton K. Janes, the *Compass*, Carbonear, Newfoundland; Paul Butler; Dr. Kathy Eden, Columbia University and the Association for Core Texts and Courses; Dr. Joanna Kafarowski; John Greene, Marjorie Doyle, Marnie Parsons, Janet Kergoat, and the late Paul O'Neill of St. John's; Tom Burke, the late Gordon Spracklin, Matilda Spracklin, the late John Waller, and other residents of Brigus, some of whom wish to remain anonymous; Bernard Kennedy and Leo Kennedy of nearby Frogmarsh; James Candow, Parks Canada; Edward Hanrahan, Cape Breton, Nova Scotia; Cathie Richardson of Barrie, Ontario; Denise Riddell, L'Amable, Ontario; Maxine King, Creighton, Saskatchewan; Dr. María Jesús Hernáez Lerena, University of La Rioja, Spain; Dr. Willeen Keough, Simon Fraser University; Elena Sánchez, Tenerife, Spain; and descendants of Leah Ings Freake, who wish to remain anonymous.

For the funding that made this book possible, I thank the Dean of Arts and Science, University of Lethbridge; the University of the Arctic north2north program, which funded my travel to Greenland; the City of St. John's Arts Jury; the Newfoundland and Labrador Arts Council; the Institute of Social and Economic Research, Memorial University; the Hakluyt Society, London, which funded my work on the Bjarne Mamen diary, Canadian Arctic Expedition; the Association for the Core Texts and Courses, which partly funded my time in New York; and the Office of the Vice-President, Grenfell Campus, Memorial University.

Short articles about Captain Bob Bartlett and his family by me were published in the St. John's *Telegram*; *The Beaver: Canada's National History Magazine*; the Russian journal *Arctic and North*; and *Antarctica and the Arctic Circle: A Geographic Encyclopedia of the Earth's Polar*

Regions; my *All Things Arctic* blog; and my facebook page Captain Bob Bartlett. Captain William Bartlett and his son Bob as a child also appeared in *Domino: The Eskimo Coast Disaster*, one of my creative non-fiction books.

I presented papers on the Bartlett family at the 10th Annual Bartlett Lecture in Brigus, 2012, and at the 2009 *Exploring Bartlett: The Legacy of an Arctic Adventurer Symposium*, also in Brigus. I presented another paper on Bartlett at the Fogo Island Inn, Joe Batt's Arm, Fogo Island, in 2016. I presented a paper on the Canadian Arctic Expedition 1914–1918 at the 2016 Inuit Studies Conference and on Bartlett's celebrity during his lifetime at the 2018 Popular Culture Association-American Culture Association Conference. Finally, I was interviewed about Bartlett and Arctic exploration for a Looking North podcast by Ted Blades of On the Go, CBC Radio Newfoundland and Labrador.

Throughout 2018, I am running a blog called *All Things Arctic* at https://captainbobbartlett.com/ and a facebook page Captain Bob Bartlett.

While many people contributed to the book, any mistakes are mine alone.

PEOPLE

Akatingwah (the Inuit mother of Henson's son)

Allakasingwah, also spelled Aleqasina, or Ally (the young Inuit mother of Peary's children)

Anaukaq (Henson's Inuit son)

Anderson, Alexander or Sandy (first officer on the *Karluk*)

Anderson, Dr. Rudolph Martin (employee of the National Museum of Canada; leader of the Southern Party of the Canadian Arctic Expedition)

Angel Crichton, Emma (Bob Bartlett's niece)

Angel, Fred (Bob Bartlett's brother-in-law; husband of Mary Elizabeth or Betty Bartlett Angel)

Angel, Jack (Bob Bartlett's nephew)

Angel Murphy, Ruperta or Paddy (Bob Bartlett's niece)

Barker, Charles (second officer on the *Karluk*)

Bartlett Dove, Beatrice or Triss (Bob Bartlett's sister; mother of Bob Bartlett's Dove nephews and niece)

Bartlett, Eleanor (Bob Bartlett's sister)

Bartlett, Elizabeth Bellamy Wilmot (Bob Bartlett's paternal grandmother)

Bartlett, Emma (Bob Bartlett's sister)

Bartlett, Ethel Sargent Hyde (Will's American wife and Bob Bartlett's sister-in-law)

Bartlett, Captain Harold (a cousin of Bob Bartlett)

Bartlett, Captain Henry or Harry (Bob Bartlett's uncle)

Bartlett, Captain Isaac (Bob Bartlett's great-uncle)

Bartlett, Captain John (Bob Bartlett's uncle)

Bartlett, Lewis (Bob Bartlett's brother)

Bartlett, Mary Jemima, nee Leamon (Bob Bartlett's mother)

Bartlett Angel, Mary Elizabeth or Betty (Bob Bartlett's sister; mother of Bob Bartlett's Angel nieces and nephews)

Bartlett, Captain Moses (Bob Bartlett's cousin, the son of Captain John)

Bartlett, Captain Robert (Bob) Abram

Bartlett, Rupert (Bob Bartlett's brother)

Bartlett, Rupert, later Judge (Bob Bartlett's nephew)

Bartlett, William, Jr. or Will (Bob Bartlett's brother)

Bartlett, William, Sr. or Captain William (Bob Bartlett's father)

Bartlett, Sam (Bob Bartlett's younger cousin, the grandson of Captain Samuel Bartlett)

Bartlett, Captain Samuel (Bob Bartlett's uncle)

Beuchat, Henri (French-born anthropologist with the Canadian Arctic Expedition)

Bird, Junius (archaeologist; American Natural History curator; sailed on the *Morrissey*)

Borden, Robert, later Sir (prime minister of Canada during the Canadian Arctic Expedition)

Boyd, Louise Arner (Arctic explorer)

Brady, John (seaman on the *Karluk*)

Breddy, George (fireman on the *Karluk*)

Butler, Constable Benjamin (Brigus official and farmer)

Butler, Mary Eliza (Constable Benjamin Butler's daughter)

Cadzow, David (Indigenous history scholar; sailed on the *Morrissey*)

Carpenter, Benjamin (son of Ruly Carpenter)

Carpenter, Robert, Sr. or Ruly (friend of Bob Bartlett; owner of the Philadelphia Phillies)

Chafe, Ernest or Charlie (mess room boy on the *Karluk*)

Cook, Dr. Frederick (Arctic explorer and Peary's rival)

Counter, S. Allen (Harvard University neuroscientist who reunited Peary's Inuit and white descendants)

Crane, Zenas (a Massachusetts industrialist and one of Peary's financial backers)

Crosbie, Jack (Bartlett's childhood friend, later a prominent merchant)

Diebitsch-Peary, Josephine (Admiral Peary's wife)

Dooling, Jim (Brigus-born crew member of the *Effie Morrissey*)

Dove, Hilda (Bob Bartlett's niece)

Dove, James or Jim (Bob Bartlett's nephew)

Dove, Robert (Bob Bartlett's nephew)

Egingwah or Enughitok (Inuit member of Peary's 1909 expedition)

Erling, P. (employee, Canadian Department of Mines and Resources)

Evans, Tom (Bartlett family employee at Turnavik, Labrador)

Ford, Commodore James B. (one of Bob Bartlett's financial backers)

Freake, Leah Mary Ings (Labrador-born woman who believed herself to be Bob Bartlett's daughter)

Freuchen, Peter (Danish explorer)

Gibbs, Sir Philip (British journalist who interviewed Bartlett for *The Graphic*)

Golightly, Edmund L., real name King (seaman on the *Karluk*)

Gould, Lawrence (geologist; sailed in the *Morrissey*)

Green, Fitzhugh (a United States naval ensign and civil engineer on the Crockerland expedition; murdered Piugaattoq)

Grenfell, Sir Wilfred (British evangelist and missionary doctor; Bartlett family friend)

Gulotta, LeRoy (Nevada-born, New Orleans-raised friend of Bartlett; fellow boarder in New York)

Gulotta, Wilhelmina (wife of LeRoy Gulotta)

Hadley, John (crew member of the *Karluk*)

Hale, Ralph T. (one of Bob Bartlett's ghost writers)

Harmsworth, Sir Alfred, later Lord Northcliffe (British newspaper magnate)

Helen (young daughter of Kiruk and Kirulek on the *Karluk*)

Henderson, Daniel (friend of Bartlett)

Henson, Matthew Alexander or Matt (African-American Arctic explorer, claimed the North Pole with Peary in 1909)

Hiscock, Gilbert (woodcutter from Victoria, Newfoundland, who worked on Peary's Greenland monument)

Hiscock, Reuben (woodcutter from Victoria, Newfoundland, who worked on Peary's Greenland monument)

Holman, John (president of the Audubon Society in Connecticut)

Horwood, Harold (journalist and author of *Bartlett: The Great Explorer*, a 1977 biography of Bob Bartlett)

Hubbard, General Thomas (a former Union Army colonel and one of Peary's financial backers)

Jerry (Inupiaq hunter with the Canadian Arctic Expedition)

Jesup, Morris Ketchum (president of the American Natural History Museum and Peary's financial backer)

Jenness, Stuart or Diamond (New Zealand-born anthropologist with the Canadian Arctic Expedition)

Jimmy (Inupiaq hunter with the Canadian Arctic Expedition)

Kataktovik, Claude (Inupiaq hunter on the *Karluk*; attempted the rescue with Bob Bartlett)

Kent, Rockwell (American artist who lived in Brigus during World War I)

Kiruk or Auntie (Inupiaq seamstress on the *Karluk*)

Kurulek (Inupiaq hunter on the *Karluk*)

Kleist, Baron (supervisor of northeastern Siberia)

Kudlooktoo (Inuit member of Peary's 1909 expedition, accused of murder)

Lane, Captain Louis (captain of the *Herman*)

Leamon, John Northway Leamon (author and Bob Bartlett's first cousin, once removed)

Leamon, Mary Norman or Grandmother Leamon (Bob Bartlett's maternal grandmother)

Leamon, Robert, Jr. (Bob Bartlett's uncle)

Lee, Hugh J. (United States marshal)

Linderberg, John (Alaskan gold mine owner)

MacMillan, Donald Baxter (Arctic explorer)

Malloch, George (Canadian ecologist with the Canadian Arctic Expedition)

Malloch, Grace (wife of George Malloch)

Mamen, Bjarne (assistant topographer with the Canadian Arctic Expedition; Norwegian)

Mann, L.B. (American friend of Bob Bartlett)

Marvin, Professor Ross (chief scientist on Peary's 1909 expedition)

Maurer, Frederick (fireman on the *Karluk*)

McConnell, Burt (secretary to Vilhjalmur Stefansson during the Canadian Arctic Expedition)

Mackay, Dr. Alistair Forbes (Royal Navy surgeon and member of the Canadian Arctic Expedition)

McKinley, William Laird (Scottish meteorologist with the Canadian Arctic Expedition)

Mill, Hugh Robert (Scottish geographer)

Morris, Stanley (seaman on the *Karluk*)

Mugpi (toddler daughter of Kiruk and Kirulek on the *Karluk*)

Murray, James (biologist and oceanographer with the Canadian Arctic Expedition; Scottish)

Norcross, Arthur Dickinson (musician-politician who sailed on the *Morrissey*)

Nutt, David Clark (mentee and friend of Bob Bartlett; faculty member, Department of Geograpy, Dartmouth College)

Nutt, Joseph Randolph or J.R. (David Nutt's father; president and board chairman of the Union Trust Company)

Ooqueah (Inuit member of Peary's 1909 expedition)

Ootah (Inuit member of Peary's 1909 expedition)

Panikpah (Inuit member of Peary's 1909 expedition)

Peary Stafford, Marie Ahnighito (Admiral Peary's daughter, known as the Snow Baby)

Peary, Admiral Robert, Sr. (Arctic explorer)

Peary, Robert, Jr. (Admiral Peary's son)

Pedersen, Captain Theodore (Danish-American whaling captain; Vilhjalmur Stefansson's first choice as captain of the *Karluk*)

Percey, Ady, Livy, and Susannah (the sisters who were Bob Bartlett's first schoolteachers)

Percy, Lord William (son of the duke of Northumberland; friend of Bartlett)

Piugaattoq (Inuit man murdered during Donald MacMillan's Crockerland expedition)

Pooadloona (Inuit member of Peary's 1909 expedition)

Putnam, David Binney (author who, as a boy, went to the Arctic with Bob Bartlett; son of George Putnam)

Putnam, George (Bob Bartlett's publisher and biographer; husband of Amelia Earhart)

Rasmussen, Knud (Greenland-born Danish explorer; the father of "Eskimology")

Robinson, Joseph (American friend of Bartlett)

Roosevelt, Theodore, II, or Teddy (26th president of the United States)

Roosevelt, Theodore, III, or Teddy (son of the 26th president of the United States)

Sando, Briant (New York-based lecture tour agent)

Seegloo (Inuit member of Peary's 1909 expedition)

Shackleton, Sir Edward (son of Sir Ernest Shackleton and an Arctic explorer)

Shackleton, Sir Ernest (Anglo-Irish polar explorer)

Smith, Courtland (Pathé News executive)

Spracklin, Gordon (Brigus resident)

Squires, Sir Richard Anderson (prime minister of Newfoundland; Bartlett family friend)

Stefansson, Vilhjalmur (Icelandic-Canadian anthropologist and explorer; leader of the Canadian Arctic Expedition)

Templeman, Robert (cook and steward on the *Karluk*)

Tuck, Sara Lee (New York-based friend and admirer of Bob Bartlett)

Whitney, Harry (millionaire sports hunter)

Wilkins, George (British cinematographer with the Canadian Arctic Expedition)

Williamson, F.H.H. (controller, Canadian Department of Mines and Resources)

ENDNOTES

PROLOGUE

1   Laura Nader, "Up the Anthropologist: Perspectives Gained from Studying Up," in *Reinventing Anthropology*, ed. Dell H. Hymes (New York: Pantheon Books, 1972), 284–311.

CHAPTER ONE

2   Robert Peary, *The North Pole* (London: Hodder and Stoughton, 1910), 34.
3   William Edward Parry, *Narrative of an Attempt to Reach the North Pole* (London: J. Murray, 1828).
4   Pierre Berton, *The Arctic Grail: The Quest for the North West Passage and the North Pole, 1818–1909* (1988; Anchor Canada, 2012).
5   Michael F. Robinson, *The Coldest Crucible: Arctic Exploration and American Culture* (Chicago: University of Chicago Press, 2006), 133.
6   Robert A. Bartlett, *The Log of Bob Bartlett: The True Story of Forty Years of Seafaring and Exploration* (1926; St. John's: Flanker Press, 2006), 153.
7   Ibid., 155.
8   Ibid., 156.
9   Ibid.
10 Ibid.
11 S. Allen Counter, *North Pole Legacy: Black, White and Eskimo* (Montpelier, VT: Invisible Citis Press, 2001), 43.
12 Bartlett, *The Log of Bob Bartlett*, 158.
13 Peary, *The North Pole*, 189.
14 Bartlett, *The Log of Bob Bartlett*, 160.
15 Ibid.
16 Harold Horwood, *Bartlett: The Great Explorer* (1977; Toronto: Doubleday Canada, 1989).
17 Peary, *The North Pole*, 47.
18 Robinson, *The Coldest Crucible*, 82; Charles Francis Hall, *Arctic Researches, and Life among the Esquimaux: Being the Narrative of an Expedition in Search of Sir John Franklin, in the Years 1860, 1861, and 1862* (New York: Harper & Bros., 1865).
19 Robinson, *The Coldest Crucible*, 82; Bruce B. Henderson, *Fatal North: Adventure Survival Aboard USS* Polaris *1st US Expedition North Pole* (Signet Books, 2001); Charles Francis Hall, *Life with the Esquimaux: The Narrative of Captain Charles Francis Hall of the Whaling Barque* George Henry *from the 29th May, 1860, to the 13th September, 1862*, vol. 2 (1864; Cambridge: Cambridge University Press, 2011).
20 Robinson, *The Coldest Crucible*.
21 Robert McGhee, *The Last Imaginary Place: A Human History of the Arctic World* (Chicago: University of Chicago Press, 2005), 22.
22 Ibid., 23.
23 P.D. Baird, "Expeditions to the Canadian Arctic," *The Beaver* 2, no. 15 (1949): 2.
24 McGhee, *The Last Imaginary Place*, 103; James McDermott, *The Third Voyage of Martin Frobisher to Baffin Island, 1578*, vol. 6 (London: Hakluyt Society, 2001).
25 James McDermott, *Martin Frobisher: Elizabethan Privateer* (New Haven, CT: Yale University Press, 2001).
26 Maura Hanrahan, "Enduring Polar Explorers' Arctic Imaginaries and the Promotion of Neoliberalism and Colonialism in Modern Greenland," *Polar Geography* 40, no. 2 (2017): 102–20.
27 Jean Malaurie, *The Last Kings of Thule: A Year among the Polar Eskimos of Greenland* (London: Allen & Unwin, 1956), 194.
28 McGhee, *The Last Imaginary Place*, 237.
29 A.R. Glen and N.A.C. Croft, *Under the Polar Star: The Oxford University Arctic Expedition, 1935–6* (London: Methuen Publishers London, 1937).
30 Matthew Henson, *A Black Explorer at the North Pole: An Autobiographical Report by the Negro Who Conquered the Top of the World with Admiral Robert E. Peary* (1912; New York: Walker and Co., 1969), 118.

31   Ibid., 123.
32   Ibid.
33   Ibid., 122.
34   Peary, *The North Pole*, 32.
35   Isaac I. Hayes, *The Land of Desolation: Being a Personal Narrative of Observation and Adventure in Greenland* (New York: Harper & Brothers, 1872).
36   Louise Bartlett Stewart, "Capt. Bob's Account of the Bartlett Family as Given to Louise Bartlett Stewart" (unpublished manuscript, Historic Sites Association of Newfoundland and Labrador, n.d.).
37   Henry Shortis, "Thomas Bartlett," 28 February 1895, unpublished papers of H.F. Shortis, Centre for Newfoundland Studies, Queen Elizabeth II Library, Memorial University [Shortis Papers].
38   James Gordon Hayes, *The Conquest of the South Pole: Antarctic Exploration, 1906–1931* (London: T. Butterworth, Ltd., 1932).
39   Alan Moorehead, *The Fatal Impact: An Account of the Invasion of the South Pacific, 1767–1840* (London: Penguin, 2000).
40   Gananath Obeyesekere, *The Apotheosis of Captain Cook: European Mythmaking in the Pacific* (Princeton, NJ: Princeton University Press, 1997).
41   James Cook and James King, *A Voyage to the Pacific Ocean*, vol. 3 (H. Hughs, 1785), 46.
42   Vanessa Collingridge, *Captain Cook: The Life, Death and Legacy of History's Greatest Explorer* (London: Ebury Press, 2003); Richard Hough, *Captain James Cook* (New York: W.W. Norton & Company, 1994).
43   "Notes on the Crustacea, Chiefly Natantia, Collected by Captain Robert A. Bartlett in Arctic Seas," *Journal of the Washington Academy of Sciences* 26, no. 8 (1936): 324–31.
44   Linda Tuhiwai Smith, *Decolonizing Methodologies: Research and Indigenous Peoples* (London: Zed, 2012); Edward Said, *Orientalism* (London: Penguin, 1978).
45   Bartlett, *The Log of Bob Bartlett*.
46   R. Chevallier, "The Greco-Roman Conception of the North from Pytheas to Tacitus," *Arctic* 37, no. 4 (1984): 341–46, quotation at 342.
47   Baird, "Expeditions to the Canadian Arctic," 2.
48   Captain Edward Fenton, "The Canadian Arctic Journal of Capt. Edward Fenton, 1578," *Archivaria* 11 (Winter 1980–81): 181–204.
49   Hayes, *The Land of Desolation*, 17.
50   Ibid.
51   Trevor H. Levere, *Science and the Canadian Arctic: A Century of Exploration 1818–1918* (Cambridge: Cambridge University Press, 1993), 245.
52   Hayes, *The Land of Desolation*, 21.
53   Smith, *Decolonizing Methodologies*, 23.
54   Stuart Banner, "Why *Terra Nullius*? Anthropology and Property Law in Early Australia," *Law and History Review* 23, no. 1 (2005): 95–131.
55   Quoted in Ariana Crachiun, *Writing Arctic Disaster: Authorship and Exploration* (Cambridge: Cambridge University Press, 2016), 224.
56   Ibid., 232.
57   Robinson, *The Coldest Crucible*.
58   Ibid., 29.
59   McGhee, *The Last Imaginary Place*, 248.
60   James Simsarian, "The Acquisition of Legal Title to *Terra Nullius*," *Political Science Quarterly* 53, no. 1 (1938): 111–28.
61   James Joll, *Nineteen-fourteen: The Unspoken Assumptions. An Inaugural Lecture Delivered 25 April 1968* (London School of Economics and Political Science: Weidenfeld & Nicolson, 1968).
62   Hanrahan, "Enduring Polar Explorers' Arctic Imaginaries."
63   Michael Elmes and Bob Frame, "Into Hot Air: A Critical Perspective on Everest," *Human Relations* 61, no. 2 (2008): 213–41, quotation at 219.

64 Gayatri Spivak, "Can the Subaltern Speak?" in *Marxism and the Interpretation of Culture*, ed. Cary Nelson and Lawrence Grossberg (Chicago: University of Chicago Press, 1988), 271–313.

65 Bjarne Mamen, 1913–1914, diary of Bjarne Mamen, MIKAN 98096, Library and Archives Canada, Ottawa, 7.

66 Elmes and Frame, "Into Hot Air," 220.

67 Ibid., 229.

68 Ibid., 232.

69 Lyle Dick, "Aboriginal-European Relations during the Great Age of North Polar Exploration," *Polar Geography* 26, no. 1 (2002): 66–81, see especially 78.

70 McGhee, *The Last Imaginary Place*, 237.

71 "Robert Edwin Peary: Memorial Meeting at the Explorers Club," typed program, Explorers Club, NY, 12 March 1920.

72 Paul Sarnoff, *Ice Pilot: Bob Bartlett* (New York: Julian Messner, 1966), 36.

73 Royal Geographical Society, "Meetings: Royal Geographical Society 1919–1920," *The Geographic Journal* 56, no. 1 (1920): 407.

74 Bartlett, *The Log of Bob Bartlett*, 11.

75 McGhee, *The Last Imaginary Place*, 237.

76 Bartlett, *The Log of Bob Bartlett*, 121.

77 Ibid.

78 Ibid.

79 Royal Geographical Society, "Meetings," 407.

80 "Robert Edwin Peary: Memorial Meeting at the Explorers Club."

81 Ibid., 14.

82 Bartlett, *The Log of Bob Bartlett*, 129.

83 Henson, *A Black Explorer at the North Pole*, 18.

84 "Robert Edwin Peary: Memorial Meeting at the Explorers Club."

85 Ibid.

86 Ibid., 14.

87 Peary, *The North Pole*, 46.

88 Vilhjalmur Stefansson, *My Life with the Eskimo* (1912; Charleston, SC: Nabu Press, 2010).

89 Knud Johan Victor Rasmussen, *Report of the First Thule Expedition 1912* (Copenhagan: C.A. Reitzels Forlag, 1915).

90 Bartlett, *The Log of Bob Bartlett*, 124.

91 Peary, *The North Pole*, 46.

92 Ibid., 48.

93 Ibid., 323.

94 Elisha Kent Kane, *Arctic Explorations: The Second Grinnell Expedition in Search of Sir John Franklin, 1853, '54, '55* (Edinburgh: T. Nelson and Sons, 1861), 221.

95 Bartlett, *The Log of Bob Bartlett,* 124.

96 Ibid., 133.

97 Ibid.

98 Board of Trade, Certificate of Competency as Master (John Bartlett), 30 July 1866, Board of Trade, National Maritime Museum, Greenock, Scotland.

99 Board of Trade, Certificate of Competency as Master (Samuel Bartlett), December 1874, Board of Trade, National Maritime Museum, Greenock, Scotland.

100 "Obituary: Captain Samuel W. Bartlett," *Geographical Review* 2, no. 5 (1916): 436.

101 Allan O. Nurse, "Captain Robert A. Bartlett," *Newfoundland Quarterly* 9, no. 4 (1910): 1.

102 "Capt. Bob Bartlett, Explorer, 70, Dies," *The Polar Times* (June 1946): 18.

103 "Robert Edwin Peary: Memorial Meeting at the Explorers Club."

104 Sarnoff, *Ice Pilot*, 60.

105 Ibid., 61.

106 Horwood, *Bartlett: The Great Explorer*, 50.

107 Ibid.

108 Ibid.

109 Bartlett, *The Log of Bob Bartlett*, 137.

110 Peary, *The North Pole*, 104.
111 Jack Angel, interview by James Candow, 27 May 1987, Parks Canada, St. John's.
112 Ibid.
113 Sarnoff, *Ice Pilot*, 66.
114 Bartlett, *The Log of Bob Bartlett*, 140.
115 Ibid., 141.
116 Ibid.
117 Ibid., 143.
118 Ibid.
119 Ibid., 148.
120 Ibid., 149.
121 "To Washington Tug and Barge Company, Seattle, Washington," 29 January 1935, Explorers Club: Robert Abram Bartlett.
122 Bartlett, *The Log of Bob Bartlett*, 122.
123 Ibid., 123.
124 Ibid., 124.
125 Robert Peary, "The Great White Journey," in *My Arctic Journal: A Year among Ice-Fields and Eskimos*, by Josephine Diebitsch-Peary (New York and Philadelphia: Contemporary Publishing Co., 1893), 221–41, quotation at 227.
126 Bartlett, *The Log of Bob Bartlett*, 132.
127 McGhee, *The Last Imaginary Place*, 238.
128 Bartlett, *The Log of Bob Bartlett*, 155.
129 Genevieve LeMoine, "Elatu's Funeral: A Glimpse of Inughuit-American Relations on Robert E. Peary's 1898–1902 Expedition," *Arctic* 67, no. 3 (2014): 340–46, quotation at 344.
130 Kane, *Arctic Explorations*, 233.
131 Dick, "Aboriginal-European Relations."
132 Peary, "The Great White Journey," 227.
133 Shannon Ryan, *The Ice Hunters: A History of Newfoundland Sealing to 1914* (St. John's: Breakwater Books, 1994), 394.
134 Diebitsch-Peary, *My Arctic Journal*, 125.
135 Ibid.
136 Linda S. Bergmann, "Woman against a Background of White: The Representation of Self and Nature in Women's Arctic Narratives," *American Studies* 34, no. 2 (1993): 53–68.
137 Heidi Hansson, "Feminine Poles: Josephine Diebitsch-Peary's and Jennie Darlington's Polar Narratives," in *Northern Studies: Monographs No. 1* (Umea, Sweden: Umea University and the Royal Skyttean Society, 2009), 105–23, see especially 112.
138 Ibid.
139 "Josephine Diebitsch-Peary," biography, n.d., Peary-MacMillan Arctic Museum, Bowdoin College, Brunswick, ME.
140 LeMoine, "Elatu's Funeral," 344.
141 Counter, *North Pole Legacy*, 53.
142 Diebitsch-Peary, *My Arctic Journal*, 41.
143 Ibid., 74.
144 Ibid., 97.
145 Said, *Orientalism*.
146 Diebitsch-Peary, *My Arctic Journal*, 2.
147 Katherine Kirkpatrick, *The Snow Baby: The Arctic Childhood of Admiral Robert E. Peary's Daring Daughter* (New York: Holiday House, 2009).
148 Counter, *North Pole Legacy*, 53.
149 Kenn Harper, *Give Me My Father's Body: The Life of Minik, the New York Eskimo* (New York: Washington Square Press, 2001).
150 Ibid.
151 Ibid.
152 Robinson, *The Coldest Crucible*, 141.
153 Peary, *The North Pole*.
154 Henson, *A Black Explorer at the North Pole*, 7.

155 Ibid., 51.
156 Ibid.
157 Jeffrey Sobal, "Men, Meat and Marriage: Models of Masculinity," *Food and Foodways: Explorations in the History and Culture of Human Nourishment* 13, nos. 1–2 (2005): 135–58.
158 Malcolm Hamilton, "Eating Death: Vegetarians, Meat and Violence," *Food, Culture & Society: An International Journal of Multidisciplinary Research* 9, no. 2 (2006): 155–77.
159 "Matt Henson, Who Reached Pole with Peary in 1909, Dies at 88," *New York Times*, 10 March 1955.
160 Booker T. Washington, introduction to *A Black Explorer at the North Pole*, by Matthew Henson, xiii–xiv, see especially xiii.
161 Ibid., xiv.
162 Ibid.
163 Henson, *A Black Explorer at the North Pole*, 3.
164 Counter, *North Pole Legacy*.
165 William Laird McKinley, *Karluk: The Great Untold Story of Arctic Exploration* (London: Weidenfeld and Nicholson, 1976), 123.
166 Counter, *North Pole Legacy*, 76–77.
167 "Matt Henson, Explorer, Dies," *New York Age*, 19 March 1955.
168 "Matt Henson, Who Reached Pole."
169 Counter, *North Pole Legacy*, 76.
170 Henson, *A Black Explorer at the North Pole*, 127.
171 Ibid., 21.
172 Peary, *The North Pole*, 238.
173 Ibid.
174 Ibid.
175 Henson, *A Black Explorer at the North Pole*, 124.
176 Ibid.
177 Peary, *The North Pole*, 241.
178 Henson, *A Black Explorer at the North Pole*, 124.
179 Bartlett, *The Log of Bob Bartlett*, 163.
180 Peary, *The North Pole*, 240–41.
181 Henson, *A Black Explorer at the North Pole*, 126.
182 Horwood, *Bartlett: The Great Explorer*, 79.
183 Ibid.
184 Bartlett, *The Log of Bob Bartlett*, 163.
185 Horwood, *Bartlett: The Great Explorer*, 80.
186 Donald B. MacMillan, "Peary as a Leader: Incidents from the Life of the Discoverer of the North Pole Told by One of His Lieutenants on the Expedition Which Reached the Goal," *National Geographic* 37, no. 4 (1920): 293–317.
187 Peary, *The North Pole*, 241.
188 Ibid.
189 "Matt Henson, Who Reached Pole."
190 Bartlett, *The Log of Bob Bartlett*, 164.
191 Ibid., 163.
192 Henson, *A Black Explorer at the North Pole*, 131.
193 Ibid., 126.
194 "Obituary: Rear-Admiral Robert E. Peary," *U.S.N. Meetings: Royal Geographical Society* (1919–1920): 407.
195 Royal Geographical Society, "Meetings," 407.
196 "Doomed Expedition to the Pole, 1912," 1999, www.eyewitnesstohistory.com.
197 Henson, *A Black Explorer at the North Pole*, 135.
198 Ibid.
199 Ibid., 136.
200 Bartlett, *The Log of Bob Bartlett*, 166.
201 McGhee, *The Last Imaginary Place*.

202 Bartlett, *The Log of Bob Bartlett*, 162.
203 Horwood, *Bartlett: The Great Explorer*, 77.
204 Bartlett, *The Log of Bob Bartlett*, 162.
205 Robinson, *The Coldest Crucible*.
206 Horwood, *Bartlett: The Great Explorer*, 88.
207 Randall J. Osczevski, "Frederick Cook and the Forgotten North Pole," *Arctic* 56, no. 2 (2003): 207–17, see especially 210–11.
208 Robinson, *The Coldest Crucible*, 82.
209 Henson, *A Black Explorer at the North Pole*, 179.
210 McGhee, *The Last Imaginary Place*, 238.
211 "Cook Tried to Steal Parson's Life Work," *New York Times*, 21 May 1910.
212 O.R. Pildt, "Mysteries of a Frozen World," *Brooklyn Daily Eagle*, 5 October 1934.
213 Dennis Rawlins, *Peary at the North Pole: Fact or Fiction?* (Washington, DC: R.B. Luce, 1973).
214 Bartlett, *The Log of Bob Bartlett*, 165.
215 Henson, *A Black Explorer at the North Pole*, 151.
216 Ibid., 152.
217 Horwood, *Bartlett: The Great Explorer*, 78.
218 Counter, *North Pole Legacy*, 27.
219 Ibid., 66.
220 Ibid.
221 Henson, *A Black Explorer at the North Pole*.
222 Bartlett, *The Log of Bob Bartlett*, 160.
223 Henson, *A Black Explorer at the North Pole*, 181.
224 Ibid.
225 Royal Geographical Society, "Meetings," 407.
226 Sarnoff, *Ice Pilot*, 159.
227 Ibid., 109.
228 Ibid., 160.
229 Edward M. Weyer, "Captain Robert Abram Bartlett, in Memory," *The Explorers Journal* (Spring–Summer 1946): 12–13.
230 Sarnoff, *Ice Pilot*, 159.
231 Marie Peary Stafford, "Greenland Men Aid in Peary Memorial," *New York Times*, 28 July 1932.
232 Ibid.
233 Angel, interview.
234 Ibid.
235 Marie Peary Stafford to Captain Robert Bartlett, 2 April 1938, Robert Abram Bartlett Papers, George J. Mitchell Department of Special Collections & Archives, Bowdoin College Library, Brunswick, ME [Bartlett Papers].
236 Ibid.
237 Eleanor Bliss to Bartlett, 16 April 1946, Explorers Club: Robert Abram Bartlett.
238 Peary, *The North Pole*, 32.
239 Ibid.

CHAPTER TWO

1 Simone de Beauvoir, *The Second Sex*, trans. Constance Borde and Sheila Malovany-Chevallier (London: Jonathan Cape, 2009); Judith Butler, "Performative Acts and Gender Constitution: An Essay in Phenomenology and Feminist Theory," *Theatre Journal* 40, no. 4 (1988): 519–31.
2 Percy H.E. Cox, Colonel Vanier, and H.R. Mill, "Oxford University Ellesmere Land Expedition: Discussion," *The Geographical Journal* 87, no. 5 (1936): 441–43.
3 Francis Spufford, *I May Be Some Time: Ice and the English Imagination* (London: Faber & Faber, 1996), 1441.
4 Ibid.
5 Ibid.

6   Quoted in Renée Hulan, *Northern Experience and the Myths of Canadian Culture* (Montreal: McGill-Queen's University Press, 2002).

7   Janice Cavell, "Manliness in the Life and Posthumous Reputation of Robert Falcon Scott," *Canadian Journal of History* 45, no. 3 (2010): 537–64.

8   Ibid., 538.

9   Rebecca Farley, "'By Endurance We Conquer': Ernest Shackleton and Performances of White Male Hegemony," *International Journal of Cultural Studies* 8, no. 2 (2005): 248.

10   Hulan, *Northern Experience*, 65.

11   Peary, *The North Pole*, 60.

12   Ibid.

13   Kari Herbert, *Polar Wives: The Remarkable Women behind the World's Most Daring Explorers* (Vancouver: Greystone Books Ltd., 2012).

14   Robert A. Barlett to Greville Haslam, Sunday night, 1943, Stefansson MSS-193, Papers of Robert Abram (Bob) Bartlett, The Stefansson Collection on Polar Exploration, Rauner Special Collections, Dartmouth College Library, Hanover, NJ [Stefansson MSS-193].

15   John Leamon, *Brigus: Past Glory, Present Splendour* (St. John's: Harry Cuff Publications, 1998), 250.

16   Bartlett, *The Log of Bob Bartlett*, 45.

17   Ibid., 41.

18   Ibid.

19   Ibid.

20   Leamon, *Brigus: Past Glory, Present Splendour*, 250.

21   Ibid.

22   John Leamon, interview by James Candow, n.d., Parks Canada, St. John's.

23   Alan F. Williams, *John Guy of Bristol and Newfoundland: His Life, Times and Legacy* (St. John's: Flanker Press, 2010), 211.

24   Ibid., 279.

25   Leamon, interview.

26   Ibid.

27   Leamon, *Brigus: Past Glory, Present Splendour*.

28   Ibid., 250.

29   Ibid.

30   Ibid.

31   Ibid., 251.

32   "Brigus United Methodist Church Marriages, 1837–1924," 9 December 1874, http://ngb.chebucto.org/Parish/brigus-mar-4-pdg.shtml.

33   Leamon, *Brigus: Past Glory, Present Splendour*.

34   Geoffrey E. Clark, *Adolphus W. Greely: Abandoned in the Arctic: The Tragic Story of the Lady Franklin Bay Expedition, 1881–1884* (Portsmouth: Portsmouth Athenaeum, 2007).

35   Robinson, *The Coldest Crucible*, 83.

36   Charles Lench, *A Souvenir of the Brigus Methodist Jubilee of the Opening of the Church 1875–1925* (Brigus: Brigus Methodist Church, 1925).

37   Family Tree Maker, "Descendants of Robert Munden," http://familytreemaker.genealogy.com/users/c/a/n/Richard-J-Cannings/GENE7-0018.html#CHILD86.

38   Leamon, *Brigus: Past Glory, Present Splendour*.

39   Bartlett, *The Log of Bob Bartlett*, 38.

40   Family Tree Maker, "Descendants of Robert Munden."

41   "Brigus United Methodist Church Marriages, 1837–1924," 9 December 1874.

42   Jenny Higgins, "Health," 2008, http://www.heritage.nf.ca/society/health.html.

43   Daniel Henderson, "The Soft Side of Skipper Bob Bartlett," *Motor Boating* 93, no. 3 (1954): 39, 120–22, 150.

44   Lovell's 1871 Provincial Business Directory Newfoundland, *Brigus* (Montreal: John Lovell's), 71, www.ngb.chebucto.org/L1871/71-brigus01.shtml.

45   Bartlett, *The Log of Bob Bartlett*, 41.

46   Leamon, *Brigus: Past Glory, Present Splendour*, 250.

47 John C. Crosbie, *No Holds Barred: My Life in Politics* (Toronto: McClelland and Stewart, 1997).
48 Bartlett, *The Log of Bob Bartlett*, 46.
49 Ryan, *The Ice Hunters*, 15; S.J.R. Noel, *Politics in Newfoundland* (Toronto: University of Toronto Press, 1971).
50 Bartlett, *The Log of Bob Bartlett*, 30.
51 Angel, interview.
52 Sir Wilfred Grenfell to Bartlett, 3 March 1938, Bartlett Papers.
53 Putnam to Bartlett, 4 July 1926, Explorers Club: George Palmer Putnam, 20.
54 Ibid.
55 Lench, *Souvenir of the Brigus Methodist Jubilee.*
56 Angel, interview.
57 Bartlett, *The Log of Bob Bartlett*, 44.
58 Thomas à Kempis, "Imitation of Christ (1418)," in *The Gospel of John: Introduction, Exposition*, notes by F.F. Bruce (Grand Rapids, MI: Wm. Eerdmans, 1994), 299.
59 Bartlett, *The Log of Bob Bartlett*, 44; Ernest Renan, *Life of Jesus* (London: Truber and Co., 1864).
60 Omar Khayyám, *The Rubāiyāt of Omar Khayyám*, trans. Edward Fitzgerald, 1859 (Project Gutenberg, 2008 edition), www.gutenberg.org/ebooks/246, 104.
61 Ibid., 112.
62 Peter Hart, *Mick: The Real Michael Collins* (London: Pan Macmillan, 2006).
63 Bartlett, *The Log of Bob Bartlett*, 42.
64 Moses Bartlett, *The Log of the* Windward, handwritten ship's log, 1902, The Rooms Provincial Archives Division, St. John's.
65 Putnam to Bartlett, Explorers Club: George Palmer Putnam.
66 Melvin Baker, "Newfoundland in the 1920s," http://www.ucs.mun.ca/~melbaker/1919-28.htm (site discontinued); Bartlett, *The Log of Bob Bartlett*, 144.
67 Bartlett, *The Log of Bob Bartlett*, 104.
68 Ibid., 105.
69 Leamon, *Brigus: Past Glory, Present Splendour,* 355.
70 Ibid.
71 Ibid.
72 Bartlett, *The Log of Bob Bartlett*, 46.
73 Angel, interview.
74 Leamon, *Brigus: Past Glory, Present Splendour*, 370.
75 Ibid.
76 Bartlett to Greville Haslam, Stefansson MSS-193.
77 Leamon, *Brigus: Past Glory, Present Splendour*, 358.
78 Gordon Spracklin, interview by author, May 2008.
79 Ruperta Angel Murphy, unpublished memoir of Hawthorne Cottage, Historic Sites Association of Newfoundland and Labrador, n.d.
80 Bartlett, *The Log of Bob Bartlett*, 88.
81 Murphy, unpublished memoir of Hawthorne Cottage.
82 Ibid.
83 Ibid.
84 Ibid.
85 "Kent Cottage at Landfall (Brigus)," http://www.heritage.nf.ca/articles/society/landfall-kents-cottage.php.
86 Mildred Brown, "House of Dread. House of Joy," *Rockwell Kent Review* 40, no. 1 (2014): 5–8.
87 Grace Glueck, "Celebrating an Artist's Spiritual Searches and Realist Findings," *New York Times*, 26 August 2005, http://www.nytimes.com/2005/08/26/arts/design/26kent.html?pagewanted=all&_r=0.
88 Ed Roberts, "Rockwell Kent—'The Brigus Spy,'" Carbonear *Compass*, 18 January 2012, http://www.cbncompass.ca/Columnists/Ed-Roberts/2012-01-18/article-2867288/Rockwell-Kent-%26mdash%3B-The-Brigus-Spy/1.

89 Frederick Lewis, "The Brigus Spy," *Newfoundland Quarterly* 107, no. 1 (2015): 17–21, quotation at 21.
90 Ibid., 21.
91 Leamon, *Brigus: Past Glory, Present Splendour.*
92 Ibid.
93 Emma Bartlett to Ward Randol, 14 January 1961, Explorers Club: Robert Abram Bartlett.
94 "The Captain's Cottage," *The Express,* 27 June 1995, 19.
95 Hugh Stewart, "Robert Bartlett (1875–1946)," *Arctic* 39, no. 2 (1986): 188–89.
96 Rupert Jackson, "The Bartletts of Benville," *Evening Telegram*, n.d. ca. 1935, Explorers Club: Flora Jo Bergstrom.
97 Ibid.
98 F.W. Angel to Bartlett, 3 November 1934, Bartlett Papers.
99 Spracklin, interview.
100 Leamon, interview.
101 Bernard Kennedy, e-mail message to author, 2008.
102 Leo Kennedy, in discussion with author, May 2009.
103 Ibid.
104 Spracklin, interview.
105 Leamon, *Brigus: Past Glory, Present Splendour*, 123.
106 Editorial, *Decks Awash* 15, no. 2 (1986): 68.
107 S.A., interview by author, May 2008.
108 Spracklin, interview.
109 Eleanor Bartlett to Bartlett, 5 January n.d., Bartlett Papers.
110 Eleanor Bartlett to Bergstrom, 9 September 1962, Explorers Club: Flora Jo Bergstrom.
111 S.A., interview.
112 Robert A. Bartlett, "Sealing—Newfoundland and Labrador," *National Geographic* 56, no. 1 (1929): 91–130, quotation at 130.
113 Ibid., 121.
114 Ibid., 123.
115 Lewis Bartlett to Bartlett, 1 March 1928, Bartlett Papers.

CHAPTER THREE

1 Horwood, *Bartlett: The Great Explorer*, 38.
2 Sarnoff, *Ice Pilot*, 125.
3 Joxe Mallea-Olaetxe, *The Basques of Reno and the Northeastern Sierra* (Chicago: Arcadia Publishing, 2009), 9.
4 George A. Rose, "Fisheries Resources and Science in Newfoundland and Labrador: An Independent Assessment," Government of Newfoundland and Labrador: Royal Commission on Renewing and Strengthening Our Place in Canada, March 2003; A.H. McLintock, *The Establishment of Constitutional Government in Newfoundland, 1783–1832: A Study of Retarded Colonisation* (London: Longmans, Green and Co., 1941), iv.
5 Roger E. Riendeau, *A Brief History of Canada* (New York: Facts on File Publications, 2007), 83.
6 Ingeborg Marshall, *A History and Ethnography of the Beothuk* (Montreal: McGill-Queen's University Press, 1996).
7 Albert Gatschet, "The Beothuk Indians," *Proceedings of the American Philosophical Society* 28, no. 132 (1890): 9.
8 Richard Budgell, "The Beothuks and the Newfoundland Mind," Journal of Newfoundland Studies 8, no. 1 (1992): 21; Francis B. Briffett, *The Story of Newfoundland and Labrador* (London: J.M. Dent, 1949), 48.
9 James Howley, *The Beothuks or Red Indians: The Aboriginal Inhabitants of Newfoundland* (Cambridge: Cambridge University Press, 1915), 181, 279.
10 Bartlett, *The Log of Bob Bartlett,* 25.
11 Gordon Hancock, "The West Country," 2000, http://www.heritage.nf.ca/society/west_country.html.
12 Counter, *North Pole Legacy.*

13 Philip Gibbs, *Adventures in Journalism* (New York: Harper and Brother Publishers, 1923).

14 Marilyn Lake and Henry Reynolds, *Drawing the Colour Line: White Men's Countries and the Question of Racial Equality* (Melbourne: Melbourne University Publishing, 2008).

15 Henderson, "The Soft Side of Skipper Bob Bartlett," 39.

16 Samuel Bartlett, interview by Susan Cummings, Historic Sites Association of Newfoundland and Labrador, 1992, 7.

17 Peary, *The North Pole*, 32.

18 Shortis, "Captain 'Bob' Bartlett Tells of Far North Fish," 1917, Shortis Papers.

19 Ibid.

20 Philip Gibbs, "The Fascination and Dangers of the Sea: Captain Bartlett, the Unchained Man," *The Graphic*, 11 June 1910.

21 "'Bob' Bartlett Back to the Arctic to Hunt Big Game. Peary's Skipper, Tired of Civilization, Is Taking an Expedition to a Sportsman's Paradise in the Polar Regions," New York *Times*, 14 May 1911.

22 Gibbs, "The Fascination and Dangers of the Sea," 852.

23 Ibid.

24 Leamon, *Brigus: Past Glory, Present Splendour*, 321.

25 Ibid.

26 *Encyclopedia of Newfoundland* (*ENL*), s.v. "Captain Abraham Bartlett."

27 Maura Hanrahan, *Domino: The Eskimo Coast Disaster* (St. John's: Flanker Press, 2006), 14; Sarnoff, *Ice Pilot*, 30–36.

28 John C. Kennedy, "Labrador's Inuit-Metis: The Historical Background," 2012, http://www.heritage.nf.ca/aboriginal/metis.html; James Hiller, "Moravian Church," 2001, http://www.heritage.nf.ca/society/moravian.html.

29 Fitzhugh Green, *Bob Bartlett: Master Mariner* (New York: G.P. Putnam's Sons, 1926), 23–24.

30 Daniel Prowse, *A History of Newfoundland from the English, Colonial, and Foreign Records* (London: Eyre and Spottiswoode, 1896), 602.

31 "The Gale off Labrador," *New York Times*, 8 November 1885, http://ngb.chebucto.org/Articles/dis-labrador-gale-1885.shtml.

32 Ibid.

33 Ibid.

34 Hanrahan, *Domino: The Eskimo Coast Disaster,* 108–9.

35 Ibid.; "The Gale off Labrador."

36 *ENL*, s.v. "Captain Abraham Bartlett."

37 "Brigus United Methodist Church Marriages, 1837–1924," 9 December 1874.

38 Ibid.

39 Ibid.

40 George Putnam, *Mariner of the North: The Life of Captain Bob Bartlett* (New York: Duell, Sloan and Pearce, 1947), 16–18.

41 Stewart, "Capt. Bob's Account."

42 Marilyn Porter, "She Was Skipper of the Shore-Crew: Notes on the History of the Sexual Division of Labour in Newfoundland," *Labour/Le Travail* 15 (Spring 1985): 105–23.

43 Putnam, *Mariner of the North*, 18.

44 Ibid.

45 Noel, *Politics in Newfoundland*, 264.

46 Higgins, "Health."

47 Melissa Hawkins, "Introduction to the Problem of Infant Mortality," *Johns Hopkins Bloomberg School of Public Health* (2006), http://ocw.jhsph.edu/courses/preventinginfantmortality/PDFs/Lecture1.pdf.

48 Putnam, *Mariner of the North*, 16.

49 Leamon, *Brigus: Past Glory, Present Splendour*, vii.

50 Noel, *Politics in Newfoundland*, 80.

51 Ibid.

52 George Story, W.J. Kirwin, and J.D.A. Widdowson, eds., *Dictionary of Newfoundland English* (Toronto: University of Toronto, 1990), 394.
53 Quoted in Prowse, *History of Newfoundland from the English, Colonial, and Foreign Records*, 419.
54 Frederick William Rowe, *A History of Newfoundland and Labrador* (Toronto: McGraw-Hill Ryerson, 1980).
55 Ibid.
56 Bartlett, "Sealing—Newfoundland and Labrador"; Bartlett, *The Log of Bob Bartlett*.
57 Dennis Flynn, "The Landfall Legacy," *Downhome Traveller*, April 2010, http://www. landfalltrust.org/pdf/Landfall%20Article%20by%20Dennis%20Flynn%20in%20PDF. pdf.
58 Roland Wells, "The Town of Brigus," http://www.brigus.net/wells.htm (site discontinued).
59 Ibid.
60 Prowse, *A History of Newfoundland*, 232.
61 Wells, "The Town of Brigus."
62 Ibid.
63 Robert Bartlett, "*Morrissey* Sails through Ice Belt," *New York Times*, 26 July 1940.
64 Wells, "The Town of Brigus."
65 Ibid.
66 Lench, *Souvenir of the Brigus Methodist Jubilee.*
67 Wells, "The Town of Brigus."
68 Bartlett, *The Log of Bob Bartlett*, 26.
69 Ibid., 39.
70 María Jesús Hernáez Lerena, "Two Voices from Newfoundland: History and Myth Addressed by Maura Hanrahan and Paul Butler," *Revista Canaria de Estudios Ingleses* 56 (April 2008): 99–119, quotation at 103.
71 Shannon Ryan, "Newfoundland Spring Sealing Disasters to 1914," *The Northern Mariner* 3, no. 3 (1993): 15–48, see especially 33.
72 David Alexander, "The Political Economy of Fishing in Newfoundland," *Journal of Canadian Studies* 11, no. 1 (1976): 32–40.
73 William E. Schrank, "The Newfoundland Fishery: Ten Years after the Moratorium," *Marine Policy* 29, no. 5 (2005): 407–20.
74 "Abram Bartlett. Indenture," 24 February 1854, The Rooms Provincial Archives Division; Abraham Bartlett, July 1852, Last Will and Testament, The Rooms Provincial Archives Division.
75 Abraham Bartlett, July 1852, Last Will and Testament.
76 Bartlett to Greville Haslam, Sunday night, 1943, Stefansson MSS-193.
77 Abraham Bartlett, July 1852, Last Will and Testament.
78 Ibid.
79 Ibid.
80 Ibid.
81 Ibid.
82 "Captain Bartlett Buried: Thousands Gather in Brigus for Funeral of Explorer," *New York Times*, 10 May 1946, Explorers Club: Robert Abram Bartlett.
83 John Edward FitzGerald, "Conflict and Culture in Irish-Newfoundland Roman Catholicism, 1829–1850" (PhD diss., University of Ottawa, 1997), http://www.ruor. uottawa.ca/en/handle/10393/9512.
84 Prowse, *A History of Newfoundland*, 232.
85 Wells, "The Town of Brigus."
86 Lench, *Souvenir of the Brigus Methodist Jubilee.*
87 Robert Bartlett, "The Kind Eskimo," lecture, ca. 1930, Pond files, Rauner Library, Dartmouth College, Hanover, NH.
88 Family Tree Maker, "Descendants of Robert Munden."
89 Leamon, *Brigus: Past Glory, Present Splendour,* 86.
90 Lench, *Souvenir of the Brigus Methodist Jubilee.*

91   Ibid.
92   Shortis, "The Voyage of Brigantine 'Albeona,'" 1919, Shortis Papers.
93   Shortis, "Captain 'Bob' Bartlett Tells of Far North Fish."
94   Lench, *Souvenir of the Brigus Methodist Jubilee*, 49.
95   Ibid.
96   Ibid., 30, 46.
97   Leamon, *Brigus: Past Glory, Present Splendour,* 82.
98   Ibid.
99   Lench, *Souvenir of the Brigus Methodist Jubilee.*
100 Ibid.
101 Leamon, *Brigus: Past Glory, Present Splendour,* 46–47.
102 Ibid.
103 George A. Rose, *Cod: The Ecological History of the North Atlantic Fisheries* (St. John's: Breakwater Books, 2007), 308; Leamon, *Brigus: Past Glory, Present Splendour*, 48.
104 Leamon, *Brigus: Past Glory, Present Splendour*, 49.
105 Ibid., 48.
106 Ibid.
107 Family Tree Maker, "Descendants of Robert Munden."
108 Solomon P. Whiteway, "Newfoundland Education until 1949," in *The Encyclopedia of Canada. Newfoundland Supplement*, by W. Stewart Wallace (Toronto: University Associates of Canada, 1949), 17–21.
109 Wells, "The Town of Brigus."
110 Leamon, *Brigus: Past Glory, Present Splendour*, 185.
111 Ibid., 359.
112 Ibid., 368–69.
113 Leamon, *Brigus: Past Glory, Present Splendour*, 359–67.
114 Ibid., 359.
115 Harold Bartlett, "Lecture of Capt. Harold Bartlett," 16 January 1940, Historical Society, St. John's, Bartlett Papers.
116 Ibid.
117 Ibid.

CHAPTER FOUR

1   Margaret MacMillan, *History's People: Personalities and the Past* (Toronto: House of Anansi, 2015).
2   Nurse, "Captain Robert A. Bartlett."
3   Bartlett, "Sealing—Newfoundland and Labrador," 101.
4   Ibid.
5   Ibid., 96.
6   Ibid.
7   Nurse, "Captain Robert A. Bartlett," 1.
8   Ibid.
9   Robert A. Bartlett, [Untitled], *Explorers Journal* 8, no. 2 (1929): 39.
10   Ibid.
11   Stafford, "Greenland Men Aid in Peary Memorial."
12   LeMoine, "Elatu's Funeral," 345.
13   Ibid.
14   David Gray and Sally Gray, *Canadian Arctic Expedition 1913–1918: Commemorating the 100th Anniversary* (Metcalfe, ON: Grayhound Information Services, 2013), http://canadianarcticexpedition.com/.
15   "The People of the Canadian Arctic Expedition. 1913–1918," Gatineau, QC: Canadian Museum of Natural History, n.d., http://www.historymuseum.ca/cmc/exhibitions/hist/cae/peo60e.shtml.
16   Gray and Gray, *Canadian Arctic Expedition.*
17   Gordon Smith, *A Historical and Legal Study of Sovereignty in the Canadian North: Terrestrial Sovereignty. 1870–1939* (Calgary: University of Calgary Press, 2014), 146.

18   Ibid., 174–75.
19   "Stefansson Has Started on Scientific Expedition into the Cold Arctic Regions," *Evening Journal*, 7 June 1913.
20   Vilhjalmur Stefansson, *The Friendly Arctic: The Story of Five Years in Polar Regions* (1921; New York: Macmillan, 1943).
21   Bjarne Mamen, "Autobiography of Bjarne Mamen," *The Karluk Chronicle*, ed. Burt M. McConnell (30 June 1913), William Laird McKinley Correspondence and Papers, Canadian Arctic Expedition—Stefansson Arctic Expedition, Library and Archives Canada, Ottawa [McKinley Correspondence and Papers].
22   George Malloch, "Autobiography of George Stewart Malloch," *The Karluk Chronicle*, ed. McConnell (2 July 1913), McKinley Correspondence and Papers.
23   Stuart Edward Jenness, ed., *Arctic Odyssey: The Diary of Diamond Jenness, Ethnologist with the Canadian Arctic Expedition in Northern Alaska and Canada, 1913–1916* (Gatineau, QC: Canadian Museum of Civilization, 1991), xvi.
24   Ibid.
25   Henri Beuchat, "Autobiography of Henri Beuchat," *The Karluk Chronicle*, ed. McConnell (29 June 1913), McKinley Correspondence and Papers.
26   Ibid.
27   Ibid.
28   "Stefansson Has Started on Scientific Expedition."
29   Burt M. McConnell, "Autobiography of Burt Morton McConnell," *The Karluk Chronicle*, ed. McConnell (6 July 1913), McKinley Correspondence and Papers.
30   Ibid.
31   McKinley, *Karluk*, 46.
32   "The People of the Canadian Arctic Expedition. 1913–1918."
33   "Stefansson Has Started on Scientific Expedition."
34   Jennifer Niven, *The Ice Master: The Doomed 1913 Voyage of the Karluk* (Basingstoke, UK: Pan Books, 2000), 8.
35   Robert A. Bartlett, "Captain Bartlett's Story of the *Karluk's* Last Voyage," *New York Times*, 19 November 1916.
36   "Stefansson Has Started on Scientific Expedition."
37   Ibid.
38   Robert A. Bartlett, *The Last Voyage of the* Karluk (1916; St. John's: Flanker Press, 2007), 2.
39   Mamen, "Autobiography of Bjarne Mamen," 5.
40   "Stefansson Has Started on Scientific Expedition."
41   McKinley, *Karluk*, 17.
42   Maura Hanrahan, "Bartlett, Robert 'Bob' Abram (1875–1946)," in *Antarctica and the Arctic Circle: A Geographic Encyclopedia of the Earth's Polar Regions*, ed. Andrew J. Hund (ABC-CLIO, 2014), 1:130–31.
43   Stefansson, *The Friendly Arctic*, 47.
44   Ibid., 48.
45   Bartlett, "Captain Bartlett's Story."
46   Burt M. McConnell, "Autobiography of William Laird McKinley," *The Karluk Chronicle*, ed. McConnell (28 June 1913), McKinley Correspondence and Papers.
47   Ibid.
48   Mamen, diary, 70.
49   Ibid.
50   Ibid., 4.
51   Ibid., 4.
52   Mamen, "Autobiography of Bjarne Mamen," 4.
53   Ibid., 7.
54   Mamen, diary, 75–76.
55   William Laird McKinley to Mr. Anderson, 14 March 1915, McKinley Correspondence and Papers, 3.

56 R.A. Bartlett, 1 August 1913, *Diary of R.A. Bartlett,* MIKAN 1641255, Canadian Arctic Expedition–Stefansson Arctic Expedition, Library and Archives Canada, Ottawa, 4.

57 Horwood, *Bartlett: The Great Explorer*, 4.

58 Bartlett, *The Log of Bob Bartlett,* 228.

59 *Diary of R.A. Bartlett*, 19 July 1913, 2.

60 Ibid., 13 August 1913, 5.

61 Bartlett, *The Log of Bob Bartlett,* 227.

62 *Diary of R.A. Bartlett*, 12 August 1913, 5.

63 William Barr, "The Voyages of *Taymyr* and *Vaygach* to Ostrov Vrangelya, 1910–15," *Polar Record* 16, no. 101 (1972): 213–34; Richard J. Diubaldo, "Wrangling over Wrangel Island," *Canadian Historical Review* 48, no. 3 (1967): 201–26.

64 Bartlett, *The Last Voyage of the* Karluk, 39.

65 Ibid.

66 Ibid., 33.

67 *Diary of R.A. Bartlett*, 20 September 1913, 5.

68 McKinley, *Karluk,* 28.

69 Ibid., 34.

70 Ibid., 56.

71 Bartlett, "Captain Bartlett's Story."

72 *Diary of R.A. Bartlett*, multiple dates.

73 *Diary of R.A. Bartlett*, 16 December 1913, 24.

74 McKinley, *Karluk.*

75 *Diary of R.A. Bartlett,* 25 September 1913, 25.

76 Bartlett, *The Last Voyage of the* Karluk, 70.

77 Bartlett, "Captain Bartlett's Story."

78 Bartlett, *The Last Voyage of the* Karluk, 69.

79 Ibid., 68.

80 Ibid., 75.

81 Ibid., 109.

82 Mamen, diary.

83 Ernest F. Chafe, "The Voyage of the 'Karluk' and Its Tragic Ending," *The Geographic Journal* 51, no. 5 (1918): 307–16, quotation at 309.

84 Ibid., 311.

85 *Diary of R.A. Bartlett*, 10 January 1914, 27.

86 Ibid., 28.

87 McKinley, *Karluk,* 66.

88 Ibid., 66.

89 Mamen, diary, 98.

90 Ibid.

91 Ibid.

92 Bartlett, "Captain Bartlett's Story."

93 Mamen, diary, 98.

94 McKinley, *Karluk*, 67.

95 Ibid.

96 *Diary of R.A. Bartlett*, 11 January 1914, 28.

97 Bartlett, *The Last Voyage of the* Karluk, 82.

98 Bartlett, "Captain Bartlett's Story."

99 *Diary of R.A. Bartlett,* 10 January 1914, 27.

100 Ibid.

101 Mamen, diary, 92.

102 Ibid., 20.

103 McKinley, *Karluk*, 55.

104 *Diary of R.A. Bartlett*, 31 January 1914, 33.

105 Bartlett, *The Last Voyage of the* Karluk, 117.

106 Janice Cavell, "Vilhjalmur Stefansson, Robert Bartlett, and the *Karluk* Disaster: A Reassessment," *The Journal of the Hakluyt Society* (January 2017), http://www.hakluyt.com/PDF/Karluk.pdf.

107 McKinley, *Karluk*, 12.

108 Bartlett, "Captain Bartlett's Story."

109 Bartlett, *The Last Voyage of the* Karluk, 97.

110 *Diary of R.A. Bartlett*, 9 February 1914, 35.

111 Bartlett, *The Last Voyage of the* Karluk, 148.

112 Bartlett, "Captain Bartlett's Story."

113 *Diary of R.A. Bartlett*, 3 February 1914, 34.

114 Bartlett, *The Last Voyage of the* Karluk, 155.

115 "Stefansson and How the *Karluk* Drifted," *New York Times,* 9 December 1913.

116 Ibid.; "Explorer Tells Story of Party Lost in Ice Pack," Indianapolis *Sunday Star*, 22 February 1914, 1 and 9.

117 "Stefansson and How the *Karluk* Drifted."

118 "May Be 'Inside Story' in Stefansson's Plight: Why Did He 'Lose' Ship?" Ottawa *Evening Journal*, 11 December 1913.

119 Ingvar Svanborg, "Chukchi," in *Antarctica and the Arctic Circle: A Geographic Encyclopedia of the Earth's Polar Regions*, ed. Andrew J. Hund (ABC-CLIO, 2014), 1:177–81, see especially 179.

120 M.K. Kos'ko, B.G. Lopatin, and V.G. Ganelin, "Major Geological Features of the Islands of the East Siberian and Chukchi Seas and the Northern Coast of Chukotka," *Marine Geology* 93 (1990): 349–67, see especially 357.

121 Horwood, *Bartlett: The Great Explorer*, 18.

122 Ibid.

123 Mamen, diary, 111.

124 *Diary of R.A. Bartlett*, 10 February, 34; 15 March, 41; 16 March 1914, 42.

125 Ibid., 16 March 1914, 42.

126 McKinley, *Karluk*, 95.

127 Ibid., 24 March 1914, 43.

128 Ibid., 25 March 1914, 43.

129 Ibid., 26 March 1914, 43.

130 Bartlett, *The Last Voyage of the* Karluk, 174.

131 Ibid., 190.

132 Claude Kataktovik to Elaoiyin (?), 30 April 1913, McKinley Correspondence and Papers.

133 *Diary of R.A. Bartlett*, 29 March 1914, 44.

134 Bartlett, *The Last Voyage of the* Karluk, 176.

135 Ibid., 154.

136 *Diary of R.A. Bartlett*, 10 April 1914, 45.

137 Bartlett, "Sealing—Newfoundland and Labrador," 128.

138 Bartlett, *The Last Voyage of the* Karluk, 204.

139 *Diary of R.A. Bartlett*, 30 March 1914, 44.

140 Ibid., 179.

141 *Diary of R.A. Bartlett*, 5 April 1914, 45.

142 T. Max Friesen, "Resource Structure, Scalar Stress, and the Development of Inuit Social Organization," *World Archaeology* 31, no. 1 (1999): 21–37, see especially 32.

143 Ernest S. Burch Jr., "The Inupiat and the Christianization of Arctic Alaska," *Etudes/Inuit/Studies* 18, nos. 1–2 (1980): 81–108.

144 Friesen, "Resource Structure," 26.

145 Ibid., 32.

146 Ibid.

147 Ibid., 31.

148 Burch, "The Inupiat," 90.

149 Ibid.

150 McKinley, *Karluk*, 49.

151 Ernest S. Burch, *Social Life in Northwest Alaska: The Structure of Inupiaq Eskimo Nations* (Fairbanks: University of Alaska Press, 2006).
152 Burch, "The Inupiat," 90.
153 Ibid.
154 Ibid.
155 Ibid.
156 Ibid., 81.
157 Bartlett, *The Last Voyage of the* Karluk, 60.
158 David Paul King, *A Brief Report of the Federal Government of Canada's Residential School System for Inuit* (Ottawa: Aboriginal Healing Foundation/Fondation autochtone de guérison, 2006); Alan R. Marcus, "Out in the Cold: Canada's Experimental Inuit Relocation to Grise Fiord and Resolute Bay," *Polar Record* 27, no. 163 (1991): 285–96.
159 Peter Bjerregaard, T. Kue Young, Eric Dewailly, and Sven O.E. Ebbesson, "Review Article: Indigenous Health in the Arctic: An Overview of the Circumpolar Inuit Population," *Scandinavian Journal of Social Medicine* 32, no. 5 (2004): 390–95.
160 Lisa Marin Wexler, "Inupiat Youth Suicide and Culture Loss: Changing Community Conversations for Prevention," *Social Science & Medicine* 63, no. 11 (2006): 2938–48.
161 Bartlett, *The Last Voyage of the Karluk,* 152.
162 Bartlett, *The Log of Bob Bartlett,* 244.
163 Peter P. Schweitzer and Evgeniy Golovko, "Traveling between Continents: The Social Organization of Interethnic Contacts across Bering Strait," *The Anthropology of East Europe Review* 13, no. 2 (1995): 50–55, see especially 52.
164 W.H. Dall, "On the So-Called Chukchi and Namollo People of Eastern Siberia," *American Naturalist* 15, no. 11 (1881): 857–68, quotation at 867.
165 Bartlett, *The Last Voyage of the* Karluk, 191.
166 Ibid.
167 Ibid., 203.
168 *Diary of R.A. Bartlett,* 6 April 1914, 45.
169 Bartlett, *The Last Voyage of the* Karluk, 194.
170 Ibid., 196.
171 Ibid.
172 Ibid., 195.
173 Ibid., 192.
174 Ibid., 204.
175 Robert A. Bartlett, "Newfoundland Seals," *Journal of Mammalogy* 8, no. 3 (1927): 207–12.
176 Bartlett, *The Last Voyage of the* Karluk, 198.
177 Ibid.
178 Ibid., 220.
179 Ibid., 218.
180 Ibid., 221.
181 Ibid., 192.
182 Ibid., 216.
183 Svanborg, "Chukchi," 178.
184 Bartlett, *The Last Voyage of the* Karluk, 196.
185 Vladislav Nuvano, "Chukchi Reindeer Herding Culture," *Inuit Studies* 31, nos. 1–2 (2007): 307–10, see especially 308.
186 Ibid.
187 Anna M. Kerttula, "Antler on the Sea: Creating and Maintaining Cultural Group Boundaries among the Chukchi, Yupik, and Newcomers of Sireniki," *Arctic Anthropology* 34, no. 1 (1997): 212–26, see especially 218.
188 "The Stefansson Expedition: Fears for the *Karluk*," *London Times*, 23 May 1914.
189 Chafe, "The Voyage of the 'Karluk,'" 314.
190 "The Stefansson Expedition."
191 Ibid.
192 Ibid.
193 Ibid.

194 Chafe, "The Voyage of the 'Karluk,'" 311.
195 *Diary of R.A. Bartlett,* 16 February 1914, 36.
196 Ibid., 22 April 1914, 46.
197 Bartlett, *The Last Voyage of the* Karluk, 248.
198 Ibid., 250.
199 Ibid., 254.
200 Ibid., 253.
201 Ibid., 255.
202 Ibid., 271.
203 Ibid., 283.
204 Ibid., 258.
205 Chafe, "The Voyage of the 'Karluk,'" 315.
206 Ibid.
207 William Laird McKinley, typewritten diary, 1914, McKinley Correspondence and Papers.
208 Ibid.
209 Ibid.
210 Ibid.
211 McKinley, *Karluk,* 59.
212 Mamen, diary, 92–93.
213 McKinley, typewritten diary.
214 Ibid.
215 Bartlett, *The Last Voyage of the* Karluk, 271.
216 *Diary of R.A. Bartlett,* 22 April 1914, 46.
217 McKinley, typewritten diary.
218 Ibid.
219 Stefansson, *The Friendly Arctic,* 729.
220 Ibid.
221 Chafe, "The Voyage of the 'Karluk,'" 315.
222 William Laird McKinley, "Typescript Work on the Life and Activities of Stefansson" (unpublished manuscript, n.d.), McKinley Correspondence and Papers.
223 Chafe, "The Voyage of the 'Karluk,'" 315.
224 Stefansson, *The Friendly Arctic,* 730.
225 Ibid.
226 Chafe, "The Voyage of the 'Karluk,'" 315.
227 *Diary of R.A. Bartlett,* 22 April 1914, 46.
228 Bartlett, *The Last Voyage of the* Karluk, 277.
229 Ibid., 277–78.
230 Ibid., 287.
231 Ibid., 278.
232 Dugald McConnell, "Marooned at the End of the World," 14 July 2013, http://www.cnn.com/2013/07/13/world/americas/deadly-arctic-expedition/.
233 Mamen, diary.
234 Bartlett, *The Last Voyage of the* Karluk, 278.
235 Ibid.
236 John Hadley, "Appendix: The Story of the Karluk," in *The Friendly Arctic,* 720.
237 McKinley, *Karluk,* 136.
238 Ibid.
239 Ibid., 142.
240 Cavell, "Vilhjalmur Stefansson."
241 Grace Malloch to Mr. (William Laird) McKinley, 19 April 1915 (?), McKinley Correspondence and Papers, 1.
242 Bartlett, *The Last Voyage of the* Karluk, 281.
243 Hampton Sides, *In the Kingdom of Ice: The Grand and Terrible Polar Voyage of the U.S.S.* Jeannette (Doubleday: 2014).
244 Gershom Bradford, "Captain Robert A. Bartlett Personal Recollections," *Explorers Journal* (September 1965): 149–53, quotation at 150.

245 Bartlett, "Captain Bartlett's Story."
246 Bartlett, *The Last Voyage of the* Karluk, 240.
247 Ibid.
248 Ibid., 186.
249 Bartlett, *The Log of Bob Bartlett*, 244.
250 Bell Bannerman Finley to William L. McKinley, 18 March 1921, McKinley Correspondence and Papers.
251 William Laird McKinley to Mr. Anderson, 14 March 1915, 1.
252 McKinley to Anderson, 1.
253 Ibid., 2.
254 McKinley, *Karluk*.
255 Ibid., 115.
256 Ibid., 98.
257 Ibid., 107.
258 Mamen, diary, 100.
259 "Death Camp Found in Arctic Solves Fate of Four Adventurers Lost in 1914. Scientists of *Karluk* Perished on Herald Isle," *Winnipeg Evening Tribune*, 14 October 1924.
260 Ibid.
261 Ibid.
262 Ibid.
263 Ibid.
264 Ibid.
265 "Steam Whaler Will Search for Missing *Karluk*," Vancouver *Daily World*, 24 March 1914.
266 McKinley, *Karluk*, 76–77.
267 Bartlett, *The Last Voyage of the* Karluk, 33.
268 Vilhjalmur Stefansson to Bartlett, 20 September 1913, McKinley Correspondence and Papers, 1–2.
269 Ibid., 2.
270 Cavell, "Vilhjalmur Stefansson."
271 William Herbert Hobbs, review of *The Friendly Arctic*, by Vilhjalmur Stefansson, *The Journal of Geology* 31, no. 2 (1923): 154–58.
272 Bartlett to Dr. Townsend Thorndyke, n.d. ca. 1914, Stefansson MSS-193.

CHAPTER FIVE
1   Peary, *The North Pole*, 289.
2   Stanley A. Freed, "Fate of the Crocker Land Expedition: One Hundred Years Ago, the Search Began for a Mysterious Arctic Territory," *National History Magazine* (2012), http://www.naturalhistorymag.com/features/092248/fate-of-the-crocker-land-expedition.
3   Ibid.
4   John Franch, "The Search for Crockerland: Doom, Death and Drama Infuse a University of Illinois Expedition to the Arctic," *Illinois Alumni Magazine* (January/February 2008).
5   Ibid.
6   Ibid.
7   Ibid.
8   Green, *Bob Bartlett*.
9   Fitzhugh Green, *Peary: The Man Who Refused to Fail* (New York: G.P. Putnam's Sons), 1926.
10   Franch, "The Search for Crockerland."
11   Horwood, *Bartlett: The Great Explorer*, 105.
12   Franch, "The Search for Crockerland."
13   Horwood, *Bartlett: The Great Explorer*, 105.
14   Service Record: Rupert Bartlett. The Newfoundland Regiment and the Great War Database, The Rooms Provincial Archives Division. http://www.therooms.ca/regiment/soldier_files/Bartlett_Rupert_W_rnr-0118.pdf (discontinued).
15   Ibid, 35.
16   Ibid.
17   Ibid, 23.

18 R.A. Squires, colonial secretary, telegram to Edith Bartlett, 11 December 1917, Service Record: Rupert Bartlett, 20.

19 Service Record: Rupert Bartlett, 5, 8, 14.

20 Emma Bartlett to Major Rendall, 5 April 1918, Service Record: Rupert Bartlett.

21 P.J. Summers to Captain J.M. Howley, 8 October 1918, Service Record: Rupert Bartlett.

22 "Gallant Allan Crawford," *Toronto Globe*, 3 September 1923, typed editorial, Bartlett Papers.

23 "Wrangel Island and Mr. Stefansson," Montreal *Standard*, 23 August 1923, typed editorial, Bartlett Papers.

24 Stefansson, *The Friendly Arctic*, 271.

25 McKinley, "Typescript Work on the Life and Activities of Stefansson," 40.

26 Ibid., 41.

27 Ibid, 39.

28 Stefansson, *The Friendly Arctic*, 739.

29 Hadley, "Appendix: The Story of the *Karluk*," 710.

30 Bartlett to McKinley, 21 April 1922, McKinley Correspondence and Papers.

31 Ibid.

32 Ibid.

33 Ibid.

34 Ibid.

35 Ibid.

36 Charles Camsell, "The Friendly Arctic Letter," *Science* 57, no. 1484 (1923): 665–66.

37 Diamond Jenness, "The Friendly Arctic Letter," *Science* 56, no. 1436 (1922): 8–12.

38 Bartlett to William Laird McKinley, McKinley Correspondence and Papers.

39 M. Young to Bartlett, 25 April 1938, Bartlett Papers.

40 Bradford, "Captain Robert A. Bartlett Personal Recollections," 149.

41 Tom Henighan, *Vilhjalmur Stefansson: Arctic Adventurer* (Toronto: Dundurn Press, 2009).

42 Knud Rasmussen, telegram to Bartlett, 2:30 p.m. 19 January 1931, Bartlett Papers.

43 Sarnoff, *Ice Pilot* 117.

44 Ibid., 115.

45 Ibid., 112.

46 Ibid., 129.

47 David Binney Putnam, *David Goes to Greenland* (New York and London: G.P. Putnam's Sons, 1926).

48 Horwood, *Bartlett: The Great Explorer*, 114.

49 Ibid.

50 Sarnoff, *Ice Pilot*, 123.

51 Horwood, *Bartlett: The Great Explorer*, 113.

52 Ibid., 115.

53 Sarnoff, *Ice Pilot,* 127.

54 E.W. Nelson, chief, Bureau of Biological Survey, United States Department of Agriculture, to Bartlett, 4 December 1924, Bartlett Papers.

55 "Grandniece of Capt. Bartlett Cherishes Province-wide Celebrations," *Western Star*, 14 August 2009, http://www.thewesternstar.com/Festivals-events/2009-08-14/article-1480196/Grandniece-of-Capt-Bartlett-cherishes-provincewide-celebrations/1.

56 "Captain Bob Bartlett Spends an Arctic Summer Digging in the Ice for Archaeological Specimens," *New York Times* online, 9 November 1930.

57 Ibid.

58 Hilda Dove to Bartlett, 6 September, 1938, Bartlett Papers.

59 Ibid.

60 Ibid.

61 Ibid.

62 Sammy Bartlett to Bartlett, 18 January 1938, 1.

63 Emma Angel Crichton to Bartlett, 3 March 1938, 2.

64 Angel, interview.

65 Ibid.

66 Ibid.

67 Ibid.
68 Ibid.
69 Ibid.
70 Ibid.
71 Mary Jemina Bartlett to Bartlett, 9 December 1938, Bartlett Papers.
72 Angel, interview.
73 Ibid.
74 Ibid.
75 "Captain Bernier Dies. Arctic Explorer," *The Polar Times* (June 1935): 15.
76 https://www.canadapost.ca/web/en/blogs/collecting/details.page?article=2009/07/10/captain_robert_a_bar&cattype=collecting&cat=stamps.
77 http://www.historicplaces.ca/en/rep-reg/place-lieu.aspx?id=2634&pid=0.
78 James Barron, "David Binney Putnam, Sr., 79. Wrote of Adventures as a Youth," *New York Times*, 3 June 1992, http://www.nytimes.com/1992/06/03/us/david-binney-putnam-sr-79-wrote-of-adventures-as-a-youth.html.
79 Horwood, *Bartlett: The Great Explorer*, 124.
80 Putnam to Bartlett, 4 July 1926, Explorers Club: George Palmer Putnam.
81 Ibid.
82 Ibid.
83 Ibid.
84 Bartlett, 29 June 1933.
85 Bartlett to Greville Haslam, June Sunday n.d. early 1930s, Stefansson MSS-193.
86 Jim Hearn to Bartlett, 27 October 1931, Bartlett Papers.
87 Putnam, *David Goes to Greenland* 161.
88 Ibid., 162.
89 Ibid., 161.
90 Ibid., 163.
91 Ibid.
92 Ibid., 160.
93 Robert A. Bartlett, foreword to *David Goes to Greenland*, viii.
94 Putnam, *David Goes to Greenland*, 72.
95 Ibid., 74.
96 Ibid., 87.
97 Franch, "The Search for Crockerland."
98 Henry E. Armstrong, "Captain Bob Bartlett's Rousing [word missing]," *New York Times*, 4 November 1934, Explorers Club: Robert Abram Bartlett.
99 Jeff A. Webb, "Lewis Varrick Frissell," *Dictionary of Canadian Biography* (Toronto: University of Toronto Press, 2013–15), http://www.biographi.ca/en/bio/frissell_lewis_varick_16E.html.
100 Ibid.
101 Ibid.
102 "Fifty Years Ago Today," *Evening Telegram*, 22 February 1980.
103 Webb, "Lewis Varrick Frissell."
104 "Life in the Sealing Fleet Is Battle," *New York Times Magazine* 22 March 1931.
105 Webb, "Lewis Varrick Frissell."
106 S.A., interview.
107 B.E., interview.
108 S.A., interview.
109 Samuel Bartlett, interview.
110 Ibid.
111 Robinson, *The Coldest Crucible*, 135.
112 Ibid.
113 Ibid., 138.
114 Briant Sando to Bartlett, 17 November 1938, Bartlett Papers.
115 Bartlett to Sando, 5 December 1938.
116 Bartlett to D.S. Kennedy, Charles Daniel Frey Company, Chicago, 27 January 1938.

117 Ibid.
118 Ibid.
119 James A. Pond to Bartlett, 13 February 1931, Stefansson MSS-193.
120 Pond to Bartlett, 29 January, 25 September, and 7 October 1929; 18 October 1932.
121 Pond to Bartlett, 30 June 1932.
122 Pond to Bartlett, 20 December 1929.
123 Pond to Bartlett, 11 March 1931.
124 Charles Scribner's Sons, royalty statement, March 1938, Bartlett Papers.
125 Sarnoff, *Ice Pilot*.
126 Charles Scribner's Sons, royalty statement, 1 August 1938, Bartlett Papers.
127 Max (?) Smith to Bartlett, 25 January 1938.
128 Ibid.
129 Ibid.
130 Royal Bank of Canada, bank statement, January 1939.
131 E. Broughton to Bartlett, 1 December 1938.
132 Ibid.
133 Bassett Jones to Bartlett, 1 October 1938.
134 Bill Province to Bartlett, 28 March n.d.
135 Agnes M. Hull to Bartlett, 2 October 1938.
136 Sister M. Rita to Bartlett, 24 January ca. 1938.
137 Myrtle Hefferton to Bartlett, 18 February 1938.
138 Spracklin, interview.
139 Angel, interview.
140 Ibid.
141 Ibid.
142 Samuel Bartlett, interview.
143 Angel, interview.
144 Samuel Bartlett, interview.
145 Angel, interview.
146 New York Athletic Club, Yachting Department, "America's Outstanding Ice Pilot" (typewritten manuscript, 22 October 1938), Bartlett Papers.
147 Jack Rose to Bartlett, 13 January 1938.
148 Henry Woodhouse to Bartlett, 1 January 1938.
149 Margaret Ockev to Bartlett, 2 February 1938.
150 Eleanor Cushman to Bartlett, 10 February 1939.
151 Isabel Campbell Daily (?) to Bartlett, n.d.
152 F.D. Frisbie to Bartlett, n.d. 1937.
153 Ruth M. Morrison to Bartlett, 13 January 1938.
154 John K. Howard to Bartlett, 22 December 1937.
155 Bartlett to President Kempton, Johns Hopkins University, 7 April 1938.
156 James A. Pond to Bartlett, 10 March 1933, Stefansson MSS-193.
157 Pond to Bartlett, 4 December 1931.
158 Pond to Bartlett, 16 March and 28 November 1931.
159 Pond to Bartlett, 8 May 1931.
160 Pond to Bartlett, 13 February 1931.
161 Howard A. Denbo to Bartlett, 18 March 1937, Bartlett Papers.
162 Llewella Kitchell to Bartlett, 9 December 1937.
163 Ibid.
164 Kitchell to Bartlett, 29 November 1937.
165 Edward Tabbert to Bartlett, 24 November 1937.
166 Tabbert to Bartlett, 17 March 1938.
167 Angel, interview.
168 Bartlett to D.S. Kennedy, Charles Daniel Frey Company, Chicago, 27 January 1938, Bartlett Papers.
169 Remington Arms Company, Remington gun tag: "Here's what Captain Bob Bartlett, famous arctic explorer and adventurer says about Remington firearms," n.d., Bartlett Papers.

170 Willeen Keough, e-mail message to author, 2015; Keough, "The Creation of Capt. Bob Bartlett: A Man's Man in an Age of Masculine Uncertainty," presentation at *Exploring Bartlett: The Legacy of an Arctic Adventurer Symposium*, Brigus, Newfoundland, 23 May 2009.
171 General Mills, Inc., contract, 8 May 1942, Bartlett Papers.
172 Bartlett to Mr. Swats (?), n.d. 1938.
173 John W. Doyle, *Riddle Me This One: A Treasury of Newfoundland Trivia* (Portugal Cove-St. Philip's: Boulder Publications, 2016), 118.
174 A.G. Nast to Richard Van Dyck Knight, M.D., 22 May 1937, Bartlett Papers.
175 G.E. Dunbar to Knight, 14 June 1937.
176 Field Museum of Natural History, Chicago, to Bartlett, 17 June 1935.
177 Madge C.L. McGuinness to Bartlett, 30 September 1938.
178 Reynold Spriggs to Bartlett, n.d.
179 Ibid.
180 Sarnoff, *Ice Pilot,* 162.
181 Bartlett to Greville Haslam, 30 September 1938, Stefansson MSS-193.
182 Ibid.
183 Bartlett to Haslam, 27 May n.d.
184 "Captain Bob Bartlett's Arctic Movies," 5 March 1940, Bartlett Papers.
185 Bartlett to Haslam, 16 April n.d., Stefansson MSS-193.
186 Bartlett to Haslam, 14 April n.d.
187 Sophie Drinker to Bartlett, 16 February ca. 1938.
188 George Moffett to Bartlett, n.d.
189 Ibid.
190 Alfred G. Reid to Bartlett, n.d. ca. 1938.
191 Hugh K. Myers to Bartlett, n.d. 1938.
192 Ibid.
193 Thomas K. McIntyre to Bartlett, n.d. 1938.
194 William Quinn to Bartlett, 19 April 1938.
195 Ibid.
196 Richard Van Dyck Knight to Bartlett, April 1938.
197 Bartlett to Honourable (Niels) Daugaard-Jensen, Greenland Department, Ministry of State, Copenhagen, Government of Denmark, 15 June 1935.
198 Geoffrey O'Hara to Bartlett, 26 April 1938.
199 Ibid.
200 Bartlett to W.B. Willison, 7 May 1938.
201 Bartlett to Frank Crowin Shields, H.I. Phillips, and Mrs. Ogden Reid, 12 May 1938.
202 Arnold Knauth, telegraph to Bartlett, 3 June 1938.
203 Bob Wurz to Bartlett, 8 June 1938.
204 Carl Sferrazza Anthony, *The Kennedy White House: Family Life and Pictures 1961–1963* (New York: Touchstone, Simon & Schuster, 2002), 256.
205 Gladys Tartière to Bartlett, n.d. 1938, Bartlett Papers.
206 David Munsell to Bartlett, 16 January ca. 1938.
207 Ibid.
208 David Munsell to Bartlett, 23 January ca. 1938.
209 Bob Wurz to Bartlett, 11 October ca. 1937.
210 Arthur Manice to Bartlett, n.d.
211 Weyer, "Captain Robert Abram Bartlett, in Memory."
212 S.A. Morse, "David C. Nutt (1919–2008)," *Arctic* 61, no. 2 (2008): 222–23.
213 Ibid.
214 Ibid.
215 Ibid.
216 "Joseph Randolph Nutt," *Encyclopedia of Cleveland History* (n.d.), http://ech.case.edu/cgi/article.pl?id=NJR1.
217 Ibid.
218 J.R. Nutt to Bartlett, 24 January 1938, Bartlett Papers.

219 David Nutt to J.R. Nutt, 30 January 1938.
220 Ibid.
221 Ibid.
222 Ibid.
223 Ibid.
224 David Nutt to Bartlett, 28 February 1938.
225 Nutt to Bartlett, 18 April 1938.
226 Ibid.
227 Bartlett to Dr. William Mann, director, National Zoological Park, 6 May 1938.
228 Mann to Bartlett, 30 September 1938.
229 David Nutt to Bartlett, 14 October 1938.
230 Ibid.
231 F.H.H. Williamson, controller, Lands, Parks and Forests Branch, Department of Mines and Resources, Government of Canada, to Bartlett, 18 January 1939.
232 Ibid.
233 Williamson to Bartlett, 26 January 1939.
234 Waldo L. Schmit to Bartlett, 8 May 1935.
235 P. Erling to Bartlett, 5 January 1939.
236 Williamson to Bartlett, 26 January 1939.
237 Ibid.
238 North Winship to the Honorable the Secretary of State, Government of Denmark, 28 May 1937.
239 Nutt to Bartlett, 14, 15, 19, and 28 December 1938; 10 January 1939.
240 Nutt to Bartlett, 15 December 1938.
241 Ibid.
242 Nutt to Bartlett, 28 February 1938.
243 John W. Aldrich and David Nutt, "Birds of Eastern Newfoundland," *Scientific Publications Cleveland Museum Natural History* 4, no. 2 (1939): 13–42.
244 Inez M. Haring, "Mosses Collected by the Robert A. Bartlett Greenland Expedition 1940," *The Bryologist* 46, no. 3 (1943): 88–91.
245 Ibid., 89.
246 William W. Fitzhugh, "Elmer Harp Jr. (1913–2009)," *Arctic* 63, no. 2 (2010): 252–54.

CHAPTER SIX

1   "Bartlett off for Arctic. Seven Students in Scientific Party aboard *Morrissey*," *New York Times* online, 27 June 1937.
2   A. Wetmore to Bartlett, 21 September 1935, Bartlett Papers.
3   "Bob Bartlett off on 15th Arctic Voyage. 11 Students Pay Way as Crew Members," *New York Times*, 21 June 1940.
4   Ibid.
5   Robert A. Bartlett, "*Morrissey* Sails through Ice Belt," *New York Times* online, 26 July 1940.
6   Bartlett to Don Uphall, 23 November 1944, Explorers Club: Robert Abram Bartlett.
7   Bartlett, "*Morrissey* Sails through Ice Belt."
8   Robert A. Bartlett, "Greenland from 1898 to Now," *National Geographic* 78, no. 1 (1940): 111–40, quotation at 112.
9   Ibid.
10   Ibid.
11   Dennis Raphael, *Social Determinants of Health: Canadian Perspectives* (Toronto: Canadian Scholars' Press, 2009).
12   Charlotte Loppie Reading and Fred Wien, *Health Inequalities and the Social Determinants of Aboriginal Peoples' Health* (Prince George, BC: National Collaborating Centre for Aboriginal Health, 2009).
13   Wexler, "Inupiat Youth Suicide and Culture Loss."
14   Bjerregaard et al., "Review Article: Indigenous Health in the Arctic."

15 Avery F. Gordon, *Ghostly Matters: Haunting and the Sociological Imagination* (University of Minnesota Press, 2008).
16 Bowdoin College, Robert Abram Bartlett *Honoris Causa*, MASTER OF ARTS, 1920, Bartlett Papers.
17 Jack White, "Bartlett: Man of the Arctic," St. John's *Evening Telegram* 30 January 1993.
18 "Centre for Cold Ocean Resources Engineering. C-CORE," Memorial University *Gazette*, 23 April 1981, 6–7.
19 Pildt, "Mysteries of a Frozen World."
20 Joseph A. Cushman, "New Arctic Foraminifera Collected by Capt. R.A. Bartlett from Fox Basin and off the Northeast Coast of Greenland," *Smithsonian Miscellaneous Collection* 89, no. 9 (1933): 1–8.
21 Edward Said, *The Edward Said Reader*, ed. Moustafa Bayoumi and Andrew Rubin (New York: Vintage Books, 2000), 104.
22 "Robert Abram Bartlett," Name File, Centre for Newfoundland Studies, Queen Elizabeth II Library, Memorial University.
23 Ellsworth P. Killip to Dr. (Waldo L.) Schmit, 29 September 1938, Bartlett Papers.
24 Sarnoff, *Ice Pilot*, 16.
25 Robert A. Bartlett, "Servicing Arctic Airbases," *National Geographic* 89, no. 5 (1946): 602–16.
26 Ibid., 603.
27 McKinley, *Karluk*, 51.
28 Bartlett, "Servicing Arctic Airbases."
29 Bartlett, "Sealing—Newfoundland and Labrador"; Bartlett, "Newfoundland Seals."
30 Bartlett, "Newfoundland Seals."
31 Ibid., 210.
32 Ibid., 212.
33 Philip F. Frank to Bartlett, 7 November 1938, Bartlett Papers.
34 Courtland Smith, Pathé News contract with Bartlett, 19 March 1931, Bartlett Papers.
35 Ibid.
36 Armstrong, "Captain Bob Bartlett's Rousing [word missing]."
37 Sarnoff, *Ice Pilot*, 158.
38 William Bartlett to Bartlett, 9 February 1938, Bartlett Papers.
39 William Bartlett to Bartlett, 31 October 1938.
40 Ethel Bartlett to Bartlett, 22 February 1938.
41 Ethel Bartlett to Bartlett, 4 January 1939.
42 William Bartlett to Bartlett, 6 March 1938.
43 F.W. Angel to Bartlett, 3 November 1934.
44 Lewis Bartlett to Bartlett, 22 January 1939.
45 Eleanor Bartlett to Bartlett, 7 February 1935.
46 E. Broughton, "Mary Jemima Bartlett," n.d. January 1943, unpublished eulogy, Explorers Club: Robert Abram Bartlett.
47 Ibid.
48 Mary Jemima Bartlett to Bartlett, 2 November 1927, Bartlett Papers.
49 Mary Jemima Bartlett to Bartlett, 11 February 1929.
50 Mary Jemima Bartlett to Bartlett, 15 August 1888.
51 Broughton, "Mary Jemima Bartlett."
52 Bartlett to Flora Jo Bergstrom, 8 February 1943, Explorers Club: Flora Jo Bergstrom.
53 Ibid.
54 Ibid.
55 Robert A. Bartlett, Last Will and Testament of Robert Abram Bartlett, 27 November 1931, Bartlett Papers.
56 Bartlett to Don Uphall, n.d., Explorers Club: Robert Abram Bartlett.
57 Ibid.
58 Robert A. Bartlett, "Bob Bartlett Sees Sun Set behind Ice," *New York Times* online, 9 September 1933.
59 Henderson, "The Soft Side of Skipper Bob Bartlett."

60 Ibid.
61 Ibid.
62 Sister M. Rita to Bartlett, 20 September 1937, Bartlett Papers.
63 Gibbs, "The Fascination and Dangers of the Sea," 852.
64 Henderson, "The Soft Side of Skipper Bob Bartlett," 39.
65 Gibbs, "The Fascination and Dangers of the Sea," 852.
66 McGhee, *The Last Imaginary Place,* 239.
67 Henderson, "The Soft Side of Skipper Bob Bartlett," 121.
68 Reynolds Spriggs to Bartlett, 6 June 1938; L.M. Mann to Bartlett, 23 June 1938; Frank Hagner to Bartlett, 5 October 1938; H.C. Haas to Bartlett, 2 November 1938; John McGrath to Bartlett, 9 November 1938; Eileen McGrath to Bartlett, n.d. 1938; Tom [no surname provided] to Bartlett, n.d. 1938, Bartlett Papers.
69 Spriggs to Bartlett.
70 Mann to Bartlett.
71 Angel, interview.
72 Ibid.
73 Joseph Robinson to Bartlett, 7 November 1938, Bartlett Papers.
74 Barry Lopez, *Arctic Dreams: Imagination and Desire in a Northern Landscape* (New York: Charles Scribner's Sons, 1986).
75 Annie Dillard, *Pilgrim at Tinker Creek* (New York, NY: HarperCollins, 1974).
76 McKinley, *Karluk,* 56.
77 Ibid.
78 "A Gathering Place," club brochure, Explorers Club, n.d. ca. 2014, 1.
79 Ibid.
80 "History of European/White Settlement," Virtual Museum of Labrador (n.d.), 1. http://www.labradorvirtualmuseum.ca/home/white_settlement.htm.
81 Ibid.
82 Burton K. Janes, "Captain Bob Bartlett's Favourite Recipe," *The Telegram,* 16 May 2009.
83 Sarnoff, *Ice Pilot,* 115.
84 Emma Bartlett to Bud, 14 April 1953, Explorers Club: Robert Abram Bartlett.
85 Robert A. Bartlett, agenda of Robert Abram Bartlett, 1919, Bartlett Papers.
86 Bartlett, agenda, 2 May and 1 June 1919.
87 Bartlett, agenda, 10 and 11 December 1919.
88 Bartlett, agenda, 22 November 1939.
89 Bartlett, agenda, 23 November 1939.
90 Bartlett, agenda, 27 November 1939.
91 Bartlett, agenda, 27 October 1939.
92 Bartlett, agenda, 11, 12, and 13 November 1939.
93 Bartlett, agenda, 25 December 1939.
94 Karl K. Kitchen, Untitled, *New York Sun,* n.d. October 1931.
95 Sarnoff, *Ice Pilot,* 37.
96 S.A., interview.
97 Paul O'Neill, in discussion with author, March 2008.
98 Henderson, "The Soft Side of Skipper Bob Bartlett."
99 Valentine card to Bartlett, 12 February 1938, Bartlett Papers.
100 Valentine to Bartlett, n.d.
101 Henderson, "The Soft Side of Skipper Bob Bartlett," 39.
102 Anne [surname?] to Bartlett, 27 October 1938, Bartlett Papers.
103 Sara Lee Tuck to Bartlett, n.d.
104 Bartlett to Greville Haslam, Monday night n.d., Stefansson MSS-193.
105 Joanna Kafarowski, "Louise Arner Boyd," presentation at *Exploring Bartlett: The Legacy of an Arctic Adventurer Symposium*, Brigus, Newfoundland, 23 May 2009.
106 Louise A. Boyd, *The Coast of Northeast Greenland with Hydrographic Studies in the Greenland Sea* (New York: American Geographical Society, 1948).
107 Ena L. Yonge to Bartlett, 29 January 1938, Bartlett Papers.
108 Ibid.

109 Kafarowski, "Louise Arner Boyd."
110 Ibid.
111 Catherine Dempsey, in discussion with author, January 2009; personal communication with Greenland family.
112 D.Y., e-mail message to author, 2015.
113 C.T., e-mail message to author, 11 and 14 March 2009.
114 Horwood, *Bartlett: The Great Explorer*, 163.
115 Ibid.
116 Robert A. Bartlett to Greville Haslam, 18 March n.d., Stefansson MSS-193.
117 Bartlett to Haslam, 16 April n.d.
118 Ancestry.com, New Orleans Ward 14, Orleans, Louisiana; Roll: 575; Page: 8A; Enumeration District: 0132; FHL microfilm: 1240575. *1900 United States Federal Census* [database on-line]. Provo, UT, USA: Ancestry.com Operations Inc, 2004.
119 Ancestry.com, New Orleans Ward 14.
120 Ancestry.com, New Orleans Ward 14; Ancestry.com, Shreveport Ward 4, Caddo, Louisiana; Roll: T624_510; Page: 12A; Enumeration District: 0041; FHL microfilm: 1374523. 1910 *United States Federal Census* [database on-line]. Provo, UT, USA: Ancestry.com Operations Inc, 2004.
121 Ancestry.com, Manhattan Assembly District 10, New York, New York; Roll: T625_1203; Page: 17B; Enumeration District: 771; Image: 1040. 1920 *United States Federal Census* [database on-line]. Provo, UT, USA: Ancestry.com Operations Inc, 2004.
122 Ancestry.com, Manhattan Assembly District 10.
123 Adrian Room, *Dictionary of Pseudonyms: 13,000 Assumed Names and Their Origins*, 5th ed. (Jefferson, NC: McFarland & Company, 2012), 514.
124 http://www.friendsofhuntleymeadows.org/News%20and%20Events/ Newsletter/2015/2015_FOHMP_June.pdf and https://web.archive.org/ web/20051025114432/http://www.rcls.org/jkuntz/woodhouse.html.
125 LeRoy Baker Gulotta to Bartlett, 9 October 1920, Bartlett Papers, 1.
126 Ibid.
127 Ibid., 2.
128 Ibid.
129 Ibid.
130 Evelyn Waugh, *Brideshead Revisited* (1945; Boston: Little, Brown, and Co., 2000).
131 Gulotta to Bartlett, 1.
132 LeRoy Baker Gulotta to Eleanor Bartlett, 27 December 1938, Bartlett Papers, 1–2.
133 Ibid., 2.
134 Ibid.
135 Ancestry.com, Chicago, Cook, Illinois; Roll: 494; Page: 5B; Enumeration District: 1892; Image: 456.0; FHL microfilm: 2340229. 1930 *United States Federal Census* [database on-line]. Provo, UT, USA: Ancestry.com Operations Inc, 2004.
136 Ancestry.com, Chicago, Cook, Illinois.
137 Ibid.
138 Ancestry.com, Lincoln, Nebraska City Directory 1940, United States City Directories 1822–1989, n.d., 228.
139 Memorial Cemetery, Fremont, Dodge County, Nebraska, n.d., http:// billiongraves.com/pages/cemeteries/MemorialCemetery/66934#cemetery_ id=66934&lim=0&num=20&order=asc&action=browse.
140 Gulotta to Bartlett, Bartlett Papers, 2.
141 Kennedy, discussion.
142 Ruly Carpenter to Bartlett, 29 April 1938, Bartlett Papers.
143 Waldo L. Schmit to Bartlett, n.d.
144 Bradford, "Captain Robert A. Bartlett Personal Recollections," 149.
145 McKinley, "Typescript Work on the Life and Activities of Stefansson," 37.
146 Bartlett to Greville Haslam, Sunday April 1944, Stefansson MSS-193.
147 Sarnoff, *Ice Pilot*, 9.
148 Ibid., 10.

149 Henderson, "The Soft Side of Skipper Bob Bartlett," 39, 120.
150 Ibid.
151 Ibid.
152 Dorothy Brooks to Bartlett, 13 September 1938, Bartlett Papers.
153 Friedrich Nietzsche, *Nietzsche: Untimely Meditations* (Cambridge: Cambridge University Press, 1983), 129.
154 Samuel Bartlett, interview, 7.
155 Ibid.
156 Eleanor Bartlett to Bergstrom, 23 May 1946, Explorers Club: Flora Jo Bergstrom.
157 Angel, interview.
158 "Captain Bartlett Buried: Thousands Gather in Brigus for Funeral of Explorer," *New York Times*, 10 May 1946.

EPILOGUE: THE *EFFIE MORRISSEY*
1 Sarnoff, *Ice Pilot*, 176.
2 Ibid.
3 Ibid., 178.
4 Ibid., 180.
5 Ibid.
6 Schooner Ernestina-Morrissey Association, Patrick Administration Announces Funding for Rehabilitation of the Schooner Ernestina-Morrissey, 19 December 2014, http://www.ernestina.org/news/patrick-administration-announces-funding-for-rehabilitation-of-the-schooner-ernestina-morrissey/.

BIBLIOGRAPHY

DOCUMENT COLLECTIONS

Centre for Newfoundland Studies, Queen Elizabeth II Library, Memorial University, St. John's.
Brigus. Community file.
"Robert Abram Bartlett." Name file.
Shortis, H.F. Unpublished papers.

Explorers Club, New York.
Bergstrom, Flora Jo. Collection.
Deceased Members Files: Robert Abram Bartlett, George Palmer Putnam.

George J. Mitchell Department of Special Collections & Archives, Bowdoin College Library, Brunswick, ME.
Bartlett, Robert Abram. Papers.

Historic Sites Association of Newfoundland and Labrador, St. John's.
Angel, Jack. Interview by James Candow. Parks Canada. Unpublished, 27 May 1987.
Bartlett, Samuel. Interview by Susan Cummings. 1992.
Leamon, John. Interview by James Candow. Parks Canada. Unpublished, n.d.
Murphy, Ruperta Angel. Unpublished memoir of Hawthorne Cottage, n.d.
Stewart, Louise Bartlett. "Capt. Bob's Account of the Bartlett Family as Given to Louise Bartlett Stewart." Unpublished manuscript, n.d.

Library and Archives Canada, Ottawa.
Canadian Arctic Expedition—Stefansson Arctic Expedition.
Mamen, Bjarne [textual record].

Caird Library and Archives, National Maritime Museum, Greenwich, UK.
Board of Trade. Certificates of Competency.

Rauner Special Collections, Dartmouth College Library, Hanover, NH.
Bartlett, Robert Abram (Bob). Papers. The Stefansson Collection on Polar Exploration.

The Rooms Provincial Archives Divisions, St. John's.
The Newfoundland Regiment and the Great War Database, www.rnr.therooms.ca/part3_database.asp.
Abraham Bartlett Family Fonds.
Rupert Wilfred Bartlett album.

Scott Polar Research Institute, University of Cambridge, Cambridge, UK.
Alister Forbes Mackay collection.
Robert Bartlett collection.
James Murray collection.
Vilhjalmur Stefansson collection.
Storker Storkerson collection.

PRINTED SOURCES

Aldrich, John W. and David Nutt. "Birds of Eastern Newfoundland." *Scientific Publications Cleveland Museum of Natural History* 4, no. 2 (1939): 13–42.

Alexander, David. "The Political Economy of Fishing in Newfoundland." *Journal of Canadian Studies* 11, no. 1 (1976): 32–40.

Anthony, Carl Sferrazza. *The Kennedy White House: Family Life and Pictures 1961–1963.* New York: Touchstone, Simon & Schuster, 2002.

Baird, P.D. "Expeditions to the Canadian Arctic." *The Beaver* 279 (March 1949): 44–47; 280 (June 1949): 41–47; 280 (September 1949): 44–48.

Banner, Stuart. "Why *Terra Nullius*? Anthropology and Property Law in Early Australia." *Law and History Review* 23, no. 1 (2005): 95–131.

Barr, William. "The Voyages of *Taymyr* and *Vaygach* to Ostrov Vrangelya, 1910–15." *Polar Record* 16, no. 101 (1972): 213–34.

Bartlett, Robert (Bob) A. Untitled. *Explorers Journal* 8, no. 2 (1929): 39.

———. Foreword to *David Goes to Greenland*, by David Binney Putnam, v–viii. New York and London: G.P. Putnam's Sons, 1926.

———. "Greenland from 1898 to Now." *National Geographic* 78, no. 1 (1940): 111–140.

———. *The Last Voyage of the* Karluk. St. John's: Flanker Press, 2007. First published 1916 by Small, Maynard & Company.

———. *The Log of Bob Bartlett: The True Story of Forty Years of Seafaring and Exploration.* St. John's: Flanker Press, 2006. First published 1928 by G.P. Putnam's Sons.

———. "Newfoundland Seals." *Journal of Mammalogy* 8, no. 3 (1927): 207–12.

———. *Sails over Ice.* New York: Charles Scribner's Sons, 1934.

———. "Sealing—Newfoundland and Labrador." *National Geographic* 56, no. 1 (1929): 91–130.

———. "Servicing Arctic Airbases." *National Geographic* 89, no. 5 (1946): 602–16.

Bergmann, Linda S. "Woman against a Background of White: The Representation of Self and Nature in Women's Arctic Narratives." *American Studies* 34, no. 2 (1993): 53–68.

Berton, Pierre. *The Arctic Grail: The Quest for the North West Passage and the North Pole, 1818–1909.* Anchor Canada, 2012. First published 1988 by Viking Books.

Bjerregaard, Peter, T. Kue Young, Eric Dewailly, and Sven O.E. Ebbesson. "Review Article: Indigenous Health in the Arctic: An Overview of the Circumpolar Inuit Population." *Scandinavian Journal of Social Medicine* 32, no. 5 (2004): 390–95.

Bown, Stephen R. *White Eskimo: Knud Rasmussen's Fearless Journey into the Heart of the Arctic.* Madeira Park, BC: Douglas and McIntyre, 2015.

Boyd, Louise A. *The Coast of Northeast Greenland with Hydrographic Studies in the Greenland Sea.* New York: American Geographical Society, 1948.

Bradford, Gershom. "Captain Robert A. Bartlett Personal Recollections." *Explorers Journal* (September 1965): 149–53.

Briffett, Francis B. *The Story of Newfoundland and Labrador.* London: J.M Dent, 1949.

Brown, Mildred. "House of Dread. House of Joy." *Rockwell Kent Review* 40, no. 1 (2014): 5–8.

Budgell, Richard. "The Beothuks and the Newfoundland Mind." *Journal of Newfoundland Studies* 8, no.1 (1992): 21.

Burch, Ernest S. *Social Life in Northwest Alaska: The Structure of Inupiaq Eskimo Nations.* Fairbanks: University of Alaska Press, 2006.

Burch, Ernest S., Jr. "The Inupiat and the Christianization of Arctic Alaska." *Etudes/Inuit/ Studies* 18, nos. 1–2 (1994): 81–108.

Butler, Judith. "Performative Acts and Gender Constitution: An Essay in Phenomenology and Feminist Theory." *Theatre Journal* 40, no. 4 (1988): 519–31.

Butler, Paul. *The Good Doctor.* St. John's: Pennywell, 2014.

Cadigan, Sean. *Newfoundland and Labrador: A History.* Toronto: University of Toronto Press, 2009.

Camsell, Charles. "The Friendly Arctic Letter." *Science* 57, no. 1484 (1923): 665–66.

"Capt. Bob Bartlett, Explorer, 70, Dies." *The Polar Times* (June 1946): 18.

"Captain Bernier Dies. Arctic Explorer." *The Polar Times* (June 1935): 15.

Cavell, Janice. "Manliness in the Life and Posthumous Reputation of Robert Falcon Scott." *Canadian Journal of History* 45, no. 3 (2010): 537–64.

———. "Vilhjalmur Stefansson, Robert Bartlett, and the *Karluk* Disaster: A Reassessment." *The Journal of the Hakluyt Society* (January 2017). http://www.hakluyt.com/PDF/Karluk. pdf.

"Centre for Cold Ocean Resources Engineering. C-CORE." Memorial University *Gazette* (St. John's), 23 April 1981.

Chafe, Ernest F. "The Voyage of the 'Karluk' and Its Tragic Ending." *The Geographic Journal* 51, no. 5 (1918): 307–16.

Chevallier, R. "The Greco-Roman Conception of the North from Pytheas to Tacitus." *Arctic* 37, no. 4 (1984): 341–46.

Clark, Geoffrey E. *Adolphus W. Greely: Abandoned in the Arctic: The Tragic Story of the Lady Franklin Bay Expedition, 1881–1884.* Portsmouth, NH: Portsmouth Athenaeum, 2007.

Collingridge, Vanessa. *Captain Cook: The Life, Death and Legacy of History's Greatest Explorer.* London: Ebury Press, 2003.

Cook, James and James King. *A Voyage to the Pacific Ocean.* Vol. 3. London: H. Hughs, 1785.

Counter, S. Allen. *North Pole Legacy: Black, White and Eskimo.* Montpelier, VT: Invisible Citis Press, 2001.

Cox, Percy H.E., Colonel Vanier, and H.R. Mill. "Oxford University Ellesmere Land Expedition: Discussion." *The Geographical Journal* 87, no. 5 (1936): 441–43. doi: 10.2307/1785644.

Crachiun, Ariana. *Writing Arctic Disaster: Authorship and Exploration.* Cambridge: Cambridge University Press, 2016.

Crellin, John K. *Home Medicine: The Newfoundland Experience.* Montreal and Kingston: McGill-Queen's University Press, 1994.

Crosbie, John C. *No Holds Barred: My Life in Politics.* Toronto: McClelland and Stewart, 1997.

Cushman, Joseph A. "New Arctic Foraminifera Collected by Capt. R.A. Bartlett from Fox Basin and off the Northeast Coast of Greenland." *Smithsonian Miscellaneous Collection* 89, no. 9 (1933): 1–8.

Dall, W.H. "On the So-Called Chukchi and Namollo People of Eastern Siberia." *American Naturalist* 15, no. 11 (1881): 857–68.

De Beauvoir, Simone. *The Second Sex.* Translated by Constance Borde and Sheila Malovany-Chevallier. London: Jonathan Cape, 2009. First published 1949 by Editions Gallimard.

Dick, Lyle. "Aboriginal-European Relations during the Great Age of North Polar Exploration." *Polar Geography* 26, no. 1 (2002): 66–86.

———. "'Pibloktoq' [Arctic Hysteria]: A Reconstruction of European-Inuit Relations." *Arctic Anthropology* 32, no. 2 (1995): 1–42.

Diebitsch-Peary, Josephine. *My Arctic Journal: A Year among Ice-Fields and Eskimos.* New York and Philadelphia: Contemporary Publishing Co., 1893.

Dillard, Annie. *Pilgrim at Tinker Creek.* New York: HarperCollins, 1974.

Diubaldo, Richard J. "Wrangling over Wrangel Island." *Canadian Historical Review* 48, no. 3 (1967): 201–26.

Doyle, John W. *Riddle Me This One: A Treasury of Newfoundland Trivia.* Portugal Cove-St. Philip's: Boulder Publications, 2016.

Elmes, Michael and Bob Frame. "Into Hot Air: A Critical Perspective on Everest." *Human Relations* 61, no. 2 (2008): 213–41.

Farley, Rebecca. "'By Endurance We Conquer': Ernest Shackleton and Performances of White Male Hegemony." *International Journal of Cultural Studies* 8, no. 2 (2005): 248.

Fenton, Captain Edward. "The Canadian Arctic Journal of Capt. Edward Fenton, 1578." *Archivaria* 11 (Winter 1980–1981): 181–204.

FitzGerald, John Edward. "Conflict and Culture in Irish-Newfoundland Roman Catholicism, 1829–1850." PhD diss., University of Ottawa, 1997. http://www.ruor.uottawa.ca/en/handle/10393/9512.

Fitzhugh, William W. "Elmer Harp Jr. (1913–2009)." *Arctic* 63, no. 2 (2010): 252–54.

Flynn, Dennis. "The Landfall Legacy." *Downhome Traveller* (April 2010): 68–71. http://www.landfalltrust.org/pdf/Landfall%20Article%20by%20Dennis%20Flynn%20in%20PDF.pdf.

Franch, John. "The Search for Crockerland: Doom, Death and Drama Infuse a University of Illinois Expedition to the Arctic." *Illinois Alumni Magazine* (January/February 2008).

Freed, Stanley A. "Fate of the Crocker Land Expedition." *Natural History Magazine,* June 2012. http://www.naturalhistorymag.com/features/092248/fate-of-the-crocker-land-expedition.

Friesen, T. Max. "Resource Structure, Scalar Stress, and the Development of Inuit Social Organization." *World Archaeology* 31, no. 1 (1999): 21–37.

Gatschet, Albert. "The Beothuk Indians." *Proceedings of the American Philosophical Society* 28, no. 132 (1890): 9.

Gibbs, Philip. *Adventures in Journalism*. New York: Harper and Brother Publishers, 1923.

Glen, A.R. and N.A.C. Croft. *Under the Pole Star: The Oxford University Arctic Expedition, 1935–6*. London: Methuen Publishers London, 1937.

Gordon, Avery F. *Ghostly Matters: Haunting and the Sociological Imagination*. Minneapolis: University of Minnesota Press, 2008.

Gosling, W.G. *Labrador: Its Discovery, Exploration and Development*. London: Alston Rivers Limited, 1910.

Gray, David and Sally Gray. *Canadian Arctic Expedition 1913–1918: Commemorating the 100th Anniversary*. Metcalfe, ON: Grayhound Information Services, 2013. http://canadianarcticexpedition.com/.

Green, Fitzhugh. *Bob Bartlett: Master Mariner*. New York: G.P. Putnam's Sons, 1929.

———. *Peary: The Man Who Refused to Fail*. New York: G.P. Putnam's Sons, 1926.

Hadley, John. "Appendix: The Story of the *Karluk*." In *The Friendly Arctic: The Story of Five Years in Polar Regions*, by Vilhjalmur Stefansson, 704–22.

Hall, Charles Francis. *Life with the Esquimaux: The Narrative of Captain Charles Francis Hall of the Whaling Barque* George Henry *from the 29th May, 1860, to the 13th September, 1862*. Vol. 2. Cambridge: Cambridge University Press, 2011. First published 1864 by S. Low, Son and Marston.

———. *Arctic Researches, and Life among the Esquimaux: Being the Narrative of an Expedition in Search of Sir John Franklin, in the Years 1860, 1861, and 1862*. New York: Harper & Bros., 1865.

Halpert, Herbert and George Morley Story. *Christmas Mumming in Newfoundland: Essays in Anthropology, Folklore, and History*. University of Toronto Press, 1969.

Hamilton, Malcolm. "Eating Death: Vegetarians, Meat and Violence." *Food, Culture & Society: An International Journal of Multidisciplinary Research* 9, no. 2 (2006): 155–77.

Hanrahan, Maura. "Enduring Polar Explorers' Arctic Imaginaries and the Promotion of Neoliberalism and Colonialism in Modern Greenland." *Polar Geography* 40, no. 2 (2017): 102–20.

———. "Bartlett, Robert 'Bob' Abram (1875–1946)." In *Antarctica and the Arctic Circle: A Geographic Encyclopedia of the Earth's Polar Regions*, 130–31. Edited by Andrew J. Hund. Vol. 1. ABC-CLIO, 2014.

———. *Domino: The Eskimo Coast Disaster*. St. John's: Flanker Press, 2006.

Hansson, Heidi. "Feminine Poles: Josephine Diebitsch-Peary's and Jennie Darlington's Polar Narratives." In *Northern Studies: Monographs No. 1*, 105–23. Umea, Sweden: Umea University and the Royal Skyttean Society, 2009.

Haring, Inez M. "Mosses Collected by the Robert A. Bartlett Greenland Expedition 1940." *The Bryologist* 46, no. 3 (1943): 88–91.

Harper, Kenn. *Give Me My Father's Body: The Life of Minik, the New York Eskimo.* New York: Washington Square Press, 2001.

Hart, Peter. *Mick: The Real Michael Collins.* London: Pan Macmillan, 2006.

Hawkins, Melissa. "Introduction to the Problem of Infant Mortality." Johns Hopkins Bloomberg School of Public Health, 2006. http://ocw.jhsph.edu/courses/ preventinginfantmortality/PDFs/Lecture1.pdf.

Hayes, Isaac I. *The Land of Desolation: Being a Personal Narrative of Observation and Adventure in Greenland.* New York: Harper & Brothers, 1872.

Hayes, James Gordon. *The Conquest of the South Pole: Antarctic Exploration, 1906–1931.* London: T. Butterworth Ltd., 1932.

Henderson, Bruce B. *Fatal North: Adventure Survival Aboard USS* Polaris *1st US Expedition North Pole.* Signet Books, 2001.

Henderson, Daniel. "The Soft Side of Skipper Bob Bartlett." *Motor Boating* 93, no. 3 (1954): 39, 120–22, 150.

Hendrik, Hans. *Memoirs of Hans Hendrik, the Arctic Traveller, Serving under Kane, Hayes, Hall and Nares, 1853–1876.* Edited by George Stephens. Cambridge: Cambridge University Press, 2014. First published 1878 by Trubner & Co.

Henighan, Tom. *Vilhjalmur Stefansson: Arctic Adventurer.* Toronto: Dundurn Press, 2009.

Henson, Matthew. *A Black Explorer at the North Pole: An Autobiographical Report by the Negro Who Conquered the Top of the World with Admiral Robert E. Peary.* New York: Walker and Co., 1969. First published 1912 by Frederik A. Stokes.

Herbert, Kari. *Polar Wives: The Remarkable Women behind the World's Most Daring Explorers.* Vancouver: Greystone Books Ltd., 2012.

Hobbs, William Herbert. Review of *The Friendly Arctic* Vilhjalmur Stefansson. *The Journal of Geology* 31, no. 2 (1923): 154–58.

Horwood, Harold. *Bartlett: The Great Explorer.* Toronto: Doubleday Canada, 1989. First published 1977.

Hough, Richard. *Captain James Cook.* New York: W.W. Norton & Company, 1994.

Howley, James. *The Beothucks or Red Indians: The Aboriginal Inhabitants of Newfoundland.* Cambridge: Cambridge University Press, 1915.

Hulan, Renée. *Northern Experience and the Myths of Canadian Culture.* Montreal & Kingston: McGill-Queen's University Press, 2002.

Ikonen, Hanna-Mari and Samu Pehkonen. "Explorers in the Arctic: Doing Feminine Nature in a Masculine Way." In *Encountering the North: Cultural Geography, International Relations and Northern Landscapes,* 127–52. Edited by Frank Möller and Samu Pehkonen. Aldershot, UK: Ashgate, 2003.

Jelinski, Jamie. "Kakiniit and Other 'Strange Blue Speckles': Self-Representation and Qallunaat Images of Inuit Tattooing." PhD diss., Concordia University, 2015.

Jenness, Diamond. "The Friendly Arctic Letter." *Science* 56, no. 1436 (1922): 8–12.

Jenness, Stuart Edward, ed. *Arctic Odyssey: The Diary of Diamond Jenness, Ethnologist with the Canadian Arctic Expedition in Northern Alaska and Canada, 1913–1916*. Gatineau, QC: Canadian Museum of Civilization, 1991.

Joll, James. *Nineteen-fourteen: The Unspoken Assumptions. An Inaugural Lecture Delivered 25 April 1968*. London School of Economics and Political Science: Weidenfeld & Nicolson, 1968.

Kafarowski, Joanna. "Louise Arner Boyd." Paper presented at *Exploring Bartlett: The Legacy of an Arctic Adventurer Symposium*, Brigus, NL, 23 May 2009.

Kane, Elisha Kent. *Arctic Explorations: The Second Grinnell Expedition in Search of Sir John Franklin, 1853, '54, '55*. Edinburgh: T. Nelson and Sons, 1861.

Keels, Janice. "Hawthorne Cottage Is Officially Opened." *Newfoundland Herald*, 15 July 1995, 12.

à Kempis, Thomas. "Imitation of Christ (1418)." In *The Gospel of John: Introduction, Exposition*. Notes by F.F. Bruce. Grand Rapids, MI: Wm. Eerdmans, 1994.

Keough, Willeen. "The Creation of Capt. Bob Bartlett: A Man's Man in an Age of Masculine Uncertainty." Paper presented at *Exploring Bartlett: The Legacy of an Arctic Adventurer Symposium*, Brigus, NL, 23 May 2009.

Kerttula, Anna M. "Antler on the Sea: Creating and Maintaining Cultural Group Boundaries among the Chukchi, Yupik, and Newcomers of Sireniki." *Arctic Anthropology* 34, no. 1 (1997): 212–26.

Khayyám, Omar. *The Rubáiyát of Omar Khayyám*. Translated by Edward Fitzgerald, 1859. Project Gutenberg, 2008. http://www.gutenberg.org/ebooks/246.

King, David Paul. *A Brief Report of the Federal Government of Canada's Residential School System for Inuit*. Ottawa: Aboriginal Healing Foundation/Fondation autochtone de guérison, 2006. http://www.ahf.ca/downloads/kingsummaryfweb.pdf.

Kirkpatrick, Katherine. *The Snow Baby: The Arctic Childhood of Admiral Robert E. Peary's Daring Daughter*. New York: Holiday House, 2009.

Kos'ko, M.K., B.G. Lopatin, and V.G. Ganelin. "Major Geological Features of the Islands of the East Siberian and Chukchi Seas and the Northern Coast of Chukotka." *Marine Geology* 93 (June 1990): 349–67.

Lake, Marilyn and Henry Reynolds. *Drawing the Colour Line: White Men's Countries and the Question of Racial Equality*. Melbourne: Melbourne University Publishing, 2008.

Leamon, John. *Brigus: Past Glory, Present Splendour*. St. John's: Harry Cuff Publications, 1998.

LeMoine, Genevieve. "Elatu's Funeral: A Glimpse of Inughuit-American Relations on Robert E. Peary's 1898–1902 Expedition." *Arctic* 67, no. 3 (2014): 340–46.

Lench, Charles. *A Souvenir of the Brigus Methodist Jubilee of the Opening of the Church 1875–1925*. Brigus: Brigus Methodist Church, 1925.

Lerena, María Jesús Hernáez. "Two Voices from Newfoundland: History and Myth Addressed by Maura Hanrahan and Paul Butler." *Revista Canaria de Estudios Ingleses* 56 (April 2008): 99–119.

Levere, Trevor H. *Science and the Canadian Arctic: A Century of Exploration 1818–1918*. Cambridge: Cambridge University Press, 1993.

Lewis, Frederick. "The Brigus Spy." *Newfoundland Quarterly* 107, no. 1 (2015): 17–21.

"Life in the Sealing Fleet Is Battle." *New York Times Magazine*, 22 March 1931.

Little, John M. "An Eskimo Deficiency Disease." *Boston Medical and Surgical Journal* 176, no. 18 (1917): 642–43.

Lopez, Barry. *Arctic Dreams: Imagination and Desire in a Northern Landscape*. New York: Charles Scribner's Sons, 1986.

MacMillan, Donald B. "Peary as a Leader: Incidents from the Life of the Discoverer of the North Pole Told by One of His Lieutenants on the Expedition Which Reached the Goal." *National Geographic* 37, no. 4 (1920): 293–317.

MacMillan, Margaret. *History's People: Personalities and the Past*. Toronto: House of Anansi, 2015.

Malaurie, Jean. *The Last Kings of Thule: A Year among the Polar Eskimos of Greenland*. London: Allen & Unwin, 1956.

Mallea-Olaetxe, Joxe. *The Basques of Reno and the Northeastern Sierra*. Chicago: Arcadia Publishing, 2009.

Marcus, Alan R. "Out in the Cold: Canada's Experimental Inuit Relocation to Grise Fiord and Resolute Bay." *Polar Record* 27, no. 163 (1991): 285–96.

Marshall, Ingeborg. *A History and Ethnography of the Beothuk*. Montreal: McGill-Queen's University Press, 1996.

McDermott, James. *Martin Frobisher: Elizabethan Privateer*. New Haven, CT: Yale University Press, 2001.

———. *The Third Voyage of Martin Frobisher to Baffin Island, 1578*. Vol. 6. London: Hakluyt Society, 2001.

McGhee, Robert. *The Last Imaginary Place: A Human History of the Arctic World*. Chicago: University of Chicago Press, 2005.

McKinley, William Laird. *Karluk: The Great Untold Story of Arctic Exploration*. London: Weidenfeld and Nicholson, 1976.

McLintock, A.H. *The Establishment of Constitutional Government in Newfoundland, 1783–1832: A Study of Retarded Colonisation*. London: Longmans, Green and Co., 1941.

Mills, William J. *Exploring Polar Frontiers: A Historical Encyclopedia*. Vol. 1. ABC-CLIO, 2003.

Möller, Frank. "Shades of White: An Essay on Political Iconography." In *Encountering the North: Cultural Geography, International Relations and Northern Landscapes*, 57–74. Edited by Frank Möller and Samu Pehkonen. Aldershot, UK: Ashgate, 2003.

Moorehead, Alan. *The Fatal Impact: An Account of the Invasion of the South Pacific, 1767–1840*. London: Penguin, 2000.

Morse, S.A. "David C. Nutt (1919–2008)." *Arctic* 61, no. 2 (2008): 222–23.

Nader, Laura. "Up the Anthropologist: Perspectives Gained from Studying Up." In *Reinventing Anthropology*, 284–311. Edited by Dell H. Hymes. New York: Pantheon Books, 1972.

Nietzsche, Friedrich. *Nietzsche: Untimely Meditations*. Cambridge: Cambridge University Press, 1983.

Niven, Jennifer. *Ada Blackjack: A True Story of Survival in the Arctic*. New York: Hyperion, 2003.

———. *The Ice Master: The Doomed 1913 Voyage of the* Karluk. Basingstoke, UK: Pan Books, 2000.

Noel, S.J.R. *Politics in Newfoundland*. Toronto: University of Toronto Press, 1971.

"Notes on the Crustacea, Chiefly Natantia, collected by Captain Robert A. Bartlett in Arctic Seas." *Journal of the Washington Academy of Sciences* 26, no. 8 (1936): 324–31.

Nurse, Allan O. "Captain Robert A. Bartlett." *Newfoundland Quarterly* 9, no. 4 (1910): 1.

Nuvano, Vladislav. "Chukchi Reindeer Herding Culture." *Inuit Studies* 31, nos. 1–2 (2007): 307–10.

Obeyesekere, Gananath. *The Apotheosis of Captain Cook: European Mythmaking in the Pacific*. Princeton, NJ: Princeton University Press, 1997.

"Obituary: Captain Samuel W. Bartlett." *Geographical Review* 2, no. 5 (1916): 436.

"Obituary: Rear-Admiral Robert E. Peary." *U.S.N. Meetings: Royal Geographical Society* (1919–1920).

Osczevski, Randall J. "Frederick Cook and the Forgotten North Pole." *Arctic* 56, no. 2 (2003): 207–17.

Parry, William Edward. *Narrative of an Attempt to Reach the North Pole*. London: J. Murray, 1828.

Peary, Robert. *The North Pole*. London: Hodder and Stoughton, 1910.

———. "The Great White Journey." In *My Arctic Journal: A Year Among Ice-Fields and Eskimos*, by Josephine Diebitsch-Peary, 221–31.

Porter, Marilyn. "She Was Skipper of the Shore-Crew: Notes on the History of the Sexual Division of Labour in Newfoundland." *Labour/Le Travail* 15 (Spring 1985): 105–23.

Prowse, D.W. *A History of Newfoundland from the English, Colonial, and Foreign Records*. London: Eyre and Spottiswoode, 1896.

Putnam, David Binney. *David Goes to Greenland.* New York and London: G.P. Putnam's Sons, 1926.

Putnam, George. *Mariner of the North: The Life of Captain Bob Bartlett.* New York: Duell, Sloan and Pearce, 1947.

Raphael, Dennis. *Social Determinants of Health: Canadian Perspectives.* Toronto: Canadian Scholars' Press, 2009.

Rasmussen, Knud Johan Victor. *Report of the First Thule Expedition 1912.* Copenhagen: C.A. Reitzels Forlag, 1915.

Rawlins, Dennis. *Peary at the North Pole: Fact or Fiction?* Washington, DC: R.B. Luce, 1973.

Reading, Charlotte Loppie and Fred Wien. *Health Inequalities and the Social Determinants of Aboriginal Peoples' Health.* Prince George, BC: National Collaborating Centre for Aboriginal Health, 2009.

Renan, Ernest. *Life of Jesus.* London: Truber and Co., 1864.

Richardson, Boyce. *People of* Terra Nullius*: Betrayal and Rebirth in Aboriginal Canada.* Douglas & McIntyre, 1993.

Riendeau, Roger E. *A Brief History of Canada.* New York: Facts on File Publications, 2007.

Robinson, Michael F. *The Coldest Crucible: Arctic Exploration and American Culture.* Chicago: University of Chicago Press, 2006.

Robinson, Rusty. "Why Matt Is Special." January 2000. http://www.matthewhenson.com/whymatt.htm.

Rompkey, Ronald. *Grenfell of Labrador: A Biography.* Montreal: McGill-Queen's University Press, 2009.

Room, Adrian. *Dictionary of Pseudonyms: 13,000 Assumed Names and Their Origins.* 5th ed. Jefferson, NC: McFarland & Company, 2012.

Rose, George A. *Cod: The Ecological History of the North Atlantic Fisheries.* St. John's: Breakwater Books, 2007.

———. "Fisheries Resources and Science in Newfoundland and Labrador: An Independent Assessment." In *Royal Commission on Renewing and Strengthening Our Place in Canada.* Government of Newfoundland and Labrador, March 2003.

Rosner, Victoria. "Gender and Polar Studies: Mapping the Terrain." *Signs* 34, no. 3 (2009): 489–94.

Rowe, Frederick William. *A History of Newfoundland and Labrador.* Toronto: McGraw-Hill Ryerson, 1980.

Royal Geographical Society. "Meetings: Royal Geographical Society 1919–1920." *The Geographical Journal* 56, no.1 (1920): 407.

Ryan, Shannon. *The Ice Hunters: A History of Newfoundland Sealing to 1914.* St. John's: Breakwater Books, 1994.

———. "Newfoundland Spring Sealing Disasters to 1914." *The Northern Mariner* 3, no. 3 (1993): 15–48.

Said, Edward. *The Edward Said Reader.* Edited by Moustafa Bayoumi and Andrew Rubin. New York: Vintage Books, 2000.

———. *Orientalism.* London: Penguin, 1978.

"Samuel Bartlett." *The Geographic Journal* 48 (July–December 1916): 436.

Sarnoff, Paul. *Ice Pilot: Bob Bartlett.* New York: Julian Messner, 1966.

Schrank, William E. "The Newfoundland Fishery: Ten Years after the Moratorium." *Marine Policy* 29, no. 5 (2005): 407–20.

Schweitzer, Peter P. and Evgeniy Golovko. "Traveling between Continents: The Social Organization of Interethnic Contacts across Bering Strait." *The Anthropology of East Europe Review* 13, no. 2 (1995): 50–55.

Sides, Hampton. *In the Kingdom of Ice: The Grand and Terrible Polar Voyage of the U.S.S. Jeannette.* Doubleday, 2014.

Simsarian, James. "The Acquisition of Legal Title to *Terra Nullius.*" *Political Science Quarterly* 53, no. 1 (1938): 111–28.

Smith, Gordon. *A Historical and Legal Study of Sovereignty in the Canadian North: Terrestrial Sovereignty. 1870–1939.* Calgary: University of Calgary Press, 2014.

Smith, Linda Tuhiwai. *Decolonizing Methodologies: Research and Indigenous Peoples.* London: Zed, 2012.

Sobal, Jeffrey. "Men, Meat and Marriage: Models of Masculinity." *Food and Foodways: Explorations in the History and Culture of Human Nourishment* 13, nos.1–2 (2005): 135–58.

Spivak, Gayatri. "Can the Subaltern Speak?" In *Marxism and the Interpretation of Culture,* 271–313. Edited by Cary Nelson and Lawrence Grossberg. Chicago: University of Chicago Press, 1988.

Spufford, Francis. *I May Be Some Time: Ice and the English Imagination.* London: Faber & Faber, 1996.

Stefansson, Vilhjalmur. *My Life with the Eskimo.* Charleston, SC: Nabu Press, 2010. First published 1912.

———. *The Friendly Arctic: The Story of Five Years in Polar Regions.* New York: Macmillan, 1943. First published 1921 by Macmillan.

Stewart, Hugh. "Robert Bartlett (1875–1946)." *Arctic* 39, no. 2 (1986): 188–89.

Story, George Morley, William James Kirwin, and John David Allison Widdowson, eds. *Dictionary of Newfoundland English.* Toronto: University of Toronto Press, 1990.

Svanborg, Ingvar. "Chukchi." In *Antarctica and the Arctic Circle: A Geographic Encyclopedia of the Earth's Polar Regions,* 177–81. Vol. 1. Edited by Andrew J. Hund. ABC-CLIO, 2014.

Ulfstein, Geir. *The Svalbard Treaty: From* Terra Nullius *to Norwegian Sovereignty*. Oslo: Scandinavian University Press, 1995.

Waugh, Evelyn. *Brideshead Revisited*. Boston: Little, Brown, and Co., 2000. First published 1945.

Washington, Booker T. Introduction to *A Black Explorer at the North Pole: An Autobiographical Report by the Negro Who Conquered the Top of the World with Admiral Robert E. Peary*, by Matthew Henson, xiii–xiv.

Webb, Jeff A. "Lewis Varrick Frissell." In *Dictionary of Canadian Biography*. Toronto: University of Toronto Press, 2013–15. http://www.biographi.ca/en/bio/frissell_lewis_varick_16E.html.

Welch, Charles E. *Oh! Dem Golden Slippers: The Story of the Philadelphia Mummers*. Book Street Press, 1991.

Wexler, Lisa Marin. "Inupiat Youth Suicide and Culture Loss: Changing Community Conversations for Prevention." *Social Science & Medicine* 63, no. 11 (2006): 2938–48.

Weyer, Edward M. "Captain Robert Abram Bartlett, In Memory." *The Explorers Journal* (Spring–Summer 1946): 12–13.

Whiteway, Solomon P. "Newfoundland Education until 1949." In *The Encyclopedia of Canada. Newfoundland Supplement*, by W. Stewart Wallace, 17–21. Toronto: University Associates of Canada, 1949.

Williams, Alan F. *John Guy of Bristol and Newfoundland: His Life, Times and Legacy*. St. John's: Flanker Press, 2010.

Williams, E.W. *Frozen Foods: Biography of an Industry*. Boston: Cahners Publishing, 1963.

INDEX

Maura Hanraham is a best-selling Canadian author whose writing has won awards in the US, Britain, and Canada. Of Irish, English, and Mi'Kmaw ancestry, Maura was born and raised on the island of Newfoundland and spent two years in the Canadian naval reserve as a teenager. She is currently Board of Governors Research Chair and Associate Professor in the Department of Indigenous Studies, University of Lethbridge, Alberta. Her research interests include drinking water policy, the Newfoundland Mi'Kmaq, and Arctic history. She is also adjunct professor with the Environmental Policy Institute, Memorial University, Newfoundland and Labrador. Maura earned her PhD from the London School of Economics and Political Science where she was a Rothermere Fellow and London School of Economics Fellow. She also has degrees from Memorial University and Carleton University. Maura lives in Alberta with her husband, novelist Paul Butler, and their daughter and horseback-riding companion, Jemma.

ALSO BY MAURA HANRAHAN

Sheila's Brush: A Novel

Spirit and Dust: Meditations for Women with Depression

The Alphabet Fleet: The Pride of the Newfoundland Coastal Service

Domino: The Eskimo Coast Disaster

Tsunami: The Newfoundland Tidal Wave Disaster

The Doryman

Rogues and Heroes with Paul Butler

A Faith that Challenges: The Life of Jim McSheffrey

A Veritable Scoff: Sources on Foodways and Nutrition in Newfoundland and Labrador. Co-edited with Marg Ewtushik

Uncertain Refuge: Lectures on Newfoundland Society and Culture

Through a Mirror Dimly: Essays on Newfoundland Society and Culture. Editor

PRAISE FOR *UNCHAINED MAN*

Maura Hanrahan has written a fine book about one of Newfoundland's most famous seamen and arctic explorers, Bob Bartlett. *In Unchained Man*—meticulously researched and finely written—she has come closer than any writer yet to solving the enigma of the great Bob Bartlett. From the haunting sinking of the *Karluk* to the epic struggle to reach the North Pole with Admiral Peary, Hanrahan depicts Bartlett as a flawed but extraordinary human being. This book is unforgettable, a must-read for lovers of the literature of exploration and the still uncharted region of the Arctic.

– Wayne Johnston, author *First Snow, Last Light* and *The Colony of Unrequited Dreams*

A riveting, comprehensive portrait of one of the most dynamic and enigmatic sea captains the Arctic has ever seen. Robert Abram Bartlett was larger than life, his adventures the stuff of legends. Maura Hanrahan expertly recounts the long overdue, very true story of this understated polar hero in engaging, dramatic prose.

– New York Times bestselling author Jennifer Niven, *The Ice Master*